美国科技与中文教学

2012

Technology and Chinese
Language Teaching in the U.S.
TCLT

许德宝　主编

De Bao Xu
Editor-in-Chief

中国社会科学出版社

图书在版编目（CIP）数据

美国科技与中文教学 – 2012 – ／许德宝主编 . —北京：中国社会科学出版社，2012.5
ISBN 978 – 7 – 5161 – 0873 – 4

Ⅰ.①美… Ⅱ.①许… Ⅲ.①计算机辅助教学 – 文集 Ⅳ.①G434 – 53

中国版本图书馆 CIP 数据核字 (2012) 第 094983 号

出 版 人	赵剑英	
责任编辑	任 明	
责任校对	邓晓春	
责任印制	李 建	

出 版	中国社会科学出版社	
社 址	北京鼓楼西大街甲 158 号 （邮编100720）	
网 址	http：//www. csspw. com. cn	
	中文域名：中国社科网 010 – 64070619	
发 行 部	010 – 84083685	
门 市 部	010 – 84029450	
经 销	新华书店及其他书店	

印 刷	北京奥隆印刷厂	
装 订	北京市兴怀印刷厂	
版 次	2012 年 5 月第 1 版	
印 次	2012 年 5 月第 1 次印刷	

开 本	710 × 1000 1/16	
印 张	27.5	
插 页	2	
字 数	485 千字	
定 价	78.00 元	

序　言

电脑语言教学（Computer-assisted language instruction，简称 CALI）开始于 20 世纪 60 年代，后来被电脑语言学习（Computer-assisted language learning，简称 CALL）一词所代替。原因是前者不能反映以学习者为中心的教学理念。电脑语言学习（CALL）的研究开始于 20 世纪 80 年代，是随着个人电脑（PC）的出现而出现、随着电脑技术的飞速发展和教学理论的发展而不断发展的。电脑语言学习（CALL）的研究可以分成三个阶段：

一、行为主义 CALL - 与行为主义教学理论、大型计算机（Mainframe）相对应，60—70 年代

二、交际交流 CALL - 与交际交流教学理论（Communicative Approach）、个人计算机相对应，80—90 年代

三、整体教学 CALL - 与整体教学理论（Integrative，Holistic Approach）、多媒体、网络相对应，21 世纪[1]

中文电脑技术教学开始于 20 世纪 70 年代（1970—1985），与电脑语言学习（CALL）的研究有重合，也有交错。开创者是美国伊利诺州立大学的郑锦泉教授 - 首创用地方计算机系统（PLATO）教授汉字。其后中文电脑技术教学又经历了起步（1986—1993）、发展（1994—1999）和全方位开拓（2000—现在）几个阶段。[2] 其中全方位开拓是中文电脑技术教学的成熟和深入发展阶段。

中文电脑技术教学的成熟和深入发展的一个重要标志就是中文电脑技术教学国际研讨会、专业研究协会和专业研究期刊的出现。《21 世纪国际汉语电脑教学研讨会》、美国科技与中文教学协会（TCLT，http：//tclt. us）与美国

---

① 见 Mark Warschauer 1996 "Computer-assisted language learning：an introduction"，in Fotos S. (ed.) Multimedia language teaching，Tokyo：Logos International：pp. 3—20 与 "CALL for the 21st Century"，IATEFL and ESADE Conference，2 July 2000，Barcelona，Spain。

② 见许德宝 2005 年 6 月 3 日在《第四届全球华文网络教育研讨会》大会演讲 "35 年中文多媒体电脑教学发展之回顾与展望"（ICICE，2005，台北）和 2011 年 8 月 7 日在中央民族大学演讲《中文多媒体电脑教学之发展 1970—2011》。

《科技与中文教学》期刊（JTCLT，http：//tclt. us/journal/）就是这种成熟和深入发展的产物。① 国际专业研讨会、专业研究协会和专业研究期刊的出现标志着中文电脑技术教学在理论上和实践上都进入了一个崭新的阶段。

《21 世纪国际汉语电脑教学研讨会》（原名《21 世纪北美汉语电脑教学研讨会》）于 2000 年由美国纽约州汉弥尔顿大学发起，是美国科技与中文教学协会的双年会，以专门讨论中文电脑技术教学，发表该领域最新研究成果，并在会上提供多种电脑技术教学工作坊教授最新电脑教学技术与软件应用著称。《科技与中文教学》期刊是美国科技与中文教学协会的会刊，创刊于 2010 年，宗旨是与《21 世纪国际汉语电脑教学研讨会》一起从理论上、实践上全面介绍、研究和推广中文电脑技术教学。

《21 世纪国际汉语电脑教学研讨会》自 2000 年以来已举办七届会议，第一届大会在汉弥尔顿大学召开（2000）、第二届大会在耶鲁大学召开（2002）、第三届大会在哥伦比亚大学召开（2004）、第四届大会在南加州大学召开（2006）、第五届大会在澳门大学召开（2008）、第六届大会在俄亥俄州立大学召开（2010）、第七届大会在夏威夷大学召开（2012）。第一届至第七届大会参会院校达 200 余所，与会人员 800 余人，来自 19 个国家和地区；大会共发表专业论文 500 余篇，提供免费电脑技术教学工作坊 40 余个。《科技与中文教学》期刊自 2010 年创刊以来，已发表专业论文 20 余篇，内容包括电脑技术教学专题研究、电脑技术教学前沿技术介绍、电脑技术教学实践和电脑技术教学教材研究等。12 年来，美国《21 世纪国际汉语电脑教学研讨会》和《科技与中文教学》期刊（与其他国际专业研讨会一起）从理论和实践上全面带动了中文电脑技术教学的研究和发展，起到了全面介绍、研究和推广中文电脑技术教学的作用。

《21 世纪国际汉语电脑教学研讨会》的参会者以北美各大院校代表为主，但近年来（2004 年以来）由于中文电脑技术教学和"汉语作为第二语言教学"的迅速发展，其他国家和地区特别是欧洲、澳洲以及东南亚地区比如新加坡、台湾、香港、澳门、日本等地的代表也不断增加。《科技与中文教学》期刊的投稿、撰稿人也从美国扩大到澳大利亚、新加坡和中国台湾、香港等地区。虽然近年来国内学者也开始参加《21 世纪国际汉语电脑教学研讨会》（比如 2006 年在澳门大学举办的《第五届国际汉语电脑教学研讨会》），但人数并不太多。因此，《21 世纪国际汉语电脑教学研讨会》与《科技与中文教

---

① 《全球华文网络教育研讨会》（台湾）、《中文电化教学国际研讨会》（北京）也是全方位开拓阶段的产物。

学》期刊代表了除中国大陆以外其他主要国家和地区中文电脑技术教学的研究、发展和实践。

它山之石，可以攻玉。为了促进国外与国内中文电脑技术教学的交流和发展，有必要把中文电脑技术教学的最新研究成果和最新教学实践尽快介绍进来。而代表最新研究成果和最新教学实践的就是国际上每两年举办一次的《21 世纪国际汉语电脑教学研讨会》和每年出版两期的《科技与中文教学》期刊所发表的论文。如果能从中选取精华论文数十篇编辑成书，按年份在国内出版，必将对国内中文电脑技术教学的研究和发展起到促进作用。另外，迄今国内还没有一本有关中文电脑技术教学研究的专业期刊或专业图书，各大专院校、图书馆（包括中国大陆、台湾、香港、澳门和新加坡等地区）均需要这样的图书作为教科书和参考书，因此，编辑、出版此书就更有必要了。

令人欣慰的是，中国社会科学出版社作为人文社会学科的出版带头人，大力支持这一出版计划，尤其是责任编辑任明先生的支持，得以使出版此书成为事实。这不仅是对中文电脑技术教学和研究的一大重要贡献，也是对"汉语作为第二语言教学"的一大贡献。在此谨向中国社会科学出版社表示衷心的感谢。

本书即从《21 世纪国际汉语电脑教学研讨会》每届大会论文（100 篇）①和每年出版两期的《科技与中文教学》期刊发表的论文（15—20 篇）中精选有代表性的论文 30 篇左右，每篇由两名编委审稿并提出修改意见，然后再由作者进行修改、整理，再次成文，最后编订成书，按年份出版。

由于《21 世纪国际汉语电脑教学研讨会》的参会者以北美各大院校代表为主，《科技与中文教学》期刊发表的论文也主要是以美国各大院校学者撰写的为主，所以书名定为《美国科技与中文教学》。由于计划每年出版一册，所以再加上出版年代。书中所选论文的中、英文形式不拘，以原文书写语言为准。其原因之一是为了反映论文原貌，翻译恐有失原义；其二是国内学者现在也阅读英文原文，以原文书写语言为准，更便于理解、沟通。另外所选中文论文用词不拘（汉语普通话、台湾国语等），其原因亦同。每篇冠以中、英文摘要，以便阅读。同时附有作者电邮，以便与作者联系。

这里要特别感谢编辑委员会的辛勤工作，论文作者同意编委审稿并进一步修订原文以符合要求，在此一并致以衷心的感谢。

————————

　　① 近年来《21 世纪国际汉语电脑教学研讨会》的规模不断扩大，参选论文增多。以今年在夏威夷举办的《第七届国际汉语电脑教学研讨会》为例，大会共收到参选论文 162 篇，实选宣读论文 101 篇。

　　最后，希望本书能起到促进国外与国内中文电脑技术教学交流和发展的作用。整理编辑期间，中、英文，简、繁体转换编码多次，版式、插图、表格转换时亦有出入，错误、疏漏之处在所难免，敬请批评指正。

许德宝

《美国科技与中文教学》主编

美国科技与中文教学协会常设委员会主席

美国《科技与中文教学》期刊主编

纽约汉弥尔顿大学东亚语言文学系教授、主任

目　录

汉语语料库开发

CALL 与传统教法之比较研究

自然语言处理文献述评

前沿技术探讨

网络参与式学习工具、虚拟课堂、第二人生

在虚拟世界进行汉语教学的工具
Tools for Teaching Chinese in the Virtual World

谢天蔚　Xie，Tianwei　美国长堤加州州立大学

California State University，Long Beach，United States txie@ csulb. edu

摘　要：虚拟世界是电脑网络发展的一个新阶段。在虚拟世界里可以进行各种商业和教育活动。语言教育也可以在虚拟世界里得到一席之地。本文广义定位虚拟世界，介绍网络上已有的虚拟世界工具，并且分享在汉语教学中使用网上工具的经验，以引起进一步的探讨。

关键词：虚拟世界，网上工具，汉语教学，合作学习

Abstract：Virtual word is the new stage of development of computer technology. People engage in all types of activities in the virtual world such as business and education. Language education can take advantage of this new technology. This article defines the virtual world in a broader sense. Some tools that can be used for teaching in the virtual world are introduced. The author also shares his own experience of using these tools in teaching Chinese. More in-depth study and discussion are needed in the future.

Keywords：Virtual world, online tools, teaching Chinese, collaborative learning

"当今世界殊"，虚拟世界（virtual world）、虚拟现实（virtual reality）已经进入了人们的生活，在商业、教育、通讯等领域里开始发挥巨大的作用。虚拟世界对语言教学，包括汉语教学也开始发挥影响力。本文试图说明：一、虚拟世界是什么；二、虚拟世界中有什么工具可以在汉语教学中运用；三、汉语教师如何使用这些工具。由于虚拟世界的许多软件出现的时间不长，运用的实例不多，理论研究和实证研究都很少。此文仅以本人的实际经验对虚拟世界以及试验性的运用作一粗略介绍。

一 虚拟世界是什么

按照网上词典的定义，"虚拟世界"（virtual word）是一个由网际网络计算机模拟的虚拟空间，用户可以通过自己的虚拟形象（化身 avatar）栖息其中，并可以与其他虚拟形象展开互动、交往（维基百科，http://zh. wikipedia. org/zh/虚拟世界，2010 年 6 月 12 日查询）。虚拟现实（virtual reality，简称 VR，又译作灵境、幻真）是近年来出现的高新技术，也称灵境技术或人工环境。虚拟现实是利用电脑模拟产生一个三维空间的虚拟世界，提供使用者关于视觉、听觉、触觉等感官的模拟，让使用者如同身历其境一般，可以及时、没有限制地观察三度空间内的事物（百度百科，http://baike. baidu. com/view/7299. htm，2010 年 6 月 12 日查询）。

这种定义实际上颇为狭窄。我们这里要探讨的不只是三维空间的虚拟世界，而是一切采用网络进行商业或教学活动的虚拟世界。这种虚拟世界是广义的"网络空间 cyberspace"，包含三维空间和非三维空间的软件，Web2.0 互动式网络工具，如虚拟教室、网络会议等。

网络上的实时（synchronous）与非实时（asynchronous）交际工具已经有很多。最先应用是商业部门，例如大公司利用网络课堂进行业务培训，航空公司利用语音识别和语音合成提供人际对话服务，可以用语音查询航班信息等。银行也提供实时的线上服务，顾客随时可以在线上找到服务人员，解决银行的业务问题。电脑公司利用实时与非实时的软件开展售后服务，甚至可以远端控制客户电脑提供技术支援。本人就曾经在线上与美洲银行（Bank of America）的业务员进行过线上交谈，解决了账户出现的问题。电脑技术首先在商业活动中得到普遍应用毫不奇怪，因为电脑技术有提高工作效率、节约成本、方便顾客三大优点。虚拟世界技术的出现使人际互动在网上更为方便。

这些技术在教育上的应用也随之跟进。学校在普遍建立网页的基础上向互动转化，网页不再只提供资讯，而且提供互动服务。现在已经不是在网上可以"看"什么，而是在网上可以"做"什么。虚拟教室，网上教学和各种网上会议（webinar）如雨后春笋一样出现。每个星期都可以收到各种网上会议的通知。例如在中文教学领域，IQChinese 从 2008 年起就在网上开办中文教学网上会议，介绍软件的使用和网上学习的问题[①]。全世界的中文教

---

① IQChinese 免费网上中文讨论会：http://www. iqchinese. com/Promotion/onlineseminar2010. html。

师，无论身处何方都可以在同一时间上网分享该领域里的进展。澳大利亚 Monash University 的网上学校用三维的"第二人生"（Second Life）建立了虚拟课堂（Chinese Island，2009）。又如 2009 年 University of Oregon 实验性地用"第二人生"举办了暑期汉语夏令营。美国的学生与中国苏州大学的辅导员共同就环境保护议题进行汉语学习。这样的应用实践与日俱增，给汉语教学带来了新的教学方法和手段。

　　然而科学技术的出现并不保证教师和学生就能自动利用这些技术并且在教学实践中应用。虽然现在的学生是"网上一代"the Net Generation（Oxford，2009），是"天生数位人"digital native（Bennett，2008）（与"移民数位人"digital immigrant 相对），他们成长在科技包围之中。"第二人生"一类虚拟世界对他们并不陌生。他们会花许多时间在网上与同侪聊天，玩电动游戏，然而这也不表明他们就能自动把技术和时间用到学习中去。因此研究如何在语言教学中应用虚拟世界就成为一个重要的课题。最近几年以来这方面研究已经逐渐出现，英语作为二语教学及西班牙语教学就走在前列。例如 Tanyeli 研究用虚拟世界帮助法学院学生提高英语阅读水平（Tanyeli，2008）。同时出现的还有一些文集如《通过技术学语言》（*Learning Languages through Technology*，Hanson-Smith，2007），《网络时代的二语教学》（*Second Language Teaching and Learning in the Net Generation* Oxford，2009）等。利用网上资料库来搜索这方面的研究可以很容易地得到相当多的资讯。

二　中文教学中可以使用的各种工具

　　可以运用的网络软件非常多，大部分的软件都可以支持中文，因而可以在汉语教学中使用。下面举例说明有哪些软件可以使用。其中有的是免费的，有的是付费的。教师可以先使用免费的软件，试验一下实用性和可用性，然后决定是个人出资购买还是向学校申请经费购买。

（一）Second Life

Second Life（第二人生）是一个典型的三维游戏软件，由 Linden 公司开发（http://secondlife.com/）。在这个虚拟世界里，每个人都是本尊的"化身"（avatar）。人人可以在这个虚拟世界里购地置屋，进行买卖。虽然这个软件本义是游戏，但是语言教师对此有很大的兴趣，试图在这个虚拟世界找到自己的"第二人生"。在第二人生中一个人可以更换自己的服饰，可以在虚拟空间中跑、跳、飞，做出各种姿势，跟人用打字或语音交谈。如果创建了一个教室，可以在课堂里放置各种学习资料，学习、观看所学语言国家的图片和视频。如果设定时间，师生可以在这个空间上课、活动。演示片（PPT）和视频可以在课堂里播放。总之，这个软件模拟的是人们在真实空间中的活动，对于青年人有很大的吸引力。根据 Linden 公司的资料，到2009 年 9 月 23 日为止玩家在这个虚拟世界中度过的总时间已经超过 10 亿小时，或者是 115 年（第二人生）。然而由于这个软件对电脑和使用者的电脑知识技能要求较高，建立自己的"岛屿"（Island）① 也颇费钱费时，至今在语言学习方面的应用始终停留在试验阶段。

图1　俄勒冈大学 2009 年虚拟暑期汉语夏令营
学生在第二人生课堂作报告
（坐在椅子上的人左一为笔者，是学生演示报告的评判员之一。）

（二）网上会议软件

相比之下网上会议软件就发展得比较快。网上会议虽然不像"第二人生"那样在色彩动画上吸引人，但是在人际交流上可以基本起到相同的作用，而且脱离了游戏的色彩，更加职业化、专业化。比较常见的几个软件是：

1. Elluminate（Eluminate, Inc, http://www.elluminate.com/）
2. ConnectNow（Acrobat, https://acrobat.com/welcome.html）
3. Webex（Cisco, http://www.webex.com/）

---

① 在第二人生中自己的领地称为"岛屿"（island）。

4. JoinNet（HomeMeeign，Inc.，http://www.homemeeting.com/en_ US/ download.asp#jeditor）

这些工具也称为网上会议与合作工具（web conferencing and collabora-tion）。这四个软件很相似，都提供实时的线上会议功能，如桌面共享①，白板②，线上交谈（online chat），还可以播放演示片（PPT）或者 Youtube 视频片段。主持人或主讲人的声音和视频可以根据需要开启或关闭，听讲人需要发言可以由主持人来确认，提供话筒。这样的虚拟会议室对于讲座一类的课型很适合。一个主讲人发言，大部分参加者只是听众，不需要人人同时发言，如有问题可以通过打字进行交流。

图 2　ConnectNow 虚拟课堂界面

中国大陆和台湾也开发类似的软件，功能都相似，但是对电脑和使用者的技术要求不同。因此在选择软件的时候要多咨询专家的意见。

（三）两个免费的虚拟课堂软件 WizIq 和 DimDim

上面说的四个软件收费不赀，因此除非是由学校出资购买，汉语教师一般很难使用。本人经常使用的两个软件是 WizIq（http://www.wiziq.com）和 DimDim（http://www.dimdim.com），更多使用 WizIq，因为虽收费，但

---

①　Desktop sharing，参与者可以同时看到主讲人的电脑屏幕，也可以从远端在主讲人的电脑上操作。

②　Whiteboard，可以共同在白板上打字画图贴照片等。

年费仅 49 美元，且有免费的版本。DimDim 是免费的，如果需要增加服务项目，如增加参加人数就需要付费升级。WizIq 和前面所说的几个网上会议软件差不多，但是功能没有那么齐全，例如不能共同浏览同一网页。但是课堂教学需要的几个基本功能都有。DimDim 除了基本功能以外，还可以共同浏览网页。

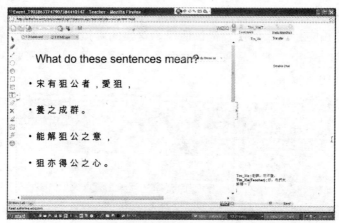

图 3　用 WizIq 进行文言文教学

除了采用上面的工具以外，也可以将免费的通讯工具变成虚拟教室。例如通讯工具 Skype（http://www.skype.com）可以和桌面共享软件 Mikogo（http://www.mikogo.com）同时使用，成为一个线上课堂。Skype 有打字聊天和语音会议功能，最多可以容纳 24 个人同时上线讨论。但是 Skype 不能播放 PPT。因此，同时启动 Mikogo 就可以让教师或者主持人把自己电脑的屏幕显示给学生看，可以播放演示片，也可执行其他软件，学生可以看到教师的电脑演示的一切。如果需要，还可以把主电脑的控制权给学生，让学生进行演示或者操作同一个软件。Mikogo 是免费软件，但是只能允许 10 个人同时上线。如果要增加参加者，就要注册付费使用。

（四）其他合作学习（协同工作）软件、"写板"（writeborad）、"谷歌文件"（google docs）和"维久"（wiggio）

合作学习目前已经是教育界的一个有共识的理念。学生通过合作学习来获得所需要的知识与技能。在外语教学中，教师经常将学生分成小组，让各组完成一定的任务。在这种合作学习活动中线上的"文件共享"（document sharing）软件就可以起到事半功倍的效果。

图4　Skype + Mikogo 也可以成为虚拟课堂

"写板"（Writeboard，http: //writeboard. com）是一个使用方便且免费的工具。使用者不需要注册新账户，只要在每次建立新的任务时由第一个主持人启动一个"写板"（writeboard），先起草一个文件，然后通知其他合作人。合作人收到邀请以后，按照提供的地址和密码即可进入修改文件。文件每次修改以后，旧的版本自动保留，新旧版本全部留存在这个"写板"里，随时可以调用、比较、查对。合作人确定最后版本以后可以将此版本输出，进行最后的编排。这个软件的好处是可以让数人实时或非实时共同编辑一个文件，不需要用电子邮件来回传输草稿。

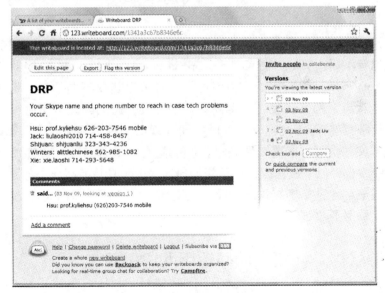

图5　"写板"截图

"谷歌文件"（Google docs，http: //www. google. com）可以起同样的作用，而且可以处理的文件类型更多。谷歌文件可以处理 Word、Excel、PPT

和 pdf 等文件，功能比较复杂，而且需要建立个人的账户。因此比较复杂的任务可以选用谷歌文件，较简单的任务可以使用"写板"。

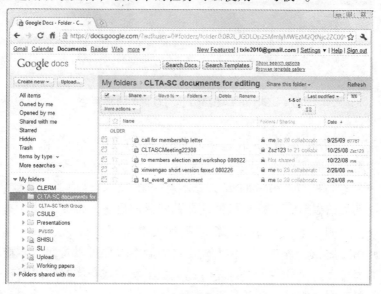

图 6　"谷歌文件"截图

"维久"（Wiggio，http://www.wiggio.com）也是免费工具，但跟前面两个工具稍有不同。Wiggio 的意思是 work in group（小组工作），因此对团队工作（team work）很有用处。利用这个工具可以建议不同的项目组，每个组有行事日历、网上会议室、文件夹、留言板、通讯区（电子邮件、语音留言、打字交流等）。小组成员可以共同处理的文件类型有 Word、Excel 和 PPT。pdf 文件也可以存在文件夹里，但不能直接处理修改。文件可以在网上直接修改也可以下载修改以后重新上传。这个工具是教师合作备课，编写教材，制定文件的有效工具。UCLA 孔子学院主持制定美国中小学汉语教学标准时就采用了"维久"。

三　如何运用网络工具

前面已经说到"天生数位人"也不见得会自动用网上工具来学习，因此作为"移民数位人"的教师更要进行研究、学习和实践，探索如何在汉语教学中利用这些工具。事实上如果利用得法，可以有事半功倍的效果。但有时候盲目地跟从也会使人迷茫，跌入五里雾中，白白浪费宝贵的时间。因

图 7 "维久"截图

此有一些建议或许可以考虑。

（一）根据实际需要选择软件

面对那么多的网上软件如何选择就是首要的任务。要考虑的因素有：功用、价格、使用方便程度。例如在选择网上教室的时候就要考虑是否的确需要进行网上远程教学。在美国很多城市，大、中、小学都有中文课，学生希望来到课堂与教师面对面地学习。在这种情况下就不需要用网上教室。不过有一两次的网上实时讨论也可以提高学生的兴趣。本人就曾经利用打字交谈在电脑室里跟学生打字交流。然而如果偏远的地区缺乏汉语师资，远程网上的虚拟课堂就成为一个很好选择。分散在各地的学生要学习汉语也只能采用虚拟教室来上课。笔者所在的长堤加州州立大学有一个暑期中文项目，学生来自南加州各个学校。第一个暑期去中国考察以后回到美国继续学习汉语。此时学生已经分散到各地，我们采用 WizIq 和 Skype 进行网上学习，取得较好的效果，有效地维持了学生在暑假学到的语言能力。

价格方面要考虑教师、学生是否能够承受。学校一般购买的是通用软件，不可能专门为汉语教学购买所需要的网上工具。汉语教学所需要的网上工具需要教师自己申请经费，或者自我消化。另外现在有一些网上学校（收费）可以提供辅导。如果教师要求学生参加网上辅导，就要考虑学生承受的能力。今年春季长堤州大与网上学校 SpeakChinese.com 进行了一个实验性的网上辅导项目。SpeakChinese 每周向长堤州大学习汉语的学生提供一个小时的免费网上辅导，得到学生的欢迎。在最后的评估中有这样一个问题：如果收费你是否会继续参加网上辅导？收费多少能够接受？学生的反馈表明他们对收费可以理解，但参加意愿大为降低。一般来说一个月收费不超 20 美元尚可接受。

最后是工具使用的方便程度。一个软件功能虽强，使用不方便也不宜采用。有的软件需要安装，注册新的账号，有的安装指示过于复杂，让人望而止步。最适宜的是不需安装，直接可以在网上运行的软件。目前电脑科技发展迅速，云计算技术（cloud computing）可以让用户直接在自己的电脑上运行云端软件，把资料存储在远端的服务器上。

（二）根据教学目的和任务选择软件

选择工具的第二个建议是根据教学的目的和任务选择软件。WizIq 一类的虚拟网上教室对讲座性的课比较适合，因为这个软件在理论上可以接受上百个听众，但是显而易见这上百个听众不能同时进行语音交流。语言课一般都是小班，需要经常的语音交流，多人能否同时进行语音交流就是一个重要的选择功能。例如 Skype 可以同时允许 24 个人进行语音会议，对于口语课就非常合适。网上一对一的辅导完全可以采用 Skype。因为 Skype 在语音对话的同时，可以用打字进行交流，传送文件。当然一对一的辅导也可以用其他网上教室，但"杀鸡何须用牛刀"。在一般的辅导中并不需要用演示片或者视频，只要双方可以对话，可以打字就行。今年秋季，长堤州大试图与上海外国语大学合作，请中国对外汉语专业的学生担任美国学生的辅导员，免费提供一周一个小时的网上辅导，采用的软件就是 Skype。小规模的实验已经结束。评估表明学生和网上辅导员比较满意，都表示可以继续进行。此类活动在虚拟世界中跨越了时空的限制，使语言学习更为有效。

学生的合作学习需要"写板"类的合作工具。我们曾在二年级汉语课和高年级的文言文课分别采用"写板"来进行学习活动。在二年级要求学生两人组成一组，合作就一个题目写出一段对话，并且通过 Skype 进行口头练习。这样学生不需坐在一起，只要利用晚上的时间在家里共同准备练习会话。在文言文课，将学生分成三至四人的小组，将一篇文言文翻译成英语。一人先起草，然后由小组成员不断修改，直到达成一个大家都满意的版本。

在虚拟中文夏令营中，学习任务比较复杂，因此要采用"第二人生"这样的软件。因为在夏令营中学习任务包括了实地调查、文章阅读、集体报告准备和课堂演讲演示。因此一种软件并不能满足多项任务的需要。学生必须在虚拟的环境中对"实地"进行环境污染状况调查，通过电子邮件和 Skype 进行讨论和沟通，然后利用其他软件准备报告，最后到虚拟课堂进行报告和演示。总之，活动需要哪一种方便的软件就可以使用哪一种软件。

（三）虚拟办公和备课活动

上面所说的都是学生和教师的课堂和课外活动。此外，教师还需要备课和接待学生（office hours）。教师共同备课或者建立共享资料库采用"维久"比较方便。因为各种教学资料可以分门别类存入"维久"的文件夹。教师随时可以提取修改，或者将自己新建的资料贡献出来存入共享库。

虚拟办公室（virtual office 或称行动办公室 mobile office）也是虚拟世界中一种可以使用的技术。台湾太御科技采用 JoinNet 的行动办公室 http://weboffice. joinnet. tw/enus. php 就是一个商用的例子，公司职员可以在任何地方任何时间进入行动办公室处理公司的事务。教师需要的行动办公室没有那么复杂，所需要的功能不多。最常用的是教师资讯、课程信息、行事日历、电子邮件、预约系统，如果需要也可以加入课程入门链接，使学生可以方便地进入课程。此类行动办公室只要网页就可以满足需要①，如果奢侈一点，在"第二人生"建立一个虚拟的办公室也是不错的。

四 结语与展望

前面介绍了虚拟世界和在语言教学中的应用。综合起来可以说，电脑技术的飞速发展不断给教育提供了先进的手段。语言教学中采用什么样的软件取决于实际的需要和教学活动与任务的性质。教师应该不断地学习、探索和研究，在实践中找到最适合自己的工具。

教育技术的潮流向着两个方面发展：云计算（cloud computing，港台称云端运算）与移动（mobile）技术。所谓云计算就是电脑程序和资料都可以存储在远端的大服务器上，如同高高在上的云端，个人电脑通过网络接入远端服务器就可以处理资料。例如教师在学校办公室接入远端服务器处理资料，不需要在自己的办公室电脑或 U 盘上储存。回到家里或者别的地方可以通过网络接入远端电脑，调出资料进行再处理。云计算技术为虚拟世界活动提供技术上的保证。

移动技术使虚拟世界更为自由方便。手机和平板电脑一类移动设备让虚拟世界更是如虎添翼。如今在 iPhone 和 iPad 一类的平台已经出现了不少软件帮助学习汉语。本人已经收集了几十个免费的学中文软件。虽然这些软件还不够成熟，但是已经显示出生命力。例如供手机和 iPhone 使用的汉语词

---

① 请参考本人建立的虚拟办公室网页：http://xietianwei. net。

典已经出现不少。有的免费，有的收费。其中最引人注目的是 Pleco① 中文词典"鱼"。因为这个词典不需要输入任何中文字词，只要将 iPhone 或者 iPod Touch 的摄像头对准文字，词典就会利用 OCR 转换成代码，立即显示出英文解释和读音。如果学生有这样的工具，无论在哪里阅读中文都不必用键盘输入，只要把手机对准文字就可以。这种词典显然是我们梦寐以求的。我们梦寐以求的不仅是"即照即译"词典，还有语音会话、自动翻译等技术。

虚拟世界很精彩，但需要我们共同努力。教师有很多的"梦"，希望电脑工程师和软件开发者来听听教师的声音，让这个梦实现。

参考文献

Bennett, S.; Maton, K. and Kervin, L. (2008). The 'digital natives' debate: A critical review of the evidence". British Journal of Educational Technology, 39 (5), 775—786.

Chinese Island. Initiative by the Chinese Studies Program at Monash University in Melbourne, Australia. Available: http://secondlife. com/destination/chinese-island.

Hanson-Smith, Elizabeth. (Ed.) 2007. Learning Languages through Technology. Teachers of English to Speakers of Other Languages, Inc.

IQChinese. Free Online Chinese Language Seminar. Available: http://www. iqchinese. com/Promotion/onlineseminar2010. html.

MyChina Village: The Third Paradigm of Language Learning. Available: http://casls. uoregon. edu/mychina. php.

Oxford, Raquel (Ed.) 2009. Second Language Teaching and Learning in the Net Generation Hawaii: National Foreign Language Resource Center.

Tanyeli, Nadiran. (2008). The Efficiency of Online English Language Instruction on Students' Reading Skills. Paper presented at the International Technology, Education and Development Conference, Spain, 2008.

虚拟教室 (Virtual Class)，参见：http://skycn. com/soft/4038. html。

第二人生 (Second Life)，参见：http://zh. wikipedia. org/zh/第二人生。

---

① 在 AppStore 用 Pleco 搜索就可以下载。

网络参与式学习工具的评测与
虚拟课堂软件的选择标准[①]
The Evaluation of Web Participatory Learning
Tools and the Criteria for Selectiong
Virtual Classroom Software

许德宝　Xu, De Bao　美国纽约州汉米尔顿大学

Hamilton College, Unites States dxu@ hamilton. edu

摘　要：网络参与式学习工具在第二语言习得中的显著优势以及虚拟课堂在网络教学和远程教学中的必不可少性使网络参与式学习工具的评测与虚拟课堂软件（Virtual Classroom Software，VCS）的选择成为科技与语言教学中的两个重要课题。本文根据 Fortin（1997）提出的参与度和互动性的定义，在许/靳（2009）提出的测量参与度和互动性六项标准数字化的基础上对六种常见网络参与式学习工具（讨论板、Discussion board、博客 Blogs、Skype 型软件、Moodle 型服务网、LiveMocha 和第二人生，Second Life）进行了评测。同时，把测量参与度和互动性的六项标准运用到虚拟课堂软件的选择上，筛选出了九种适合于语言教学的虚拟课堂软件并在此基础上提出了选择虚拟课堂软件的四项标准。本文共分四部分，一是研究动机，二是网络参与式学习工具的评测，三是虚拟课堂软件的选择标准，四是结语。

关键词：网络参与学习，网络参与式学习工具，参与度，互动性，虚拟课堂，虚拟课堂软件

Abstract：The advantage of web participatory learning tools in second language acquisition and the cruciality of virtual classrooms in distance learning have raised two questions for the study of technology-based language teaching and learning：（1）how to evaluate the web participatory

---

① 本文部分内容曾以会议论文形式在《第六届全球华文网络教育研讨会》（ICICE' 09，台北，台湾，2009 年 6 月 19—21 日）和《第六届国际汉语电脑教学研讨会》（TCLT6，俄亥俄州立大学，2010 年 6 月 12—14 日）上发表。

learning tools, and (2) how to select the virtual classroom software (VCS) for language teaching and learning. Based on the concepts of participation and interaction established by Fortin (1997) and the six numerical measures of participation and interaction proposed by Xu & Jin (2009), this paper evaluates six commonly used web participatory learning tools (discussion board, blogs, Skype-type software, Moodle-based service network, LiveMocha, and Second Life). Meanwhile, it extends the six numerical measures of participation and interaction to the selection of VCS by filtering out nine VCS for language teaching and learning and summarizing four criteria for VCS selection. §1 is motivation, §2 is the evaluation of web participatory learning tools, §3 is the criteria for VCS selection, and §4 is conclusion.

Keywords: Web participatory learning, participatory learning tools, participation, interaction, virtual classroom, virtual classroom software

一　研究动机

电脑技术以及数码媒体的迅速发展使网络成为一种重要的国际交际平台，在这个交际平台上，世界各地人士都可以通过各种网络媒体工具进行交流合作。这种借助网络媒体工具所进行的交际方式以及参与互动活动逐渐形成了一种全球性的特殊文化——"网络参与文化"（Participatory culture）或者"网络参与学习"（Participatory learning）（许/靳，2009）。

第二语言习得从交流的角度讲，就是发展学习者的交际能力，因此参与性网络学习具有显著的优势——既能为学习者提供远程学习和与母语者面对面的真实互动交流，达到语义协商的目的，又能将语言学习变为有目的、有意义的参与交际过程，所以选择具有显著优势的参与性网络学习工具用于第二语言教学是语言教师所面临的一个问题。但是迄今为止，很少有人有系统地调查研究过不同的网络工具所能提供的参与度和互动性。要充分利用网络工具进行外语教学，选择最有利于语言教学的网络工具，有必要对不同网络工具所能提供的参与度、互动性进行有系统的研究。

虚拟课堂（Virtual classrooms）是指学生与老师身处异地、异时而利用高科技、应用软件、多媒体、电视电话会议技术等在电脑网络上打造的一种同步（Synchronous）教学环境，同时又有异步（Asynchronous）重播共用功能（Kurbel，2001）。虚拟课堂是远程教学、网络教学最重要的和最基本的工具，也是语言教学必不可少的辅助工具。在今后 5 到 10 年内，每一个语言教师、每一所学校大概都要面临一个选择适合于自己教学的虚拟课堂问题。另外，由于科技的飞速发展，可以打造虚拟课堂的网络平台（Internet platforms）不可数计，虚拟课堂软件也如雨后春笋，层出不穷。如何选择适合于语言教学的虚拟课堂软件是所有语言教师所面临的一个问题。但是到目前为止，对虚拟课堂和虚拟课堂软件有系统的研究并不多，尤其是对适合语言教学的虚拟课堂软件的研究。因此要充分利用虚拟课堂进行外语教学，有必要对这个问题进行研究，提出一套适合于语言教学的虚拟课堂软件的标准。

本文即讨论网络参与式学习工具的评测与虚拟课堂软件（VCS）的选择标准问题。

二　网络参与式学习工具的评测

（一）参与度与互动性的定义（Fortin，1997）

根据 Fortin（1997）的研究，参与度是指在高科技环境下，人们为达到目标或完成任务所投入的程度。参与可分为主动型参与或被动型参与，一对多型参与或多对多型参与，接收型参与或输出型参与。

互动性是指交流程度。互动性的高低取决于交流是允许一个终端用户还是多个终端用户；交流是双向还是单向，即交流者是信息发出者还是接收者或二者都是；交流对象是一个还是多个。此外，互动性还取决于交流方式，即互动是同步（Synchronous）即时的，还是异步（Asynchronous）存储转发式的（如电话会议记录和电子邮件）；信息传播是用户自控式还是预录转发式的（亦即用户是否可以控制交流内容、时间、顺序等，是统一制作，还是是独家控制）。

（二）评测标准

靳/路（2009）把 Fortin（1997）对参与度与互动性下的定义总结成六项标准，即：

（1）参与类型（主动参与还是被动参与）

（2）参与范围（一对多参与还是多对多参与，非母语者之间的交流还是非母语与母语者之间的交流）

（3）交流模式（信息接收还是输出，或两者兼备；单一形式还是多重形

式，即人际交流、理解诠释、表达演说全部涵盖）

（4）交流方向（单向还是双向）

（5）交流方式（文本即时交流、视频面对面交流还是存储转发式交流）

（6）信息传播方式（用户自控式还是预录转发式）

为了便于运用，许/靳（2009）又把上述参与度与互动性六项标准数字化，即：

（1）参与类型共3分，其中主动参与得2分，被动参与得1分

（2）参与范围共6分，其中一对多参与得1分，多对多参与得2分，使用目标语在非母语者间的交流得1分，使用目标语在非母语与母语者间的交流得2分

（3）交流模式共6分，其中用户终端为信息接收者得1分，用户终端为信息输出或接收、输出两者兼备得2分，采用单一交流模式得1分，采用三种完整交流模式即人际交流、理解诠释、表达演说三种模式全部覆盖得2分

（4）交流方向共3分，其中信息交流为单向得1分，信息交流为双向得2分

（5）交流方式共5分，其中即时同步交流得2分，面对面交流得2分，存储转发式交流得1分

（6）信息传播方式共3分，其中用户自控式得2分，预录转发式得1分

六项标准总共26分，各项得分超过半数达标，以"√"为记号。得分高、达标项目多的工具更符合参与度和互动性的标准，因此更适于网络语言教学；反之则较不符合参与度和互动性的标准，较不适于网络语言教学。列表如下：

表1   评测网络参与式学习工具参与度和互动性的六项标准

类别	网络工具特征描述（总分：26分）	总得分	达标与否
1）参与类型（3）	a）主动参与（2） b）被动参与（1）		
2）参与范围（6）	a）一对多参与（1） b）多对多参与（2） c）使用目标语在非母语者间的交流（1） d）使用目标语在非母语者和母语者之间的交流（2）		
3）交流模式（6）	a）用户终端为信息接收者（1） b）用户终端为信息输出者，或是两者兼有（2） c）采用单一交流模式（1） d）采用三种完整交流模式（2）：即人际交流、理解诠释、表达演说三种模式全部涵盖		
4）交流方向（3）	a）信息交流为单向（1） b）信息交流为双向（2）		
5）交流方式（5）	a）即时同步交流（2） b）面对面交流（2） c）存储转发式交流（1）		
6）信息传播方式（2）	a）用户自控式（时间、顺序、内容）（2） b）预录转发或直播式，独家控制（1）		

（三）　网络参与式学习工具的评测

　　本文选择了六种常见网络参与式学习工具，根据许/靳（2009）网络参与式学习工具参与度和互动性的六项数字化标准进行了评测。评测结果如下。

　　1. 讨论板（Discussion board）

　　讨论板是一种常见的网络参与式学习工具，可以上传、下载目标语文本信息，可进行跨时空、一对多、多对多文本讨论，但不能同步，也不能提供其他媒体比如视频、音频等。

表2　　　　　　　　　　讨论板参与度和互动性的评测

（每项超过半数达标，以"√"为记号）

类别	网络工具特征描述（总分：26 分）	得分：13 分	三项达标
1）参与类型（3）	a）主动参与（2） b）被动参与（1）	2	√
2）参与范围（6）	a）一对多参与（1） b）多对多参与（2） c）使用目标语在非母语者间的交流（1） d）使用目标语在非母语者和母语者之间的交流（2）	2 2	√
3）交流模式（6）	a）用户终端为信息接收者（1） b）用户终端为信息输出者，或是两者兼有（2） c）采用单一交流模式（1） d）采用三种完整交流模式（2）：即人际交流、理解诠释、表达演说三种模式全部涵盖	2 1	
4）交流方向（3）	a）信息交流为单向（1） b）信息交流为双向（2）	2	√
5）交流方式（5）	a）即时同步交流（2） b）面对面交流（2） c）存储转发式交流（1）	1	
6）信息传播方式（3）	a）用户自控式（时间、顺序、内容等）（2） b）预录转发或直播式，独家控制（1）	1	

　　讨论板在参与度和互动性的六项标准上有三项达标，即参与类型（主动参与）、参与范围（多对多参与和使用目标语在非母语者和母语者之间的交流）和交流方向（信息双向交流），共得13分。

　　在语言教学方面，由于讨论板可提供目标语言在文本方面的输入与交流，可提供多对多、双向参与式互动，因此有益于语义协商；同时讨论板鼓励主动参与式学习，因此是一种有用的参与式网络学习工具。

讨论板的局限是不允许面对面交流，也不允许口头交流。在交流方式上，不能同步交流，因此反馈不即时。另外信息传播仅允许预录转发或直播式，也不能提供其他媒体比如视频、音频方面的帮助以提供交际交流的真实性。

2. 博客（Blogs）

博客也是一种常见的网络参与式学习工具，可以上传、下载目标语音频、视频、文本信息，可以进行跨时空、一对多、多对多即时文本交流讨论，但不允许面对面真实话语交流。

表3   博客参与度和互动性的评测（每项超过半数达标，以"√"为记号）

类别	网络工具特征描述（总分：26 分）	得分：17 分	六项达标
1）参与类型（3）	a）主动参与（2） b）被动参与（1）	2	√
2）参与范围（6）	a）一对多参与（1） b）多对多参与（2） c）使用目标语在非母语者间的交流（1） d）使用目标语在非母语者和母语者之间的交流（2）	2 2	√
3）交流模式（6）	a）用户终端为信息接收者（1） b）用户终端为信息输出者，或是两者兼有（2） c）采用单一交流模式（1） d）采用三种完整交流模式（2）：即人际交流、理解诠释、表达演说三种模式全部涵盖	2 2	√
4）交流方向（3）	a）信息交流为单向（1） b）信息交流为双向（2）	2	√
5）交流方式（5）	a）即时同步交流（2） b）面对面交流（2） c）存储转发式交流（1）	2 1	√
6）信息传播方式（3）	a）用户自控式（时间、顺序、内容等）（2） b）预录转发或直播式，独家控制（1）	2	√

博客在参与度和互动性的六项标准上全部达标，共得 17 分。总结起来，博客有如下几个特点：

就参与度而言，博客可以做到多对多的参与互动，可以允许多人上传目标语音频、视频、文本信息，并可同步阅读、听取、观看、讨论等。

就交流模式而言，博客可以提供多种交流模式来完成学习任务，比如阅读、听取、理解、诠释、采访（文本）和评论交流（文本），以及用目标语口头和书面表达（文本演说）等交流模式。

就互动性而言，使用者可阅读博客文章，听取其他人的录音，并能进行多对多的文本互动和双向交流。

就交流方式而言，博客可实行实时性采访（文本即时性采访），也可使用存储转发设备（网络博客）来交换信息，进行互动。博客能提供跨时空与母语者进行的密集交流互动。

就目标语的使用而言，博客可使学生有目的地、大量地使用目标语，比如分配阅读任务，网上采访，网上工作坊、出版社和辩论室等。

博客是一种具有高度参与性、互动性的网络学习工具。局限是不允许面对面视频真实交流，只允许即时同步文本交流和存储转发式交流。

3. Skype 型软件 [①]

Skype 型软件是一种网络视频交际工具，允许与目标语国家的母语者进行跨时空视频音频互动，并允许话筒通话、同步文本信息显示等。

表4 Skype 型软件参与度和互动性的评测（每项超过半数达标，以"√"为记号）

类别	网络工具特征描述（总分：26分）	得分：17分	五项达标
1）参与类型（3）	a) 主动参与（2） b) 被动参与（1）	2	√
2）参与范围（6）	a) 一对多参与（1） b) 多对多参与（2） c) 使用目标语在非母语者间的交流（1） d) 使用目标语在非母语者和母语者之间的交流（2）	2 2	√
3）交流模式（6）	a) 用户终端为信息接收者（1） b) 用户终端为信息输出者，或是两者兼有（2） c) 采用单一交流模式（1） d) 采用三种完整交流模式（2）：即人际交流、理解诠释、表达演说三种模式全部涵盖	2 2	√
4）交流方向（3）	a) 信息交流为单向（1） b) 信息交流为双向（2）	2	√
5）交流方式（5）	a) 即时同步交流（2） b) 面对面交流（2） c) 存储转发式交流（1）	2 2	√
6）信息传播方式（3）	a) 用户自控式（时间、顺序、内容等）（2） b) 预录转发或直播式，独家控制（1）	1	

---

① 包括 MSN Messenger 等类似软件。

　　Skype 型软件在参与度和互动性的六项标准上有五项达标，传播方式未达标，共得 17 分。

　　Skype 型软件基本上具备博客的所有功能，但不能上传和储存目标语音频、视频、文本信息。与博客不同，Skype 型软件可提供真实的面对面交流和互动。这种可看到交流对方面部表情和手势等的参与互动最有利于语义协商。一对一的互动是语言教学最需要的一种双向交流，也是最真实的人际交流。Skype 型软件也可提供多方面对面的即时交流和互动。Skype 型软件还允许学习者使用多种交流工具（如话筒对话、文本对话）同步进行与母语者的互动和语义协商。由于 Skype 型软件允许与目标语国家的母语者进行跨时空视频、音频互动，具有高度参与性、互动性和真实性，并允许话筒通话、同步文本信息显示等以帮助语义协商，因此是一种比较理想的远程教学工具。

　　Skype 型软件的局限是往往适合有一定语言水平的学生，比如中、高级水平。其有效使用与网络连接速度、设备质量以及使用者对时间差的容忍度有关（如中美时差）。因此，在交流方式方面，会受限于其他条件而影响即时交流，与存储转发的交流方式一样，不易由人完全掌控。

　　4. Moodle [①] 型服务网

　　Moodle 型服务网可以用来制作网上课程、打造网页等，具有讨论板、博客等多项功能，其中 Wiki 可以供多人共时合作同一网页或文本文件（例如，Google 也提供 Wiki 服务）。

表5　　　　　　　　　　　**Moodle 型服务网参与度和互动性的评测**
（每项超过半数达标，以"√"为记号）

类别	网络工具特征描述（总分：26 分）	得分：17 分	六项达标
1）参与类型（3）	a）主动参与（2） b）被动参与（1）	2	√
2）参与范围（6）	a）一对多参与（1） b）多对多参与（2） c）使用目标语在非母语者间的交流（1） d）使用目标语在非母语者和母语者之间的交流（2）	2 2 2	√
3）交流模式（6）	a）用户终端为信息接收者（1） b）用户终端为信息输出者，或是两者兼有（2） c）采用单一交流模式（1） d）采用三种完整交流模式（2）：即人际交流、理解诠释、表达演说三种模式全部涵盖	2 2	√

---

　　① 参见 http：//moodle．org/。其他类似平台有 Blackboard（http：//www．blackboard．com/）等。

续表

类别	网络工具特征描述（总分：26 分）	得分：17 分	六项达标
4）交流方向（3）	a）信息交流为单向（1） b）信息交流为双向（2）	2	√
5）交流方式（5）	a）即时同步交流（2） b）面对面交流（2） c）存储转发式交流（1）	2 2 1	√
6）信息传播方式（3）	a）用户自控式（时间、顺序、内容等）（2） b）预录转发或直播式，独家控制（1）	2	√

Moodle 型服务网在参与度和互动性的六项标准上全部达标，共得 17 分。

Moodle 型服务网的主要功能是用来制作网上课程，合作网页，同时又具有讨论板、博客的功能。

Moodle 有安装好的课程模具（modules），用户可根据自己的需要加以调整。课程模具可设置学生密码和使用时间；可运用文本、录音、录像等设置各种课堂活动，也可移植其他软件制作的课堂活动（例如，Hot Potatoes）。

Moodle 课程形式比较完整：包括作业（Assignment）、讨论（Chat）、意见回收（Poll and questionnaire）、课堂内容储存（Database）、自由论坛（Forum）、词汇检索（Glossary）、课程内容（Lessons）、课程日记（Journal）、考试及成绩（Quizzes and tests）、网上合作（Webquests）以及 Wiki 文本合作和网页开发等。

就六项标准来讲，Moodle 可提供多方面文本即时交流和互动，并能提供与母语者之间的语义协商，是很好的免费远程教学工具。

Moodle 的局限是不能提供真实的面对面视频、音频交流和互动。作为语言教学工具还可以进一步改进。

5. LiveMocha①

LiveMocha 是 Web 2.0 的产物，由 Shirish Nadkani 于 2007 年建立，具有 Skype 型软件所有优点，同时又具有博客的功能。

表6　　　　　　　　LiveMocha 参与度和互动性的评测

（每项超过半数达标，以"√"为记号）

类别	网络工具特征描述（总分：26 分）	得分：18 分	五项达标
1）参与类型（3）	a）主动参与（2） b）被动参与（1）	2	√

---

① http://www.livemocha.com, Shirish Nadkani, 2007.

续表

类别	网络工具特征描述（总分：26 分）	得分：18 分	五项达标
2）参与范围（6）	a）一对多参与（1） b）多对多参与（2） c）使用目标语在非母语者间的交流（1） d）使用目标语在非母语者和母语者之间的交流（2）	2	
3）交流模式（6）	a）用户终端为信息接收者（1） b）用户终端为信息输出者，或是两者兼有（2） c）采用单一交流模式（1） d）采用三种完整交流模式（2）：即人际交流、理解诠释、表达演说三种模式全部涵盖	2 2	√
4）交流方向（3）	a）信息交流为单向（1） b）信息交流为双向（2）	2	√
5）交流方式（5）	a）即时同步交流（2） b）面对面交流（2） c）存储转发式交流（1）	2 2 1	√
6）信息传播方式（3）	a）用户自控式（时间、顺序、内容等）（2） b）预录转发或直播式，独家控制（1）	2 1	√

　　LiveMocha 在参与度和互动性的六项标准上有五项达标，参与范围未达标，共得 18 分。LiveMocha 与 Skype 型软件非常相似，加以比较，其特点更容易说明：

　　（1）与 Skype 相同，LiveMocha 可提供真实的面对面视频交流和一对一的互动。但不能提供一对多、多对多交流。

　　（2）同样与 Skype 相同，LiveMocha 的视频互动具有高度参与性，是第二语言习得最需要的练习方式。

　　（3）还是与 Skype 相同，LiveMocha 的网上视频互动允许学生同时使用其他交流工具，比如用话筒对话、文本对话等进行同步语义协商。

　　另外，LiveMocha 还为初学者提供了网上互动教学软件，因此既适合有一定语言水平的学生，也适合于初学者。因此是理想的网上语言教学工具。

　　LiveMocha 的局限是要收费，只能提供一对一的互动，信息传播可能会受网络连接速度、设备质量的影响。

6. 第二人生（Second Life）①

Web 2.0 的产物，属虚拟世界，可打造三维虚拟课堂、虚拟校园等。具有上述软件所有的功能。

表 7　　　　　　　　　第二人生参与度和互动性的评测
（每项超过半数达标，以 "√" 为记号）

类别	网络工具特征描述（总分：26 分）	得分：20 分	六项达标
1）参与类型（3）	a）主动参与（2） b）被动参与（1）	2	√
2）参与范围（6）	a）一对多参与（1） b）多对多参与（2） c）使用目标语在非母语者间的交流（1） d）使用目标语在非母语者和母语者之间的交流（2）	2 2	√
3）交流模式（6）	a）用户终端为信息接收者（1） b）用户终端为信息输出者，或是两者兼有（2） c）采用单一交流模式（1） d）采用三种完整交流模式（2）：即人际交流、理解诠释、表达演说三种模式全部涵盖	2 2	√
4）交流方向（3）	a）信息交流为单向（1） b）信息交流为双向（2）	2	√
5）交流方式（5）	a）即时同步交流（2） b）面对面交流（2） c）存储转发式交流（1）	2 2 1	√
6）信息传播方式（3）	a）用户自控式（时间、顺序、内容等）（2） b）预录转发或直播式，独家控制（1）	2 1	√

第二人生在参与度和互动性的六项标准上均达标，共得 20 分。

第二人生可提供三维虚拟教学环境，可模拟老师、学生、教室等进行实地教学，也可进行多种仿真语境教学。从功能上来讲，第二人生具有讨论板、博客、Skype、LiveMocha 的所有相似功能，可提供即时音频、视频对话、上传文本信息、电子邮件，提供群组、个人对话，播放 PPT 和电视录像，举行电话会议，模拟黑板、电脑打字，提供网络搜索等一对一、一对多、多对多的仿真互动交流。因此是理想的网上语言教学工具。

第二人生的局限与 LiveMocha 相同，即要收费。另外用户需要自己打造

---

① http://secondlife.com, Linden Lab, 1999.

教师、学生的化身（avatar）等，比较费时费力。再有信息传播也可能会受网络连接速度、设备质量的影响。

7. 六种网络参与式学习工具评测结果比较

如上所述，六种网络参与式学习工具在语言教学方面各有利弊长短，用户可根据不同需要选择使用或搭配使用。为方便起见，兹将上述六种网络参与式学习工具缺点和问题列表如下，以备查询。

表8   六种网络参与式学习工具缺点和问题

讨论板 13	博客 17	Skype 型软件 17	Moodle 型服务网 17	LiveMocha 18	第二人生 20
1）不允许面对面交流 2）不允许口头交流 3）网上交流非同步，反馈不即时 4）信息传播仅允许储存转发 5）无其他媒体（视频、音频）帮助以提供真实性	不允许面对面视频真实交流	仅适合有一定语言水平的学生，如中高级水平	不能提供面对面即时视频、音频交流和互动	1）只能提供一对一的互动 2）要收费	1）须打造虚拟情境、教师学生 av-atar 等，学习使用较费时力 2）要收费

三　虚拟课堂软件的选择标准

（一）选择虚拟课堂软件的第一个标准

1. 虚拟课堂与真实课堂的比较

虚拟课堂与真实课堂比较，有不同点，也有相同点。虚拟课堂与真实课堂的不同首先是打破了真实课堂的时空限制，可以提供异地、异时的课堂交流。其次是班级的大小伸缩性很大，可以一对一，也可以一对无限。再次是课程内容的讲解深化是靠文本上的交流合作、音频视频会议、讨论板、博客、聊天室、电子邮件、课程日记等网上形式和工具。虚拟课堂的目的就是极大限度地模拟真实课堂，因此需要有相应的教学理论、教学大纲、教学方法；要以学生为中心，也要有详细课程、作业、考试等；而且要更强调师生互动、生生互动，合作学习。

虚拟课堂的优点首先是具有灵活性（Flexibility）：课程时间、课程长短、课程内容、学习进程（Pace）均由学生决定。其次是费用低，注册、入学容易，选择性高，不受时地限制。虚拟课堂的缺点是缺乏真实的面对面的参与和互动，缺乏社会交际交流的这个重要过程。再次是使用虚拟课堂不论是教师还是学生都要有一个学习过程。另外虚拟课堂高度依赖计算机网络、线路、软件、硬件、系统、程序的畅通运行，稍有差错，即会影响教学、学习。

2. 网络参与度、互动性的六项标准

鉴于虚拟课堂（特别是适合于语言教学的虚拟课堂）的课程内容讲解、深化主要是靠文本上的交流合作，靠音频、视频会议、讨论板、博客、聊天室、电子邮件、课程日记等网上形式和工具。其目的是极大限度地模拟真实课堂，同时更强调师生互动、生生互动、合作学习，因此网络参与度、互动性也应该是衡量选择适合于语言教学虚拟课堂软件的第一标准。

许德宝（2010）在参与度、互动性的每项标准上又细分为文本、音频、视频、仿真情境互动四项用以检查衡量虚拟课堂软件的参与度和互动性，因此衡量虚拟课堂软件参与度和互动性的六项标准总分从 26 分增加到 104 分，见表9。

表9   **虚拟课堂软件参与度和互动性的六项标准**
每项超过 52 分达标

类别（各项总分）	参与度和互动性特征描述及具体分数（总分：104 分）	评测得分
1）参与类型（12）	a）主动参与：文本、音频、视频、仿真情境互动（8）（每项2分，下同） b）被动参与：文本、音频、视频、仿真情境互动（4）	
2）参与范围（24）	a）一对多参与：文本、音频、视频、仿真情境互动（4） b）多对多参与：文本、音频、视频、仿真情境互动（8） c）使用目标语在非母语者间的交流：文本、音频、视频、仿真情境互动（4） d）使用目标语在非母语者和母语者之间的交流：文本、音频、视频、仿真情境互动（8）	
3）交流模式（24）	a）用户终端为信息接收者：文本、音频、视频、仿真情境互动（4） b）用户终端为信息输出者，或是两者兼有：文本、音频、视频、仿真情境互动（8） c）采用单一交流模式：文本、音频、视频、仿真情境互动（4） d）采用三种完整交流模式：即人际交流、理解诠释、表达演说三种模式全部涵盖：文本、音频、视频、仿真情境互动（8）	
4）交流方向（12）	a）信息交流为单向：文本、音频、视频、仿真情境互动（4） b）信息交流为双向：文本、音频、视频、仿真情境互动（8）	

续表

类别（各项总分）	参与度和互动性特征描述及具体分数（总分：104 分）	评测得分
5）交流方式（20）	a）即时同步交流：文本、音频、视频、仿真情境互动（8） b）面对面交流：文本、音频、视频、仿真情境互动（8） c）存储转发式交流：文本、音频、视频、仿真情境互动（4）	
6）信息传播方式（12）	a）用户自控式（时间、顺序、内容等）：文本、音频、视频、仿真情境互动（8） b）预录转发或直播式，独家控制：文本、音频、视频、仿真情境互动（4）	

3. 通过网络参与度、互动性六项标准选出的虚拟课堂软件

本文在许德宝（2010）的基础上，根据上述虚拟课堂软件参与度和互动性的六项标准对网上 21 种虚拟课堂软件进行了试用筛选，[①] 包括 Acrobat Connect 8、B-Live、Saba Centra、Click-to-Meet、eLECTA Live、Elluminate、GoToTraining、INSORS、Wimba Classroom、iLinc、Lotus Sametime、Macromedia Breeze、Marratech、Microsoft Lync Online、Polycom Web Office、Question Mark、Second Life、Tegrity、Voluxion、Virtual Language Lab、WebEx，得出以下九种（具体出版公司、厂家、价格等从略，有兴趣的读者可以根据网址自行了解）：

1. Acrobat Connect 8 （http：//www. adobe. com/products/acrobatconnect-pro/）54 分

2. Elluminate Live [②]（http：//www. elluminate. com）57 分

---

① 一些后起的虚拟课堂软件未能包括进去，比如 WizIQ，Verxact LMS，dexway Language courses，Global Virtual Classroom，Fenix Language Institute，EasyCampus，Integrated Language Solutions，BigBlueBotton，JigsawMeeting，Vmukti 等。

② 现在 Elluminate Live （http：//www. answers. com/topic/elluminate#ixzz1Paif46B6）、Wimba Classroom 和 Blackboard 合并成了一个公司，叫 Blackboard Collaborate http：//www. wimba. com/。

3. iLinc（http：//www. ilinc. com/）57 分

4. Microsoft Lync Online （http：//office. microsoft. com/en-us/live-meeting/）57 分

5. Saba Centra（http：//www. saba. com/products/centra/）57 分

6. Wimba Classroom（http：//www. horizonwimba. com）57 分

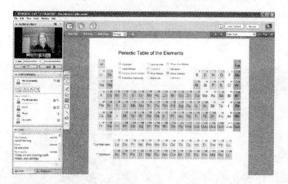

7. WebEx（http：//www. webex. com）57 分

8. eLECTA Live（http：//www. e-lecta. com/features. asp）57 分

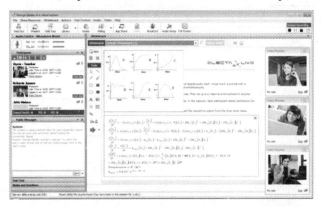

9. Second Life（http：//www. secondlife. com/）76 分

上述九种虚拟课堂软件都达到了参与性、互动性的六项标准，积分都在52 分以上。具体评测得分如下：

表 10　　　　　九种达标虚拟课堂软件参与度和互动性六项标准得分

类别（各项总分）	虚拟课堂特征描述及具体分数（总分：104 分）	评测得分
1）参与类型（12）	a）主动参与：文本、音频、视频、仿真情境互动（8） b）被动参与：文本、音频、视频、仿真情境互动（4）	1—8（6），9（8）
2）参与范围（24）	a）一对多参与：文本、音频、视频、仿真情境互动（4） b）多对多参与：文本、音频、视频、仿真情境互动（8）	1—8（6），9（8）
	c）使用目标语在非母语者间的交流：文本、音频、视频、仿真情境互动（4） d）使用目标语在非母语者和母语者之间的交流：文本、音频、视频、仿真情境互动（8）	1—8（6），9（8）

续表

类别（各项总分）	虚拟课堂特征描述及具体分数（总分：104 分）	评测得分
3）交流模式（24）	a）用户终端为信息接收者：文本、音频、视频、仿真情境互动（4） b）用户终端为信息输出者，或是两者兼有：文本、音频、视频、仿真情境互动（8） c）采用单一交流模式：文本、音频、视频、仿真情境互动（4） d）采用三种完整交流模式：即人际交流、理解诠释、表达演说三种模式全部涵盖：文本、音频、视频、仿真情境互动（8）	1—8（6），9（8） 1—8（6），9（8）
4）交流方向（12）	a）信息交流为单向：文本、音频、视频、仿真情境互动（4） b）信息交流为双向：文本、音频、视频、仿真情境互动（8）	1—8（6），9（8）
5）交流方式（20）	a）即时同步交流：文本、音频、视频、仿真情境互动（8） b）面对面交流：文本、音频、视频、仿真情境互动（8） c）存储转发式交流：文本、音频、视频、仿真情境互动（4）	1—8（6），9（8） 1—8（6），9（8） 1—8（3），9（4）
6）信息传播方式（12）	a）用户自控式（时间、顺序、内容等）：文本、音频、视频、仿真情境互动（8） b）预录转发或直播式，独家控制：文本、音频、视频、仿真情境互动（4）	2—8（6），9（8） 1（3）

　　数字 1—9 代表不同的虚拟课堂软件，其具体名称见前页。括号内数字是各个虚拟课堂软件在六项标准中相应条款上的具体得分。汇总起来，Second Life 共得 76 分（九项 8 分，一项 4 分），得分最高；①Elluminate Live、iLinc、Microsoft Lync Online、Saba Centra、Wimba Classroom、WebEx 和 eLECTA Live 各软件均各得 57 分（九项 6 分，一项 3 分），只有 Acrobat Connect 8 共得 54 分（八项 6 分，两项 3 分），得分最低。Second Life 得分最高

---

　　① 本文旨在选出符合网络参与度、互动性六项标准的虚拟课堂软件，进而证实网络参与度、互动性的六项标准可以作为选择适合于语言教学的虚拟课堂软件的标准，但并不具体比较选出的虚拟课堂软件哪种最适合于语言教学。有兴趣的读者可以参考《美国科技与中文教学》2010 年 12 月特刊号"虚拟课堂软件研究"。具体文章见刘（2010）、陈（2010）、谢（2010）、Grant 与黄（2010）。

的原因是具备"仿真情境互动"①一项而其他虚拟课堂软件不具备。Acro-bat Connect 8 得分最低的原因是在用户自控方面只能是直播式或预录转发式，用户不能自控。上述九种虚拟课堂软件在六项标准相应条款上的得分都在52 分以上，所以都达到了参与性、互动性的六项标准。

4. 相关研究参照

CERMUSA（2005）② 对十五种虚拟课堂软件（iLinc、Click-to-Meet、IN-SORS、Question Mark、Macromedia Breeze、Horizon Wimba、Marratech、Ellu-minate、Centra、Tegrity、WebEx、B-Live、Polycom Web Office、MS Live Meet-ing、Lotus Sametime）进行适用研究。研究分成三阶段。第一阶段对每种虚拟课堂软件使用四个月，筛选出的八种虚拟课堂软件［Centra、Click-to-Meet、Horizon Wimba、iLinc、Macromedia Breeze、Marratech、Microsoft Live Meeting（亦即 Microsoft Lync Online）和 WebEx］，其中六种与我们的相同（没有 Second Life、Elluminate Live，但有 Macromedia Breeze、Marratech）。第二阶段对第一阶段筛选出的八种虚拟课堂软件再进行筛选，得出三种（Wimba、iLinc、Microsoft Live Meeting）也都在我们的选择之中。

Schullo 等（2007）从十种虚拟课堂软件中挑选了 Elluminate Live 和 Ado-be Connect 进行比较。这两种虚拟课堂软件也在我们的选择之中。

Cogburn 和 Kurup（2006）经过研究，给 Elluminate Live 打了 A-，给 Adobe Connect 打了 B。我们的评测结果是 Elluminate Live 57 分，Adobe Con-nect 8 54 分，也比较相符。

因此，网络参与度、互动性的六项标准可以作为选择虚拟课堂软件特别是适合于语言教学虚拟课堂软件的标准之一。

（二）选择虚拟课堂软件的第二个标准

通过网络参与度、互动性六项标准筛选出的九种适合于语言教学的虚拟课堂软件大都具备以下十项功能和特点：

---

① "仿真情境互动"是指仿真模拟情境互动。比如用 Second Life 制作的"英语城市"（ht-tp：//www. youtube. com/watch? v = 8hJZ2bre_ FI）。学习者可以去这个英语城市中的任何地方，所遇到的人都是英语母语者，可以直接通过与母语者的化身进行仿真情境互动学习英文。又如"英语课堂" http：//www. youtube. com/watch? v = kO6FBbw69dc，其中所有的学生都是真实英文学习者，由英文母语教师带领在仿真情境中实地学习英文。

② 见 Griffin et al（2005）。

　1. 文本合作功能

　2. 音频多向共用功能

　3. 视频多向共用功能

　4. 白板（White Board）共用功能

　5. 投影片（Power Point）共用以及上传下载功能

　6. 网页浏览器共用功能

　7. 小组多向合作功能

　8. 储存、录制、重放功能

　9. 跨平台（多数能够运用在 Windows 和苹果机上，有的还可以在 Linux 上使用，比如，Elluminate Live）

　10. 易用、界面直观

这十项功能和特点可以说是从技术角度反映了虚拟课堂软件特别是适合于语言教学的虚拟课堂软件应该具备的条件，也可以说是虚拟课堂软件特别是适合于语言教学的虚拟课堂软件应该达到的技术标准。

CERMUSA（2005）、Finkelstein（2006）也这样认为。CERMUSA（2005）让员工从以下九个方面使用检查所收集的十五种虚拟课堂软件：

　1. 易用（Ease of Use）

　2. 音频（Audio）

　3. 视频（Video）

　4. 白板（White Board）

　5. 投影片（Power Point）

　6. 浏览器共用（Shared Web Browser）

　7. 小组合作（Team/Group Collaboration）

　8. 应用软件共用（Application Sharing）

　9. 界面直观（Interface Intuitive）

其中八项与我们总结出的十项功能和特点相同/相似；只有"应用软件共用"与我们"文本合作功能"稍有差异。

Finkelstein（2006）在讨论同步共时网上教学时，认为虚拟课堂软件应具备如下九项功能：

　1. 视频共用（videoconferencing ability）

　2. 实时音频共用（real-time voice and visual contact between all participants）

　3. 白板共用（shared whiteboard）

　4. 投影片共用（integrated area for the projection of slides or other visuals）

5. 文本合作共用（capacity for text-based interaction，including side conver-sations or note-passing）

6. 师生交流功能（means for learners to indicate that they have questions or are confused）

7. 学生感觉、观点、理解评价（tools for assessing current moods，opin-ions，and comprehension as well as for soliciting）

8. 反馈搜集（questions or feedback，and the ability to gauge virtual body language，or a sense of how）

9. 易用（engaged learners are in the activity at hand）

这九项功能也与我们总结的十项功能和特点基本相同。

因此，上述十项功能和特点从技术角度反映了虚拟课堂软件应该具备的条件，是虚拟课堂软件特别是适合于语言教学的虚拟课堂软件应该达到的技术标准。这十项功能和特点应该是选择虚拟课堂软件特别是适合于语言教学的虚拟课堂软件的第二标准。

（三）选择虚拟课堂软件的第三个标准

Andreessen（2009）把互联网平台（Internet platforms）分成三级：① 一级互联网平台只可以使用该平台所提供的使用软件（Applications）、功能，该平台负责提供软件系统、计算机语言、数据和数据库、服务器、网络系统、宽带、安全控制等，比如 eBay，Paypal；二级互联网平台是在一级互联网平台的基础上允许使用者插用其他使用软件作为"插件"（plug-ins），比如 Facebook；三级互联网平台则允许使用者根据个人需要在这个平台上自己再编码，自己再写程序，当然也可以在这个平台上直接运用其他平台所提供的使用软件，如 Ning、Second Life、Amazon's FPS、Salesforce 等。Andreessen（2009）所说的三级互联网平台就是现在所谓的云平台 PaaS（见下）。An-dreessen（2009）认为三级互联网平台是互联网的将来。一级、二级互联网平台可能会失去竞争力。因此，从发展角度讲，虚拟课堂软件应该植根于三

---

① 3 levels of Internet Platforms（Marc Andreessen 2009）：A Level 1 platform's apps run elsewhere, and call into the platform via a web services API to draw on data and services—this is how Flickr does it. A Lev-el 2 platform's apps run elsewhere，but inject functionality into the platform via a plug-in API—this is how Fa-cebook does it. Most likely，a Level 2 platform's apps also call into the platform via a web services API to draw on data and services. A Level 3 platform's apps run inside the platform itself—the platform provides the "runtime environment" within which the app's code runs.

级互联网平台。换句话讲，虚拟课堂软件的第三标准是应植根于三级互联网平台（云平台 PaaS）。原因有二：第一，如果是一级、二级互联网平台提供的虚拟课堂软件，平台没有了，那它们提供的虚拟课堂软件也就没有了。第二，要给自己的虚拟课堂软件留有发展的余地，如有需要，应该可以再编码、再写程序，不断提高。

斯坦福大学的互联网专家 Parulkar（2010）认为互联网已经到了亟待更新的时候，五至十年内互联网会与现在大不相同。互联网的使用环境和基本设置（Infrastructure）将由用户、所有者及其使用软件来决定和控制，也会受到公开检查。[①] Parulkar（2010）预测的由用户、所有者及其使用软件来决定和控制并受到公开检查的互联网环境其实就是我们现在谈的不同用户可以根据自己的需求来选择不同的云计算（Cloud Computing）服务，比如 IaaS、PaaS、SaaS。[②]因此，虚拟课堂软件也要适合于这种由用户、所有者及其使用软件来决定和控制并受到公开检查的互联网环境（不同的云计算服务）。

最后，虚拟课堂软件还应该适用于不同的计算机平台，比如苹果、Windows、Linux，也应该能在 iPod、iPad、iPhone 等移动式接收器上使用。这些也应该纳入选择虚拟课堂软件的第三个标准。

因此，选择虚拟课堂软件的第三个标准应该是植根于三级互联网平台（云平台 PaaS），适合于由用户、所有者及其使用软件来决定和控制并受到公开检查的不断发展的互联网环境（云服务），而且能在不同计算机平台、不同移动式接收器上使用。

（四）选择虚拟课堂软件的第四个标准

虚拟课堂软件应该符合用户自己语言教学的特点、要求、技术需要、自己的购买能力等。大多数虚拟课堂软件都可以免费试用，所以购买虚拟课堂软件时要先进行试用，然后再购买。

（五）虚拟课堂软件选择标准小结

总结起来，虚拟课堂软件特别是适合于语言教学的虚拟课堂软件的选择

---

① Internet will look very different in five to ten years. Internet Infrastructure will be under the control of the users, owners and their applications, and is open to public scrutiny（Guru Parulkar, 2010）.

② IaaS 通过网络提供计算机的使用环境和基本设置（Infrastructure）服务（比如网上服务器），PaaS 提供互联网平台及其应用软件开发（platforms）服务（比如第二人生），SaaS 提供网络使用软件（applications）服务（比如 Gmail）。

标准共有四个：

1. 虚拟课堂软件须达到网络参与式学习工具参与度和互动性的六项标准（得分 52 分以上）。

2. 虚拟课堂软件须达到十项技术标准（十项功能和特点）。

3. 虚拟课堂软件应植根于三级互联网平台（云平台 PaaS），应适合于由用户、所有者及其使用软件来决定和控制并受到公开检查的不断发展的互联网环境（不同的云计算服务），而且能在不同计算机平台、不同移动式接收器上使用。

4. 虚拟课堂软件要符合用户自己语言教学的特点、要求、技术需要、自己的购买能力等，用户对所要购买的虚拟课堂软件先进行试用，然后再购买。

四　结语

综上所述，参与度和互动性的六项标准不但可以评价网络参与式学习工具在语言教学方面的利弊长短，选择出具有显著优势、适合于第二语言教学的网络参与式学习工具，也可以用来选择虚拟课堂软件特别是适合于语言教学的虚拟课堂软件，而且是选择虚拟课堂软件特别是适合于语言教学的虚拟课堂软件的主要标准。

参考文献

Andreessen, Marc, 2009. "The three kinds of platforms you meet on the Internet", http：//pmarca-archive. posterous. com/the-three-kinds-of-platforms-you-meet-on-the-0.

Chen, Dongdong, 2010, "Enhancing the learning of Chinese with Second Life", *Journal of Technology and Chinese Language Teaching*, Vol. 1, No. 1, December 2010, pp. 14—30.

Cheng, Hsiu-Jen, Hong Zhan, Andy Tsai, 2010. "Integrating Second Life into a Chinese language teacher training program：A pilot study", *Journal of Technology and Chinese Language Teaching*, Vol. 1, No. 1, December 2010, pp. 31—58.

Cogburn, Derrick L., Divya Kurup, 2006. "Tech U：The World Is Our Campus", Derrick L. Cogburn and Divya Kurup, *Network Computing*, *For it by it.* April 2006.

Finkelstein, Jonathan, 2006. *Learning in Real Time：Synchronous Teaching and*

Learning Online. San Francisco, CA. Jossey-Bass.

Fortin, David R, 1997. *The Impact of Interactivity on Advertising Effectiveness in the New Media*, unpublished dissertation. Kingston, RI: College of Business Administration, The University of Rhode Island.

Grant, Scott, Hui Huang, 2010. "The integration of an online 3D virtual learning environment into formal classroom-based undergraduate Chinese language and culture curriculum", *Journal of Technology and Chinese Language Teaching*, Vol. 1, No. 1, December 2010, pp. 2—13.

Griffin, Robert E., Dana Parrish, Michael Reigh, 2005. "Using Virtual Classroom Tools In Distance Learning: Can The Classroom Be Re-created At A Distance?" http://commons.internet2.edu.

Jin, Hong Gang, Lu Shengjie, 2009. "Participatory Learning in Internet Web Technology: A Study of Three Web Tools in the Context of CFL Learning", *Journal of the Chinese Language Teachers Association*, Vol. 44, No. 1, pp. 25—49.

Kurbel, Karl, 2001. "Virtuality on the Students' and on the Teachers' sides: A Multimedia and Internet based International Master Program, ICEF Berlin GmbH (Eds.), *Proceedings of the 7th International Conference on Technology Supported Learning and Training-Online Educa*; Berlin, Germany; November 2001, pp. 133—136

Liu, Shijuan, 2010. "Second Life 及其在中文教学中的应用", *Journal of Technology and Chinese Language Teaching*, Vol. 1, No. 1, December 2010, pp. 71—93.

Parulkar, Guru, 2010. Overview of Programmable Open Mobile Internet POMI 2020 Program, Stanford Computer Forum, Annual Meeting: POMI 2020 Workshop, http://forum.stanford.edu/events/2011cleanslate.php.

Schullo, S., Hilbelink, A., Venable, M., Barron, A. E., 2007. "Selecting a Virtual Classroom System: Elluminate Live vs. Macromedia Breeze (Adobe Acrobat Connect Professional)", *Journal of Online Learning and Teaching*. Vol. 3, No. 4, pp. 331—345.

Xie, Tianwei, 2010. "在虚拟世界进行汉语教学的工具", *Journal of Technology and Chinese Language Teaching*, Vol. 1, No. 1, December 2010, pp. 59—70.

Xu, De Bao, Hong Gang Jin, 2009. "网络参与式学习工具的评测", paper presented at 第六届全球华文网络教育研讨会（ICICE09，台北，台湾，2009 年 6 月 19 日—21 日）

Xu, De Bao, 2010. 网络参与式学习工具的评测与虚拟课堂软件的选择标准, Keynote speech at *the 6th International Conference on Technology and Chinese Language Teaching*（TCLT6, Ohio State University, June 12—14, 2010）.

The Integration of an Online 3D Virtual Learning Environment into Formal Classroom-based Undergraduate Chinese Language and Culture Curriculum

Scott Grant   Monash University Australia scott. grant@ arts. monash. edu. au

黄 慧 Huang, Hui   Monash University Australia

Hui. huang@ arts. monash. edu. au

Abstract: This paper discusses the integration of "Second Life", an online 3D multi-user virtual environment, into a formal classroom-based undergraduate Chinese language and culture teaching program. The paper identifies a range of limitations with the formal curriculum from the perspective of educational theory and language acquisition theory. It then goes on to discuss the theoretical mechanism by which such integration can be achieved and finally discusses the viability and benefits of integration.

摘　要：本文探讨了如何将"第二人生"这个网络三维多用户虚拟环境融入大学本科汉语语言文化课堂教学。从教育和语言习得理论出发，本文揭示了传统课程设置的系列不足并讨论了如何将"第二人生"融入传统课堂的理论体系以及融入的可行性和益处。

Introduction

The Monash University Chinese Studies Program (CSP) is one of the largest Chinese language and culture programs in Australia, with over 800 students enrolled in any one semester. The formal classroom-based curriculum for first year beginner students provides a reasonable mix of rules-based learning, drill and pattern-based learning, and conversation practice. Implementation of the curriculum also involves a mix of teacher-centred and learner-centred learning, although the balance has generally been biased towards the former. The curriculum provides learners with exposure to a range of linguistic and non-linguistic 'inputs' and with opportunities to generate 'outputs', but these are confined to a classroom-based, textbook-centred learning context that involves little spontaneous or meaningful communication in the target language.

The Formal Classroom-based Curriculum-Structure, Nature and Limitations

The formal classroom-based curriculum is made up of four parts: lecture, seminar, tutorial and computer lab classes.

The two-hour lecture is essentially an 'input' based activity focused on explanations of new grammar, vocab and content, most of which is in English. 'Input' in the target language is essentially limited to modelling of pronunciation and sentence patterns. Due to class numbers, time limits and class format, there is little opportunity for students to generate 'output' in the target language during class. The main opportunity for 'output' comes in the form of periodic written assessment. Lecture classes are essentially teacher-focused and a passive learning activity for learners.

While still predominantly teacher-focused, seminar classes are designed to have a higher level of interactivity. 'Input' in the target language takes the form of language modelling and simple instructions from the teacher and exercises in the textbook. Learners have some opportunity to generate 'output' in the target language, though it is often limited to reading out answers to set exercises or set passages and drill and skill type exercises. With a few exceptions, learner 'output' in the target language is generally only produced when requested by the teacher, and thus tends to be passive. Due to the numbers involved and time limits, not every student gets an opportunity to generate 'output' and receive feedback each time they attend a seminar class.

The spoken tutorials have generally provided the best opportunity for students to receive 'input' and to generate 'output' in the target language. These classes are more learner-centred, with the teacher playing more of a facilitating role, and learners working together to create and perform topic-based dialogues. 'Input' comes via instructions and feedback in the target language from the tutor and through interaction with fellow students. 'Output' in the target language is mostly limited to performance of the dialogues in the artificial context of the classroom. 'Meaningful communication' in the target language is very limited in that use of the language in this context is an end in itself (practicing language), rather than a means to an end (using the language to achieve something else). Again, due to numbers and limited time, not all students have the opportunity to perform their 'output' and receive feedback from the tutor and their peers every time.

The web-based exercises undertaken by learners in computer lab classes, while very much learner-centred, have in the past generally not been well received by students. As interaction with fellow learners and the teacher is limited, students have expressed a preference for doing these exercises in their own time.

Questions for consideration

The limitations of the formal classroom-based curriculum for first year Chinese language and culture students described above have thus raised several questions. How could the formal classroom-based curriculum be made more learner-centred and better reflect widely accepted educational principles such as those of constructivism? What opportunities for 'meaningful communication' in the target language could be created within the formal classroom-based curriculum? If, as proposed by a number of language acquisition theorists, the role of 'comprehensible input' (Krashen, 1985) and 'comprehensible output' (Swain, 1985, 1995) is essential to the language learning process (see discussion below), how could more of these two elements be incorporated within the formal classroom-based curriculum?

In an attempt to answer these questions, it was decided that the computer lab classes would be used to conduct lessons in the 3D online virtual world Second Life. In 2007, Monash University purchased its first 'region' for general educational and research use[1]. In 2008, after the purchase of a 'region' dedicated to the learning and teaching of Chinese language and culture [2], first year and third year undergraduate students began classes in Second Life as an integrated part of their formal classroom-based curriculum.

Second Life as an Online 3D Virtual Learning Environment

Recent years has seen a continual growth of interest and investment of time and resources in 3D simulations, games and virtual environments for teaching and learning across a broad range of disciplines and institutions (education. au, 2009; ALTC, 2009/2010; Henderson et. al. , 2009; Dalgarno, 2010). Educators and educational institutions around the world see great potential for these platforms as 3D virtual learning environments (3D VLEs) that provide the possibility of rich learner engagement, as well as the ability to explore, construct and manipulate virtual objects, structures and metaphorical representations of ideas (Dalgarno, 2010).

Second Life is one of over 250 online virtual worlds (Association of Virtual Worlds, 2008 in Henderson et. al. , 2009). An online virtual world is a three-dimensional graphical space that resides on a computer server (s) connected to the Internet and accessed via three-dimensional graphical representations of the users (avatars). While often perceived of as being similar to 3D computer games or massively multiplayer online role-playing games, some virtual worlds like Second Life, Croquet, Project Wonderland, Olive, Active Worlds, web. alive, etc. , are not per se games (Ondrejka, C. , 2008). They do not have pre-set game rules, objectives, roles and environments, but rather are flexible 3D virtual spaces that can be, to a lesser or greater degree, configured by the users themselves to suit their specific needs. These needs can be game-like, but are

---

① secondlife: //monash%20university/123/136

② secondlife: //monash%20university%202/83/89/26

increasingly oriented towards social networking, education and training, and business (Ondrejka, C., 2008; Salt et. al., 2008).

While not unique to virtual worlds, there are two other important affordances offered by these online spaces. The first is the high level of synchronous interactivity (via text and voice chat, gesture and movement) that greatly facilitates peer-to-peer and student-to-instructor real-time interaction regardless of actual physical location of the participants. The second is the potential for asynchronous interactivity via persistent digital objects such as whiteboards, bulletin boards, slideshows, notecards and programmed non-player characters, which the learners/avatars can interact with even though the 'owner' is absent or offline (Henderson et. al., 2009). It is this high level of synchronous and asynchronous interactivity and configurability of the virtual environment that has provided a unique opportunity for meaningful communication in the target language and for creating an environment rich in 'comprehendible input' and 'comprehendible output' for the first year Chinese language and culture students at Monash University.

Constructivism-three Perspectives

In a paper entitled *The Potential of 3D Virtual Learning Environments: A Constructivist Analysis* (2002), Dalgarno summarises and re-casts Moshman's (1982) discussion of three broad approaches to constructivist learning. Moshman calls these approaches endogenous, exogenous and dialectical constructivism. Each approach is underpinned by several basic principles at the heart of constructivism: knowledge is actively 'constructed' by the learner and not simply passively absorbed; new knowledge is constructed on the foundation of, and at times in contrast with, existing knowledge and experience; each learner constructs knowledge in their own way.

The three approaches differ in terms of the locus of learning. In the exogenous category "knowledge is derived from one's environment" and is a "reconstruction of structures (empirical relationships, presented information, observed behaviour patterns, etc.) pre-formed in the external reality" (Moshman, 1982). For endogenous learning, the "locus of activity in the construction of new knowledge is⋯the organism rather than the environment" (Moshman, 1982). In other words, new knowledge is developed through "a reflective abstraction of new structures via intercoordination of, and/or metacognitive reflection on, current structures" and not via an "empirical abstraction of information from the environment" (Moshman, 1982). Dialectical constructivism involves, as the name suggests, "continuing interactions between organism and environment". "New knowledge is a constructed synthesis which resolves the inevitable contradictions arising during the course of such interactions" (Moshman, 1982). Interaction with the environment clearly includes social interaction with peers and instructors (and others in society in general), and indeed it is this social interaction as the source of new knowledge that forms the core of many of the modern applications of constructivist learning theory.

We would argue that with the addition of interactive lessons in a 3D virtual learning environment like Second Life these three perspectives can be effectively combined within the overall structure of a formal language and culture curriculum with large class sizes to address some of the limitations of the existing curriculum outlined above. Indeed, Moshman sees exogenous and endogenous learning almost as a subset of dialectical constructivism, and certainly argues for a partial integration of the three paradigms (Moshman, 1982).

Integrating Second Life into the Formal Classroom-based Curriculum

An educational perspective

Integrating learning in a 3D VLE like Second Life into a formal undergraduate language and culture curriculum is one way of effectively bringing together the three constructivist paradigms and addressing some of the limitations outlined above. Lectures provide the structures "pre-formed in the external reality" by presenting the rules of the target language and examples of those rules in action, and are thus of an "exogenous" nature. Seminars provide "exercises requiring the learners to be cognitively active" and to "form and refine their knowledge representations" through formal pattern exercises (Dalgarno, 2002), and are thus also mainly exogenous in nature. We would argue that the speaking-based tutorials fulfil the requirements of endogenous constructivism as outlined by Dalgarno in that the role of the tutor is as a "facilitator in providing experiences that are likely to result in challenges to learners' existing models". The experiences are the topics set for the dialogues that students create and perform, with the challenges coming from both the linguistic and cultural content inherent in each topic, as well as the instructive feedback provided by the tutor. We would argue, however, that the tutorials only fulfil the requirements of dialectical constructivism outlined in Dalgarno in a 'weak' form in that the dialogues performed by students are (a) not 'meaningful communication' and (b) out of context, and therefore not realistic. The collaboration engaged in by students is essentially limited to the construction and performance of artificial dialogues and is usually restricted to pairs. We would thus argue that this is a 'weak', and ergo inadequate, form of dialectical constructivism.

This is where we see a role for the task-based learning undertaken by students in Second Life in completing the picture/framework. The tasks undertaken by students in their lessons in Second Life fulfil the requirements of dialectical constructivism (and thus comply with the basic principles of constructivist learning) in a 'strong' from by facilitating broader and deeper collaborative work and by providing a realistic, meaningful context for the use of the vocabulary, grammar and cultural knowledge learned in the lectures, seminars and tutorials. Because tasks are performed in a context that generally reflects the context of the real world and in an environment that simulates the real world with a reasonable degree of fidelity[1], engagement in and completion of the tasks do provide a "realistic experience" (Honebein et. al., 1993). Opportunities for 'comprehensible input', 'comprehensible output', and 'meaningful communication' are also thereby increased greatly. We would argue that this is a 'strong' from of dialecti-

---

① For a more detailed discussion of 'fidelity', see Dalgarno and Lee (2010).

cal constructivism.

A language acquisition perspective

Comprehensible input' is a hypothesis first proposed by Stephen Krashen. (Krashen, 1981) He purports that language learners acquire language by hearing and understanding messages that are slightly above their current second language level. In everyday contexts the degree to which 'input' is comprehensible is extremely variable. The multiple information channels available in 3D VLEs like Second Life enable the level of 'input' to be better tailored to the comprehension levels of specific groups of learners than is possible in similar contexts in real life. What a learner might not understand from text-based information might be better understood from visual observation of the surrounding environment or through interaction with objects in the environment (clicking an object to hear an audio file for pronunciation) or agents within the environment (other learners, automated non-player characters).

We would argue that Krashen's concept of i + 1 is not incongruous with the Piagian idea embodied in exogenous constructivism of learning being seen as "fundamentally an accommodation of the organism's prior structures to those imposed by its current environment" (Moshman, 1982). In Krashen's formulation of i + 1, "i" includes extra-linguistic "knowledge of the world and of the situation, that is, the context" (Wikipedia, Comprehensible Input). Thus, 'comprehensible' input' includes both linguistic and contextual information. The content of our Second Life lessons is based closely on content students have previously encountered in their textbooks. When designing the task scenarios, in addition to incorporating as much material as possible that students are already familiar with, extra linguistic and contextual material drawn from real life scenarios is also incorporated. Learners thus construct new knowledge and structures through using existing knowledge and structures to explore and interact with the multi-channel 'input' they encounter when completing the set tasks.

Developed by Merrill Swain (1985, 1995), the 'comprehensible output' hypothesis states that learning takes place when encountering a gap in the linguistic knowledge of the L2. By noticing this gap the learner becomes aware of it and might be able to modify their output so that they learn something new about the language. Although Swain does not claim that comprehensible output is solely responsible for all or even most language acquisition, she does claim that under some conditions, 'comprehensible output' facilitates second language learning in ways that differ from and enhance input due to the mental processes connected with the production of language (production forces learners to pay some attention to form and to process syntactically). Swain defines three functions of output: 1. Noticing function: Learners encounter gaps between what they want to say and what they are able to say and so they notice what they don't know or only know partially in this language. 2. Hypothesis-testing function: When a learner says something there's always a hypothesis behind it e. g. about grammar. By uttering something the learner tests this hypothesis and receives feedback from an interlocutor. This feedback enables them, if necessary, to reprocess his hypothesis. 3. Metalinguistic function: Learners reflect about the language they learn and hereby the output enables them to control and internalize linguistic knowledge.

Again, we would argue that Swain's concept of 'comprehensible output' correlates well to the principles of constructivist learning. The task-based learning that takes place in Second Life provides excellent conditions for the implementation of each of the three functions outlined by Swain. As in real life, learners are required to interact with the 3D VLE and the objects and agents within it to complete the set task, giving them the opportunity to test linguistic and non-linguistic knowledge learned in the classroom and receive direct and immediate feedback as a consequence of their 'output'. In the case of our Second Life lessons, failure to produce 'comprehensible output', to communicate appropriately, can lead to a learner being unable to move towards completion of the set task. In order to move forward, learners have re-assess their communicative strategy ('notice' where any gaps in communication might exist) and develop a new strategy that will enable them to continue to progress to the end of the task.

The communication engaged in by the students in the target language is 'meaningful' in that it is a means to an ends, which in crude terms is the completion of the set task. In the process of completing the set task, students are required to explore and understand information provided in written, graphical and/or auditory form and through the surrounding environment in teams, and are thus exposed to a variety of meaningful 'inputs' that contribute to the forming of new knowledge essential to completing the task. They in turn have to generate meaningful 'output' as part of their interaction with their peers, teaching staff, a range of digital artefacts that form part of the environment and the lesson, and with the non-player characters imbedded in the environment.

Student-focused Learning in Second Life-an Example

In the constructivist view of learning, collaborative work is important with 'learners working together and developing their understanding of concepts through a social learning process' (Dalgarno, 2002). From the very first lesson on basic Second Life skills, our first year Chinese language and culture students are asked to form teams, and indeed the process of forming teams itself becomes a step in their acclimatisation to the virtual environment and to interacting with their peers.

One lesson in Second Life requires learners to complete two tasks. Students are divided into teams using a system of coloured flags that resemble ancient Chinese battle flags[①] and are required to wear coloured team T-shirts for easy identification. To complete the tasks in time and successfully team members need to work together closely. The tasks consolidate previously learned vocabulary and concepts as well as introduce learners to new linguistic and non-linguistic information. Completion of each task requires a combination of reading textually-based information, listening to audio-based information, visually scanning the virtual environment, conducting conversations with automated non-player characters ('bots') and interacting with automated objects in the environment (e. g. restaurant menus, automatic ticket selling machine, air conditioners, etc.). The role of the teachers is (a) to create the environment / task / in-

---

① For a description of ancient Chinese battle flags, see: http: //big5. china. com/gate/big5/military. china. com/zh_ cn/episteme/jz/070. html

structions / experience (b) scaffold learners as they work towards completion of the task and (c) confirm that learners have successfully completed the set tasks.

The first task involves purchasing a train ticket to Beijing from the Chinese Island railway station. Each team of students is provided with a different set of criterion (purpose of travel, budget, desired arrival time) which determines what ticket they should buy. Success is measured by purchasing of the correct tickets for the whole team (the tickets can be visually inspected by the teacher). The second task involves enquiring about long-term accommodation for a foreign student studying in China. Teams are given the address of a real estate agent on the island and a list of information they have to gather. Visual inspection of potential accommodation is also required. Success is measured by answering a series of questions with correct information.

The advantages of this kind of team arrangement are obvious. Firstly, it puts the students at the centre of the learning process. Secondly, with more experienced student-mentors in each team to take care of many of the problems encountered and to keep the teams moving, the teachers are to some extent freed up to move amongst the learners, both virtually and in the computer lab, and provide more individualised assistance as required. Thirdly, the forming of teams facilitates the socialisation and peer-to-peer communication process. Fourthly, it makes the teacher's task of managing and keeping track of a large number of learners a good deal easier.

Student Feedback

A post-lesson survey was carried out on 112 first year Chinese language and culture students after one lesson in Second Life in 2009 focused on familiarising them with the environment and the skills necessary to function in the environment. The survey focused on the question of whether or not students saw learning Chinese in Second Life as an 'acceptable' mode of learning, and in particular, whether they felt there was any benefit from the type of collaborative learning advocated by dialectical constructivism and outlined above. Analysis of the survey data has clearly shown that students are on the whole comfortable with the platform/environment and importantly, 90% of students surveyed felt that they benefited from collaborative interaction with the other members of their group during completion of the set task (see Table 1 below).

Table 1　　　　　　　　　　**Results from Student Survey**

Question	Results				
1. How much access do you have to a computer at home / where you spend most of your time?	Very limited	Limited, but enough to do what I need	As much time as I need		
	7. 1% (8people)	26. 8% (30people)	66. 1% (74people)		
2. Do you have a fast broadband Internet connection (at home)?	None	Excruciatingly slow - even pages of text take a long time to load onto my screen	Slow - text loads but I have to wait for images to appear	Medium - I don't have to wait for pages too often but videos and other large files take a while	Fast - I rarely have to wait for files (including watching long you tube videos)
	2. 7% (3people)	1. 8% (2people)	5. 4% (6people)	59. 8% (67people)	30. 4% (34people)
3. Have you spent time in a 3D virtual world or played a 3D game with an avatar before?	Never	A few times	Many times	Frequently	No response
	44. 6% (50people)	36. 6% (41people)	11. 6% (13people)	5. 4% (6people)	1. 8% (2people)
4. Did you find mastering the basic skills (for example flying, zooming your camera, 'wearing' clothes and other items, etc.) difficult?	Very difficult	Difficult	Easy	Very easy	No response
	2. 7% (3people)	22. 5% (25people)	56. 8% (63people)	18% (20people)	0. 9% (1 person)
5. Do you feel comfortable in the Second Life 3D environment?	Very uncomfortable	Uncomfortable	Comfortable	Very comfortable	No response
	0% (0people)	18% (20people)	65. 8% (73people)	16. 2% (18people)	0. 9% (1people)
6. Was having peer support helpful learning the basic skills?	Not relevant	Only sometimes	Most of the time	All of the time	
	8. 9% (10people)	2. 7% (3people)	49. 1% (55people)	39. 3% (44people)	

In order to establish a base-line for measuring the level of comfort or otherwise students might have with learning in the Second Life environment from a technical / skills perspective, a number of questions were asked about access to computers and the Internet at home, previous experience with similar virtual environments and actual perceived level of difficulty in mastering skills specific to operating within the environment. The majority of students appear to have relatively good access to computers and the Internet at home (66.1% and >90%) and thus were reasonably familiar with both these basic requirements for using an online 3D VLE. Despite the majority of students having had little or no contact with similar virtual environments previously (approx. 80%), over 70% did not find mastering basic skills necessary for engaging in learning in the Second Life environment difficult to master and over 80% felt 'comfortable' in the environment. With respect to the collaborative nature of the environment and the tasks concerned, over 90% of students felt that scaffolding provided by peers was indeed helpful, which is consistent with the dialectical constructivist view of learning.

A second survey was carried out after a lesson on eating in a virtual Chinese restaurant which focused on the issue of what the students themselves thought was their biggest gain from the specific lesson in Second Life. Detailed findings have been published in the conference proceedings of the 8th International Conference on Chinese Language Pedagogy held in Kunming, China in June 2010, however, it should be noted that a significant number of students (approximately 50%) believe that they benefited from the lesson not just in terms of linguistic knowledge, but also in terms of having had a realistic linguistic and cultural experience that linked classroom-based learning with real life (Huang and Grant, 2010).

Another important measure of the efficacy of language and culture learning in 3D VLEs like Second Life Further is that of self-efficacy. In 2009 a research project was conducted that aimed to explore the proposal that a language lesson in Second Life could sustain or improve students' self-efficacy beliefs through learning activities favouring selective language performance. The quantitative results from the pre and post questionnaires supported the research proposal by indicating a statistically significant increase in student' self-efficacy beliefs in using Mandarin in real-life Chinese settings (Henderson et. al., 2009). Further follow up research is planned for 2010.

Conclusion

Over a period of a number of years, faculty engaged in the teaching of Chinese language and culture to first year undergraduate students at Monash University observed a number of pedagogical and logistical limitations in the formal classroom-based curriculum. The curriculum was perceived to be overly teacher-focussed. Due to the structure of the curriculum and large class sizes, inadequate opportunities were available for students to construct new linguistic and non-linguistic knowledge and skills in other than classroom-based and textbook-based contexts. In particular, few opportunities were available for learners to engage in meaningful communicative activities based in realistic contexts that could potentially consolidate existing knowledge and generate new knowledge.

In 2008 the decision was made to incorporate learning in the rich online 3D virtual environment of Second Life as one way of addressing these issues. Since then over 400 hundred Monash Chinese language and culture students (first and third year) have undertaken Chinese language and culture lessons in Second Life and these lessons are ongoing. Formal and informal feedback from students has shown that these lessons are popular and have gone some way to addressing the limitations outlined. However, the authors believe that further research is needed to look at issues such as the effectiveness of learning in such an environment in terms of language and culture learning outcomes and the transferability of linguistic and non-linguistic knowledge and skills learned in the virtual environment to the real world environment.

Bibliography

Association of VirtualWorlds (2008). The Blue Book: A Consumer Guide to Virtual Worlds Available from: http://www. associationofvirtualworlds. com/pdf/Blue% 20Book%204th%20Edition%20August%202008. pdf.

china. com（中华网），http://big5. china. com/gate/big5/military. china. com/ zh_ cn/episteme/ jz/070. html.

Collins, A. , J. S. Brown, & Newman, S. E（1989）. Cognitive Apprenticeship： Teaching the crafts of reading, writing and mathematics. In L. B. Resnick（Ed. ）, *Knowing, learning and instruction： Essays in honour of Robert Glaser*, Hillsdale NJ： Lawrence Erlbaum Associates.

Dalgarno, B. , （2002）*The Potential of 3D Virtual Learning Environments： A Constructivist Analysis.*

www. usq. edu. au/electpub/e-jist/docs/Vol5_ No2/Dalgarno％20-％20Final. pdf.

Dalgarno, B. & Lee, M. J. W. （2010）. What are the learning affordances of 3-D virtual environments? *British Journal of Educational Technology*, 41, 1, 12.

Ellis, R 1994. *The Study of Second Language Acquisition.* Oxford： Oxford University Press.

Ellis, R 2008. *The Study of Second Language Acquisition, Second Edition.* Oxford： Oxford University Press.

Honebein, P. , T. M. Duffy& Fishman, B. （1993）. Constructivism and the design of learning environments： Context and authentic activities for learning. In Thomas M. Duffy, Joost Lowyck, and David Jonassen（Eds. ）*Designing environments for constructivist learning.* Heidelberg： Springer-Verlag.

Henderson, M. , Huang, H. , Grant, S. , Henderson, L（2009）. Language acquisition in Second Life： improving self-efficacy beliefs. Presented at the 26th AS-CILITE conference held in New Zealand from December 6-9, 2009.

Huang & Grant（2010），不出国门的文化侵入和语言学习：第二人生"作为汉语语言文化教学平台 in *Chinese as a Foreign Language Teaching Practice and Reflections* （*Selected Papers for the 8th International Conference on Chinese Language Pedagogy*）, pp. 417—421. Foreign Language Teaching and Research Press.

Krashen, S. D. （1982）*Principles and Practice in second Language Acquisition.* Oxford： Pergamon.

Krashen, S. D. （1985）*The Input Hypothesis： Issues and Implications.* Harlow： Longman.

Moshman, D. （1982）Exogenous, Endogenous, and Dialectical Constructivism. *Developmental Review 2*, 371—384.

Ondrejka, C. （2008）Education Unleashed： Participatory Culture, Education, and Innovation in Second Life. *The Ecology of Games： Connecting Youth, Games, and Learning.* Katie S. The John D. and Catherine T. （Eds. ）Cambridge, MA： The MIT Press.

Salt, B. , C. Atkins, & Blackall, L. （2008）Engaging with Second Life： Real Education in a Virtual World Literature Review. *The SLENZ Project for the New Zealand Tertiary Education Commission.* http: //slenz. files. wordpress. com/2008/12/slliteraturereviewa1. pdf.

Savery, J. R. , & Duffy, T. M. (2001) Problem Based Learning: An instructional model and its constructivist framework. *CRLT Technical Report No.* 16—01. Centre for Research on Learning Technology, Indiana University.

Schumann, J. H. (1978). The acculturation model for second language acquisition. In R. C. Gingras (Ed.), *Second language acquisition and foreign language teaching* (pp. 27—50). Arlington, VA: Center for Applied Linguistics.

Swain, M. (1985) Communicative competence: some roles of comprehensible and comprehensible output in its development, in: S. Gass & C. Madden (Eds) *Input in Second Language Acquisition* (Rowley, MA, Newbury House).

Swain, M. (1995) Three functions or output in second SLA learning, in: G. Cook & B. Seidhofer (Eds) *Principle and Practice in Applied Linguistics.* Oxford: Oxford University Press.

Swain, M. (1998) Focus on form through conscious reflection, in: C. Doughty & J. Williams (Eds) *Focus on Form in Classroom Second Language Acquisition.* Cambridge: Cambridge University Press.

Swain, M. (2000) The output hypothesis and beyond: Mediating acquisition through collaborative dialogue. , in: C. Lantolf (Ed) *Sociocultural Theory and Second Language Learning.* Oxford: Oxford University Press.

Swain, M. & Lapkin, S. (1995) Problems in output and the cognitive processes they generate: a step towards second language learning. *Applied Linguistics*, 16 (3), pp. 371—391.

Swain, M. & Lapkin, S. (1998) Interaction and second language learning: Two adolescent French immersion students working together. *Modern Language Journal*, 82 (3), pp. 320—337.

Vygotsky, L S. (1978) Interaction between learning and development in *Mind in Society.* (L. S. Vygotsky). Cambridge: Harvard University. (This chapter originally published in 1935.)

Vygotsky, L. S. . In L. S. Vygotsky, Mind in society: The development of higher psychological processes. Cambridge, Mass. : Harvard University Press, 1978.

Wikipedia, Comprehensible Input, http: //en. wikipedia. org/wiki/Comprehensible_ input

Enhancing the Learning of Chinese with Second Life

陈东东　Chen, Dongdong　美国西东大学

Seton Hall University United States dongdong. chen@ shu. edu

Abstract: This article reports on a study that incorporates SL into the curriculum of university Introductory Chinese course in Fall 2009, including its implementation and evaluation. Using the existing resources of the SL Chinese School created by Michigan State University, 7 learning tasks were designed to supplement teaching throughout the semester. Along with the face-to-face instruction in class, students were required to study by completing the tasks alone, or with their peers or the teaching assistant in the SL Chinese School outside of the classroom. In performing the tasks, students practiced what was being learned in the classroom, and explored cultural aspects relating to the language. We will discuss both the teaching experience of including SL in the curriculum from the instructor's perspective, and the feedback from students on the learning of Chinese within the virtual world. Recommendations are provided for researchers for future directions as well as for practitioners for effective use of SL in the Chinese classroom.

Introduction

Multiuser virtual environments (MUVEs) have become an emerging tool in the field of education in this information era. Second Life (SL) developed by Linden Lab, is the best known and the most popular MUVEs with over 4000 people registered on the SL Educators List as of the summer 2009. They are people who are interested in exploring SL, or who are currently engaged in SL-supported education (Kingsley and Wankel 2009). This is not to mention millions of other account-registered users. As a development space in the format of online 3-D virtual world, SL is, in terms of content, exclusively user-generated. Anyone can enter SL for free. Residents, i. e., those who inhabit the SL world, are able to create a digital character (avatar) to represent themselves, using it to interact with others from around the world. They can not only create almost anything they can imagine but also share the result with others and, thereby, develop interactive and immersive environments. This interaction is unique in that users can fully participate in a virtual world in real time just like they do in the real world. For instance, they can communicate with each other by sending an instant message, verbal exchange, or gesture; they can read a note card and keep it for future use if necessary; they can even watch multimedia presentations. Because of these user-created, community-driven features, SL has, since its inception in 2003, attracted increasing and considerable attention from researchers and practitioners, including foreign language educators (e. g., Clark, 2009; Cooke-Plagwitz, 2008, 2009; Kuriscak and Luke, 2009; Wang et al., 2009). Using six criteria proposed by Jin and Xu (2009), Xu (2010) found that the SL environment, as compared to other computer programs, achieved the highest scores with respect to its effectiveness in the teaching and learning of foreign languages. Some unique potentials of SL as compared to the traditional classroom-based language teaching are well summarized by Cooke-Plagwitz (2008, 2009). Among many other advantages of using SL in foreign language education, there are three that should be highlighted. First, SL enables learners to create their own avatars, which can effectively help introverted students to participate and learn. Second, SL provides a collaborative learning setting, which encourages students to co-construct knowledge. Third, SL forms an immersive environment, which makes students' language practice contextualized.

A major reason for the growing attention to the use of MUVEs like SL for educational purposes is that the students whom we teach nowadays are part of the "Net Generation" —a term first coined by Tapscott (1998) and later used by Oblinger and Oblinger (2005). Though different from each other with respect to the definition of the timeframe during which the Net Generation was born, they noted some characteristics of this particular group: (i) preferring to work as part of a group or team; (ii) enjoying the learning by doing; and (iii) desiring to access information immediately and easily. This kind of learning behavior is the direct result of recent advances in information technology, such as television, computer, Internet, iPhones, MP3, iPod, iPad, etc. , as well as video games. Having grown up with various entertaining digital gadgets, most of which are designed to help them learn, Net Generation students or "digital natives" (Prensky, 2001) come to school with an expectation that they are learning for fun (Hay, 2000). Consequently, as observed by Oxford and Oxford (2009), in order to reach and teach these native speakers of the digital languages associated with computers, video games and Internet, educators must revisit and revise traditional pedagogy, and design and develop new techniques using the media and methodology that they understand. Trevett-Smith (2010) made a similar remark, "At a time when students will turn to Google rather than visit the library, or search Wikipedia instead of asking for a reference librarian, professors need to rethink how we use technology in our classrooms. "

It is readily apparent that educators of the 21st- century must explore the use of technology to support learning. Nonetheless, how to effectively apply technology in educational settings in order to advance learning outcomes remains a question to be answered. In particular, how should the MUVEs like SL be integrated·into the Chinese curriculum so as to make the learning of the language more effective and enjoyable? Oxford and Oxford (2009, p. 3) claim that "teachers cannot simply use technology for technology's sake; they must take advantage of specific age- and content-appropriate tools to accomplish specific pedagogical objectives. " This research attempts to examine whether the SL virtual environment supports the learning of Chinese for university students. The ultimate goal of the study is to identify appropriate ways to use SL in order to enhance student learning.

Second Life in Education

According to Clark (2009), there are at least 250 colleges and universities in the world that apply SL to promote teaching, support learning, and/or facilitate research in nearly all disciplines. Much work has been done exploring and examining the function of virtual world for higher education. *Higher Education in Virtual worlds* (Kingsley and Wankel, 2009) is one of the first serious publications that targets educators who are interested in using MUVEs in their teaching practice. Covering both the theoretical perspectives and the practical case studies of the use, and the potential use of virtual work in higher education, their book offers a wide range of valuable insights, and suggestions for educators, whether they are novice or experienced in technology-supported teaching.

At the university where the author is working, the educational benefits of SL have been exploited since 2007 when a piece of "land" was leased, which was later built into virtual Pirate Island for the sole use of the university community. Instructors of different disciplines have thus been able to engage students to learn by either creating things or using the resources specially developed on Pirate Island. For example, graduate students in the English Program were able to co-create a learning environment, i. e., House of 7 after Hawthorne's novel, The House of Seven Gables, within SL, while taking a literature course (Balkun et al., 2009). This case study shows, among other results that, with the integration of SL, the orientation of the course undergoes a transformation from teacher as "communicator of knowledge" to student as "builder of knowledge", which is difficult to achieve in the real-world classroom. Salt Marsh Dynamics (Trotta and Marian, forthcoming) is a case-based learning scenario, which makes the learning of endangered eco-systems possible for college students taking Ecology and Environment Geology courses. Such community and situated learning effectively supports team building and creative problem solving skills. In a series of studies (Hewitt et al. 2008; 2009; 2010), healthcare administration faculty used the Play2Train simulation, a virtual world platform to conduct training in SL adopted by a variety of academic and health institutions, to help both on-campus and online students in the Master of Healthcare Administration to learn how to prepare for, and manage crisis and emergency risk communication. By applying the emergency preparedness best practices in a real-time virtual learning scenario, students learned how to communicate during a crisis, think critically, and develop collaborative leadership as well as decision making skills.

With respect to foreign language education, there has been extensive research on the effects of virtual world learning. For example, Clark (2009) explored teaching hybrid Spanish courses with the instructor teaching grammar and organizing communicative activities in class while students discussing topics and completing projects in SL outside of the classroom. By building a Spanish *hacienda* in SL which provided additional elements of language and culture, the author was able to create an immersion experience for students. Clark further argues that with students being able to meet either in a real or virtual world to perform activities, SL can be an ideal place to teach single lessons or an entire course of a traditional Spanish 1. Sykes (2009) reports on an empirical study that examines the interlanguage pragmatic development by learners of Spanish in MUVEs with respect to making appropriate requests in Spanish. The findings obtained from interview data and in-class presentation indicate that, through the use of a synthetic immersive environment, learners became more aware of the complicated pragmatic issues. Although the study showed little improvement from pre- to posttest, anecdotal evidence suggests that students who were examined learned the subtleties of making appropriate requests in Spanish. Wang et al. (2009) discuss an ongoing research collaboration between an American university and a Chinese university, which explored the integration of SL into a program of teaching English as a foreign language during two semesters in China. They found that the Chinese students of English were able to, through the SL platform, conveniently exchange ideas and opinions with English native speakers on issues that both groups found interesting, a valuable learning experience that would not be easily achieved in real life, if at all. Besides work that involves the teaching of Spanish or English, there are two published studies relating to the teaching of Chinese as a foreign language. One is Henderson et al. (2009) 's empirical research on a collaborative activity to identify and order Chinese food in Mandarin in a virtual Chinese restaurant. The study found that there was a significant improvement between students' pre and post self-efficacy ratings which, the authors believe, was the result of a lesson incorporated in SL that enriches the students' experiential learning opportunities. The other study is Grant and Huang (2010) that discussed the integration of SL as one way of addressing some issues that exist in college level Chinese language instruction. That is, the pedagogical and logistical limitations of formal classroom-based curriculum, textbook-centered context, and teacher-focused methodology. The authors suggest that incorporating learning in an online 3D virtual environment like SL provides learners with valuable opportunities to actively communicate in realistic and, therefore, meaningful ways. According to Cooke-Plagwitz (2009), SL works particularly well for the students of the Net Generation whose learning styles have been greatly affected by the evolution of information technology. Kuriscak and Luke (2009), after investigating language learners' attitudes toward SL, report similar findings: students welcomed the opportunities afforded by SL to interact with native speakers.

There are two well-developed SL sites which offer free resources specially designed for the teaching and learning of Chinese as a foreign language. One is Second Life Chinese School developed by Michigan State University (MSU). This virtual Chinese School is a place where individuals can independently learn the Chinese language and experience its culture at their own pace. Embedded in the restaurant, park, apartment building, museum, stores as well as classroom, bookstore, and office are challenging but entertaining quests, all serving as great teaching materials. Thus learners can come to practice as many times as they want until they pick up the patterns of usage. For more information about the design concept of this Chinese school, please check into the site, http: //confucius. msu. edu/secondlife/overview. html. With a registered account in SL, anyone can log in to experience the beauty of this virtual Chinese School.

A second well-developed SL site is Chinese Island by Monash University, Australia, available from http: //slurl. com/secondlife/Monash% 20University/72/170/28. On this island, the railway station, airport, bank, inn with tea house, clinic, multi-purpose building, village, as well as traditional Chinese college, courtyard house, and garden, are "used as a basis for Chinese language classes in both first-year and media studies classes" (http: //www. monash. edu. au/international/dvc/virtual-worlds/monashsecondlife. html). The aforementioned research by Henderson et al. (2009) and the study by Grant and Huang (2010) utilized the resources in this site.

In the section below we will report on a study that incorporates the resources available on MSU's Second Life Chinese School in the teaching of Introductory Chinese at college level. We will talk about the rationale of the research and its implementation, evaluation, implications, and recommendations.

Integrating SL in Chinese Language Instruction

Research questions and logistics

There are three particular questions that we were interested in for this study: (i) is it feasible and plausible to integrate the SL resources into a one-semester university introductory Chinese? (ii) does SL support students' learning? (iii) do students welcome the use of SL as part of their Chinese learning process?

A total of 26 university students in two sections of beginning Chinese were involved in this Fall 2009 study. Except for four students who had some Chinese backgrounds due to either being born in a Chinese family or taking some Chinese before, the rest had zero Chinese skills. All the students except one belonged to the Net Generation, with an age range of 18 to 24 years old. On the first day of class, students were informed of the mandatory SL project for which they would receive 16 points toward the total grade of the course upon satisfactory completion of all the required SL activities.

Before elaborating on the details of methods, a note is in order about the conditions under which the author conducted the project using SL. First, the author's university is a "most wired" campus, which not only supplies wired and wireless access to the internet, but also provides a laptop to each full-time undergraduate student. The models of the laptops which students have received are either Thinkpad T500/T61 or X200/X61. These models are, configurationally speaking, sufficiently sophisticated to run the SL application. Additionally, the university offers a Language Resource Center, furnished with all the basic language learning tools, including the SL platform. With such a ubiquitous computing environment where students can get online anywhere and anytime, optimum learning outcomes can be expected. Besides good infrastructure, help-desk support technicians who can fix any issues with laptops concerning hardware or software are available during normal office hours. Finally, the university has Teaching, Learning and Technology Center (TLTC), where knowledgeable instructional designers regularly provide training and, thereby, assist faculty to employ emerging technology to maximize student learning.

The author of this study first received training on SL. With some familiarity with the basics of the SL application, the author was able to brainstorm with two instructional designers from TLTC to identify strategies for the best use of SL for the teaching of Chinese. The discussion and technical support from the experienced instruction designers made it easier to initiate the project. Kuriscak and Luke (2009) recommended that an in-class SL tutorial for students be provided in advance so that all will be uniformly informed of what is available in the SL platform, and what they need to know in order to be able to complete the learning tasks assigned. Inspired by this recommendation, we planned a 75-minute in-class hands-on crash course on SL in the second-day class of the semester. Conducted by said instructional designers, students were shown, step by step, how to (i) download the SL application, (ii) install it onto their own laptop, (iii) create account to log in, and (iv) navigate in SL. For their convenience, the tutorial documents and links were made accessible online. In addition, any other in-class follow-up or walk-up support was available either in the Language Resource Center or at the university Helpdesk whenever students need assistance.

Tasks and requirements

To make the project support the curriculum, meaningful tasks were created that incorporated resources of the SL Chinese School of MSU. The primary purposes of including these tasks were (i) to engage students to review what was being taught in the classroom, and (ii) to enable exploration of culture and language outside the class. There are two reasons why MUS's SL Chinese School was particularly chosen for this study. First, the site of the SL Chinese School was developed under the design-based research methods for an embodied experience for learners of Chinese. The author of the current study attended Zheng et al. (2009)'s presentation about this virtual school at CALICO 2009. Second, as a virtual learning facility developed and sponsored by a higher institution, the site was not only free, but relatively safe for students.

Table 1   **Tasks for SL Project**

Tasks	Weeks	Goals	Students required to
1. Know your way	Week 2	Practice the basics of SL	Dress up oneself; walk & fly
2. Visitor Center	Week 4	Practice pronunciation	Say place names
3. Look for radicals	Week 6	Practice radicals & Characters	Identify radicals/ characters
4. Self-introduction	Week 8	Learn to introduce oneself	Introduce oneself
5. Ask questions	Week 10	Learn to say Zhè shì shénme? Nà shì shénme	Describe things in rooms
6. Tour cities in China	Week 12	Learn to say Wǒ xǐhuān··· Yīnwéi	Watch PPT and make sentences
7. Talk about hobbies	Week 14	Learn to talk about hobbies	Ask each other questions
8. Let's have a party at Mr. Li's	Week 16	Learn to say things at a friend's place	Reply when welcomed or offered with drinks

As can be seen from the comprehensive list of tasks in Table 1, each task spanned two weeks consistently in order to provide the students with sufficient time to review what they had learned in the classroom and then to practice by doing the task. Each task had a theme which included the pronunciation of Chinese sounds, the ability to identify and write Chinese radicals and characters before proceeding, to the 5 topics that are related to Greeting, Family, Date and Time, Hobbies, and Visiting Friends. These 5 topics are the first 5 chapters from *Integrated Chinese Level 1 Part 1* (Liu et al., 2008), which were used as part of teaching materials in that semester.

The first task was to familiarize students with the SL platform and the SL

Chinese School. While this task did not involve any Chinese, learning to be able to walk around with appropriate dress, and getting to know how to chat through instant message or voice is the first set of basic skills that students must grasp in order to carry out the virtual learning activities in the SL Chinese School. This task was added to increase students' level of comfort with the virtual learning technology. However, as we will see in the next section, just performing one task might not be enough to prepare for an efficient virtual learning.

Tasks 2 to 8 were created for enhancing the learning of materials covered in the class. Since the subjects were beginners of Chinese, they just finished learning *pinyin* by the end of the 4th week. Task 2 offers them an opportunity to become familiar with the SL Chinese Island by getting to know where each place is located, and learning how to say the place names correctly in Chinese. In doing the task, students reviewed *pinyin* and used it for a real function. In order to assist students with this task, an audio file was made and posted online in advance, which contains the reading of all the place names recorded by a teaching assistant. To utilize the road signs and places names written in Chinese characters as well as in *pinyin*, we had students look for, and identify the radicals that they had learned in the classroom by doing Task 3 after they were introduced radicals around the 6th week. With characters associated with *pinyin* and English presented in the visual landscapes on the Island, all these adding authenticity and meaningfulness, the learning of Chinese radicals and characters became a less daunting task. After students learned the topics of Greeting, and Family, we encouraged them to learn the lessons offered by the SL Chinese School by doing Task 4. For this task, students were guided to explore different ways of introducing oneself, and greeting each other. Tasks 5, 6 and 7 all required paired work. Task 5 expected students to learn extra vocabulary related to furniture and objects in an apartment, and to learn to ask the questions *Zhè shì shénme* "What is this?" *Nà shì shénme* "What is that?" and answer the questions. For Task 6, students must first of all watch a PPT slide available on the site, which is an itinerary of travelling in China. After watching the PPT slide, students were required to talk about which city they wanted to see if they were offered an opportunity to visit China, and provided a reason. Students were instructed to do some research, in advance, on the places of historical interests in China, and include the sentence pattern such as "Wǒ xǐ huān⋯ yīnwéi" in their conversation. Task 7 concerns hobbies, which the majority of students were interested in talking about. Task 8 is a group activity, which required everyone in the class to go to Mr. Li's to have a party. This task was scheduled at the last-day of class, when students had finished the chapter *Visiting Friends*, and had obtained a good grasp of basic structures and vocabulary to carry a simple conversation.

For a better understanding of how tasks work, take a look at the requirements of Task 5 in Table 2. For this task, students were required to visit, in pairs, the apartment in Lianhua Apartment Building. While in the room, students must first learn the new vocabulary about each of the objects that they saw in the rooms, and then learn how to ask and answer questions using *Zhè shì shénme* "What is this? *Nà shì shénme* "What is that?" What is nice about this virtual apartment is that not only does it consist of different rooms, such as the living room, bedroom, and the kitchen, each room is furnished with furniture or objects that one would usually see in a real-world apartment. Furthermore, each piece of furniture or object has *pinyin*, and character embedded behind the scene, which will pop up after being clicked. For instance, after clicking the pot on the oven in the kitchen, as shown in Figure 1, one will see *guō* 锅 showing up. When the cupboard above the counter is clicked, the door will open, and *yán* 盐, *yóu* 油 will show up if they are clicked respectively. This kind of interactive way of presenting the vocabulary helps students to learn and memorize new words.

Table 2 **Requirements of Task 5**

Now that we finish Chapter 1 *Family*, teleport to Lianhua Apartment Building of Second Life Chinese School with your partner, and do the following:
a. Visit each of rooms in the building, i. e. , R101, R102, R201, R202, R301, R302
b. Learn the new words for things/objects inside the rooms by clicking each of them
c. Learn to say the wh- question, *Zhè/Nà shì shénme*? (What is this? What is that?)
d. Learn to answer the questions by using each of the new words just learned
e. Submit your dialogue via email

Figures 2 and 3 show the two screen shots of Task 8 when it was in

Figure 1   Bedroom and Kitchen in an Apartment

progress. In Figure 2, the instructor, as a hostess, stands at the door, greeting each student when s/he enters Mr. Li's home. Figure 3 shows the scene of students at the party in the living room.

Figure 2   Instructor Greeting Each Student

Task 8 was completed in Language Resource Center, where each computer was fully powered, so that during the process of the task, students would not run into the potential problem of losing batteries. Another advantage of using the Language Resource Center was that each workstation was equipped with a headset, so that students could talk

Figure 3   In the Living Room of Mr. Li's

to one another with a good quality voice.

As instructed, all the tasks had to be completed outside of class. Each task was posted on Blackboard, a course management application, in due time. A reminder of the assignment was also sent to students via email reminding them to do the task. Depending on the nature of task, students must perform Tasks 1, 3, 4, 6 alone; they must complete Task 2 with the teaching assistant; they must finish Tasks 5, 6, 7 in pairs; they must participate in Task 8 with the whole class. There were two ways for the instructor to check students' assignment. One was through a follow-up in class, asking students questions about the task. The other was to have students submit their work via email. Thanks to the built-in function available in SL, students, after chatting, can easily copy and paste the record of their dialogue, located in the 'history' window of the local chat box, and email it to the instructor. Students must submit their dialogue for the tasks involving a partner, for which they received comments or corrections.

Learner attitudes and performance

As mentioned above, except for one, all other students who were involved in this study belonged to the Net Generation. Although only a very few of them had heard about the SL program, this group appeared very excited on the first day when they were informed of the project. Some students picked up navigation skills right away in the tutorial class; some were able to modify their avatar's appearance so as to look great.

Figure 4 shows the work from a pair of students for Task 5, asking and answering questions about the objects and furniture in both living room and the kitchen.

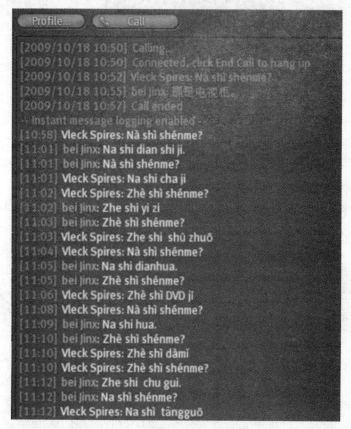

Figure 4   Student Work for Task 5

However, to our surprise, as the time passed by, some students gradually became late in doing the assigned tasks as required, and some even did not bother to try. An examination of the students' general perform-ance on tasks, as shown in Table 3, indicates that only 7 out of 26 students completed all the tasks properly, for which they received full credit, i. e., 16 points. 15 students did the tasks ok, but left some tasks incomplete, thus, receiving 12 to 14 points. 4 students did only a few tasks.

Table 3   **General Performance of Tasks**

No. of Students	No. of Students	No. of Students
perform very well	perform OK	did not perform well
7 (27%)	15 (58%)	4 (15%)

Given that this group, except for one student, was a part of Net Generation, why did only one third of them perform well with the technology-related tasks? Why did some students not complete the tasks as expected? Was that because of difficulty with the language or was that because of problems with their computer? Was the failure of completing the tasks an indication of a lack of capability, or a lack of learning motivation? Furthermore, what was students' learning experience? Did they learn? In order to find out what students thought about the project, the author administered a questionnaire at the end of the project.

Here the discussion will focus on the two particular questions in the questionnaire: (i) *What do you think of the Second Life tasks developed for this semester?* (ii) *Do you want me to continue to integrate Second Life in the teaching/learning of Chinese in Spring 2010?* The feedback from the students was mixed regarding the first question. On the one hand, some students expressed a positive experience about the virtual learning. For example, one student wrote, "it helps learn, and it's fun". One said, "it was a fun interactive way to learn Chinese". Another student said, the tasks "allowed me to talk to others in the class and I get to know them". These students enthusiastically suggested continuing the tasks in the following semester when answering the second question. For example, some even provided such suggestion as designing tasks that have "more interactions and tasks with incentives to encourage students to go on to Second Life", or having students "do some of the gamed tasks, like find a girl-friend". On the other hand, there were less encouraging comments from students. For instance, I "couldn't get navigation around the Island, —— couldn't always find the location", or "couldn't find a partner", or "I felt that technical difficulties were much", or "my computer didn't work properly", or "I got too frustrated and confused on technology rather than Chinese". Not surprisingly, this last comment was from the student who was not part of Net Generation, and who did not perform any other learning tasks except for the first and the last one. It is obvious that this student did not feel comfortable with the technology. Those students who commented negatively suggested not continuing the project, because (i) they did not have time to do assignments; (ii) they could not find a partner to work with. Out of these negative comments, the complaint about the difficulty of using the computer technology in SL, which had prevented them from completing tasks, was beyond our expectation. However, this finding is along the lines of the observation made by Kuriscak and Luke (2009, p. 193). That is, the Net Generation students may be strong with playing special technology, i. e. , the technology that is involved in the programs especially designed for generating funs, but they are less experienced or motivated with utilizing technology for learning. While the SL technology has been shown to be effective for beginners of Spanish, as observed by Clark (2009), the current study suggests that the technology seemed to discourage some of our students from trying it enthusiastically.

Discussion and Conclusion

With respect to the three questions that we raised above, here are some tentative answers. In terms of whether it is feasible and plausible to integrate SL in Chinese language instruction, the answer is obviously YES. While the learning experience with SL is mixed, there are some observations on the benefits of using the SL from the teaching perspective. First, SL offers an opportunity for students to interact with each other easily. This kind of interaction in SL will make the learning a co-constructive and enjoyable social experience if the instructor can develop a workable strategy to help students find their partners. For today's students who are busy with working as well as studying, the SL platform offers them a convenient and comfortable place to meet and practice the language if the tasks designed can assist them with learning and progressing. Secondly, explorations of cultural aspects such as objects, buildings, landscapes, places of interest, etc. in the virtual world make visitation of the country possible without costing anything. Here, again, tasks are crucial in the sense that they must be interesting enough to attract students to explore the authentic contexts on their own, and engaging sufficiently to sustain their motivation for repeated exploration. Thirdly, SL presents creative ways for students to learn the language meaningfully in a context. With contextualized interactions and meaningful communications, language learning is no longer merely repetition, and recitation, which are usually boring, and less effective (e. g. , Lee and Vanpatten, 2003). It is no doubt that SL plays a significant role in connecting students for social and experiential learning.

In regards to the question to what extent SL supports the learning of Chinese, further empirical research is required. Possible directions would be to conduct an experimental study, which should examine and compare the learning of Chinese in two different conditions: one is the regular teaching without the use of SL; the other is the teaching plus the support from the SL. Only when the quantitative data on the effect of the learning is obtained can a substantial conclusion be made. However, caution must be exercised to avoid a hasty conclusion or overgeneralization. Sometimes just one empirical research may not be sufficient enough to offer a conclusion about the effects of technology-supported language teaching. In the study of the second language acquisition of Spanish pragmatics, as the data obtained did not support any significant progress from pre- to posttest, Sykes (2009) suggested some further considerations for future studies in design, implementation and research.

In terms of the question whether students welcome the use of SL in their learning of Chinese, responses and reactions varied. We speculate that many unknown factors could be at work in that regard. Maybe the tasks are time-consuming, therefore many students could not afford time to do. It was possible that the technology involved in SL was a bit complicated so that students had to give up. Another possibility is that the percentage of the overall marks for the SL project is a bit too low so students felt that their efforts were not worthwhile, or they were not motivated enough to explore on their own. There might be some other reasons involved. Thus, it would be informative and helpful, for future study, to require students to write up journals recording their frustration and excitement with the virtual learning. In exploring the use of SL in Chinese language instruction, instructors need to be aware of students' thoughts and reflections. In the case of those students who did not perform certain tasks as assigned, it would be necessary for the instructor to find out immediately why students failed to do the work, and address the issue right away. If it involves the language, the instructor should go over the difficult points again and make them clear to students. If it is a technology-related problem, the instructor should help by arranging a better support service. If it is related to the lack of time or the lack of partners, the instructor should work with students to resolve the issue. Using the virtual world to support the teaching of Chinese is much like having students perform task-based learning. In order to achieve effective outcomes, the instructor should play multiple roles: a teacher, an architect, a chairperson, a resource person, or a facilitator (e. g., Willis, 1996; Lee and Vanpatten, 2003). As pointed out by Clark (2009, p. 168), "If students are living and working within the Second Life community, they are discovering knowledge on their own. Our role as teacher will change from being authority figures and knowledge-keepers to being guides".

For the teachers who are interested in including SL into their Chinese teaching program, here are three important suggestions. First, increase the weighting of marks for the SL project so as to raise students' awareness of the significance of performing the tasks in the virtual world. The current study shows a small number of students who completed all the tasks satisfactorily, while many others left some tasks incomplete. Such a result could be derived from the possibility that the students did not have much incentive to make their best efforts for a time-consuming, challenging, but lower-weighted project.

Second, in addition to arranging learners to practice with their own peers, try to recruit native speakers to participate in the project so that learners could access the expertise of native Chinese speakers. It would be very helpful for learners to be exposed to the authentic Chinese in addition to the limited exposure to the formal language in the classroom. College students in China or Chinese students studying in the same American university would serve as best partners, as they are in the same generation group as the learners, thus showing the same interests to communicate with each others. The earlier and richer exposure to the native language that students receive, the better learning outcomes they achieve.

From the current study, we find that more research is required with respect to the designing of tasks that can serve "curricular goals and instructional models". While SL is a powerful tool, tasks or activities form the crucial part of the pedagogy. That means the instructor needs to develop pedagogically-sound tasks to motivate learners to learn. With so many resources available on SL islands, instructors must identify and select right materials, and use them to create engaging activities. To that end, instructors must take into account learner backgrounds, pedagogical issues, and teaching goals. The purpose of utilizing SL is to enrich and extend real-world classroom teaching and learning. As remarked by Oxford & Oxford (2009, p. 2), "successful integration of technology into the classroom in a pedagogically sound manner involves more than simply introducing a software program or other innovation to the students in a classroom. Technology integration must be thoughtfully planned out based on curricular goals and instructional models". Our study highly suggests that more planning is required before such a project is undertaken. For example, to run a successful group activity on the SL platform like "Let's have a party at Mr. Li's", we suggest the following. (i) Try to meet students in a bigger space. If that is not possible, break the class in small groups so that each time the instructor is with a small group instead of the whole class. This way, the interaction between the instructor and students is easier and more effective. (ii) Give clear directions to students as to what to do and what not to do while the instructor is having a dialogue with one student or there is a conversation between two students. Just like the natural conversation taking place among a group ofpeople in the real world, everyone should follow a rule in terms of who at what time takes a turn to speak. Maybe the instructor can run a Round-Robin activity by asking one question and having each student respond. This practice is even more important in the virtual world; otherwise, it will be too noisy with two or more than two persons speaking at the same time. (ⅲ) Prepare some activities in advance and assign the activities to those students who are waiting to have a dialogue or who have done a dialogue with other students. (ⅳ) Make sure that everyone including the instructor test out the built-in microphone so that when doing a group activity, the equipment works properly. There is a button beneath TALK on the SL viewer, which can be clicked to enable the avatar to speak hands free. This feature is very useful for the instructor who has to use hands to navigate in order to interact with students. Unfortunately we did not know the availability of that function until the task was completed.

To conclude, this study has shown an integration of SL in one-semester university beginning Chinese course. It is found that some students enjoyed the virtual learning, while others were discouraged for various reasons. However, the author observed some benefits of the SL-supported teaching, and intends to conduct further research to explore its effectiveness along the lines of the suggestions recommended. As an emerging tool, SL has much to offer the field of Chinese language instruction, and learns of Chinese. For its best practice, focus should be on developing tasks that aim to enhance students' learning.

Acknowledgements

I gratefully acknowledge the tremendous assistance from Melissa Mc-Dowell, Heidi Trotta, instructional designers from Teaching, Learning, and Technology Center, Seton Hall University, and Wendy Sue Williams, Director of Language Resource Center of Seton Hall University. Without their help, this project would not have been completed. I also thank my teaching assistant, Ms. Jingyu Zhao, for her help throughout the project during Fall 2009. Part of the paper was presented at NEALLT/NERALLT Fall 2009 Joint Conference in Yale University on October 30, 2009, and at the 6th International Conference and Workshops on Technology and Chinese Language Teaching in the 21st Century held at Ohio State University, Columbus during June 12—14, 2010. I thank the audience for their feedback. Special thanks to the anonymous JTCLT reviewers for suggestions and comments on the revision of this article. All remaining errors are mine.

References

Balkun, Mary, Zedeck, Mary, and Trotta, Heidi (2009). Literary Analysis as Serious.

Play in Second Life, in Charles Wankel and Jan Kingsley (Eds.), *Higher Education in Virtual Worlds*. UK: Emerald, pp. 141—157.

Clark, Gloria B (2009). These Horses Can Fly! And Other Lessons From Second Life: The View from a Virtual Hacienda. In Raquel Oxford and Jeffrey Oxford (Eds.), *Second Language Teaching and Learning in the Net Generation* (pp. 153—172), University of Hawai'i.

Cooke-Plagwitz, Jessamine (2009). A New Language for the Net Generation: Why.

Second Life Works for the Net Generation. In Raquel Oxford and Jeffrey Oxford (Eds.), *Second Language Teaching and Learning in the Net Generation*, National Foreign Language Resource Center, University of Hawai'I, pp. 173—180.

Cooke-Plagwitz, Jessamine (2008). New directions in Call: an objective introduction to Second Life. *CALICO Journal*, 25 (3), 547—557.

Grant, Scott and Huang, Hui (2010). The Integration of an Online 3D Virtual Learning.

Environment into formal Classroom-Based Undergraduate Chinese Language and Culture Curriculum. In De Bao Xu, Jun Da and Phyllis Zhang (Eds.), *Proceedings of the 6th International Conference and Workshops on Technology and Chinese Language Teaching in the 21st Century*, Ohio State University, pp. 91—99.

Hay, Leroy E. (2000). Educating the Net Generation. *School Administrator*, 57 (4).

Retrieved November 9, 2010, from http://www.aasa.org/SchoolAdministratorArticle.aspx?id=14422.

Henderson, Michael, Huang, Hui, Grant, Scott, Henderson, Lyn. (2009). Language.

acquisition in Second Life: Improving self-efficacy beliefs. *Proceedings ascilite Auckland 2009*, pp. 464—474.

Hewitt, Anne, Spencer, Susan, Mirliss, Danielle and Twal, Riad. (2010). Incident and Disaster Management Training: Collaborative Learning Opportunities Using Virtual World Scenarios. In Eleana Asimakopoulou and Nik Bessis (Eds.), *ICTs for Disaster Management and Threat Detection: Collaborative and Distributed*

Frameworks. Harrisburg, PA: IGI Publishers, pp. 179—199.

Hewitt, Anne, Spencer, Susan, Mirliss, Danielle and Twal, Riad. (2009). Preparing Graduate Students for Virtual World Simulations: Exploring the Potential of an Emerging Technology. *Innovate Vol* 5 (6). Available at: http://www. innovateonline. info/pdf/vol5_ issue6/Preparing_ Graduate_ Students_ for_ Virtual_ World_ Simulations_ _ Exploring_ the_ Potential_ of_ an_ Emerging_ Technology. pdf.

Hewitt, Anne, Spencer, Susan, Ramloll, Rameshsharma and Trotta, Heidi. (2008).

Expanding CERC beyond Public Health: Sharing Best Practices with Healthcare Managers via Virtual Learning. *Health Promotion Practice*, 9: 4 (Supplement), pp. 83—87.

Jin, Hong Gang and Xu, De Bao (2009). Wǎngluò Cānyùshì Xuéxí Gōngjù de Píngcè, presentation given at 2009 International Conference on Internet Chinese Education, Taipei (ICICE'09) June 19, 2009.

Kuriscak, Lisa M. , and Luke, Christopher L (2009). Language Learner Attitudes toward

Virtual World: An Investigation of Second Life, *CALICO Monograph Series* Vol. 8, 173—198.

Lee, James and VanPatten, Bill (2003). *Making Communicative Language Teaching Happen*. McGraw-Hill, pp. 3—19.

Liu, Y. et al. (2008) *Integrated Chinese Level* 1 *Part I*, Boston: Cheng & Tsui Company.

Oblinger, Diana and Oblinger, James. (2005). Is it age or IT: First steps toward understanding the Net Generation. In Diana Oblinger and James Oblinger (Eds.), *Educating the Net Generation*, pp. 2. 1—2. 20. Retrieved October 30, 2010, from http://www. educause. edu/Resources/EducatingtheNetGeneration/IsItAgeorIT-FirstStepsTowardUnd/6058? bhcp = 1.

Oxford, Raquel and Oxford, Jeffrey. (2009). (Eds.), *Second Language Teaching and Learning in the Net Generation*. National Foreign Language Resource Center, University of Hawai'l, pp. 1—8.

Prensky, Marc (2001). Digital native, digital immigrants: A new way to look at ourselves and out kids. *On the Horizon*, 9 (5), 1— 6. Retrieved on October 24, 2020, from http://www. marcprensky. com/writing/Prensky% 20—% 20Digital% 20Natives, % 20Digital% 20Immigrants% 20—% 20Part1. pdf.

Sykes, Julie M (2009). Learner Requests in Spanish: Examining the Potential of.

Multiuser Virtual Environments for L2 Pragmatics Acquisition, *CALICO Monograph Series Vol.* 8, 199—234.

Tapscott, Don (1988). *Growing up digital: The rise of the Net Generation.* New York: McGraw-Hill.

Trevett-Smith, Matthew (2010). Second Life Provides Real-World Benefits, *Teaching and Learning.* Retrieved on October 24, 2010, from http: // www. facultyfocus. com/articles/teaching-and-learning/second-life-provides-real-world-benefits/.

Trotta, Heidi and Glenn, Marian. (Forthcoming). Salt Marsh Dynamics: A Problem-Based Learning Scenario, in Charles Wankel and Randy Hinrichs (Eds.), *3D Virtual World Learning Handbook*, UK: Emerald in press.

Wang, Charles X., Song, Hongbo, Stone, David and Yan, Qiaoqiao (2009). Integrating.

Second Life into an EFL Program in China: Research Collaboration across the Continents, *TechTrends*, November/December 2009, 14—19.

Wankel, Charles and Kingsley, Jan (2009). (Eds.), *Higher Education in Virtual Worlds*.

UK: Emerald.

Willis, Jane (1996). *A Framework for Task-Based Learning.* London: Longman.

Xu, De-Bao (2010). Wǎngluò Cānyùshì Xuéxí Gōngjù de Píngcè Yú Xūnǐ Kètáng Ruǎnjiàn de Xuǎnzé Biāozhǔn, Keynote speech given at The 6th International Conference and Workshops on Technology and Chinese Language Teaching in the 21st Century, Ohio State University, Columbus, OH, June 12—14, 2010.

Zheng, Dongping, Dirkin, Kenneth Wade and Zhao, Yong (2009). Second Life Chinese

School: Iterative Design for Embodiment and Game Play, Presentation given at CALICO 2009, Arizona State University, Tempe, March 10—14, 2009.

Integraing Second Life into A Chinese Teacher Training Program—A Pilot Study

郑秀仁　Cheng, Hsiu-Jen Chung Yuan Christian University Taiwan hsiujen@ cycu. edu. tw
战　红　Zhan, Hong Embry-Riddle Aeronautical University United States zhan121@ erau. edu
蔡德禄　Tsai，Andy The Institute for Information Industry Taiwan andy@ iii. org. tw

Abstract：Second Life （SL），a 3-D Multi-User Virtual Environment, has been found beneficial to foreign language education because of its immersive and interactive environments. This cross-continental study explored feasibilities of using Second Life to provide field experiences to pre-service Mandarin teachers in a program of Teaching Chinese as a Foreign Language in Taiwan. This study also investigated pre-service teachers' insights of teaching Chinese in such a virtual environment，as well as the difficulties these teachers encountered when integrating Second Life in teaching Chinese. The study found that the more teaching experiencethe pre-service teachers gained in teaching Chinese in Second Life，the more positive an attitude they would develop toward adopting Second Life in teaching Chinese virtually，and in contrast，the less frustrations they would have for technical challenges when teaching in Second Life.

Key words：Second Life, Virtual learning environment, Mandarin teacher training, Teaching Chinese as a foreign language

摘　要：因3-D 虚拟第二人生所提供互动式及沉浸式环境的特质已被许多研究证实有利于外语教学，本研究以跨国合作的模式设计融合第二人生及实境教学培训台湾的华语师资，同时调查学生教师对在网络虚拟实境教学的观感及其所遭遇的困难。结果发现若学生教师于第二人生的教学经验值增加，他们对于此类教学模式的态度就越正面，尤其是在技术上及教学上遇到困难的时候。

关键词：第二人生，虚拟世界，华语/中文教师培训，对外汉语教师培训，华语/中文作为外语教学

Introduction

Virtual reality (VR) is a combination of technologies which allow multiple users to interact with each other in a computer-simulated environment that can be a replica of the real world or an imaginary cyber world. Seventy-five virtual worlds existed in the Internet (Johnson, 2008, cited in Gregory & Tynan, 2009), for example, Second Life, World of Warcraft, the Sims 3, IMVU, and Active Workds, etc. . Since VR was adopted into education in West Danton High School in England in 1991, researchers and educators have investigated applications of VR technology from its potentials for general education to its integration to specific subject areas. Researchers found that, compared with traditional two-dimension interactive web tools, such as Skype, Google Doc, digital Whiteboards, and Google Wave, the three-dimension VR promotes more authentic and physical interactions, immersion, students' awareness of the target culture, knowledge construction, and learning (O' Brien & Levy, 2008; Von et al. , 2001).

One of the emerging VR drawing increased attention is a 3-D virtual world-Second Life. Second Lifewas developed and launched in 2003 inthe California-based Linden Research Lab (http: //lindenlab. com). In this virtual world, replica of any objects in the real world can be built and operated by so-called "residents" or the users, through their own digital representatives-avatars. The avatars can fly, move, and walk, and quickly relocate on different islands, which are rich in graphic illustrations by using teleport functions. In addition, the avatars can communicate with other avatars by text or voice chat (Hislope, 2008; Schiller, 2009; Theodore, 2009). Because of these immersive, interactive, physical and graphic capabilities of Second Life, it has grown explosively to become the second best thing to a face-to-face meeting. Up to 2009, Second Life had 21, 332 islands from over a 100 countries (Schiller, 2009). Back to 2007, Garner Inc. predicted that by the end of 2011, 80 percent of active Internet users will have an avatar in any of the virtual worlds, which indicates the era of virtual reality is upon us.

Because of Second Life capabilities for communication and interaction, as well as its affordance of immersive simulations, many companies and organizations have purchased and created their own virtual space, called islands in Second Lifefor various purposesincluding business, educational use, political use, and special group use. Many organizations have chosenSecond Life to provide professional training, especially training that can be dangerous or simply impossible to do in the real world.

For example, some key IT companies including Cisco, Dell, and Samsung have built their learning and training virtual spaces in Second Life. In 2008, IBM's Academy of Technology held a Virtual World Conference and an annualmeeting drawing over 200 participants. The virtual world training and conferences haveproven to be a cost effective model. Children's Memorial Hospital in Chicago, Illinoishas replicated its facilities to successfully provide disaster drills to train doctors, nurses, and other related staff for emergence response planning. Because Second Life can engage learners in simulated experiential activities, "Second Life is the next realm of delivery for training" (http：//www. secondlife. com).

Second Life also provides an arena for educators to seek innovative ways to provide engaging and constructive learning in virtual environments. Since Linden Lab released "Campus：Second Life" in 2004, more and more educational institutions have built their virtual campuses for teaching, learning, training, or advertising purposes. For educational use, USA Today reported that more than 300 universities have utilized Second Life as an educational tool, with some for distance education courses, and some for use by professors to supplement existing face-to- face courses (Sussman, 2007). A report in 2008 (Lester, 2008, cited inGregory & Tynan, 2009) claimed there are approximately 1, 000 educational institutions using Second Life in different ways to serve different needs. Such innovation can be easily found from literature and Second Life websites：Harvard law school and Harvard Extension School's Cyber One：Law on the Court of Public Opinion (Schiller, 2009), Ohio University's Nutrition Games, Healthinfo Island and VNEC (Virtal Neurological Education Centre) developed by University of Plymouth, UK (Boulos, et al., 2007), Second China from University of Florida, 3D Collaborative Learning owned by Graz University of Technology, Austria (Chang, et al., 2009). Many of the universities have their own Second Life virtual campuses such as Harvard, Princeton, Drexel, Ball State, Stanford, Ohio, and Bowling Green (Descy, 2008; Schiller, 2009). University of Central Florida has received a National Science Foundation grant to teach science and physics in Second Life (Cart & Elseth, 2009).

When adopting Second Life for education, pedagogical possibilities for extending traditional classroom activities and learning become enormous. Applications of Second Life in the classroom are as innovative as the virtual technology itself. Conklin (2007) suggested 101 uses for Second Life in the college classroom to encourage learning in a more collaborative and social way. The VR technology has proven to be a useful educational tool by studies over the decades in terms of promoted interactions, resources sharing, increased motivation, a sense of realism, the student-centered nature of interactions, identification with a target culture and reduction in anxiety levels (Billings, 2009; Bricken, et al., 1992; O'Brien & Levy, 2008; Shim, 2003).

However, among various applications of Second Life in education, conducting teacher training in this engaging virtual spaceis still anew territory that has not yet been thoroughly investigated. Foreign language teacher training, especially Mandarin Chinese language teacher training, in Second Life is even more sparse. Web technology has opened new horizons for teaching Chinese using computers and the Internet (Yao, 2009). Understanding how to use emerging technology to enhance teaching and learning in Chinese becomes essential in order to engage 21st century learners who are digital natives (Bennett, Maton, & kervin, 2008). This pilot study pioneered a Mandarin Chinese teacher training model which utilized Second Life as a platform allowing teacher education students in Taiwan to gain field experiences teaching Chinese to American students and to understand how to integrate emerging technology in teaching Mandarin as a foreign language. Based on surveys and an open-ended question (see Appendix I), this study investigated perceptions of pre-service teachers ina Teaching Chinese as a Foreign Language Program in Taiwan regarding using Second Life asa learning and teaching platform. This study adds to the understanding of benefits and drawbacks of using Second Life in teaching and learning Mandarin Chinese, and it also provides practical suggestions for integrating Second Life into a Mandarin Chinese teacher training program.

Related Studies

Teacher Training and Field Experiences

Tsui (2003) stated that teacher' knowledge is embedded in and developed through their reflective and personal daily practices. Teachers' knowledge includes five categories: knowledge of subject matter (subject disciplines and learning theories), curriculum (the structuring of learning), instruction (classroom routines and student needs), self (individual's characteristics), and knowledge of the milieu of schooling (the social structure of school). When discussing the relationship of these five categories of knowledge, Tsui stressed the dynamic features of the relationships: "teacher' knowledge shapes practices, but it is also shaped by the practices" (Tsui, 2003, p. 46). Therefore, educators of Chinese teacher education argue thatChinese teacher training should include content knowledge, curriculum and instruction, and practical training (Chien, 2008).

Tsui (2003) also pointed out that the nature of teacher knowledge is situated in the specific context in which teachers operate. Teacher's knowledge can contextuallydevelop as they respond to the specific contextof the school and classroom setting in which they interact with students. Thus, providing pre-service teachers authentic teaching contexts to gain some field experiences is critical to developing teacher knowledge. Through field experiences, pre-service teachers can obtain first-hand experience through one-to-one encounters in classrooms, so that they may developgood teaching practices. For this reason, field experiences are frequently an integral part of courses in teacher education (Grable, Kiekel, &Hunt, 2010).

Teacher Education in Second Life

Despite the explosive use of Second Life in many aspects of life, the body of knowledge related to teacher education in the virtual world is very sparse. Two studies that addressed this topic applied a comparative approach to explore pre-service teachers' beliefs and field experiences that theydeveloped in both the physical and virtual classrooms. Gregory and Masters (2010), in their pilot study exploring learning of different kinds of thinking skills (known as Six Thinking Hats), found that some students preferred the traditional face-to-face lesson; others could see the benefits of using a virtual world in the right circumstances. The researchers compared prospective teachers' beliefs and experiences regarding their learning and engagement in a virtual environment andthose in a face-to-face situation. Thiscomparison yieldeda positive correlation to perceptions of using virtual world as a teaching and learning tool. This study suggested that Second Life is a feasible environment for teacher training and real life activities can be duplicated or improvised in the virtual environment.

A strong argument for the need and possibility to conduct teacher training in the virtual world was presented by a group of researchers (Grable, et al. , 2010). These researchers asserted that since doctors, pilots, and military staff can be trained virtually, teachers could also be trained through digital field placements. This assertion was aimed to solve a problem in the researchers' online teacher training degree program: the online program could not offer field experience courses. To solve this problem, the researchers (Grable et al. , 2010) implemented distance learning technologiesto their online secondary education teacher training courses. The technologies such as compressed interactive videos and a video-conferencing software that incorporates an interactive whiteboard and communication tools allowed pre-service teachers in secondary math, physics, business and Spanish to completetheir field experiences in the virtual classroom. Four pre-service teachers' field experiences in a traditional thirty-hour field observation are compared to their virtual field experiences. The researchers compared the two types of field experiences in three domains: planning, classroom management, and instruction. Their study found that-the students majoring in physics, business, and math showed a mixed attitude in the three domains no matter where their field experiences were gained. However, the students majoring in Spanish showed a more positive attitude in all three domainsin their virtual field experiences than those in the traditional settings. These results suggested that the virtual environment was feasible for prospective Spanish teachers to obtain valuable field experiences.

A current study (Mahon, Bryant, Brown, & Kim, 2010) looked into a specific aspect of teacher training-using Second Life to enhance classroom management practice. The researchers created their management simulators of 30 middle school students, and used artificial intelligence methods to infuse the simulation with random student behavior that would arise in a real classroom. In this mixed method study, the researchers found that participating students perceived the simulation to be a useful learning experience because Second Life provided a creative and intriguing approach to studying classroom management skills. The real-like classroom setting and behavior simulators put pre-service teachers in the situation where they had to make culturally and linguistically appropriate responses to address those behaviors. A shared opinion observed from the above three studies indicated that, regardless of technical challenges, Second Life is promising a "non-judgmental, risk-free environment" (Gregory &Masters, 2010, p. 2) for pre-service teachers to practice their teaching skills.

Demand for Mandarin Teacher Training in Second Life

Positive Foreign Language Learning Experiences in Second Life

Before Second Life was launched, foreign language educators had applied other types of game-based virtual reality technologiesto foreign language education for decades. Researchers agreed that VR can enhance foreign language learning (Salies, 2002; Schwienhorst, 2002; Von der Emde, et al. 2001). Von et al. (2001) identified pedagogical benefits of using VR in foreign language learning in five aspects: (1) authentic communication and content, (2) autonomous learning and peer teaching in a student-centered classroom, (3) individual learning, (4) importance of experimentation and play, and (5) students as researchers.

Different from the game-based VR, Second Life is a multi-user-created cyber environment wherepeople around the world carry out social interactions for certain purposes such as commerce, business, and education. This emerging 3-D virtual world allows immersive and interactive real-life communications withpeople around the world, thus bringing great benefits to foreign language education. Second Life has added new dimensions to second language study (Sweley, 2008).

Through visiting foreign islands, real communication with native speakers of target languages becomes highly possible and feasible for the foreign language learners (Swelley, 2008). Additionally, exchanging different cultures becomes attainable in Second Life (Hislope et al. , 2008; Thompson & Garetty, 2009). For these reasons, an increasing number of language educators start to view Second Life as a tool for supplementing foreign language classes.

Some empirical studies have tested the effectiveness of teaching foreign languages in Second Life. Hislope, et al. (2008) reported the perceived benefits and drawbacks of using Second Life in her intermediate Spanish course in Spring 2008 as a way to promote more out-of-class contact with native Spanish speakers. Results of a survey with 20 open-ended questions administered to15 students showed both positive and negative experiences with learning Spanish in Second Life. Students liked interactive, creative, and gaming-like aspects of Second Life. The reported negative experiences with Second Life focused heavily on technical issues and the high learning curve of navigating in Second Life. Regardless of challenges, 13 of 15 students reported that Second Life could help them improve their comprehension of Spanish.

Wang et al. (2009) conducted an international cooperative study to investigate students' technology readiness for and their perception of using Second Life as a language learning platform, as well as students' perceptions of integrating Second Life into a Teaching English as a Foreign Language (EFL) program. Sixty one EFL learners in China met weekly with American partners to complete assigned learning tasks. This evaluation research showed that EFL learners positively perceived Second Life as a language learning tool, and they perceived the EFL program in Second Life to be interesting and successful.

Garcia-Carbonellet al. (2001) stated that in traditional classrooms, language teachers normally control the students' conversation frequency, topics and responding time; therefore, language input to promote communicative competency seemed very limited. Simulation and gaming, however, seem to provide a nice solution to the problem that lackslanguage exposure outside of the classroom.

Demand for Teaching in the Virtual Environment

One significant impact of advanced technologies on 21st century education is the increasing demand for teaching via alternative and innovative methods. Learners in the 21st century are digital natives (Bennett, et al., 2008), therefore teaching in the virtual environment via internet teleconferencing and other types of learning management systemis one effective way to engage students. With the needs for qualified teachers, it is important that teacher candidates be exposed to alternative delivery methods to learn a different set of skills for future career opportunities. The effective use of technology in the classroom depends on teachers beingfamiliar with the technological options that are available and suitable to particular learning goals. Therefore, it is necessary for teachers to develop some experiences with the technology by stepping into any classroom, virtual or traditional (Grable, et al., 2010).

The best situation for learning teaching skills is through teaching in the real classroom (Tsui, 2003). However, Chinese teacher training programs in Taiwan have faced a challenge for not being able to provide enough opportunities and environments for pre-service teachers to teach Chinese as a foreign language to non-native Chinese speakers. As a solution to this practical problem, Second Life is found to be feasible for pre-service Mandarin teachers to practice teaching to non-native Chinese speakers in a one-to-one format (Cheng, Zhan& Chen 2010).

Second Life Capabilities for Language Teacher Training.

Second Life allows almost unlimited imagination and imitations of reality. This affordance of Second Life technology makes it feasible to conduct teacher training in this virtual world. Specifically, Second Life offers a very immersive and interactive instructional context, along with various means for instructional design, communication, and teaching observation and reflection. All of these components in Second Life contribute to the effectiveness of language teacher training.

Instructional Context

Second Life users can build almost anything their skills allow and interact with objects and other residents from all over the world within the environment (Carter & Elseth, 2009). Depending on the learning objectives, Second Life classrooms can be built to illustrate an instructional context where specific language learning topics are presented by rich graphics and colorful objects to satisfy learners with different learning styles. The virtual avatar presence of teachers and students adds a real feeling of being in a class. In addition, avatars can fly, move, and walk as well as teleport to relocate at an instructional context in different islands within the environment. It can provide a friendly, appealing, and contextually relevant space for native speakers of a target language to interact with learners (Wang, et al. , 2010).

Means for Instructional Design

Because Second Life is a user-generated virtual world with built-in tools for constructing and scripting, language teachers can create an immersive and interactive learning environment by using different instructional design strategies. Many instructional strategies commonly used in the traditional classroom are also available in Second Life. For example, depending on the needs for instructional activities, animations, audio or video clips, PowerPoint Presentation, note cards containing any information, words or phrases can be developed outside and easily be uploaded to Second Life. These materials can be attached to any object in Second life and retrieved with a simplemouse click. The micro-worlds allow users to interact with others and build objects within the environment, thus adding to the interactive nature of the world (Carter & Elseth, 2009).

Means for Communication

Communication in Second Life takes place via two avenues: text-based chat （ can be asynchronous or synchronous ） and live voice chat. The communication can be conducted individually or in a group format. Users can communicate verbally in real time, which adds another layer of authenticity to the text-based interaction. In addition to communications through text messages and audio conversations, avatars can also communicate with simple non-verbal gestures （ e. g. , waving, thumbs-up）. These forms of communication allow language teacher to create an engaging and interactive learning environment that helps language learners practice speaking a target language, such as Mandarin Chinese, that many CFL learners have a very limited opportunity to hear, use, and practice in the real world.

Means for observation and reflection.

SecondLife also offers capabilities to record events taking place within the environment. This allows teacher training programs to capture screen shots and to record entire lesson in Second Life. Teacher trainers and pre-service teachers can later review and reflect on their personal performances and interactions with others by watching their own recorded video clips in Second Life （Cheng, Zhan, & Chen, 2010）.

Statement of Problem and Research Questions

Based on a review of the literature, researchers believe that virtual reality can be a very useful environment for Mandarin pre-service teachers to obtain some field experience and to learn special skills for teaching in the virtual environment. These special skills may be translated to teaching in not only other types of virtual environments but also in the classrooms. Yet, data-based research to support this belief is very limited. Three sets of questions triggered the researchers to conduct this collaborative study between two institutions, one in Taiwan and the other in the United States, with technical support from Institute for Information Industry （ III）, a non-profit information technology association in Taiwan. This pilot study pioneeredconducting a Mandarin Chinese teacher trainingin the virtual world. In this study, a special virtual space the Virtual Living Lab （ the VLL） was built in Second Lifeby III, and the VLLis used as an instructional environment in which pre-service teachers design, develop, and deliver learning tasks tailored to learners of Chinese in the U. S. The researchquestions are:

1. How doMandarin pre-service teachers perceive the Second Life as reflected in the Virtual Living Labafter training? Is there any difference of perceptions between their 1st time and 2nd time teaching?

2. How do Mandarin pre-service teachers perceive teaching Mandarin in a virtual environment? Do their perceptions change between 1st time and 2nd time teaching experiences?

3. What difficulties do Mandarin pre-service teachers encounter when teaching in theVirtual Living Lab?

The purpose of paper is to report results of the pilot study of integrating Second Life into a teacher training program. Based on surveys of objective items supplemented with one open-ended question, this study investigated how pre-service teachers of Mandarin Chinese in Taiwan perceived Second Life as a teaching platform. This study adds to the understanding of benefits and drawbacks of using Second Life in teaching and learning Mandarin Chinese, and it also provides practical suggestions for integrating Second Life into Mandarin Chinese curriculum.

Theoretical Framework

Researchers of the study believed that creating social and authentic interactions could enhance language production, promote communication and assist language acquisition in foreign language settings. Therefore, Communicative Language Teaching (CLT) and constructivism are adopted as the main theoretical frameworks of this study.

Communicative Language Teaching approach in a foreign language classroom enables students to communicate in the target language, and to actively negotiate meaning (Gass & Selinker 2008; Larsen-Freeman, 2000). One tenet of CLT approach requires a maximum use of target language in language teaching, thus bringing the following benefits to foreign language classrooms: (a) the more the students are exposed to the target language, the more they learn, (b) students' motivation is increased, and (c) higher exposure to the target language positively associated with student language proficiency（Turnbull, 2001）. Second Life can provide such a high exposure to language learners who maynot have access to n-ative speakers of the target language in real life.

Constructivists believe that learning occurs through interactions in the learning environment rather than messages transmission from the instruc-tors. It is throughinteraction thatpeople construct meaningful knowledge（Mcdonough, 2001）. Jonassen et al.（1995）pointed out that construc-tive environments involved four attributes: context, construction, collabo-ration and conversation. These four attributes, which also are key elements in Second Life, are interwoven in a learning process. Constructivism has been widely adopted to support Computer Assisted Language Learning（CALL）. Some examples included using e-mail, websites, and videoco-nferencing as venues to help learners to construct knowledge via interaction in the cyber space（Mcdonough, 2001）. Beyond the functions of these tools for knowledge construction in the virtual world, Second Life allows learners to be "physically" situated in the virtual context where they can construct their linguistic and cultural knowledge through the authentic inter-action with native speakers of the target language. As Rieber（1992）pointed out, visually based virtual environments are an extension of con-structivist learning theories, and the virtual world is an immediate applica-tion of the infusion of constructivism into instructional design.

Method

Research Context—the Virtual Living Lab（VLL）（http: //slurl. com/sec-ondlife/Virtual%20Living%20Lab/119/186/21）.

The primary Second Life island/region for this study, the Virtual Living Lab, was an on-going construction island designed for Mandarin Lan-guage learning built by a non-profit association in Taiwan, Institute for In-formation Industry. The target users of the VLL were Mandarin learners in the United States. According to Institute forInformation Industry（2010）, the mission of this 3D virtual learning environment is to build up a culture-enhanced Mandarin language environment to best simulatereal-life learning experiences. The islands, scenes, as well as specific objects in the Living Lab were built around common topics including an airport, duty free shops, hotels, restaurants, a night-time market, streets, and a subway station.

Figure 2   Airport and duty free shops

Figure 3   Night market

Research Process

The literature suggestedthree essential elements contributing to the success of teaching and learning in Second Life: teacher presence in the virtual activities, training on Second Life skills, and the effectiveness of group activities (Wang et al. , 2009; Wang & Braman, 2009). Based on these three elements, the research processof this study was divided into fivestages as illustrated in Figure 9.

Figure 4   Hotel

Figure 5   Street and shops

Figure 6   Restaurants

Preparation stage. During this stage, researchers first analyzed the Mandarin learners' language background and pre-service teachers' teaching background, and then decided the themes for Second Life activities. All the activities were integrated in the existing curriculumfor the teacher training class and the Mandarin Chinese class. Based on the teaching and learning needs, the IT group built possible objects that could be used

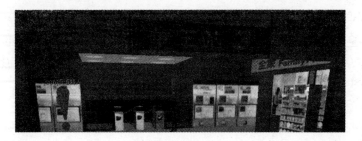

Figure 7　Subway

as instructional tools. Since this cross-continental study involved three institutions located in two time zones with a15-hour difference, establishing a carefully planned schedule and matching the pre-service teachers in Taiwan and the Mandarin learners in the States were also very importanttasks that were completed in the preparation stage.

Second Life training stage. Hislope, (2008) and Wang and Braman, (2009) all pointed out that in-class training on "getting around" in Second Life could reduce the frustration of users. Therefore, the two researchers arranged some in-class, hands-on activities to help pre-service teachers (6 hours total) and the Mandarin students (2 hours total) familiarize themselves with the Second Life environment and functions, such as registration, manipulating the avatar, teleporting to different locations, and chatting in text and voice. Pre-service teachers were expected to be more familiar with these functions because they were todirect the students to complete tasks in the virtual Mandarin class.

Lesson planning stage. Based on the themes and context (such as shopping, hotel reservations, food, and night-time market) in the Virtual Living Lab, the pre-service teachers designed the lessons and created tasks for their matched Mandarin students. All of the lessons matched the students' language levels referring to their textbook, *Integrated Chinese Level 2 Part* 1. Before teaching, the lesson plans were reviewed by the professor in Taiwan. Then, the pre-service teacher modified their lessons anddelivered them in the VLL. Each of the lessons was taught twice to different Mandarin learners in different weeks.

Technical testing stage. Before meeting with Mandarin learners in the Virtual Living Lab, all of the pre-service teachers practiced teaching in the

Living Lab to test their uploaded instructional PowerPoint slides, functions of objects, and functions of hardware, such as headsets, graphics display, and Internet connections. The technicians from III provided immediate assistance when problems occurred.

Virtual teaching stage. The teaching in the virtual world in this study was designed in a one-to-one format (one leading teacher and one student). Chung Yuan University requires undergraduate students to take a minimum of 36 hours of tutoring in order to satisfy the teaching training component in the program of study, so such trainingformat enhanced students' professional knowledge of one-to-one tutoring. Researchers believe that theteacher training model involved in providing field experience was a better way to train pre-service teachers to prepare for authentic professional life. In the study, the pre-service teachers were undergraduate students who did not have much teaching experience, so their teaching skills were not matured enough to handle many of the unexpected issues that can arise in class. To help the participating teachers reduce their anxiety, the researchers grouped 5 to 6 pre-service teachers to teach one Mandarin learner. Such group work was designed to reduce teaching anxiety and increase teaching effectiveness. Group members played different roles such as teachers, technicians or other roles that were needed in scenarios and tasks. When teaching a session, some of the members were teachers who took turns to provide instruction on vocabulary, grammar, or tasks. Some members acted as technicians to videotape the whole teaching session. Some members played specific roles needed in scenariosor tasks to assist learners in accomplishingthe task. Each group taught two sessions to different students in different weeks. Each teaching session lasted about one hour. During the teaching hour, the class was videotaped and observed by the two professors. Technicians fromIII were also virtually presentto provide technical support.

Participants

The study was implemented as a cooperative project between Taiwan and the United States. The target population of this study was a group of pre-service teachers in Taiwan. To administrate this study, in Fall 2009,

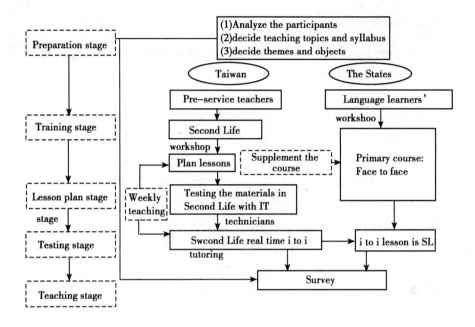

Figure 9   The Research Design

the 3rd-year pre-service teachers from anundergraduate Mandarin Teacher Training Program in a mid-size private university in Taiwan were selected. Pre-service teachers who were junior standing or above were preferred because many of them hada certain level of tutoring credit hours or some teaching experience. Since group work could create more scenarios and reduce 'technology anxiety' for first time user of Second Life, the researchers grouped pre-service teachers for this project. Thirteen Mandarin learners (intermediate level) froma mid-size university in the United States were willing to participate in this international project, and accordingly, the sixty five pre-service teachers were divided into 13 groups (with 5-6 trainee teachers in one group) to match the 13 American students.

The research team consisted of one professor from the Teacher Training Program in Taiwan, one Chinese professor teaching the 13 American students, and a few technicians from a non-profit technology organization in Taiwan. The two professors also participated inthis study as trainers of pre-service Mandarin teachers.

Instruments

A two-part survey was designed to solicit information about pre-service teachers' perceptions ofthe VLLas a teaching platform and their teaching experiences in using such a platform to teach during project implementation. The survey was carried out after each session of teaching Mandarin Chinese in the VLL. The survey included four sections: (1) demographic information (1 item), (2) attitudes toward *Virtual Living Lab* (9 items), (3) readiness for teaching in a virtual environment (12 items), and (4) one open-ended question. Demographic information only had one itemasking for the name of the pre-service teacher's avatar, which was aimed to match two data sets from the survey which was distributedafter each teaching sesson. Sections (2) and (3) were five-level-Likert- scale questions (strongly disagree = 1, disagree = 2, neural = 3, agree = 4, strongly agree = 5). Survey items 5 and 8 were negative statements, indicating a reverse five-level-Likert-scale: "1 = strongly agree" and "5 = strongly disagree." The open-ended question, "*Have you met any difficulties in terms of technical and instructional issues?*" was to collect qualitative data soliciting any challenges and difficulties the pre-service teachers encountered in their virtual teaching process. In order to investigate pre-service teacher' attitudes and perceptions in-depth, the survey was given in Chinese, and then was translated into English for the purpose ofthis paper.

Data Analysis

This study had a total of 65 participants who were in the Mandarin teacher training program in a university in Taiwan. Thirty nine participants completed two sets of survey. After data screening, these 39 participants were included in the data analysis. The collected data was run through SPSS for both descriptive and statistical analysis. The descriptive analysis looked into means, frequencyand percentage of each item from survey section (2) (*the attitudes toward Second Life as reflected in the VLL*) and section (3) (*readiness for teaching in a virtual environment*). In order to investigate whether any changes occurred in pre-service teachers' perceptions of the VLL and their teaching experience in such an environment, a paired-*t* test was employed to compare the means of the teachers' first and second teaching sessions. Qualitative data from survey section (4) (the open-ended question) was analyzed by the two professors. During the analysis process, emerging themes regarding the difficulties were formed and frequencies of types of difficulties were counted (Punch, 2005).

Results

Results of Research Question # 1: How Do Mandarin Pre-service Teachers Perceive the Second Life as reflected in Virtual Living LabAfter Training? Is There Any Difference in Perceptions Between Their 1st Time And 2nd Time Teaching?

Since this research group createdthe VLL, for instructional purposes, collecting the insights of the pre-service teachers was seen as crucial for its future improvement. The first research question in this study sought to fulfill this purpose. Table 1 presents results of the descriptive analysis and significance levels of paired-t tests which indicate changes in pre-service teacher's perceptions of the VLLas a teaching environment and of their experiencesteaching in the Lab. The data showed that, when teaching the second lesson, about 17.9% more of the pre-service teachers found that they enjoyed using their avatar ($mean_1$ =3.36, $mean_2$ =3.95, p <0.05).

After the second session of authentic teaching, 26.5% more of the pre-service teachers strongly believed that the VLLoffered an interesting setting for language communication ($mean_1$ =3.54, $mean_2$ =3.95, p < 0.05); 25.6% more of the teachers enjoyed chatting with other avatars in the VLL ($mean_1$ =3.13, $mean_2$ =3.72, p <0.05); 30.8% more of the participating pre-service teachers thought working with the gestures and actions of their avatars became easier ($mean_1$ = 3.00, $mean_2$ = 3.69, p <0.05); about half of the pre-service teachers (48.1%) believed that the VLLwas good for Mandarin teaching and learning ($mean_1$ = 2.97, $mean_2$ =3.44, p <0.05). However, after the second teaching session, even though 7.8% more of the pre-service teachers believed that the VLL offered great possibilities for teaching Mandarin Chinese, there was no significant difference in the participating teachers' attitudes between the two teaching sessions ($mean_1$ =3.54, $mean_2$ =3.85, p >.05).

Survey item 5 (*I still cannot get use to the virtual environment*) and item 8 (*The features in Virtual Living Lab seem to be hard for me to manipulate*) were negative statements. Regarding these two negative statements, after teaching the second lesson, fewer pre-service teachers agreed to item 5 (15.4%) and item 8 (20.5%). Perceptions reflected in the responses to items 5 (mean$_1$ = 3.26, mean$_2$ = 2.51, $p < 0.05$) and item 8 (mean$_1$ = 3.28, mean$_2$ = 3.00, $p < 0.05$) showed significant differences between the first and second sessions of teaching. These results indicated that pre-service teachers gradually overcame the difficulties and challenges as they gained more experience.

Table 1　　　**Results of the Differences in the Attitudes to Second Life as Reflected in the Virtual Living Lab**

Items	1st Mean	%	2nd Mean	%	P value
Changing avatar's appearance is very enjoyable.	3.36	56.4	3.95	74.3	0.00 *
Working on the gestures and actions of my avatar is easy to me.	3.00	38.4	3.69	69.2	0.00 *
The virtual living lab offers an intenerating environment for language communication.	3.54	56.5	3.95	82.1	0.01 *
I enjoy chatting with other avatars in the virtual living lab.	3.13	38.5	3.72	64.1	0.00 *
I still cannot get use to the virtual environment.	3.26	48.7	2.51	15.4	0.00 *
In terms of Mandarin learning, I believe virtual living lab offers great possibilities.	3.54	58.9	3.85	66.7	0.97
Virtual living lab is good for Mandarin learning.	2.97	33.3	3.44	48.7	0.04 *
The features in virtual living lab seem to be hard for me to manipulate.	3.82	66.7	3.00	20.5	0.00 *
Overall, I do enjoy time in this virtual living lab.	2.87	30.7	3.64	71.8	0.00
Mean	3.03		3.63		

* significance $p < 0.05$

Results of Research Question #2: How do Mandarin Pre-service Teachers Perceive Teaching Mandarin in a Virtual Reality? Do Their Perceptions Change Between the 1st Time and 2nd Time Teaching Experiences?

Teaching in a virtual reality environment is an innovativeinstructional delivery method, especially in the field of teaching Mandarin Chinese. The researchers believe that although this different teaching environment may develop a unique set of teaching skills, pre-service teachers still need fundamental professional knowledge, such as understanding the teaching objectives and teaching strategies such as when and how to correct students' errors. Therefore, some items in the survey could be common in other studies of teaching Mandarin Chinese in a traditional face-to-face situation.

As shown in Table 2, after teaching the second lesson, pre-service teachers' perceptions of teaching in the VLL had significantly and positively changed. 10.3% more of pre-service teachers believed that teaching in the VLLwas as effective as teaching in a face-to-face environment ($mean_1 = 2.92$, $mean_2 = 3.47$, $p < 0.05$). 10 % more of the pre-service teachers believed their "teacher talk" was more appropriate for their student in the second lesson ($mean_1 = 3.46$, $mean_2 = 3.74$, $p < 0.05$). 10.2% more of the pre-service teachers came to better understand one-to-one format teaching ($mean_1 = 3.79$, $mean_2 = 3.4.13$, $p < 0.05$). In addition, 28.2% more of the pre-service teachers believed that, after teaching the first session, they came to be prepared for the unpredictable issues in the future class ($mean_1 = 3.38$, $mean_2 = 3.89$, $p < 0.05$), 23.1% more of the pre-service teachers believed they were qualified for teaching the VR class ($mean_1 = 3.05$, $mean_2 = 3.55$, $p < 0.05$), 5.1% more of pre-service teachers agreed that they had come to know more about how to evaluate their own teaching proficiency ($mean_1 = 3.28$, $mean_2 = 3.61$, $p < 0.05$).

However, regardless of the increased means, some aspects of pre-service teachers' perspectives of teaching in the world did not show significant differences ($p > .05$). In specific, regarding item 2, 20.5% fewer of pre-service teachers thought teaching in the virtual world was less stressful than teaching in a face-to-face setting ($mean_1 = 2.79$, $mean_2 = 2.71$). Similarly, a high percentage of the pre-service teachers believed that they knew the objectives of both lessons (item3, $mean_1 = 3.82$, $mean_2 = 4.05$), but there was no statistically significant difference ($p > .05$). When asking the pre-service teachers whether they were well-prepared for both classes, 12. 9 % more of them thought they were well-prepared in the second lesson (item 4, $mean_1 = 3.74$, $mean_2 = 4.00$), but there was no significant difference between first lesson and second lesson ($p > .05$). A good number of pre-service teachers believed that they understood the process of their teaching in both sessions (item 6, $mean_1 = 3.97$, $mean_2 = 4.16$), and there was no significant difference ($p > .05$). The results of item 8 showed that a small number of the pre-service teachers ($mean_1 = 3.28$, $mean_2 = 3.39$) hadsufficient confidence to correct students' errors, but there was no significant difference. Of course, since the pre-service teachers were all inexperienced teachers, such results were predictable. Item 9showed that a good number of pre-service teachers believed that they were well prepared for teaching in terms of presenting class content, forming questions and providing examples ($mean_1 = 3.77$, $mean_2 = 4.03$) and there was no significant difference ($p > 0.05$).

Table 2   Results of Pre-service Teachers Perceptions toward Teaching in the Virtual Environment

Items	1st %	1st mean	2nd %	2nd mean	P value
I believe that teaching in a VR environment is as effective as teaching in a face-to- face environment.	41.0	2.92	51.3	3.47	0.004 *
I believe it is less stressful to teach in a VR environment than in a face-to-face environment.	43.6	2.79	23.1	2.71	0.562
I know the objectives of this VR lesson very well.	74.4	3.82	82.1	4.05	0.146
I am well-prepared for the 1st/ 2nd VR lesson.	69.2	3.74	82.1	4.00	0.067
I understand one-to-one format teaching.	79.5	3.79	89.7	4.13	0.007 *
I understand the teaching process of this lesson.	87.2	3.97	87.2	4.16	0.128
I believe my "teacher talk" is appropriate for my student.	48.7	3.46	59.0	3.74	0.010 *

Items	1st %	1st mean	2nd %	2nd mean	P value
I know how to correct my student's errors	30. 8	3. 28	43. 6	3. 39	0. 378
I am well prepared for this class in terms of class content, questions, and examples.	74. 4	3. 77	79. 5	4. 03	0. 077
I have prepared for the unpredictable issues in the class.	48. 7	3. 38	76. 9	3. 89	0. 001 *
I believe I am qualified for this VR class.	33. 3	3. 05	56. 4	3. 55	0. 001 *
I know how to evaluate my own teaching efficiency.	48. 7	3. 28	53. 8	3. 61	0. 010 *

* significance $p < 0.05$

Results of Research Question #3: What Difficulties Do Mandarin Pre-service Teachers Encounter WhenTeaching in the Virtual Living Lab?

Regarding difficulties that the pre-service teachers encountered at two timeswhen teaching Chinese in the VLL two categories of difficulties emerged from the detailed qualitative responses to the third research question. The first category is related to technical challenges, and the second category is related to instruction.

Difficulties Encountered During the First Teaching Session
Technical Challenges

Technical problems were mentioned by many participants. Low Internet speeds and insufficient computer capacity werethe most common problems. When these problems occurred in the VLL, these problems blocked out the users, reduced the speed of graphics display and PowerPoint slide shows, and froze the computer or audio effects. In the data, 17 participants addressed the problems associated with PowerPoint and audio effects, five participants had been blocked out, seven had difficulties with graphics display, and nineexperienced situations where their computers froze. When teaching in Second Life, both teachers and students relied heavily on quality voice connections and high speed graphic displays to exchange information. If one userdid not hear other users, the lesson was delayed for long periods or canceled. The following comments from pre-service teacher illustrate some of these problems.

" *the process of my lesson was serious delay due to the issues of dis-*

playing PowerPoint slides" （*Participant ID #24*）.

"*the capacity of my computer was not sufficient to run* ［the VLL］ *in Second Life*, *so it was very easy to be blocked out or get my computer freeze while teaching*" （*Participant ID #25*）.

"*I can't hear the voice*, *so I could not communicate with others*, *but my speakers and microphone were running perfectly with other software*" （*Participant ID #28*）.

Using Power Point slide shows in Second Life is one of a number of instructional strategies used to transfer information, such as presenting new vocabulary and new sentence structures, or explaining exercises or tasks. The Internet bandwidth and computer visual card capacities may influence the speed of PowerPoint display in Second Life. Sometime, the pre-service teachers and students could not view the same slide at the same time. When this issue happened, a lot of pre-service teachers felt panic and they believed such problem affected the effectiveness of teaching. The following comments reflected this problem.

"*my student and I could not view the same slide due to my poor computer*" （*Participant ID #53*）.

"*Second Life requires high capacity hard ware*, *my computer and school computers cannot run Second Life smoothly*, *a lot of graphics and PowerPoint sidescannot be displayed*" （*Participant ID #59*）.

"*the problem of displaying PowerPoint slides caused serious delay of the lesson*" （*Participant ID #37*）.

Instructional Challenges

The instructional challenges faced by the pre-service teachers derived from three sources: the lack of the knowledge of the students' language proficiency level, undeveloped skills ofhow to clearly explaintasks to the students, and inability ofhow to communicate with the students in teacher'slanguage. Before teaching, the pre-service teachers did not have opportunities to talk with their students. The teachers referred to the textbook used by the students to figure out the students' language proficiency level. Therefore, seven pre-service teachers mentioned that they were not sure about the language level of their students, even though they were given the copies of students' textbook. Due to the fact that some pre-service teachers either were not familiar with the textbook, or had very limited ex-perience teaching Mandarin, theiranxieties in the first time lesson were very high. Although this problem is a planning issue that is separate from the technology, this problem affected teaching results.

"*my student's language level were better than I expected, our lesson seemed to be too easy to the student*" (Participant ID #29) .

" *I was not confident about the student's language level, so part of the content was too easy to my student and the usage of language from me seemed to be too hard*" (Participant ID #25) .

Difficulties Encountered in the SecondTeaching Session
Technical Challenges

After teaching the first class, the pre-service teachers developed some strategies to cope with technical issues and to improve their instruc-tion. The responses to the open-ended question after the second time teaching showed that all of the teachers had made some pro-gress. Regarding technical issues, four participants were temporarily blocked out by the system, three had difficulties viewing the graphics, three had problems displaying PowerPoint slides, four had computers freeze, ten had audio issues, and ten did not have any technical prob-lems. Even though the same technical problems still occurred, the pre-service teachers understoodthey could solve the problem by some simple ways such as switching to computers with high speed internet connection or testing all possible technical devices before teaching. The following re-sponses from the pre-service teachers provide details of how they coped with problems when they arose.

" *for second class, most of the problems associated with software and hardware have not happened, because we have done millions of tests and got a nice computer*" (Participant ID #15) .

" *even though my account was blocked* 10 *minutes before class be-gan, I got it back on time and the system was more stable than the one at the first class. We also used better computers and no audio problems. It became easy to communicate with the student⋯*" (Participant ID #30) .

Instructional Challenges

Instructional issues in the second time teaching dramatically dropped. With experience from the first teaching session, a lot of the participants had a better idea of the students' language proficiency level, so they were more comfortable teachingthe second lesson. Only two participants mentioned that they still had problems with instruction due to uncertainty about their students' language level.

"*I still have difficulties to catch the language level of my student*" (*Participant ID #13*).

Discussion

This study found that using the VLL in Second Life as a platform for Mandarin teacher training in Taiwan is promising. This finding supports previous studies (Grable, et al., 2010; Mahon, Bryant, & Kim, 2010; Mullin, Beilke, & Brooks, 2007) which found that Second Life was a feasible and meaningful context to offer field experiencein teacher education. The collaborative teacher training model of this study utilized a specially designed virtual space in Second Life (the VLL) to provide real teaching opportunities for pre-service Mandarin teachersin Taiwan to teach learners of Chinese in the United States. Such field experience also served as a promising solution to solve a practical problem in Mandarin teacher training programs in Taiwan, where teaching practice normally has to be a mock dry-runbecause of the lack oftarget foreign students in real classrooms. The training model investigated in this study enabled pre-service Mandarin teachers to experience teaching target students abroad without even stepping out of their home campus.

The findings yielded from the surveys showed that teacher training in Second Lifepreparedparticipating pre-service Mandarin teachers for their profession in the following three aspects, which may help them better meet the demand for teaching digital natives in the 21st century to via different instructional delivery methods. First, through the training onintegrating Second Life in virtual teaching, the pre-service teachers learned how to effectively use different applications in the virtual classroom. They became more skillful at using applications such as PowerPoint and audio software to enhance instruction and to engage students. Second, the pre-service teachers developed anawareness of the complexity of using technology in the classroom and learned how to copewith unpredictable technical and instructional issues that may not directly occur in technologically based instructional environment. They came to understand that to teach effectively in the virtual environment, or indeed using any kind of technology to teach, it was not enough to just haveappropriate technical facilities such as a high speed Internet connection and powerful computers with high definition graphic cards. Before teaching takes place, it is necessary to test the hardware and software to assure interactive instruction. Third, the pre-service teachers developed positive attitudes toward using the emerging technology for teaching Chinese in virtual environments such as Second Life. This attitude will empower them to integrate new technologies in an innovative and meaningful way to enhance their teaching in the 21st century in which technology has become an integral component of teaching and learning.

The carefully planned virtual training not only helped the pre-service teachers grow in terms of their knowledge about integrating technology into teaching, more importantly, it helped them develop pedagogical strategies that would benefit their professional life in both virtual and physical situations. First, the virtual training helped the pre-service teachers develop self-confidence inteaching. Self-confidence may help these teachers to more actively interact with their students, teaching contexts, and teaching materials. The pre-service teachers came to understand that teaching in the virtual environment and in physical situations can be equally effective as long as teachers have clear instructionalobjectives and are prepared thoroughly for the lessons and for unpredictable issues.

Such results may be associated with two carefully planned stages of this research: *lesson planning stage and virtual teaching stage*. During the lesson plan stage, a group of pre-service teachers were required to prepare their lessonstogether and their lessons were further reviewed by the professor in Taiwan. During the virtual teaching stage, both professors in Taiwan and in the United States observed the entire class and provided immediate feedback on site at the end of each lesson for future improvement. With such an intensive training process, pre-service teachers improved very quickly in their teaching.

One very encouraging and important finding of this study is that, through the one-to-one teaching format, the pre-service teachers learned how to effectively communicate with students by using "teacher talk." Language teachers need to adjust their language use for instruction based on student language proficiency level, but it is a difficult task for teacher training if there is no authentic teaching takes place. Through the real teaching experience in the virtual environment, the pre-service teachers learned how to assist communication in the target language. They learned to use topics familiar to the students to stimulate language output; used more standard pronunciation and expressions to model language use; used simplified vocabulary and sentence structures to provide comprehensible input; carried out regular checks for understanding. The pre-service teachers might not be able to develop their teacher talk skills so quickly if they did not teach target students in a real class, even if the class was in the virtual world.

Last but not the least, an important finding of this study was that pre-service teachers learned how to self-evaluate the effectiveness of their teaching by observing responses from their students' achievement of their instructional objectives, and by reflecting the whole teaching process. This set of skills will help the pre-service teachers be able to analyze various factors contributing to the success of teaching.

Implications for Chinese Language Teacher Training

This study has echoed other studies which believed Second Life as a "worthwhile venue for virtual learning in teacher education" (Mahon, Bryant, Brown, & Kim, 2010, p. 131). In terms of pre-service language teacher training, this study has the following implications where teacher training is carried out in a virtual world.

1) Utilizing the virtual reality technology to provide an authentic teaching experience is an alternative and effective way for pre-service Chinese teachers in a Chinese-speaking environment to obtain valuable field experience. The authentic teaching experience gained in the virtual classroom

can certainly help pre-service teachersunderstand what is going on in a real Chinese language classroom, thus helping them to develop strategies for solving technical and instructional problems as a result of the training.

2) Teaching and learning with technology as a tool can help pre-service teachers develop positive attitudes toward emerging technologies and help them better understand how to use technology to enhance instruction.

3) When conducting teacher training in a virtual world such as Second Life, "onsite" observations and timely feedback from teacher trainers are crucial to training efficiency. The feedback and comments provided "on site" will help pre-service teachers develop contextualized knowledge so that they reflect on the weakness in their teaching for future improvement.

Limitations and Suggestions for Future Research

This study was a pilot studydesigned to pioneerconducting a Mandarin Chinese teacher training model in the virtual world. Although some findings are encouraging, this study reveals the following limitations in the research design and process, thus the findings may not be simply generalized to other situations where teacher training is conducted in a different virtual world.

1) Issues with the credibility and reliability of the survey: This study was a pilot study in which the two researchers created the survey to explore pre-service teachers' perceptions of teaching Chinese in Second Life. The credibility and reliabilityof the survey items were not tested. Therefore, the data from the survey may not fully reflect the attributes of teaching Chinese in the virtual world.

2) Issues with teaching improvement: In this study, the pre-service teachers taught the same class twice todifferent target students who had the samelevels of language proficiency. This design did not allow the pre-service teachers to demonstrate their improvement in teaching different levels of students. In addition, the pre-service teachers only taught two hours in the virtual environment. Such a short time of teacher training may not be long enough to lead substantial improvement in teaching.

3) Issues with group teaching: This study arranged five to sixpre-

service teachers in one group. Although only one leading teacher taught the lesson to one American student, all other team members had to log in at the same time to assist the role-play during the instruction. Such design caused log-in problems. Second Lifeblocked out some users during the instruction. For future research, using computers with a stable internet connection with high speeds is suggested.

4) Issues with the VLL: As a Region within Second Life, the VLL has its agent limit. For example, a high number of avatars on a Region can significantly reduce the Region's performance. In addition, since the VLL is specially designed to promote teaching and learning Mandarin Chinese in a virtual world, the VLL also incorporated other types of technologies that may have influenced Second Life performance. For example, instead of using Second Life built-in PowerPoint Viewer, the VLL used Moodle, an open-source virtual learning environment) to upload and download PowerPoint slides. This type of file transfer may be slower than using the PowerPoint Viewer.

Conclusion

This study pioneered integrating Second Life intoa Chinese teacher training program. The researchers developed a collaborative training model involving a Chinese teacher training program in Taiwan, an existing Chinese language course in the United States, and a technology institution in Taiwan. The three parties collaboratively created a virtual world for pre-service Mandarin Chinese teachers to gain field experiences. This study found that this training model benefited the participating pre-service Chinese teachers in Taiwan in many aspects. Particularly, through the virtual training, the pre-service teachers developed positive attitudes toward teaching in the virtual world, and they also improved teaching strategies for effective instruction. This training model is worth further development through implementations to other Chinese teacher training programs which have the *need* for authentic teaching. The*realpractical need* for using Second Life to enhance teacher training may break through the barriers between using Second Life and its challenges in terms of technical skills and instructional strategies for teaching in a virtual world.

References

Bennett, S. , Maton, K. , & Kervin, L. (2008). The 'digital natives' debate: A critical review of the evidence. British Journal of Educational Technology, 39 (5), 775—786.

Billings, D. M. (2009). Teaching and learning in virtual worlds. The Journal of ContinuingEducation in Nursing, 40 (11), 489—490.

Boulos, M. N. K, Hetherington, L. , & Wheeler, S. (2007). Second Life: An overview of the potential of 3-D virtual worlds in medical and health education. Health Information and Libraries Journal, 24, 233—245.

Bricken, M. , & Byrne, C. M. (1992). Summer students in virtual reality: A pilot study on educational applications of virtual reality technology. [Eric Document 38 853]

Carter, B. , & Elseth, D. (2009). The usefulness of Second Life for language learning, in R. Marriott & P. Torres (Eds.), Handbook of research on E-Learning methodologies for language acquisition, pp. 443—455. New York: Hershey.

Chang, V. , Gütl C. , Kopeinik S. , Williams, R. (2009). Evaluation of collaborative learning settings in 3D virtual worlds. International Journal of Emerging Technology, 4 (3), 6—17.

Cheng, H-J. , Zhan, H. , Chen, X. (2010). Using virtual reality space in training Mandarin pre-service teachers: An Innovative method. Chung Yuan Journal of Teaching Chinese as a Second Language, 5, 157—177.

Chien, Y-H. (2008). Oversea Chinese internship and cross culture communication-Active Research, Chung Yuan Journal of Teaching Chinese as a Second Language, 2, 243—269.

Conklin, M. (2007). 101 uses of Second Life in the college classroom. Retrieved May, 24, 2009, from http: //trumpy. cs. elon. edu/metaverse.

Descy, D. E. (2008). All aboard the InternetSecond Life. TechTrends, 52 (1), 5—6.

Gartner Inc. (2007). Garner says 80 percent ofactive Internet users will have a "second life" in the virtual world by the end of 2011". Retrieved on December 23, 2009 from http: //www. gartner. com/it/page. jsp? id =503861

Garcia-Carbonell, A. , Rising, B. , Montero, B. , & Watts, F. (2001). Simulation/ gaming and the acquisition of communicative competence in another language. Simulation & Gaming, 32 (4), 481—491.

Gass, S. , & Selinker, L. (2008). Second language acquisition: An introductory course. N. Y. : Routledge Taylor & Francis Group.

Grable, C. , Kiekel, J. , & Hunt, A. (2010). Digital pre-service teacher education: Field experiences as a possible augmentation to the traditional brick and mortar field experience. Retrieved on November 10, 2010 from http: //www. journaleic. com/article/viewFile/3392/2464

Gregory, S. , & Masters, Y. (2010). Six hats in Second Life: Enhancing pre-service teacher learning in a virtual world. Conference proceeding of International Conference for Teaching and Learning with Technology, 2010, 2—6 March, Singapore. Retrieved on Nov. 10, 2010.

Gregory, S. , & Tynan, B. (2009). Introducing Jass Easterman: My Second Life learning space. Proceedings ASCILITE, Auckland, 2009.

Hislope, K. (2008). Language learning in a virtual world. The International Journal of Learning, 15 (11), 51—58.

Jonassen, D. , Daidson, M. , Colins, M. , Campbell, J. , & Haag, B. B. (1995). Constructivism and computer-mediated communication in distance education. American Journal of Distance Education, 9 (2), 7—26.

Larsen-Freeman, D. (2000). Techniques and principles in language teaching. Oxford: Oxford University Press.

Mahon, J. , Bryant, B. , Brown, B. , & Kim, M. (2010). Using Second Life to enhance classroom management practice in teacher education. Educational Media International, 47 (2), 121—134.

Mcdonough, S. K. (2001). Way beyond drill and practice: Foreign language lab activities in support of constructivist learning. International Journal of Instructional Media, 28 (1), 75—81.

Mullen, L. , Beilke, J. , & Brooks. N. (2007). Redefining field experiences: Virtual environments in teacher education. International Journal of Human and Social Science, 2 (1), 22—28.

O'Brien, M. , & Levy. R. (2008). Exploration through virtual reality: Encounters with the target culture. Canadian Modern Language Review, 64 (4), 663—691.

Punch, K. F. (2005). Introduction to social research: Quantitative and qualitative approaches (2nd ed.). Thousand Oaks, CA: SAGE publications.

Rieber, L. P. (1992). Computer-based microworlds: A bridge between constructivism and direct instruction. Educational Technology Research & Development, 40 (1), 93—106.

Sanchez, J. (2007). Second Life: An interactive qualitative analysis. In C. Crawford et al. (Eds.), Proceedings of Society for Information Technology and Teacher Education International Conference 2007 (pp. 1240—1243). Chesapeake,

VA: AACE

Salies, T. G. (2002). Promoting strategic competence: What simulations can do for you. Simulation & Gaming, 33 (3), 280—283.

Schiller, S. Z. (2009). Practicing learner-centered teaching: Pedagogical design and assessment of a Second Life project. Journal of Information Systems Education, 20 (3), 369—381.

Schwienhorst, K. (2002). Why virtual, why environments? Implementing virtual reality concepts in computer-assisted language learning. Simulation and Gaming, 33 (2), 196—209.

Sege, I. (2006). Leading a double life in a user-created universe, alter egos bridge the gap between fantasy and reality. Retrieved on December 16, 2009 from http: //www. boston. com/news/globe/living/articles/2006/10/25/leading _ a _ double_ life/

Shim, K. , Park, J. , Kim, H. , Kim, J. , Park, Y. , & Ryu, H. (2003). Application of virtual reality technology in biology education. Journal of Biology Education, 37 (2), 71—74.

Sussman, B. (2007, August 1). Teachers, college students lead a second life. USA Toda. Retrieved on November 23, 2009 from http: //www. usatoday. com/news/education/2007-08-01-second-life_ N. htm.

Sweley, M. H. (2008). Unreal world: Second Lifeadds new dimensions tosecond language study, The Language Educator, 3 (2), 22—25.

Institute for Information Industry (2010). Institute for Information Industry: 3D Virtual Learning environment. Taipei, Andy Tsai.

Theodore, P. A. (2009). Real education in virtual space: Look at a multi-user virtual environment through a Deweyan lens. Journal of Philosophy & History of Education, 59, 118—121.

Thompson, A. D. & Garetty, C. (2009). Second Life: A tool for teacher educators. Journal of Computing in Teacher Education, 25 (4), 118.

Tsui, A. B. (2003). Understanding expertise in teaching: Case studies of ESL teachers. N. Y. : Cambridge University Press.

Turnbull, M. (2001). There is a role for the L1 in second language and foreign language teaching, but ⋯ . The˙ Canadian Modern Language Review, 57 (4), 531—540.

Von der Emde, S. , Schneider, J. , & Kotter, M. (2001). Technically speaking: Transforming language learning through virtual learning environments (MOOs). The Modern Language Journal, 85 (2), 210—225.

Wang, Y. , & Braman, J. (2009). Extending the classroom through Second

Life. Journal of Information Systems Education, 20 (2), 235—147.

　　Wang, C. X. , Song, H. , Xia, F. , & Yan, Q. (2009). Integrating Second Life into an EFL program: Students' perspectives. Journal of Educational Technology Development and Exchange, 2 (1), 1—16.

　　Yao, T-C. (2009). The current status of Chinese CALL in the United States. Journal of the Chinese Language Teaching Association, 44 (1), 1—23.

Appendix I　Research Survey

Demographic Information

Second Life Avatar account:　＿＿＿＿＿＿＿

Part 1　　　　　　　　　**Attitudes Toward theVirtual Living Lab**

Changing avatar's appearance is very enjoyable.	5	4	3	2	1
Working on the gestures and actions of my avatar is easy to me.	5	4	3	2	1
The virtual living lab offers an intenerating environment for language communication.	5	4	3	2	1
I enjoy to chat with other avatars in the virtual living lab.	5	4	3	2	1
I still can not get use to the virtual environment.	5	4	3	2	1
In terms of Mandarin learning, I believe virtual living lab offers great possibilities.	5	4	3	2	1
Virtual living lab is good for Mandarin learning.	5	4	3	2	1
The features in virtual living lab seem to be hard for me to manipulate.	5	4	3	2	1
Overall, I do enjoy time in this virtual living lab.	5	4	3	2	1

Part 2　　　　　**Readiness for Teaching in a Virtual Environment**

I believe that teaching in a VR environment is as effective as teaching in a face-to- face environment.	5	4	3	2	1
I believe it is less stressful to teach in a VR environment than in a face-to-face environment.	5	4	3	2	1
I know the objectives of this VR lesson very well.	5	4	3	2	1
I am well-prepared for the 1st/ 2nd VR lesson.	5	4	3	2	1
I understand one-to-one format teaching.	5	4	3	2	1
I understand the teaching process of this lesson. .	5	4	3	2	1
I believe my "teacher talk" is appropriate for my student.	5	4	3	2	1
I know how to correct my student's errors	5	4	3	2	1
I am well prepared for this class in terms of class content, questions, and examples.	5	4	3	2	1
I have prepared for the unpredictable issues in the class.	5	4	3	2	1
I believe I am qualified for this VR class.	5	4	3	2	1
I know how to evaluate my own teaching efficiency.	5	4	3	2	1

Part 3   **Open-ended Question**

Have you met any difficulties in terms of technical and instructional issues?

_____

_____

_____

_____

"第二人生"及其在中文教学中的应用
Second Life and Its Application in
Chinese Teaching and Learning

刘士娟　Liu，Shijuan　美国宾州印第安那大学
Indiana University of Pennsylvania United States laurelsliu@ gmail. com

摘　要：本文共分五部分。文章首先介绍了什么是 Second Life，包括其缘起、发展历史和近几年在教育、商业、健康卫生等领域的影响。同时比较了它和 3D 大型多人在线角色扮演游戏的异同，阐述了它和互联网第二代技术的关系。此外，还介绍了与之同属一类的其他 3D 虚拟世界。文章第二部分简单概括了 Second Life 在语言教学中的运用情况、相关学术会议和网上讨论小组等。文章第三部分重点介绍了三个利用 Second Life 进行中文教学的实际案例。接着，文章总结了将 Second Life 运用于中文教学的五大优点和五大缺点及相关问题。文章最后为有意将 Second Life 或其他类似 3D 虚拟世界运用于中文教学与研究的教师和研究人员提了几点建议。

关键词：第二人生，Second Life，三维（3D），虚拟世界，语言教学，中文教学

Abstract：This article first introduces what Second Life is，including its origin，similarities and differences with Massively Multiplayer Online Role-Playing Games（e. g.，World of Warcraft），and its influences in such areas as business，health，and education. The first section also discusses the relations between Second Life and other social Web 2. 0 tools（e. g.，Wikis），and points out that Second Life is not the only 3D virtual worlds. There are other similar 3D virtual worlds such as Active Words，Twinity，and HIPIHI（a Chinese virtual world developed by a Chinese company at Beijing）as well as new emerging ones（e. g.，Opensim，and Open Cobalt）. Next，the article briefly describes the history of applying Second Life in language education，such as when and who started to use Second Life in language teaching and learning，and listed some examples of using Second Life in teaching different languages (e. g. , Spanish and Italian). This section also introduces the existing wikis and listserv on the use of Second Life in education, as well as the related annual conferences (e. g. , SLanguages) and proceedings.

In the third section, the article introduces real cases of using Second Life in Chinese teaching and learning, such as the online Chinese language courses taught at the Confucius Institute of Michigan State University. This section describes three cases in more detail. One is the courses taught by Professor Scott Grant at the Chinese Programs of Monash University, Melbourne, Australia. The second case is the MyChina Village project, a virtual summer camp held in Second Life in August 2009, led by The Center for Applied Second Language Studies at the University of Oregon. The third case is a collaborative project between a class on multimedia and Chinese pedagogy offered to preservice teachers of Mandarin Chinese from the Chung Yuan Christian University, Taiwan, and an intermediate Chinese class offered to Chinese language students at Embry—Riddle Aeronautical University-Prescott. The three cases all used Second Life in improving Chinese teaching and learning, and all built their virtual facilities in Second Life.

In the fourth section, the article discusses the advantages and disadvantages in using Second Life in Chinese language teaching and learning. The first advantage is reflected in teaching and learning online. For example, Second Life can help make online teaching and learning more engaging as well as provide a way to organize learning resources in multiple dimensions. In addition, it can help strengthen connections among online students and make synchronous group discussions more effective. This section also discusses the other four important advantages. For instance, using Second Life helps create a realistic situated context for role play and authentic communication. It also becomes easier in Second Life to act out the language and use the Total Physical Response strategies. Additionally, students can experience studying abroad in the virtual worlds while staying home. Another benefit is that it is easier to find topics and less awkward to start a conversation with a stranger in the virtual worlds. On the other hand,

the major disadvantages of using Second Life include: the technical barriers such as the high requirements of the users' computers; the high learning curves that demand time and energy in mastering the use of this tool;
the monetary cost for purchasing the virtual space and building the virtual
facilities; the need for technical and teaching support; and the potential
unexpected disturbing behaviors because of the open nature of the virtual
environments.

The last section provides suggestions for instructors and researchers
interested in using Second Life in Chinese language teaching and learning,
such as knowing the tool well before using it; weighing the investment and
outcomes in using the tool; Finally, the author encourages interested researchers to conduct a review of the studies on the use of Second Life in
teaching different languages, and encourages interested instructors and
researchers to explore the use of HIPIHI, the Chinese 3D virtual worlds, in
Chinese language teaching and learning.

一 什么是 Second Life

Second Life（中文译作"第二人生"）是由林登实验室（Linden Lab）
建立的互联网上的三维（3 dimensional—3D）虚拟世界（Virtual worlds）。
虽然其看起来与大型多人在线角色扮演游戏（Massively Multiplayer Online
Role—Playing Games）有些类似，但却有很多不同。具体来说，其类似之
处在于两者都可以选择虚拟的自我化身（Avatar），角色之间可以互动，参
与者还可以用文本或语音进行实时交流等。而其最大的不同之处在于，在那
些游戏里（比如有名的 World of Warcraft）有预先设置的目标、任务、情
景、角色及游戏规则，而在 Second Life 的 3D 虚拟世界空间内，却无此类
限制。如其创办人菲利普·罗斯德尔（Philip Rosedale）（2006）在介绍
Second Life 缘起的时候所说，Second Life 最大特点就是为用户提供一个平
台和工具让人们在这里尽情发挥自己的创造力①。

Second Life 的用户又叫居民（Resident）。居民可以选择自己的性别、
肤色、身高、胖瘦及其他所有外形特征，还可以购买虚拟土地并在其上面自

---

① http://www.youtube.com/watch? v = 0t1 XR-LrgyM: The Origin of Second Life and its Relation to
Real Life.

图 1 Second Life 网站上的图片

由设计构建任何城市（如莫斯科、香港），任何设施（如飞机场、火车站、图书馆），任何景物（如高山、大海、湖泊）等等。居民可走，可坐，可乘坐其他用户提供的交通工具（如自行车、汽车、轮船），还可像童话中一样自己飞行，并可利用 Second Life 提供的 Teleport① 功能在瞬间抵达该世界中的任何指定地点。此外，像现实人生一样，Second Life 的居民还可以转让自己的虚拟土地，销售自己的产品包括虚拟的服饰。

Second Life 的测试版于 2003 年 5 月发布②，经各大主流媒体报道后，在 2006 年与 2007 年间风靡一时。其注册用户人数成倍增长。在 2006 年 10 月 18 日其注册账户达到 100 万个，而至 2006 年 12 月 14 日，不到两个月注册账户达 200 万个（Terdiman，2006）。到 2007 年 2 月则又迅速达到 400 万个③。很多有名的大公司也纷纷紧跟潮流在 Second Life 占领一席之地，比如微软（Microsoft）、IBM、可口可乐（Coca—Cola）、丰田（Toyota）等，以保持在用户心中常变常新的形象及向 Second Life 的居民进一步推广其产品。各组织机构包括世界一些国家领导人也在 Second Life 注册，比如菲律宾总统阿罗约与其科技部部长 2007 年也成了 Second Life 的居民，

---

① 有人将 Teleport 译成"闪电移动"、"瞬间移动"或"远程传送"等。

② http://wiki.secondlife.com/wiki/History_ of_ Second_ Life；History of Second Life.

③ http://zh.wikipedia.org/zh/% E7% AC% AC% E4% BA% 8C% E4% BA% BA% E7% 94% 9F.

以响应其倡导的民族创新战略①。新闻、影视、医药卫生、航天、军事、建筑设计、旅游等其他各行业也都加入了这一虚拟世界浪潮中，比如路透社还在 Second Life 设立了分社。美国政府疾病控制与预防中心也用 Second Life 提供的平台宣传提高公众对公共卫生的意识（Boulos, Hetherington, &Wheeler, 2007）。

很多学校与教育机构也在 Second Life 设置虚拟校园、图书馆、教室、招生处等以扩大其影响，同时也为其教师、学生探索新教学途径和方法提供场所。如俄亥俄大学（Ohio University）在 2007 年购买了 7 个岛屿打造其虚拟校园②，斯坦福大学（Stafford University）在 Second Life 建立了虚拟图书馆③，南加州大学（University of South California）商学院在 Second Life 里提供场地让其学生经营管理虚拟资产④。据 Second Life 的教育宣传册介绍，至 2010 年已有来自世界各地超过 700 多所学校及教育机构入住 Second Life（Liden Lab, 2010）。

在一定程度上说，以 Second Life 为代表的 3D 虚拟世界可划入 Web 2.0（互联网第二代技术）的范畴。其共性之一是用户既是参与者或消费者（Consumer），同时也是生产者（Producer）。同 Youtube、Wiki 等为代表的互联网技术一样，Second Life 提供的只是一个平台。除了作为消费者可以欣赏使用或购买别人创造分享的东西外，在这里用户也可以自己作为创造者、生产者和内容提供者，让别人使用自己创造的事物。基于 3D 虚拟世界的巨大潜力，有人提倡把 Second Life 划为互联网第三代技术（Web 3.0），认为其代表了互联网将来的发展方向（Driscoll, 2007）。

这里需要指出的是 Second Life 并不是唯一的 3D 虚拟世界。其他类似的 3D 世界还有 ActiveWorld⑤、There⑥、Twinity⑦ 等。Second Life 只是迄今最有影响的一个，其市场运营策略也较为成功。中国自 2005 年开始建造

---

① http://club.classic023.com/? action-viewthread-tid-95785（《菲总统也玩〈第二人生〉推进民族创新战略》）.

② Ohio University Second Life Campus History：http://vital.cs.ohiou.edu/mediawiki2/index. php/Ohio_ University_ Second_ Life_ Campus_ History.

③ http://secondlife.com/destination/600：Stafford University's virtual library.

④ http://secondlife.com/destination/679：USC School of Business in Second Life.

⑤ http://www.activeworlds.com/.

⑥ There 公司于 2010 年 3 月 9 日因资金问题关闭（http://www.there.com/info/announcement）。

⑦ http://www.Twinity.com.

图 2 **HIPIHI** 网站上的图片

自己的 3D 虚拟世界。2007 年 3 月中国 HIPIHI[①] 公司推出 HIPIHI3D 世界有限试测版，2008 年 4 月进入公测期对大众用户开放。另外，基于各 3D 虚拟世界之间不兼容、各自为政的情况，有人提倡平台共享，并开发了相应软件如 Opensim[②]。一些教育机构认识到将数据内容放在一个商业公司服务器上对该公司产生的依附性，从而提倡开发面向教育机构且可把数据内容存在自己机构服务器的 3D 虚拟世界平台（Young，2010）。在美国国家自然科学基金及其他基金赞助下，杜克大学（Duke University）目前正在研发的 Open Cobalt[③] 就是针对这种需要的产品。

二 Second Life 在语言教学中的应用

自 2006 年开始陆续有教育工作者在 Second Life 进行教学实践。比如哈佛大学（Harvard University）法学院[④]Charles Nesson 教授和他女儿 Rebecca Nesson 2006 年秋季在 Second Life 开了一门叫做 Cyber One：Law in the Court of Public Opinion 的课（Lamb，2006）。丹佛大学（Denver University）物理系的教授在 Second Life 创建虚拟核反应实验室以帮助人们提高对核能的理解（Inside HigerEd，2007）。加拿大 Loyalist College 的教

---

① http://www.hipihi.com/.

② http://opensimulator.org.

③ http://www.opencobalt.org/.

④ http://secondlife.com/destination/597.

授们通过在 Second Life 中的模拟边防海关审查培训来提高学生毕业后在实际海关工作的技能（Hudson & Degast—Kennedy，2009）。2006 年 8 月与 2007 年 8 月，一些对 Second Life 在教育中的应用感兴趣的教育工作者及研究者就这一领域召开研讨会，并出版了论文集。此外，为了支持用户对这方面的兴趣，林登实验室（Linden Lab）还建立了一个专门的维基（Wiki）①和一个简称 SLED（Second Life in Education）的邮件列表（Mailing list）②。

图 3　Second Life 中的哈佛大学 Beckman 中心

利用 Second Life 进行语言教学方面的讨论也在 2006 年兴起。2006 年 11 月，在西班牙巴塞罗那（Barcelona，Spain）英国文化协会青少年学习活动中心（Young Learners Centre of the British Council）工作的 Graham Stanley 在 SLED 上发布一个信息③，欢迎大家参加他在 Yahoo 上建立的讨论用 Second Life 进行语言教学的用户小组④。2007 年 1 月英语教学网上电子村（TESOL Electronic Village Online）举办了"数字游戏和语言学习"

---

① http://wiki. secondlife. com/wiki/Second_ Life_ Education.

② SL Educators（The SLED List）：https：//lists. secondlife. com/cgi-bin/mailman/listinfo/educators.

③ https：//lists. secondlife. com/pipermail/educators/2006-December/004118. html.

④ http://groups. yahoo. com/group/secondlifelanguages/messages/1？l=1.

（Digital Gaming and Language Learning）网上培训①，其中 Second Life 是其重点培训内容，有很多英语教师参加。2007 年 6 月由位于西班牙巴塞罗那的 Consultants—E 公司发起赞助在 Second Life 里举办了第一届讨论 Second Life 用于语言教学（SLanguages）的网上 3D 会议②。该会议至 2010 年已举行了 4 届，最近一次于 2010 年 10 月 15—16 日召开③。

最早尝试使用 Second Life 进行语言教学的多为语言（特别是英语）培训机构，比如除了上面提到的位于西班牙的 Consultants—E 公司，还有 Avatar Languages④ 和 Languagelab. com⑤，以及一所位于意大利的意大利语语言培训学校⑥。

图 4　Second Life 中的歌德学院

各种正规教育机构从事语言教学与研究的教师和研究人员也相继开始关注并尝试将 Second Life 运用到不同语言的教学中。比如德国的歌德学院在 Second Life⑦ 提供免费德语课程⑧。印第安纳州 Ball State University 的 Lisa

① http://evo07sessions. pbwiki. com/digitalgamingELT.

② The 1st Slanguages Conference, 2007：http://www. theconsultantse. com/edunation/SLanguages2007. pdf.

③ The 4th Slanguages Conference，2010：http://www. slanguages. net/archive2010. php.

④ http://www. avatarlanguages. com.

⑤ Language Lab：http://www. languagelab. com；http://secondlife. com/destination/647.

⑥ http://secondlife. scuolaleonardo. com/.

⑦ http://secondlife. com/destination/954.

⑧ http://www. goethe. de/lrn/duw/sdl/enindex. htm.

Kuriscak 和 Christopher Luke 教授在 2007—2008 学年尝试利用 Second Life 教西班牙语。从 2008 年开始在 CALICO① 的年会上探讨利用 Second Life 进行语言教学的报告也越来越多。此外，北伊利诺伊大学的教授利用 Second Life 培训未来的语言教师。来自挪威、瑞典和意大利的研究者 Deutschmann，Panichi，& Molka—danielsen（2009）研究如何利用 Second Life 提高母语为非英语的博士生的英语口语能力。

图 5　Second Life 中的密歇根州立大学孔子学院办公楼

三　Second Life 在中文教学中的几个实例

从事有关中文教学的一些教师和研究者从 2007 年开始尝试将 Second Life 运用到中文教学中。比如密西根州立大学孔子学院在 Second Life 修建了虚拟孔子学院、教学楼、饭馆等，并于 2008 年秋天在 Second Life 开设中文 101 和 102 课程。注册的学生可得到 Saint Clair County Community College 的学分②。

下面就三个利用 Second Life 进行中文教学的实际案例做些较为详细的介绍。

案例一：

---

① Computer-Assisted Language Instruction Consortium（CALICO）：https：//www. calico. org/.

② http：//confucius. msu. edu/secondlife/enrollment. html.

澳大利亚蒙纳士大学中国研究系（Chinese Studies Program at Monash University, Melbourne, Australia）的 Scott Grant 老师自 2008 年以来一直在利用 Second Life 进行中文辅助教学。据 Grant 老师的网站①介绍，为了研究 Second Life 在教学中的应用，蒙纳士大学于 2007 年在 Second Life 购买了一个虚拟岛屿（Virtual Island）。中国研究系于 2007 年下半年在学校的虚拟岛屿上建造了具有中国文化特色的书院，比如其门口贴有中国民间传统的门神图案。另外，还建造了茶馆、医务室、旅行社、商业街、蔬菜市场等虚拟设施供情景教学使用。2009 年中国研究系又建立了一个专门为中国语言文化学习方面的活动使用的岛屿。该岛称作"中国岛"（Chinese Island）。在该岛上相继又建立了 3D 飞机场、火车站、房地产中介公司等虚拟设施。

据该网站介绍，自 2008 年开始使用 Second Life 教学以来，中国研究系已有超过 400 多个本科生使用过该虚拟空间学习中国语言文化。Grant 老师进行了多种富有创意的教学尝试。

**图6　澳大利亚蒙纳士大学中国研究系在 Second Life
中的中文学习场所**

他的尝试大致可分为三类：第一是针对一、二年级初级或中级水平的语言课而设计的活动。Grant 老师利用"中国岛"提供的接近真实的中国情景

---

① http://www.virtualhanyu.com/.

让学生复习，练习并拓展在课本及面对面课堂上学的词汇、句子及文化知识。比如，在学习与交通有关的话题时，他让学生在"中国岛"的 3D 虚拟火车站、飞机场练习买票、上车/登机，并给在中国的朋友发电子邮件通知自己所乘车次/航班及到达时间。在学习有关身体健康和看病等话题时，在精心设计的 3D 虚拟医务室，学生们可以复习（读和听）课本上学的词汇句型，并根据自己的水平和实际需要选择学习该 3D 空间提供的课本以外的有关词汇及句子。此外还可模拟如何用中文看病的全过程，包括填写病历卡，向医生描述身体不舒服的症状等，从而为在现实生活中真的需要看中国医生做准备。

第二是针对三年级中高级程度的"中文媒体课"（Chinese Media Studies）① 进行的尝试。在这门课上，Grant 老师让学生做了以下一些任务：其中一个任务是让学生们在 Second Life 采访来自中国、美国、新加坡说中文的人。采访首先在被采访人所在的虚拟地点进行，然后请被采访人来到蒙纳士大学"中国岛"专为该课建立的电视采访室接受较为正式的访谈。之后，学生们还要把采访的内容写成书面新闻报道，在虚拟的电视台播出并录下来。

第三是设立可适用于任何年级的课外聊天室。从 2009 年 7 月底到 10 月底每周日到周三晚上 8 点到 9 点（当地墨尔本 Melbourne，Australia 时间），都会有一个高年级的学生在"中国岛"的聊天室和学生们通过声音或文本聊天，包括帮助初级班的学生练习与课本有关的内容。

Grant 老师把自己使用 Second Life 教学情况做成了多媒体视频，在其网站 http://www.virtualhanyu.com 上可以看到。

案例二：

美国俄勒冈大学（The University of Oregon）第二语言应用研究中心（The Center for Applied Second Language Studies）② 在美国国家安全教育项目（National Security Education Program）的资助下，于 2009 年夏天在 Second Life 举办了"我的中国村（MyChina Village）"虚拟中文夏令营（Summer camp）③。该夏令营的目标是帮助具有中级水平的学习者进一步提高其中文水平。该项目的合作伙伴有 Centric 公司及 Avant Assessment 公

---

① 据 Scott Grant 介绍，"中文媒体课"以学习媒体语言为主，并不是对中国媒体的研究或分析。这门课相当于过去的报刊课，只是多增加了网上媒体这一新内容。

② http://casls.uoregon.edu/.

③ http://mychinavillage.uoregon.edu/.

司。Centric 公司负责在 Second Life 建立适合活动需要的虚拟的"我的中国村"，Avant Assessment 公司负责学生的标准语言水平测试。

夏令营的负责人是第二语言应用研究中心的助理主任 Sachiko Kamioka 女士，她的助手是一个来自中国在俄勒冈大学就读的博士生，担任夏令营顾问。参加该夏令营的中文学习者来自美国各地，是通过网上召集到的。申请者一般要经过两个步骤的测试以确定其中文水平。第一个是电话测试。第二个是使用 Avant Assessment 公司网上的标准化语言测试。夏令营的志愿者是苏州大学对外汉语专业的本科生。这些志愿者帮助夏令营的中文学习者学习中文。所有活动都在网上进行，对参与者免费。共有 7 个来自美国不同州的中文学习者，16 个来自苏州大学的志愿者参加。

夏令营从 2009 年 8 月 3 日到 28 日，每天在网上活动两个小时（美国太平洋时间下午 5 点到 7 点）。该夏令营以环保为活动主题。第一个星期的题目是关于水危机。参加夏令营的成员首先互相自我介绍，然后志愿者为学习者介绍苏州、附近太湖的水危机及全球的水危机情况。成员们一起做关于水危机方面的游戏。比如在虚拟中国村的大屏幕上列出 15 个关于水危机的问题及答案，让学习者选择，答对后得分。

在第二个星期里，苏州大学的志愿者制作了一个小品，模拟采访苏州市的一个官员和市民关于太湖水问题的看法。学习者可以提问。之后夏令营的参加者根据他们的理解准备一个有关的小品，并在 Second Life 里参观两个帮助人们了解生态生活和可持续性发展的场所。

图 7　夏令营成员在 Second Life 做游戏

在第三个星期，参加者分成小组，每个小组就如何将"我的中国村"

变成可持续发展的城市发表看法。参加者要求从六个题目中选择四个，比如交通，废物利用，水和土地的利用，减少二氧化碳排放量等。组织者还请了富有中文教学经验的教师志愿者作为评委为小组的演讲打分，每位参加者也可以为他们喜欢的小组投票。活动之后小组提出的好的想法（比如用风力发电，提供免费自行车等）可以在虚拟的"我的中国村"付诸实施。第四个星期活动的重点是进一步培养夏令营的参加者对"我的中国村"的主人翁感，引导他们设计夏令营结束后的一些自主学习活动，从而使"我的中国村"这一项目可以自己持续下去。

关于该夏令营的详细介绍及研究发现可参考 Sachiko Kamioka 女士在 2009 年全美外语协会上作的报告：MyChina：Summer Chinese Immersion Camp in Second Life[①]。

案例三：

台湾中原大学应用华语文学系郑琇仁老师与美国安柏瑞德航空航天大学—普雷斯科特分校（Embry—Riddle Aeronautical University-Prescott）战红老师合作，在 2009 年秋季利用 Second Life 来培训中文教师和教授中文。郑琇仁老师的学生母语是中文，需要实际教学经验，以便毕业后作中文教师。战红老师的学生是母语不是中文的美国大学生。两位教授通过 Second Life 平台，让中文为母语的台湾学生和老师教美国学生学中文，从而使得隔着太平洋的双方学生各取所需，分别得到实际教学和应用语言的机会。为了满足教学需求，两位教授与台湾资讯工业促进会（简称资促会）[②] 合作，成立研究小组共同在 Second Life 建造了属于自己的 3D 虚拟教学设施"虚拟生活实验室"（Virtual Living Lab），包括虚拟的飞机场、宾馆、商店等。

郑老师教的是为本科生高年级开设的"多媒体与华语文教学"课。班上有 63 个学生。战老师教的是中文二年级的学生，共 13 人。为了使郑老师班上的 63 个学生都有在 Second Life 实习教中文学习者的机会，这些学生被分成 13 组，每组有 4—5 个人。作为课程要求的一部分，双方学生都需要参加 Second Life 的活动。在 Second Life 的实际教学时间为期两周，每周一次，每次 30 分钟。考虑到检测双方设备（如麦克风等）和了解中文学习者的具体水平的所用时间，每次实际安排 1 个小时。教学的内容是帮助郑老

---

① Sachiko Kamioka（2009），MyChina：Summer Chinese Immersion Camp in Second Life. Presentation given at ACTFL 2009 Annual Convention and World Languages Expo. Available：http：//my-chinavillage. uoregon. edu/learn. php? section = presentations.

② http：//www. iii. org. tw.

图 8 实习老师在 Second Life 上课的情景

师的学生练习和复习他们在面对面课上学习的内容。两次教学的内容完全相同。双方学生在 Second Life 教学时，两位教授都会在旁边观看以确保教学顺利进行。在每次实习教学时间结束后，两位教授会及时给予学生反馈，并提出改进建议。一名助教负责协助教学过程的录影。

关于这一项目的具体情况及研究发现可参考她们写的文章，如"华语师资培训之教学个案研究——以虚拟实境 Second Life 为例"①。为分享教学经验和提供 Second Life 教学培训资料，她们的学生还在两位老师的指导下，制作了记录其当时在 Second Life 教学情景的影片，放在 Youtube 上②。另外，资促会和两位教授合作建立了一个网站，名为"第二课堂"（Second Classroom）③，以分享研究成果和推广运用 Second Life 的经验，并提供培训。此外，他们还在社交网站（Facebook）成立了 Second Life 的网上空间来进行这方面的讨论④。

除了以上介绍的几个案例外，美国西东大学（Seton Hall University）的陈东东老师也尝试在其中文课中使用了 Second Life。陈老师试用的班级是她教的两个初级中文班，共 30 个学生。其学生除了 4 个学生有一些中文背

① 郑琇仁、战红、陈庆萱（2010）：《华语师资培训之教学个案研究 ——以虚拟实境 Second Life 为例》，《中原华语文学报》（5），第 157—178 页：http://cycuir. lib. cycu. edu. tw/handle/310900400/45901。

② http://www. youtube. com/watch? v = Ou4Xei0DMQY&feature = related（庆祝朋友生日）；http://www. youtube. com/watch? v = 2gQznOtKPpA&feature = related（介绍新房子）。

③ 其网址为 http://www. chineseplaza. com/。

④ 其网址是 http://www. facebook. com/second。

图 9   密歇根州立大学孔子学院在 Second Life 的教室

景外，其他都为零起点的学生。在一个学期的 16 个星期内，学生们需要完成 8 个任务。每两星期一个任务。这些任务包括练习发音，寻找汉字及其字根，练习做自我介绍，问对方爱好等。这些任务占学生总成绩的 16%。陈老师用的是前文提到的密歇根大学孔子学院的虚拟场所和所建设施。其具体情况和研究发现可参考她在 2010 年 TCLT6[①] 论文集中发表的论文。

四 利用 Second Life 进行中文教学的优缺点及相关问题

Second Life 在教育包括语言教学中应用的优缺点已有人评述（如 Stevens, 2006；Erard, 2007；Cooke—Plagwitz, 2008；Nesson & Nesson, 2008；Hundsberger, 2009；郑琇仁、战红、陈庆萱, 2010）。下面，笔者根据自己从 2007 年开始对有关文献的阅读包括对一些应用 Second Life 的教学案例的观察以及自己在日常使用 Second Life 的体会，就其在中文教学运用中的优缺点及相关问题谈一下认识。

（一）利用 Second Life 进行中文教学的优点

研究一项新技术的优点，第一，先看该技术与其他相关技术比有哪些独特之处，即其他技术不能实现或不如该新技术有效的地方。以 Second Life

---

① http://nealrc.osu.edu/tclt6.

为代表的 3D 虚拟世界在教育应用方面最大的优点体现在远程（互联网）教育①方面（Liu，2008；Nesson & Nesson，2008）。而远程（互联网）教育与传统的面对面（Face to Face）教育相比存在的必要性体现在诸多方面，比如网络教育可为由于种种原因不便面对面（Face to face）上课的学生提供学习机会；可以使学生接触到由于地域限制等因素不能在传统课堂中接触到的同学或老师；老师也能通过互联网接触到来自更大范围的学生（如 Kim，Liu & Bonk，2005；Liu 等，2007）。具体到中文教学，远程教育可为在周围找不到合适老师的学生找到合适的中文老师，为学生人数不够的老师招到更多的学生。通过互联网教学还有其他益处，比如在以上提到的台湾中原大学郑琇仁老师和美国战红老师合作教学的案例中，郑老师的学生在台湾学校当地不容易找到学中文的学生来实习中文教学；战老师的美国学生在美国学校当地不容易找到说中文的人来练习中文。通过远程互联网他们的学生可以互取所需。

与其他用于远程互联网教学的技术比，Second Life 在远程教育方面有以下几个优势：（1）可以使网上学习更有趣。由于没有和老师及同学面对面接触的机会，并且网络课程中文本形式较多，学生学起来容易感到枯燥（Shih & Yang，2008）。而在 3D 虚拟世界里，学生和老师都有自己的 3D 虚拟化身，可坐可走可飞，还可以在虚拟的教室、图书馆学习（Nesson & Nesson，2008）。（2）Second Life 可以帮助加强学生们之间的联系。一些研究发现远程教育课程中的学生在学习时常会有孤独感（如 Palloff & Pratt，2007）。有时虽然两个学生同时在浏览一个课程网页，但他们并不知道两人同时在线。虽然可以用 Skype 等基于电脑间的网络电话来显示对方是否在线，但不如在 Second Life 的虚拟教室或图书馆内看到对方更直接（Nesson & Nesson，2008）。Second Life 可将分布在世界各地的学生通过虚拟空间聚在一起。他们可以像现实世界中一样和同学们在校园里散步，一起喝咖啡，坐在一起讨论问题等。（3）利用 Second Life 可以帮助远程教育课更直接和方便有效地组织小组活动如分组讨论、小组分角色辩论等。笔者曾上过网上课程，在这些课上体验过利用 Adobe Connect 这一网络实时会议工具进行小组讨论。来自美国不同地区的学生在家里通过互联网上课。举行会议的地址就是一个网址，这一网址相当于一个房间。学生登录进去后，看到的界面如下页图 10 所示。在组织小组讨论时，老师给每个小组一个不同的网

---

① 在此文中，"远程教育"（Distance Education）和"网络教育"、"互联网教育"（Online Education）所指相同。

址，进入后会看到类似的界面。只不过在会议参与者显示框里只显示登录进来的该小组成员。而在 Second Life 里由于是 3D，学生和老师可以更加直接的看到彼此的位置、在线状态，从而在开会和进行讨论时也更有真实感。（4）Second Life 可以在 3D 空间内以立体方式更有效的组合各种与课程有关的资料。比如，在讲与饮食有关的话题时，可将各种菜用 3D 虚拟体现出来，学生可听到该菜的中文名称，看到该词的汉字和拼音写法。另外，在虚拟的中国饭馆里，还可以听到以中国音乐做背景的音乐，墙上的虚拟电视机里还可播放中国电视节目。

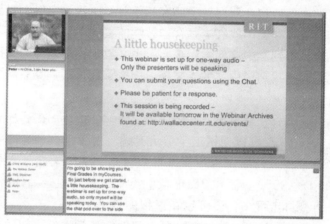

图 10   利用 Adobe Connect 上课/开会/讨论的情景

图 11   在 Second Life 上课/开会/讨论的情景

第二，Second Life 与其他用于教育的技术相比，其在运用于语言教学

图 12　密歇根州立大学孔子学院在 Second Life 的饭馆

包括中文教学方面的优越性还体现在可用于情景教学与角色扮演上（Shih & Yang，2008）。比如，在学习与就餐话题有关的课程时，可让学生到 Second Life 里建的中国餐馆里练习对话。从而让学生学起来更有情景感，更容易进入角色。

第三，在 Second Life 里，学生可以更容易按照语言给的指令做出相应动作，从而加深对语言的理解，同时教师也可以更准确的了解学生的理解掌握程度。比如在讲到与方向和问路有关的话题时，告诉学生"往前走，向左转"。虽然在面对面的教学中，也可以让学生用动作的方式来做，但做起来不太方便，特别是教室空间有限和学生人数较多时。而在 Second Life 里却很容易做到，并且还可让很多学生同时来做。另外一些在实际教室里不容易实现的动作，比如"上车"、"骑马"等可在 Second Life 里很方便地实现。笔者一直觉得 ASHER 教授提出的"全身反应法"（Total Physical Response①）应用在成人外语学习的一个局限是：与儿童相比，成年人的自我意识比较强，在他人面前做动作时有时会不好意思。对那些性格内向怕羞的人来说，更是如此。而在 Second Life 由于控制的只是虚拟化身，学习者做动作时会更自然，更少焦虑感（Hundsberger，2009）。

第四，在 Second Life 里，由于其仿真性，可使学生足不出户、不用花钱也可到"中国城"（China town）进行语言实习（Field Trip），或到中国旅行（Grant，2009），尽管这些地方都是虚拟的。比如在 Second Life 里学习者可在蒙纳士大学建的体现中国特点的火车站、飞机场体验买火车票、飞

①　http://www.tpr-world.com/.

机票，还可在 Second Life 里的虚拟中国医院里模仿看病，为以后在现实中看中国医生做准备。这些在虚拟世界里的语言实践，除了费用低、方便灵活外，老师还可通过计算机及时给学生反馈和指导（Liu，2008；郑琇仁、战红、陈庆萱，2010）。比如学生忘记一个单词怎么说或者老师希望该学生与对话者的对话还可更深入些时，老师可以通过 Second Life 的文本对话窗口，或另打开 Skype，在不打断学生对话的同时提出建议。

　　第五，在虚拟世界里人们更容易找到对话话题。如 Nesson 和 Nesson（2008）所说，在 Second Life 里除了其他很多话题外，人们还可以谈论对方选的虚拟化身。由于谈话没有现实生活中的诸多顾忌，与陌生人开口讲话也更加容易。比如如果不喜欢对方，可以连再见也不用说马上飞走，因为下次见了面双方的虚拟化身已经变了。另外对方也不会像在现实中一样觉得跟你说话你飞走不礼貌，可能会觉得你只是个新手，操作失误，或你用的计算机出了问题而已。

图 13　郑老师学生做的影片中的截图

　　利用 Second Life 还有其他一些好处，比如由于学生在 Second Life 有较高的掌控权和较高的学习主动性、自觉性，学生对学习中文的自我效能感（Self—efficacy beliefs）也会有较大提高（Henderson 等，2009）。另外，与一些网上实时会议软件（比如 Adobe Connect）功能类似，在 Second Life 里，可以很方便地将谈话过程记录下来，除了文本外，还可记录下动作过程，从而让学生事后观看，以提高自己的表现，比如上面提到的郑琇仁老师的学生制作的影片。最后，文献中（如 Kuriscak & Luke，2009；郑琇仁、战红、陈庆萱，2010）中提到了利用 Second Life 还可以和母语是目标语的人谈话，除了语言外，还可了解所学语言的文化。对于这一点笔者认为值得指出的是，除非是事先有所安排（比如像郑老师和战老师所教班级间的合作），不然在 Second Life 里随便找个时间，即使在那些虚拟中文学校和中国人建立的虚拟场所也并不能保证每次都能碰到一个会说中文的人。

（二）利用 Second Life 进行中文教学的缺点及相关问题

同其他工具一样，Second Life 也有一些不足。在其应用于教学的过程中也会出现诸多问题。在谈及 Second Life 不足的文献中，共同提到较多的是技术本身的问题。比如（1）该平台对用户计算机硬件配置有较高要求。使用该平台，第一，需要将该平台作为软件下载到用户的计算机上运行。为了使在 3D 世界里的事物图像很好显示出来，同时使用户的虚拟化身在虚拟世界里动作显得流畅，用户使用的计算机要有较快的运行速度和比较高级的图像显示和处理卡。另外，用户使用的互联网速度要快。（2）在使用过程中，有时会出现从 Second Life 被挤出，特别是当在同一空间的参与者较多时（郑琇仁、战红、陈庆萱，2010）。这种情况下，就需要再次打开运行该软件，重新登录。另外，由于各种技术原因，还会出现麦克风不工作，语音传送滞后，实现上传的文档打不开等问题。这些都会干扰教学，占用真正教学时间。

第二，同其他技术相比，特别是同第二代互联网技术相比，学习并熟练掌握 Second Life 需要花大量时间和精力。比如会用一般文档软件（如 Microsoft Word）写作的人很容易就能使用 Google Site 来制作漂亮的网页，不需要像以前那样，需要学习专业的网页制作软件。而 Second Life 使用的是 3D 虚拟技术，对于较少玩 3D 电子游戏的人来说，界面与功能全是新的。并且和日常使用互联网浏览器访问网站，搜索站点也不同，需要学习很多新东西。教语言的老师大多是文科背景，计算机基础较弱，另外，其教学工作繁忙，很多老师可能找不到足够的时间和精力来学习这门新技术，更谈不上解决使用中出现的种种技术问题。对于一般学生来说，特别是中文只为选修课的学生，他们用来学习中文的时间有限。如果他们的专业离计算机科学较远，如历史，而他们自己对计算机技术又不很热衷，在课余时间又很少玩3D 电子游戏，那么用 Second Life 来教这些学生中文是否合理或有必要？另外，学习中文需要花很多时间在学习汉字上。尽管也可在 3D 虚拟世界里设计一些学习汉字的活动，但却远非其长项。而花时间学习 Second Life 的时间，设计自己虚拟化身的长相，为自己的虚拟形象设计衣服的时间，这些时间显然与中文学习无关。如果学生学习的中文课不是全部采用网上授课的话，笔者觉得将这些时间与其花在 Second Life 的使用上，不如花在对中文的直接学习上更有效。

第三，费用问题。到目前为止，只有基本会员是免费的。作为基本会员，可在 Second Life 参观任何对外开放的地方①，可以使用其他用户免费分享的产品。如果要在 Second Life 拥有一块虚拟空间的话，需要购买②。而只有购买了空间，才可以在上面修建自己想造的风景或设施。这些虚拟空间根据大小收费不同，购买后与现实生活中的地产税一样，每月还要交 5 美元到 295 美元不等的维护费③。虽然教育和非营利机构会享受到一些折价，但据公司 2010 年 10 月宣布的最新政策④，从 2011 年 1 月开始，这些价格优惠将取消。而设计创建这些虚拟设施需要较高的计算机技术。虽然有些开放的源代码可以用，但设计者还需有一定的编程能力。并且，设计者还需要有美术功底和较高的审美能力。否则设计出来的建筑不具美感。像上面提到的俄勒冈大学的"我的中国村"就是由专门的公司设计，而郑老师和战老师的项目使用的"虚拟实验室"也是由专门机构设计。

第四，与费用有关的还有教学过程的人力支持问题（Cooke—Plagwitz，2008）。在郑老师的台湾学生教战老师的美国学生的过程中，负责提供技术的合作单位会有人在线帮助解决技术上可能出现的问题。在俄勒冈大学的网上夏令营项目中，也有技术支持。另外，陈东东老师所在的学校有语言学习技术中心和教师教学咨询服务中心。她的学生都有学校配置的较高性能的手提电脑。如果在使用过程中出了技术问题，可随时找这些中心帮助。

值得注意的是，郑老师的班上有 63 个学生，分成 13 个组，每组有 4—5 个人。这 4—5 个实习老师在 30 分钟内同时教一个美国学生。在网上夏令营项目中，有 7 个学习者，而中文是母语的来自苏州大学的志愿者则有 16 个。这意味着 1 个学中文的学生能同时和 2 个以上母语是中文的人练习。毋庸置疑，这两个项目的设计就其目的来说是合理的。项目是成功的，尤其在使用 Second Life 过程中取得的经验及发现的问题是十分宝贵和难得的。然而，在日常正常的中文教学中却很难能这么"奢侈"。在相当多的美国公立大学里，一个中文班里一个老师要教至少 15 个学生，很多情况下还要教 25 个到 30 个，甚至更多。并且没有任何助教。如果出现技术问题，如果没有专项资金资助或有关部门支持的话，意味着这些问题都要自己解决。

---

① 与现实生活一样，在"第二人生"也设有只有成人才可进去的虚拟地区。对于成人与否的判断，在网上只能靠自觉，因为用户的生日年龄都是自己填写的，无须证明。

② http://secondlife.com/corporate/pricing.php.

③ http://secondlife.com/corporate/pricing.php.

④ Two Important Updates on 2011 Land Pricing, Nelson Linden on Oct 4, 2010.

第五，如其他基于互联网的工具一样，由于 Second Life 的开放性，在 Second Life 中可能会出现一些意料不到的事情，或看到一些不当的行为。Second Life 公司对"居民"的行为规范有具体规定①，比如不可以骚扰、攻击其他居民，对信仰、性别、种族等方面的歧视采取零容忍态度；禁止在主要活动区出现使用和成人色情有关的行为事物。尽管如此，像使用其他开放网络工具（如网上论坛等）一样，有时会出现一些防不胜防的情况（Bugeja，2007）。在这里教学的老师，特别是在使用他人建造而自己没有控制权的虚拟设施时，要做好应急准备（Cooke—Plagwitz，2008）。

此外，与其他一些与社交网络（Social Networking）有关的技术（如 Facebook）一样，Second Life 还有用户所存放的数据，所创建事物的控制权、拥有权、知识权等问题（Young，2010）。最后，尽管与其他公司相比，Second Life 对于其在教育方面的应用很重视。比如设置专人负责与教育有关的事务，赞助有关会议，设置供教育工作者、研究者交流用的网上讨论组；并在教育机构购买虚拟空间时给予优惠（至 2010 年 12 月止②）等等，但如 Nesson 和 Nesson（2008）所言，Second Life 终究是一个以营利为目的的商业公司。公司在决策的时候，不会把教师教学的需要放在首位。比如，很多老师提出像其他一些网络会议一样，当"居民"在 Second Life 谈话时，可以提供一张帮助大家交流的"白板"（Whiteboard），但这一要求不一定在决策者的优先考虑之列。另外，如一些观察者指出，像其他以营利为目的的网络公司一样，Second Life 还可能存在继续提高收费标准的可能，也不能排除被其他大公司收购的情况（张晶，2010）。在决定是否利用 Second Life，是否在其中购买打造自己的虚拟空间时，这些因素都应当给予适当考虑。

五　建议及结语

本文首先介绍了什么是 Second Life，介绍了其发展历史和在近几年的影响，并列出了它的几个竞争者和新兴的几个 3D 虚拟世界；然后简单介绍了 Second Life 在教育包括语言教育方面的运用情况。此后较为详尽的介绍了三个利用 Second Life 在中文教学中的实际案例。接着，基于对有关文献的阅读和笔者的体会，总结了将 Second Life 运用于中文教学的优点和缺点

---

① http://secondlife.com/corporate/cs.php：Community Standards.

② Two Important Updates on 2011 Land Pricing，Nelson Linden on Oct 4，2010.

及有关问题。在结束文章正文之前，笔者想对有意将 Second Life 或其他类似 3D 虚拟世界运用于中文教学和研究的同仁最后提些拙见，并分享具有使用 Second Life 进行中文教学的丰富经验的 Scott Grant 老师应邀给予同仁的一些真知灼见①。

首先，决定使用一项新技术前，要对该技术有尽可能详细的了解，特别是要了解与其他相关技术比它有哪些优势和不足。如 Grant 老师（2010）所说，对技术的了解不够往往会导致对该技术不能充分利用，并会影响应用该技术的教学效果。帮助读者对以 Second Life 为代表的 3D 虚拟世界有个较为全面的了解，也正是本文写作的根本目的。另外本文附录中还列了一些笔者收集的与 Second Life 有关的资料供大家参考。

在使用一种技术用于教学时，首先要明确的是教学目的。提高学生学习效果应该是所有使用技术目标中的关键。然后围绕具体目标设计教学活动。另外，选择使用技术时，要考虑到功效，投入和产出的比例，争取做到事半功倍，而不是事倍功半。如前文所说，与其他相关技术相比，以 Second Life 为代表的 3D 虚拟世界学起来比较费时费力，打算使用这一技术的教师更要认真考虑其功效比。笔者窃以为，除非教师自己有较高的计算机水平和足够的时间与精力，不然使用该技术一定要争取得到自己所在单位有关技术人员的支持，或找到相应的合作伙伴。

关于针对以 Second Life 为代表的 3D 虚拟世界的研究，如 Grant 老师（2010）所说，关于这一领域的研究才刚开始。由于这一技术与以前其他互联网技术有很大不同（除了与之有关的 3D 网络游戏），探索这一技术在教学中的应用还有很大空间。本人觉得一个比较有意义可以写的题目是总结分析一下迄今所有研究 Second Life 或其他 3D 虚拟世界的用于语言教学包括中文教学的文章。所用方法可以参考 Hew 和 Cheung（2010）文章的写法。

最后，笔者想建议有兴趣和有条件的同仁关注并探索利用 HIPIHI 这一由中国本土开发的 3D 虚拟世界，进行中文教学。笔者自 2007 年底在网上发现 HIPIHI 公司以来，一直认为虽然 HIPIHI 的成立理念与 Second Life 类似，但与之相比，至少在中文教学方面有着得天独厚的优势。到目前为止，Second Life 还没有中文版本。在其上面建造的为学中文用的风景及设施，虽然有中国特色，但其运营的 Second Life 界面工具栏菜单仍然是英文的。另外，Second Life 中只有极少部分是由中国人建立的与中国有关的景物，所以在一定意义上说，在 Second Life 学中文严格意义上来讲，不能称作全

---

① Scott Grant 老师的建议原文在附录 1 中。

图14　HIPIHI 网站上庆祝中国春节的一张照片

部浸入式中文教学。而 HIPIHI 完全由中国人创造设计，里面的虚拟景物设施绝大多数都是由中国人特别是年轻人建造的。在里面活动的居民很多是在校的大学生。与 Second Life 相比，在 HIPIHI 里更容易找到和中国人对话交流的机会。另外，HIPIHI 平台的界面工具栏也完全是中文的。即便使用 HIPIHI 的中文教学设计不完全成功，学生们也至少可以多认识接触些生词句子，欣赏由中国人建造的直接或间接体现中国文化特色的虚拟设施，如四合院、桃花源等。

致谢：本文在撰写过程中得到许德宝博士、笪骏博士的鼓励和大力支持，在此深表谢意。笔者同时感谢 Scott Grant 老师、战红博士和郑琇仁博士慷慨分享他们的研究成果和使用 Second Life 的宝贵教学经验。另外，感谢刘晓镜博士认真阅读全文并提出诸多修改建议，Curtis Bonk 博士帮助校正英文提要。最后，对负责排版的笪骏博士的辛勤工作及他对文章格式上的诸多帮助，表示衷心感谢。

参考文献

Boulos, M. , Hetherington, L. , & Wheeler, S. （2007）. Second Life：an overview of the potential of 3—D virtual worlds in medical and health education. Health Information & Libraries Journal, 24 （4）, 233—245. Available：http://onlinelibrary. wiley. com/doi/10. 1111/j. 1471—1842. 2007. 00733. x/full.

Bugeja, M. J. （2007, September 14）. Second Thoughts About Second Life. Chronicle of Higher Education. Available：http://chronicle. com/article/Second—

Thoughts—About—Secon/46636.

Chen, D. (2010). Enhancing the learning of Chinese with Second Life. Proceedings of the Six International Conference and Workshops on Technology and Chinese Language Teaching (pp. 21—25), June 12—14, Columbus, Ohio.

Cooke—Plagwitz, J. (2008). New directions in CALL: An objective introduction to Second Life. CALICO Journal, 25 (3), 547—557.

Deutschmann, M., Panichi, L., & Molka—danielsen, J. (2009). Designing oral participation in Second Life—A comparative study of two language proficiency cour-ses. ReCALL, 21 (2), 206—226.

Driscoll, T. (2007). Welcome to the era of the free range learner.

Keynote speech at the World Conference on E—Learning in Corporate, Govern-ment, Healthcare, & Higher Education, October 15—19, 2007, Quebec City, Cana-da.

Erard, M. (2007, April 10). A boon to Second Life language schools. Technol-ogy Review, Available: http://www. technologyreview. com/printer _ friendly _ article. aspx? id =18510.

Grant, S. (2009). About (Chinese Island). Retrieved November 1, 2010, from http://www. virtualhanyu. com/? page_ id =87.

Grant, S. (2010). Personal communication, December 20, 2010.

Henderson, M. Huang, H, Grant, S. & Henderson, L. (2009). Language ac-quisitions in Second Life: Improving self—efficacy beliefs. Available: http:// www. ascilite. org. au/conferences/auckland09/procs/henderson. pdf.

Hew, K. F. & Cheung, W. S. (2010). Use of three—dimensional (3—D) im-mersive virtual worlds in K—12 and higher education settings: A review of the re-search. British journal of educational technology, 41 (1). 33—55.

Hudson, K & Degast—Kennedy, K (2009). Canadian border simulation at Loy-alist College. Journal of Virtual Worlds Research, 2 (1). Available: https: //jour-nals. tdl. org/jvwr/article/view/374/449.

Hundsberger, S. (2009). Foreign Language learning in Second Life and the im-plications for resource provision in academic libraries. Available: http://arcadia-project. lib. cam. ac. uk/docs/second_ life. pdf.

Inside HigerEd (2007, August 20). In Second Life, there is no fall out. Available: http://www. insidehighered. com/layout/set/print/news/2007/08/20/secondlife.

Kamioka, S. (2009). MyChina: Summer Chinese Immersion Camp in Second Life. Presentation given at ACTFL 2009 Annual Convention and World Languages Expo. Available: http://mychinavillage. uoregon. edu/learn. php? section = presenta-tions.

Kim, K. J. , Liu, S. , & Bonk, C. J. (2005). Online MBA students' perceptions of online learning: Benefits, challenges and suggestions. Internet and Higher Education, 8 (4), 335—344.

Kuriscak, L. M. and Luck, C. L. (2009). Language learner attitude toward virtual world: An investigation of Second Life. In L. Lomicka, L. and G. Lord (Eds) The Next Generation: Social Networking and Online Collaboration in Foreign Language Learning(pp. 173—198). CALICO Monograph. Available: https://www. calico. org/page. php? id =517.

Lamb, G. (2006, October 5). At colleges, real learning in a virtual world. Available: http://www. usatoday. com/tech/gaming/2006—10— 05—second—life—class_ x. htm.

Liden Lab (2010). Second Life education: The virtual learning advantage. Available: http://lecs static secondlife com. s3. amazonaws. com/work/SL—Edu—Brochure—112910. pdf.

Liu, S. (2008, January). Does Second Life mean anything to second/foreign language teaching and learning? Presentation given at the Department of Foreign Languages, Rochester Institute of Technology, Rochester, NY.

Liu, S. , Kim, K—J. , Bonk, C, J. , & Magjuka, R. (2007). Benefits, challenges, and suggestions: What do online MBA professors have to say about online teaching? The Online Journal of Distance Learning Administration, 10 (2). Available: http://www. westga. edu/—distance/ojdla/summer102/liu102. htm.

Livingstone, D. & Kemp, J. (2006) (Eds.). Proceedings of the Second Life Education Workshop at the Second Life Community Convention, San Francisco, CA, August 20th, 2006. Available: http://www. simteach. com/SLCC06/slcc2006—proceedings. pdf.

Livingstone, D. & Kemp, J. (2007) (Eds.). Proceedings of the Second Life Education Workshop at the Second Life Community Convention, Chicago, IL, August 24th—27th, 2007. Available: http://www. simteach. com/slccedu07 proceedings. pdf.

Nesson, R. & Nesson, C. (2008). The case for education in virtual worlds. Space and Culture, 11 (273). Available: http://sac. sagepub. com/content/11/3/273. refs. html.

Palloff, R. and Pratt, K. (2007). Building Online Learning Communities: Effective Strategies for the Virtual Classroom. Josse Bass Higher and Adult Education: San Francisco, CA.

Shih, Y, & Yang, M. (2008). A collaborative virtual environment for situated language learning using VEC3D. Educational Technology & Society, 11 (1), 56—68. Available: http://www. ifets. info/journals/11_ 1/5. pdf.

Stevens, V. (2006). Second Life in Education and Language Learning, TESL—EJ, 10 (3). Available：http://www. tesl—ej. org/ej39/int. html.

Terdiman, D. (2006, December 14). 'Second Life'hits second million in eight weeks. Cnet News. Available：http://news. cnet. com/8301—10784 _ 3— 6143909—7. html? part = rss&tag =2547—1_ 3— 0—5&subj = news.

Young, J. (2010, February 14). After frustrations in Second Life, Colleges look to new virtual worlds, Chronicle of Higher Education. Available：http://chronicle. com/article/After—Frustrations—in—Second/64137/.

张晶 (2010).《"第二人生"迷途》.《经济观察报》，2010 年 5 月 21 日。参见：http://finance. ifeng. com/opinion/cjpl/20100521/2220610. shtml。

郑琇仁、战红、陈庆萱 (2010).《华语师资培训之教学个案研究——以虚拟实境 Second Life 为例》，《中原华语文学报》，5，157—178。参见 http://cycuir. lib. cycu. edu. tw/handle/310900400/45901。

附录1
Suggestions Given by Scott Grant
（2010）on the Use of
Second Life（SL）

"If possible, could you please so generous to write one or two paragraphs to briefly summarize your experience of using SL, especially the challenges you encountered and give suggestions to fellow Chinese instructors who are interested?"

"This is a big question, not easily (or advisedly) summarized. A lot of educators in a wide range of different disciplines are using virtual worlds (VWs) like SL and OpenSim (and other platforms) to conduct a wide range of teaching and research. VWs like any other technology used in teaching and learning have their advantages and disadvantages. Assuming that we are all interested in incorporating some form of technology into our teaching practices (otherwise there is no point in talking about VWs at all), it is important to look at a range of technologies and find which one best suits your pedagogical goals. VWs like SL suit some pedagogical goals and not others. It is still early days and there is still a lot of experimenting and research that needs to be done to establish just exactly what VWs are good for pedagogically (if anything at all), but my strong belief is that they make a good compliment to formal classroom—based F2F curriculum (providing opportunities for experiential and task—based learning that may not be as easily achieved in a real classroom and where travelling to the L2 country is not easily done), and have the potential to add an important interpersonal dimension to distance education learning.

So, my advice is for educators to think about what it is they want to achieve by using a VW in their teaching, and then go ahead and give it a try. Having solidly grounded pedagogy is the absolute key, but also having a virtual environment appropriate to the goals set and that is of a good standard of quality (not necessarily complex, but for tertiary learners not cartoon or child—like or 'half—baked') is important. Understanding the platform/technology/environment thoroughly is also extremely important. Even with things like conventional LMSs (Blackboard, Moodle, etc), many educators only have a superficial understanding of how they work or their full potential, and thus have a lukewarm attitude to their use in teaching and learning, which at the end of the day results in poor use of the technological platform. Reading up on available research on the use of technology in general and of VWs specifically is also critical so that you can learn from others, avoid pitfalls and creating unrealistic expectations, and can be inspired by the potential others have found." -Scott Grant (12/20/2010), Personal communication.

附录 2

Resources for Using Second Life in (Chinese) Language Teaching and Learning

General introduction about Second Life
- http://www.youtube.com/watch?v=0t1XR—LrgyM: The Origin of Second Life and its Relation to Real Life, an interview with the founder Philip Rosedale
- http://wiki.secondlife.com/wiki/History_of_Second_Life: History of Second Life
- http://www.youtube.com/watch?v=FZAj8Cg4bLo: A video

clip about the introduction to Second Life

● http://www. slideshare. net/eduservfoundation/second—life—in—3600—seconds/: A nice PPT on Second Life

Discussion Groups and Listservs

● http://groups. yahoo. com/group/secondlifelanguages/messages/1? l = 1: Yahoo discussion group: Second Life & Languages(since Nov. 6, 2006)

● https://lists. secondlife. com/cgi—bin/mailman/listinfo/educators: Second Life in Education [SLED] Listserve

● http://www. facebook. com/second: The Facebook group for Second Classroom, discussing the use of Second Life in Chinese

Workshops and Consultation

● http://evo07 sessions. pbwiki. com/digitalgamingELT: TESOL E-lectronic Village Online offered a session on "Digital Gaming and Language Learning" featuring Second Life, January 2007

● http://www. chineseplaza. com/ : Consultation and training service provided by Second Classroom

Conferences and Proceedings

● http://www. slanguages. net/: The website for the annual SLanguages (Second Life in Languages) conference

● http://www. theconsultants—e. com/edunation/SLanguages2007. pdf: The first SLanguages Colloquium, June 23, 2007

● www. simteach. com/SLCC06/slcc2006—proceedings. pdf: Proceedings of the 1st Second Life in Education Workshop, San Francisco, CA, August 18—20, 2006

● http://www. simteach. com/slccedu07 proceedings. pdf: Proceedings of the Second Life in Education workshop, August, 2007

Comprehensive Collections

● http://www. simteach. com: SimTeach: Information and Community for Educators using MUVEs, maintained by Jeremy Kemp

● http://web. ics. purdue. edu/-mpepper/slbib # pedagogy: Bibliography of using Second Life in education, collected by Mark Pepper

● http://www. dokimos. org/secondlife/education/index. html: A collection on educational use of Second Life by Theodore Wright

- http：//www. healthcybermap. org/sl. htm：A collection on Second Life by Maged Kamel Boulos

Websites on Using Second Life in Chinese

- http：//mychinavillage. uoregon. edu/：MyChina Village，a project led by The University of Oregon's Center for Applied Second Language Studies

- http：//www. virtualhanyu. com：about the use of Second Life at Monash University's Chinese Studies Program，Melbourne，Australia

- http：//confucius. msu. edu/secondlife/enrollment. html：Use of Second Life at Michigan State University's Confucius Institute

- http：//www. chineseplaza. com/events/201008/2nd_ classroom/ about_ us. html：Use of Second Life in Chinese by Second Classroom

网络教学开发、设计与评估

在线汉语教学和资源系统 建设的问题与改进：以《网络孔子学院》 和《长城汉语》为例

Issues in the Development of Online CFL Learning and Resource Systems：A Case Study of *Great Wall Chinese* and *Confucius Institute Online*

笪　骏　Da, Jun　中田纳西州立大学

Middle Tennessee State University United States jda@ mtsu. edu

摘　要：虽然中国大陆已陆续推出了数个对外汉语在线教学和资源系统，但它们目前还难以在北美地区大学汉语教学中得到有效的应用。本文结合中田纳西州立大学汉语教学的实际情况探讨影响使用这些系统的几个教学设计和平台技术问题，并提出相应的改进建议。希望我们的分析和建议能对今后类似的对外汉语教学资源和平台开发提供一些有益的借鉴，同时也可为汉语教师评估和选择教学资源提供一个参考框架。

关键词：对外汉语教学，在线教学管理平台，多媒体教学资源

Abstract：While several CFL online learning and resource systems have been made available from mainland China，few have been adopted successfully in the CFL instruction in colleges and universities in North America. This paper examines several pedagogical and technical issues that have limited their application in North America and makes several recommendations on improving the design of those learning and resource systems. It is hoped that our analysis and recommendations will be helpful to those who are going to improve or develop similar systems. At the same time，they can also be used by CFL instructors in their evaluation and selection of CFL learning and resource systems.

Keywords：Teaching Chinese as a Foreign Language，Online Teaching and Management System，Multimedia Learning resources

一　引言

　　从 2006 年到 2009 年，美国高校选修汉语课程的学生从 51000 多人增加到近 61000 人，继续呈迅速增长趋势（Furman，Goldberg 和 Lusin，2010）。随着汉语学习者数量的不断增长，对汉语学习材料和其他教学资源的需求也在日益增加。为满足北美和世界其他地区的这种需求，中国大陆数所院校、出版社和其他机构都在制作、推出各种对外汉语①教学资源系统，比如像国家汉办的《网络孔子学院》② 和《长城汉语》③系列、外语教学和研究出版社的《外研汉语》④ 平台和中央广播电视大学对外汉语推广中心的《易校园》⑤ 等。与此同时，国家汉办还设立了数个汉语教材和教学资源研发基地（如中山大学国际汉语教材研发与培训基地⑥和武汉大学的汉语国际推广教学资源库⑦等）从事对外汉语教学资源的开发、集成和推广。在花费了不菲的人力和物力开发这些教学资源之后，接下来的一个主要问题就是如何将它们推广给它们所面向的汉语教师和学习者。

　　然而，就我们对北美地区几所大学汉语教学实际情况的了解而言，还很少听到能将上述教学资源直接和方便地应用于汉语教学的例子。一方面，北美地区高校的汉语教学主要还是以面授和纸质教材为主。为帮助学生学习，提高教学效率和效果，激发学生的学习热情，教师都在不同程度上使用了各种教学技术手段和（多媒体）教学资源⑧。而另一方面，除了大量面向母语者的（多媒体）资源（如广播、电视和互联网站等）可供选用外，能配合教材辅助汉语教学的各种（多媒体）资源又相对选择较少。这种资源的短

---

① 在本文中，对外汉语教学意指汉语作为外语/第二语言的教学。

② 参见 http://www.chinese.cn/。

③ 参见 http://www.greatwallchinese.cn/。

④ 参见 http://www.chineseplus.cn/。

⑤ 参见 http://i.myechinese.com/。

⑥ 参见 http://www.cntexts.com/。

⑦ 参见 http://www.hy123.org/。

⑧ 关于北美地区汉语教学中使用各种教学技术和多媒体资源的情况可从《第六届国际汉语电脑教学研讨会会议论文集》（Xu，Da and Zhang，2010）中窥见一斑。

缺在初、中级汉语课堂教学中尤为突出。虽然国内的数所院校、出版社和其他机构都提供了相当数量的在线汉语教学资源，但它们却很少能在美国高校的汉语教学中得到直接有效的应用。

本文通过对中田纳西州立大学汉语教学模式和各种教学技术以及资源使用情况的介绍来探讨为什么在类似中田纳西州立大学的学校中很少或基本不使用诸如《网络孔子学院》等国内开发的汉语教学和资源系统。我们将从教学模式设计、内容选取编排以及平台技术等几个方面来具体分析它们在北美高校汉语教学中使用的局限性并提出一些改进建议。我们希望本文的讨论将有助于国内同行更有针对性地开发或改进（现有的）在线教学和资源系统以适应不同地区不同用户的不同需要。同时，我们也希望本文的讨论能为汉语教师在评估和选择各种汉语教学资源时提供有益的参考。

本文以下分四个部分。在第二节中我们以中田纳西州立大学为例介绍美国大学汉语教学中使用教学技术和（多媒体）资源的情况。在第三节中我们对目前在汉语教学中可以使用的各种在线教学和资源系统进行一个简要的概述。在第四节中我们结合美国高校汉语教学的需求来探讨影响使用国内开发的汉语教学资源的几个问题并提出改进建议。第五节中为本文的结语。

二　中田纳西州立大学的汉语教学

中田纳西州立大学是美国田纳西州在校本科学生人数最多的公立大学，在 20 世纪 90 年代初期曾经开设过汉语课程，自 2005 年起又重新开设初级和中级汉语课程。现在每学期约有 30 位学生选修。除了极少数有汉语背景的华裔学生外，他们绝大多数是零起点的学生。学生选修汉语或是为满足学位课程对外语的要求，或是出于个人的兴趣。除了准备去中国留学的少数学生外，其他大部分学生对汉语学习的期待值不高，尤其是在听力和口语方面。由于相当部分的学生除了学习之外还做兼职，所以除了课堂学习时间外，他们课外学习汉语的时间很少。

中田纳西州立大学汉语课程按照学生语言水平分为初、中级班，每个学期 15 周，每周 3 个课时，每个级别分别需要 90 课时分两个学期修完。这两个级别的汉语课程不再细分为口语、听力、阅读和写作课等，而是由教师根据自己设计的教学大纲、所选教材提供的学习内容以及学生的兴趣同时教授各种语言知识、技能和文化。目前使用的教材是在北美地区由 Prentice Hall

公司出版的 *Chinese Link*（《中文天地》）（Wu 等，2006）①。该教材除纸版课本、学生练习册和汉字练习册外还提供了配套的教学资源网站②，提供课文录音以及和课文学习内容相关的词汇、语法、听力和阅读等在线练习。从第二版开始，《中文天地》还同时推出了在线课程 MyChineseLab③，提供了纸质教材的电子版和相应的在线教学平台④。

就教学硬件而言，中田纳西州立大学的教室里都配备了联网的计算机、投影仪和 DVD 播放机等多媒体播放设备。同时，学校还提供了便利的有线和无线上网环境。大部分学生都拥有自己的计算机，可以在课内和课外方便的上网。另外，学校还设有开放式的语言教学机房，提供在线分级考试，教学资源分发和外语教学软件使用等服务。同时，学校还提供了 Desire2Learn 教学管理平台⑤供教学使用。

中田纳西州立大学的汉语课程采取课堂面授的教学模式。教师在以下几个方面在不同程度上使用了各种教学技术、工具和（多媒体）资源来辅助教学：

1. 教学管理：如使用学校提供的 Luminis Platform 教务管理系统⑥、Desire2Learn 教学平台以及教师自行开发的网站（功能）来管理班级学生信息，与学生交流（如讨论版和电子邮件）和分发授课讲义等。

2. 课堂教学：在具体的课堂教学中，教师会根据教材的内容和教学实际情况借助第三方或自行开发的（多媒体）教学资源来帮助学生理解和掌握学习内容，进行各种课堂学习活动。这些教学资源包括与课文学习内容相关和语言难度相当的阅读短文，能够释义、提供真实语境或传递文化信息的图片和视频短片（如《看图学中文》⑦ 和《汉语课堂视听》（李孚嘉等，2007）等）。除了使用这些教学资源外，教师还会利用互联网上的真实语料和环境进行任务型的教学活动，帮助学生了解中国文化。比如在学习天气这

---

① 在这之前还曾经使用过《中文听说读写（*Integrated Chinese*）》（Tao 等，2005）系列教材。

② 参见 http://wps. prenhall. com。/wl_ wu_ chineselink_ 1/。

③ 参见 http://www. mychineselab. com/。

④ 《中文天地》在线课程在 2009 年中期新近推出，尚未在中田纳西州立大学采用。

⑤ Desire2Learn 系统信息可参见 http://www. desire2learn. com/。除此之外，中田纳西州立大学还曾使用过 Blackboard（c. f. http://www. blackboard. com）和 WebCT（c. f. http://en. wikipedia. org/wiki/WebCT）等教学管理平台。

⑥ 参见 http://www. sungardhe. com。/Products/Product. aspx？ id = 1042&LangType = 1033。

⑦ 参见 http://lingua. mtsu. edu/qing/signs/.

个主题时，教师会使用中国天气网①让学生了解中国各地的实时天气，模拟完成天气预报任务，了解中国天气预报和美国天气预报做法上的异同等。在学习交通旅行这个主题时，教师会利用谷歌地图②和其提供的街景功能来介绍中国地理常识，学习常用地名，让学生自制旅行地图和旅行计划等（Da，2010）。

3. 课后学习：除了教材提供的学习内容外，教师还会选择适合于学生当前语言水平的各种汉语学习网站给学习积极性较高的学生补充额外的学习内容。例如，鼓励学生使用《中文天地》配套网站③提供的课文录音和在线练习进行课后的听力学习，使用 The University of Iowa 大学的《中文阅读天地》④ 来提高学生的汉语阅读和汉字认字能力，以及借助 ChinesePod⑤ 以增加更多的听力机会和与其他汉语学习者的交流。

4. 汉语学习资源、信息和工具：教师和学生使用的多为那些互联网上提供的各种免费汉语资源、信息和学习工具。例如，在《线上学中文》⑥ 网站上教师很容易查找到各种供教师使用的工具信息。在《线上中文工具》⑦ 网站上学生可以学习汉字书写、查阅字典和使用拼音标注等。

在中田纳西州立大学的汉语教学中，影响教师和学生选择使用各种教学技术、工具和（多媒体）资源的因素主要有以下三个：

1. 就教师感兴趣的（多媒体）资源而言，它们要能配合当前使用的纸质教材，即它们的话题、词汇、语法和语言难度等要符合现有教材的内容。如果那些资源是通过在线网站的形式提供，那么需要这些网站能提供便于浏览和搜索的用户界面，即其提供的资源要按照教学实际需求（如交际功能、语言技能、语言难度和不同目标用户等）进行清晰的分类，要提供直观的链接以方便播放、下载和分发。

2. 对于那些能给学生提供额外学习内容和练习机会的网站而言，它们提供的资源和（用户界面）使用的语言要符合当前初、中级水平的学生，涵盖的话题要能使美国大学生感兴趣，足以吸引他们经常和定期地访问。

---

① 参见 http://www.weather.com.cn/。

② 参见 http://maps.google.com./http://ditu.google.cn/。

③ 参见 http://wps.prenhall.com。/wl_wu_chineselink_1/。

④ 参见 http://chinesereadingworld.org/。

⑤ 参见 http://chinesepod.com/。

⑥ 参见 http://learningchineseonline.net/。

⑦ 参见 http://www.mandarintools.com/。

3. 无论是汉语教学和资源系统或是学习工具，它们最好能操作简便，能支持不同的操作系统和浏览器，无须用户安装（太多的）插件。如果是面向集体用户使用的平台，它们最好能与全校通用的教学平台有数据对接的接口。

就我们对北美地区大学几所汉语教学实际情况的了解而言，中田纳西州立大学汉语教学和使用各种教学技术与资源的情况颇具代表性，即选修汉语的学生大部分为初、中级水平的学生，教学主要是以课堂面授和使用纸质教材为主，教师会在不同程度上借助于各种教育技术手段和（多媒体）教学资源来辅助课堂教学。

三　在线汉语教学和资源系统

从教师自制的教学工具、网站到商业型或开源型的多功能教学管理平台，从教师自己编写的多媒体教学材料到由各个出版社和其他机构推出的教学资源系统，目前有不少教学平台、工具和资源可供汉语教师和学习者选择。除了由教师或其他个人自制外，由各院校、出版社、软件公司或其他机构制作的在线教学平台、工具和（多媒体）资源可按照其功能和提供的资源内容分成以下几类：

1. 通用型教学管理平台：这类教学平台为各个科目的教学和课程管理提供相应的工具，比如用户管理、在线作业和测试、教学文件管理、用户交流和日历等，但需要教师提供具体的教学内容。比如，教师可以在这类平台上上传自己编写的课程讲义，通过标准数据接口导入由第三方提供的学习课件。美国高校常用的平台包括商业型的 Blackboard Learning System、Desire2Learn Learning Environment 和开源型的 Moodle 等①，它们一般由学校统一提供和管理。这类平台经过十多年的使用和不断完善，其系统功能已相对稳定和成熟，但与下列第二类平台相比，它们并非为（汉语）语言教学所专门设计，缺少一些语言教学特需的工具和功能。

2. 专用汉语教学平台：这类平台专为汉语学习者所设计，提供了（相对）完整的在线汉语课程和其他教学内容。为配合在线使用或结合面授的混合式使用，它们还提供与上述通用教学平台类似的教学和课程管理工具。这类平台或由出版商自行运营，或由（集体）用户自行安装运行。在美国

①　参见 http://www.edutools.info/item_ list.jsp?pj＝4。在该网站上可以进行各个平台的功能对比。

制作和出版的专用汉语教学平台包括 MyChineseLab、ActiveChinese[①] 和 IQChinese[②] 等。国内出版的有《长城汉语》和《易校园》等。和下述汉语教学资源系统不同，它们主要的设计目标是提供一站式的汉语教学解决方案，其汉语课程往往自成一体，用户无法选择其（部分）内容配合其他教材或课程的使用。

3. 汉语教学资源系统：这类在线系统提供各种（辅助）汉语教学资源供教师和学习者使用，极少或不提供类似上述通用或专用汉语教学平台的教学和课程管理工具或环境。国内出版的包括《网上孔子学院》和《外研汉语》等综合性资源系统和武汉大学在建的《汉语国际推广教学资源库》等。与上述专用汉语教学平台不同，这类教学资源系统提供的资源更丰富、多样，但并不构成相对独立的完整汉语课程。

4. 通用型辅助教学平台：这类平台主要是提供在线教学环境和工具以方便教师创建和共享教学资源，给学习者提供（互动）学习内容，如在线互动练习、问卷调查和在线测试等功能。同时，它们也会提供由第三方（如出版社）开发的教学资源。这类平台的典型代表为 Quia[③]，上面有 *Integrated Chinese*（《中文听说读写》）（Yao 等，2005）的学生练习册。和上述第一类通用教学平台相比，它们并不提供完整的教学管理环境和功能。与上述第二类专用汉语教学平台相比，它们也不提供完整的课程学习内容。和上述第三类教学资源平台不同，它们提供的教学资源除了由教师自行创建和共享外，其他由第三方提供的资源多为配合现行的教材。

5. 语言教学在线工具：这类平台为满足（汉）语言教学的特殊需求提供一种或有限的几种语言学习工具。比如在美国出版的 Lingt[④]，它提供的在线多媒体口语作业系统可以很方便地让教师发布和批改带有口语练习的作业。又如《线上中文工具》[⑤]，它提供了在线汉英字/词典、汉语拼音标注以及一些中国文化知识和工具等。

6. 汉语教师和学习者社区平台：这类平台主要通过如论坛、博客、微博和短信等交互工具为教师和学习者提供互动社区。国内开发的如《易校

---

① 参见 http://www.activechinese.com/。

② 参见 http://www.iqchinese.com/。

③ 参见 http://www.quia.com/。

④ 参见 http://lingt.com/。

⑤ 参见 http://www.mandarintools.com/。

园》和《网络孔子学院》的用户社区等。和其他社交网络（如 Facebook[①]和 Twitter[②]）相比，这类社区的目标使用对象为汉语教师和学习者，其话题更集中于汉语学习。与通用教学平台和专用汉语教学平台提供的有限社区互动功能相比，它们对参与者没有严格的限制，更注重于开放型社区的建设，提供的互动工具也更丰富。因为各种用户的参与，它们也会提供或发布一些教学资源。

7. 虚拟汉语教学环境：这类平台使用虚拟现实（Virtual reality）技术给学习者提供模拟的真实语言环境进行沉浸式的学习（Immersion learning）。目前正在研发和使用的虚拟汉语教学环境主要是采用 Second Life[③] 技术的平台，如 Michigan State University 的 *Second Life Chinese School*[④] 和 The University of Oregon 的 *MyChina Village*[⑤] 项目等。和上述几类平台相比，这类平台尚在开发和完善中，并未得到广泛的使用。

表 1 为上述前六类教学和资源系统的功能特性对比表，其中，●表示系统以提供此类功能或内容为主，▶表示系统也附带提供此类功能或内容。

表 1 　　　　　　　　　　各类平台和系统的主要特征

	教学管理系统：如用户管理、作业系统、用户交流和测试系统等	（汉语）语言教学工具：如拼音输入、笔画演示、录音等	完整教学课程：如在线或电子版教材等	部分教学内容：如与教材配套的在线互动练习内容等	辅助汉语教学资源：如文字、图片、视频和课件等	非完全封闭的互动社区
（1）通用型教学管理平台，如 Moodle/D2L 等	●					
（2）专用汉语教学平台，如《长城汉语》和 MyChineseLab 等	▶	▶	●			

---

① 参见 http://www.facebook.com/。

② 参见 http://twitter.com/。

③ 参见 http://lindenlab.com/。

④ 参见 http://confucius.msu.edu/secondlife/default.html。

⑤ 参见 http://mychinavillage.uoregon.edu/。

续表

	教学管理系统：如用户管理、作业系统、用户交流和测试系统等	（汉语）语言教学工具：如拼音输入、笔画演示、录音等	完整教学课程：如在线或电子版教材等	部分教学内容：如与教材配套的在线互动练习内容等	辅助汉语教学资源：如文字、图片、视频和课件等	非完全封闭的互动社区
（3）汉语教学资源系统，如《网上孔子学院》					●	▶
（4）通用型辅助教学平台，如 Quia 等	▶			●	▶	▶
（5）语言教学在线工具，如 Lingt 等		●				
（6）汉语教师和学习者社区平台，如《易校园》等					▶	●

从表 1 可以看出，经过十多年的开发和使用，各种教学和资源系统提供的功能和内容互有交叉，并非完全排它。就我们了解的情况而言，国内目前已推出的汉语教学和资源系统大多数还集中在第二类专用汉语教学平台和第三类汉语教学资源系统这两个类别。

四　影响使用国内开发的汉语教学和资源系统的问题及对策

我们在对中田纳西州立大学的介绍中提到美国高校的汉语教学主要还是以面授和使用纸质教材为主。为提高教学效率和效果，教师在教学的各个环节都会不同程度上使用各种教学工具、平台和（多媒体）资源。除了部分自制的内容和学校提供的通用教学平台外，它们还包括由第三方提供的工具和资源。在对国内出版的各种汉语教学和资源系统进行评估时，我们发现除营销因素外它们在教学模式设计、内容选取编排和平台技术等方面与美国高校汉语教学的实际情况不能很好地匹配，从而影响了它们的推广和使用。下面我们就以比较有代表性的《长城汉语》和《网络孔子学院》为例来具体分析国内出版的这类系统存在的共同问题，并提出一些改进建议。

（一）专用汉语教学平台：以《长城汉语》为例

目前国内开发的专用汉语教学平台包括《长城汉语》和《易校园》等。这类平台提供了完整的汉语课程以及配合这些课程使用的在线教学环境和工具，意在"向学习者提供个性化的学习方案，满足海内外汉语学习者任何时间、任何地点、任何水平的学习需求"①。然而，这种追求面面俱到的设计理念和做法却与美国高校汉语教学的需求和实际做法不能很好地匹配，具体表现在以下几个方面：

1. 课程编排模式

这类专用汉语教学平台因为要"满足海内外汉语学习者任何时间、任何地点、任何水平的学习需求"，所以提供的课程内容往往是从初级到高级，从日常汉语到专用汉语，试图涵盖各种水平、多种类别和不同需求的学习者。比如《长城汉语》（计划中）的核心课程从生存交际到自由交际包括了18个级别的学习内容。它还（计划）提供正音和汉字等辅助课程系列以及新闻和商用汉语等专门课程和文化课程系列。这些课程系列又同时需要适用于"'讲练—复练'短期强化教学模式、视听说教学模式、大综合教学模式、大小课教学模式和'面授+上机'自主学习模式"等各种教学模式。然而，我们从其网站目前公布的现有说明材料还无法获知该平台是如何选取和编排各种学习内容以适用于上述不同的教学模式。在系统的设计者尚未提供具体的课程教学大纲和教案样例的情况下，这种试图以一套教材去适应多种教学模式的设计思路不足以说服美国高校（潜在）的汉语教师采用其系统。

我们在第二节中提到美国高校的汉语课程一般为每周3—5课时，每学年约90—150课时，选修汉语课程的学生多数集中在初、中级班级。从《长城汉语》课程内容的选取上来讲，这种大而全的设计虽然可以满足少数学习积极性很高同时又有充足时间学习的用户需求，但很难为美国高校那些学习需求和时间均有限的学习者使用。同时，又因为这些课程采取了类似纸质教材的内容编排结构，其教学内容自成一体，所以学习者无法如同进超市一样自由选择和组合学习内容。这种量多但选择性较差的内容编排方式使得它们很难适用于美国高校汉语课程的设置情况。

2. 目标用户定位和教学法

这类专用教学平台的课程设计目标是为各种学习者提供个性化的学习方案，但这种大而全的设计理念却导致了其目标用户定位的不明确，不能顾及

---

① 参见 http://www.greatwallchinese.com。cn/customer/aboutCCHY/aboutCCHY_ 01.jsp。

到各种用户当地的教学理念和教学标准。比如，《长城汉语》生存交际课程6个级别的设计①使用了基于语法的描述，第一级的目标人群定义为"学习过拼音的"，第二级为"可以用简单的句子表达意思"，第五级为"能够使用较复杂的语法和句型表达自己的观点，灵活驾驭日常生活中的话题"。这种主要以语法能力为主来区分和定位用户的方法与美国外语教学中普遍采用的交际功能教学标准（如美国外语教学委员会（American Council on the Teaching of Foreign Languages）的外语能力标准②和田纳西州的中小学外语教学大纲③）不能很好的对应，从而影响了系统的采用。

　　另外，这类教学平台的设计思路是既想适用于在线学习又想适用于"面授＋在线"的混合式学习模式，但在具体学习内容的呈现上却未能顾及到两种教学模式的差异。比如《长城汉语》网站上提供的生存交际1级第9单元样课④。该单元的话题是关于时间的表达，课文为对话形式。但从其具体的语言内容来看，该对话只是一个句型操练，通篇表达的语意不构成一个（类似）真实语境的交际对话。虽然系统提供了动画视频帮助学生理解对话的内容，但学生只能一句一句地随着系统提供的单句对话往下学，无法全面观察整篇对话或选择自己感兴趣的内容，又不能同时查阅字典、课文和语法讲解等其他内容。这种颇为机械的教学方法与美国高校汉语教学中普遍采用的交际法教学有差异。虽然并非所有的美国汉语教师和学生都认同交际法的教学理念，但在课程内容的使用上能否自由选择编排以适合各种教学法的需求却是影响用户选择教材的一个重要参照因素。

　　3. 用户界面设计

　　类似《长城汉语》的专用汉语教学平台的目标用户为海内外的各种学习者。虽然它们通常也提供了多语种的用户界面，但往往却使用同一种用户界面设计，未能考虑到各种学习者的不同审美和使用习惯。比如，从《长城汉语》提供的课程样课和（有限几个）教案来看，其教学内容的呈现均结合了图片和音/视频等多媒体表现形式。但系统使用的动画人物形象对美国高校的成年大学生来说显得过于幼稚和儿童化，不足以吸引学生的注意力和提高他们的使用兴趣。

---

①　参见 http://www.greatwallchinese.com。cn/customer/individual/getixueyuan_ 01. jsp。

②　参见 http://www.actfl.org/files/public/StandardsforFLLexecsumm_ rev. pdf 和 http://www.sil. org/lingualinks/languagelearning/otherresources/actflproficiencyguidelines/contents. htm。

③　参见 http://www.tn.gov/education/ci/foreign_ lang/index. shtml。

④　参见 http://www.greatwallchinese.com。cn/trialCourse/trial. jsp。

4. 平台运行环境和用户支持

影响美国高校用户选择在线教学平台的非教学因素包括付费（方式）、服务器运行可靠性、网络速度以及对客户端的技术支持等。因为硬件和技术支持的原因和学校现有的教学平台运行环境，像中田纳西州立大学这类学校一般不会考虑在本校安装和维护由第三方提供的平台系统而是会选择使用由出版商直接负责运行的平台系统。

虽然像《长城汉语》等国内开发的专用汉语教学平台通常会提供由出版商直接运行的网络版、在当地学校局域网中安装的网络版和个人单机版供用户选择使用，但在客户端的设计和使用的技术上却往往只针对使用 Windows 操作系统和 Internet Explorer 浏览器的用户而忽略了其他平台的用户。比如，美国高校常用的操作系统除了 Windows 之外还包括 Mac 和 Linux 等平台，常用的浏览器除了 Internet Explorer 外还包括 Safari 和 Firefox 等。但《长城汉语》的客户端需要用户下载安装汉字手写识别和汉语语音识别插件，目前只能在 Windows 操作系统上的 Internet Explorer 浏览器中运行，不支持 Firefox 等其他浏览器。这就限制了其系统被采用的机会。

基于以上课程内容编排、教学法和平台设计的偏差，类似《长城汉语》的专用汉语教学平台目前尚不能在美国高校中得到有效的利用。要改变这一状况，我们建议这类平台要改变面面俱到的设计理念，根据目标用户的年龄、文化习惯以及汉语学习目标和水平有针对性地开发适用于不同地区不同目标用户的课程。例如，可以针对美国高校成年学生初、中级汉语学习专门设计一教材系列，其内容选取、编排和呈现方式要能适用于基于有限课时安排的以面授为主在线为辅的教学模式，其用户界面设计要符合美国成人学生的审美习惯，其采用的平台技术要适用于美国高校多操作系统多浏览器的技术环境。为达到这些目标，最好在教学内容编写和系统开发过程中有目标用户的参与，从他们那里获得适合当地用户需求和使用习惯的设计参考思路和试用反馈。

（二）汉语教学资源系统：以《网络孔子学院》为例

与专用汉语教学平台不同，这类系统主要是提供各种辅助教学资源而不是自成一体的完整汉语课程。目前国内开发的较有代表性的系统是《网络孔子学院》，它提供了海量的各种教学资源，包括文字资料、音乐、动画、电影（片段）和中国文化介绍等等，其目标服务对象包括从少儿到成年人。

然而，不同的用户对教学资源的需求不同。从美国高校汉语教学的实际情况来看，教师经常需要的是那些可以辅助课堂教学的资源。这些资源最好能和当前使用的教材匹配，提供的话题和语言难度能符合当前的教学内容。对美国高校的学生来说，理想的学习资源需要能符合他们当前的汉语水平，能为他们创造更多的练习机会，帮助他们进一步了解感兴趣的中国文化。就美国高校汉语教学的这些需求而言，影响《网络孔子学院》得到采用的主要因素有以下三个方面：

1. 文化资源内容多集中于中国传统文化，对现今中国社会、政治、文化和生活的介绍偏少，这与美国高校学生的兴趣点有较大偏差。比如《网络孔子学院》提供的中国文化介绍主要集中在饮食、功夫、珍宝、中医、曲艺、旅游和人物等话题，而缺少关于中国政府、法律、经济、体育和普通人生活等内容。在文化介绍内容的编排上，《网络孔子学院》首选的第一个主题是饮食文化，而非美国学生更感兴趣的体育赛事。

2. 教学和文化资源内容大都直接取自于供母语者使用的材料，其语言偏难，不能为初、中级汉语水平的学生使用。比如，《网络孔子学院》一篇关于葛优的介绍①取自于《中国网》的原文②。虽然它对原文略有修改，并添加了词汇注释，但仍然只适合高级水平的学生阅读。同时，其注解的词汇大部分是基于随意的选择，并非为影响理解该文章内容的关键词。

3. 资源缺乏明确的分类和标注，网站的浏览导向和检索功能过于简单。《网络孔子学院》提供的海量资源虽然在教学资源、学习材料和文化介绍等大的框架下进行了初步的分类，但它们更像是源于各种网站和教材资源的简单内容堆砌，没有能够按照各种用户的需求进行有针对性的分类和标注，提供准确的检索功能。比如，针对每个具体的资源对象，它未能提供诸如话题和语言难度等信息标注以及关键词索引。这种资源标注信息的缺乏导致了其网站提供的基于 Google 技术的检索功能无法让用户准确地进行资源检索。

欲提高这类资源系统在美国高校汉语教学中的可用性，可以按照以下的思路进行一些改进：

1. 要多提供适合初、中级水平用户使用的各种资源，尤其是各种音/视频等材料。这些资源最好能针对目标用户的兴趣点。对于取自于母语者使用的材料，除了提供原文外，还需要提供简化版。

2. 要对每个资源对象进行标注。标注的信息可以包括话题、交际功能、语言难度、关键字/词、语言技能、语法点、目标用户和能配套使用的教科书等。例如，语言难度的标注可以参照美国外语委员会关于各种语言能力的

---

① 参见 http://people. chinese. cn/article/2010-12/09/content_ 206608. htm。

② 参见 http://www. china. com. . cn/info/men/2010-11/26/content_ 21424434. htm。

分级描述。这些标注信息既可以为用户提供浏览上的便利，同时也可以为准确检索功能提供参照依据。

3. 网站的浏览导向要根据不同用户的需求提供有针对性的编排，并提供多种信息分类索引，便于用户进行有的放矢的浏览。例如，从汉语教师的需求考虑，可以将资源分成用于课堂教学的资源和用于科研的参考性资源。在用于课堂教学的资源下面，可以按照类别（如学习材料或教案）、话题、交际功能、目标语言技能、可匹配的常用教材内容以及适用的场合（课内或是课外）等进行进一步的编排。

4. 对于图片、音频和视频等多媒体资源，需要提供直观的链接和不同格式的文档下载，以便适用于美国高校多种操作系统和多种浏览器的技术环境，避免网络带宽或网络故障造成的使用上的不确定性和不稳定性。

5. 改进网站检索功能的设计以便用户准确地查找信息。比如，除了提供借助于 Google 技术的关键字/词搜索引擎外，还需要提供能使用不同检索条件（如上述各种资源标注信息）的检索功能。

五　结语

本文以中田纳西州立大学汉语教学和使用各种教学技术以及（多媒体）资源的实际情况为参照讨论了国内开发的汉语教学和资源系统在教学内容和平台设计中存在的几个问题，并提出了相应的改进建议。通过对《长城汉语》和《网络孔子学院》两个案例的具体分析，本文试图说明这些教学和资源系统由于大而全的设计思路在目标用户定位、教学模式、内容选取和编排以及采用的平台技术等方面不能有效地对接于美国高校汉语教学的实际环境和通常做法，从而影响了它们的使用。为能在美国高校的汉语教学中得到广泛的应用，本文建议各种汉语教学和资源系统的开发最好能得到目标用户的参与，更多地面向初、中级水平的学习者，满足以面授为主的教学需求。同时，用户界面的设计和平台技术需要顾及到多操作系统和多浏览器的运行环境以及当地的审美习惯。我们希望本文的分析和建议能对国内现有汉语教学、资源系统的改进和未来类似系统的开发起到一定的借鉴作用。

参考文献

李孚嘉等：《汉语课堂视听》，中央广播电视大学音像出版社 2007 年版。

Da, Jun. (2010). Using Google Earth and Google Maps for task—based activities and cultural knowledge. The Sixth International Conference and Workshops on Technology and Chinese Language Teaching in the 21st Century. Columbus, Ohio, USA.

Furman, Nelley, David Goldberg and Natalia Lusin (2010). Enrollments in languages other than English in United States Institutions of Higher Learning, Fall 2009. The Modern Language Association of America web publication. Available: http://www. mla. org/pdf/2009_ enrollment_ survey. pdf.

Wu, Sue—mei, Yueming Yu, Yanhui Zhang, and Weizhong Tian (2006). Chinese Link (《中文天地》). New Jersey: Prentice Hall.

Xu, Debao, Jun Da and Phyllis Zhang (eds.) (2010). Proceedings of the 6th International Conference and Workshops on Technology and Chinese Language Teaching in the 21st Century. Columbus, Ohio, USA.

Yao, Tao—chung, Yuehua Liu, Liangyan Ge, Yea—fen Chen, Nyan—Ping Bi, Xiaojun Wang, and Yaohua Shi (2005). Integrated Chinese (2nd Ed) (《中文听说读写》). Boston: Cheng & Tsui Company.

与数码时代同步——利用网络
技术训练写作技能①

Synching with the Digital Age：Using Web
Toolsto Develop Chinese Writing Proficiency

张　霓　Phyllis Zhang　美国乔治·华盛顿大学

The George Washington University United States zhang@ gwu. edu

摘　要：汉字书写的耗时费力限制了学生书写技能的发展。鉴于电脑网络交际方式逐渐成为主流，打写式的交际应成为中文技能训练的重要部分。本文提出利用网络技术强化技能训练，用打写方式在短期内覆盖较多的词汇，结合主题式技能组合训练程序，有效地提高中文书写效率与质量。本文以中高级教学实例说明网记工具的条理性、规律性和目的性，有助于建立一种循序渐进、环环相扣的训练机制。利用网络工具进行定时写作训练也可有效地提高写作效率。

关键词：书写，写作，打字，输出，表达，网记，博客，网络工具，技能训练，教学模式，逆向设计

Abstract：The complexity of the Chinese writing system has been a hindrance to the development of the learner' writing skills. Today as the web and mobile tools have become ubiquitous，written communication via typing and web applicationshas become an essential job skill and important part of literacy training. This article proposes that web tools such as blogging and Quia be used more proactively for the development of Chinese writing proficiency. The author's pilot practice has shown that using the blogging tool to improve Chinese typing output accuracy and quality is highly feasible. The typing mode coupled with a proficiency-oriented training procedure allows for more vocabulary items to be covered than in a tra-

---

① 本文部分内容基于 2010 年 6 月美国俄亥俄州立大学召开的第六届国际汉语电脑教学研讨会论文"利用博客网记训练中文写作技能"。

ditional class with the hand-writing mode，promoting output quantity and quality. The regular and focused writing structure of the blogging tool also helps build a systematic training mechanism，whereas timed-writing via online tools promotes writing efficiency.

一　引言

在语言技能中，写可以算是最难掌握的技能。对于中文作为外语教学而言（以下称"中文教学"或"汉语教学"），由于汉字读写的难度，写的技能（对没有汉字背景的学生来说），一向是学习者难以突破的瓶颈，也是令教师却步的教学领域。然而，写的技能在外语学习中至关重要，特别是在高级阶段更是衡量语言技能的一个重要标尺。作为一种综合技能，写融合说、读技能的运用，也能培养描述、叙述、比较、评论等语段乃至语篇的表达能力。书写活动不仅能练习口头表达方式，也可学习练习书面语的用法和格式。有深度的写作更是一个创意思维、独立思考、互动合作的过程，有助于培养分析、组织、概括能力，并深化对目标语及学习者自己母语文化的认识理解。从外语习得角度看，书写作为一种输出式的练习活动能促进语言能力的获得。Swain（1985，1993，1995）提出，输出式的语言训练可有效地促进学习者对语言结构的掌握，有助于表达的流利度和自动化的获得。输出活动为学习者提供了练习流利表达的机会；在输出过程中，学习者更容易注意到词句结构的用法，进而提高表达的准确性；通过输出，学习者会发现自己在表达上存在的差距和缺口，因此会在后续的语言学习中注意填补这些缺口。以此观之，书写任务不仅是目的，亦可作为一种促进语言习得的教学方式和手段。

新时代对书写技能的需求将写作训练提到一个显要的位置并注入了新的内涵。高速发展的网络技术及新型交际工具改变了人们的传统交际方式，导致以数码输入为主的书写量激增。显而易见，越来越多的日常事务、人际沟通、公务来往、商业服务乃至社会交往正在从口头交际变成同步（synchronous，也译为实时）或异步（asynchronous，也译为非实时）的网络书写交际，如电邮（Email）、网记/博客（Blog）、微博（Microblog）、维基合作撰写（Wiki）以及网上实时交际的聊天或个人网页交流（Skype、Chat、QQ、Facebook）等等。专家们在90年代中期就预测，由于大量的交际活动通过网络异步或非实时进行，因此很大程度上，口头交际方式会逐渐让位于电子书写方式（Robb，1996）。网络评论权威人士指出，未来网络的广泛运用将需要大量的网络写作人才；熟练运用网络方式进行交际沟通的技能不仅是今后职场竞争的基本要求，而且也是个人充实自我、实现自我的重要机制（Nielsen 2000，引自 Murray &Hourigan 2006）。由此可见，新时代日益增长的书写需求给教育人士提出了新的挑战：传统的写作训练方式必须与新技术相结合。

事实上，从 90 年代末开始至今，美国的外语教学界（特别是英语、法语、西班牙语等几大语种）将电邮、博客、维基等工具纳入教学计划的实例已屡见不鲜，相关的研究和报道也很多。很多研究表明，有效的电脑网络工具运用有助于提高学生表达时的准确性与流利度及书写量（Nutta，1998；Nagata，1998；Shrum&Glisan，2010）。然而，在美国汉语中文教学领域里，有关书写或写作技能训练的研究却向来稀缺，对电脑网络工具辅助写作技能训练的研究报道寥寥无几（Z. Zhang，1998，Xie，2007b；D. Zhang，2009）。因此，我们有必要加强对这一领域的关注与研究，并探索新型的写作技能训练模式。

本文针对博客及 Quia 工具的作用，探讨网络工具用于语言技能训练的必要性、合理性及可行性。讨论重点为：在美国大学的中高级阶段要达到 ACTFL 写作技能要求，训练中急需突破哪些难关？博客及 Quia 作为训练工具适用于哪类书写任务？这些工具作为非交际性写作是否有效？笔者以自己的教学实践为例，尝试提出一套写作训练的设计方案及教学建议，比较两种网络工具对于写作技能训练的辅助作用。文中所用的"书写"或"写作"均指汉语学习中的一般性写作，而非文学创作或学术性文章写作。

二 汉语教学结合网络工具的必要性与合理性

（一）打写将成为主流

对汉语教学而言，写作训练首先要解决的就是汉字教学问题。由于汉字的复杂和书写的难度，读写技能向来是汉语教学中的瓶颈。虽然手写汉字对初级学生仍然必要，但对中级以上的教学而言，手写不仅耗时费力，而且一笔一画的蜗牛行步方式极大地限制了学习者的词汇扩展及表达流利度的提高，也不能适应新时代快节奏交际的要求。要与时代同步，只能用新技术训练新时代的技能。这意味着打写将成为汉语教学的一个主要技能目标。自 90 年代末开始，美国汉语教学界就有人开始提倡并试行打写的教学方式，提出打写的诸多优势：如打写是通过语音输入，有助于巩固发音和拼音；输入时选词，有助于辨别同音字，强化认读能力；打写方式省力流畅，因此思维连续，有助于表达的连贯、集中于文章的写作而不必为笔画分神（Zhang，1998；Xie，1999；Kubler，2002；Xu，2005；He，2005）。谢天蔚（Xie，2001）对其打写教学成效做过详细报道，发现打写方式可有效地提高教学效率，促进技能发展；学生在完成作业的效率、拼音的准确率以及汉字的认读能力上均有明显提高；学生在写作能力上的明显进步表现为内容较以前丰富、深刻；而存在的主要问题是同音字偏误较为频繁。由于中文打字的逐渐普及，打写现已被很多教师视为比手写更重要的技能。不言而喻，打写将逐渐取代手写而成为主流中文书面交际方式。

（二）网络工具促进中文技能发展

从实际运用的技能角度看，写作训练不仅是打写取代手写的问题，也是一个实际语言技能运用的问题。近年来美国中文教师的一些教学尝试均显示出结合网络工具进行交际训练的益处。谢天蔚（Xie，2007a）提出电脑不应仅仅作为辅助工具，而应是师生之间、学习者之间实现真实社会交流的重要工具；学生应在实际电脑使用中学习语言。因此学生在学习过程中使用各种常见的交际工具，如电邮、博客、维基等，学习兴趣增强。许德宝、靳洪刚（Xu 与 Jin，2009；Jin，2009）针对各种网络参与式学习工具进行了研究评估，并特别针对讨论版（Discussion Board）、博客（Blog）及网络通话（Skype）三种交流方式的特点设计了参与式教学法并对其做了细致的教学实验，让学生在网络上直接进行互评交流，参与者也包括身在中国的素不相识的母语者。考察结果显示，博客交流方式的互动性最高、兼容及灵活性也最强，网络通话次之（Jin，2009）。这样的参与式机会大大增加了学生之间以真实参与、沟通、交流为目的的互动及目标语的使用。D. Zhang（2009）用教学应用软件 WebCT 讨论版来强化写作训练，发现其对学生在写作过程中形成互动合作的团体起到积极的作用，可提高学生的写作兴趣、动力及成效。除以上研究外，其他报道包括利用网络交流工具进行真实交流和讨论，用博客练习写作或用维基合作撰写旅行观感（Xie，2007b），用视频网播进行汉字读写训练（P. Zhang，2009a），或让学生通过 Wiki 合作完成期末论文（Wang，2010）。以上有限的报道以及不同程度的教学实践均表明，网络工具起到了丰富教学活动、强化读写能力、增强学生自主性、合作性的作用。

（三）新课题：探索写作训练方式

从汉语教学总体上看，写作仍然是薄弱环节。尤其是在结合网络工具方面，尚需摸索出一套行之有效的训练方式。虽然大多数教师已经承认打写方式的优势，但毕竟还处于摸索过渡阶段，教学中仍然存在诸多急需解决的问题。例如，在考试及课后作业完成中，打写还是手写、各占多少比例等问题上，教师们尚无定论，因此各行其是，这给系统规划技能训练造成困难。对大多数中文教师而言，由于对网络工具的功能及使用方式了解甚少，因此利用率很低；规律性结合网络工具的写作任务（包括电子邮件式的交流）尚未纳入教学规划。很多教师将打写方式仅仅视为完成作业的形式而已，而并未从教学法、技能训练及语言习得的角度来对其加以考虑和利用。显然，从纸本教学过渡到纸本＋网络的混合式教学、从传统的输入为主的方式转到结合输出式的教学方式，尚需要相当一段时间的心理建设和教学规划。这表明，结合网络工具的写作活动，不管是基于实际运用技能的训练还是以促进语言习得为目的的写作，都已成为我们新时期的重要课题，需要我们从多种角度来进行研究探索。

三　网络工具的利用：可行性

目前可用于写作训练的网络工具很多，工具的选择取决于教学目的。笔者认为博客网记工具及 Quia 模版系统便于进行例行写作训练，因此本文针对这两种网络工具的可行性和有效性进行讨论。

（一）网记工具用于教育的优势与益处

就写作能力发展而言，最为大众化、简便灵活的网络应用程序当属网记工具（Weblog 或 Blog），中文常称为博客、部落格、网络日志、网志等（以下通称网记或博客）。网记从 90 年代末开始逐渐在全球普及，进入 21 世纪后便一跃成为最热门的网络交际与微型发表方式。随后网记的使用及成效不断受到教学人士的关注。根据美国教育部门对青少年的调查，使用网记对青少年的写作有明显促进作用：网记使用者比其他同龄人更加投入，内容丰富，输出量也较多（Pew Internet, 2008）。英国对中小学生读写能力的调查结果与美国的基本一致，发现网记形式有助于增强写的能力及对写作的自信心（National Literacy Trust, 2009；BBC, 2009；Edublogs, 2009）。网记简单易用，为学生提供了一个课外的虚拟写作空间，让他们能够用目标语思考、评论、提问、审读与交流，从而培养他们的学习责任感和独立性，为终身学习打下良好基础（Pinkman, 2005）。因此，目前很多欧美语种已将网记方式作为培养写作技能的常用手段之一。

网记工具的特点使它成为一个理想的交际和教学工具。推特微博创始人之一 Stone 将网记的结构特点总结为三大要素：时序（Chronology），频率（Frequency），焦点/议题（Focus）（Stone，2004）。其实，网记还有另外一项最具特色的功能，即增强作者和读者互动的读者评论（Comments）。除此之外，网记的优势还在于网页的兼容性，图片、视频等都可上传，使写作的表现形式丰富多彩，图文并茂。网记之所以成为理想的教学工具，除方便好用之外，还在于以下多重功能和特点（Godwin-Jones，2003；Pinkman，2005；Tan et al. 2005；Carla 2008）：

互动性：读者可发表评论，与作者进行对话式交流。

合作性：网记的作者可以是个人或集体的，个人或集体之间均可进行互动连通，互相配合完成某一写作或报告项目。

交流性：持续的网记写作可帮助学生形成课外交流圈或团体，互观互读有利于良性竞争、促进写作质量的提高。

自主性：作者可以选择是否将所写的东西与他人交流，不公开、有限公开或者完全公开

灵活性：可随时修改，也可随时删除；可允许别人评论，也可不允许评论。

个别性：作者可利用网记写作的空间表现自己的个性特点，发挥自己的创意。

记录性：网记写作日期、主题一目了然，按反时序排列，日积月累便成为一个井井有条的作文集（writing portfolio），是展示语言技能及知识深广度的窗口

出版性：个人写作在网上发表，对个人的语言交际沟通能力具有积极推动作用，同时读者及其评语也会激发作者的写作兴趣和动力。

博客网记与维基合作式编写（Wiki，中文也称维客）不同。维基是仅次于博客网记的大众化网络写作工具，近年来迅速发展普及，使用者日益增多。维基的互动性及合作性对学生的写作能力发展以及写作动力起到极大的推动作用。关于两种工具的区别，维基软件发明人 Ward Cunningham 有一句甚为精辟的概括："The blogosphere is a community that might produce a work, whereas a wiki is a work that might produce a community."（直译：博客圈是一个可以产生作品的社团，而维基则是一个可以产生社团的作品）（Wikiquote，2010）由此可见，二者各有其用，可互补而不可互代。

从便捷灵活角度看，网记不失为培养写作习惯和能力的首选工具。一般来说，网记可用于各种写作练习：定期或非定期，命题或不命题，交际或非交际，均可根据教学需要而定。

（二）Quia 系统用于写作训练的优势

与网记工具不同，Quia 是一个为教师设计的应用系统，提供多种教学活动及测试的模版，以便教师可自编网上练习和测试、收取学生作业或进行各种问卷调查；只需教师开户，学生使用者无限制。测试模版中含有各种题型模版，包括多项选择、判断正误、开放式回答、作文等。与网记工具一样，Quia 页面可兼容插入图片、链接、音档等作为测试题目或辅助提示。同时，Quia 也是一套教学管理系统，学生的作业和考试记录都有条不紊地收录在教师账户中，可供老师随时查阅打印，很多题型可以自动阅卷给分，免去了老师繁杂的人工劳务。学生也可从学生账户中查看自己的分数或教师的评语。从写作训练上看，Quia 的几个功能有显著优势：

收取作业：教师可用测试模版中的"作文"题型出题，然后将网页链接发给学生，以便全班学生进入同一网页写作或交卷（相当于设置一个收件箱），从而省去了用电邮发送的麻烦。

定时写作：教师在布置写作任务时即可自行设置定时写作的时间限制，学生开始写作后定时器就开始倒计时，时间到即自动关闭写作框。定时写作有助于训练学生的写作效率，也可用于课上测试。

作业记录：不管是课堂测试还是课后作业，都有自动详细记录，包括学生所用的时间、开始和结束的时间、尝试次数等。可打印个别学生的记录，或全体学生的记录，按时间排列或按名字顺序排列。

问卷调查：问卷调查模版可用于了解学生背景、学习需要和对教学的反馈意见。调查结果自动统计，一目了然，亦可转为文档保存。

自动评卷：可用于打字练习，预先设定正确答案，即可在学生输入语块或句子后提供错误反馈，以训练学生打字的效率及准确度

资料保管：所有学生的资料和作文均在老师账户中，便于学生资料的储存、查阅和整理。

由此可见，网记工具的好处更多的是针对网记作者而言，网页也可供自己或别人访阅，而 Quia 则主要是针对老师的需要所设计，从这里收取的作业或测试只有老师和学生本人能看到。两种工具各有好处，配合使用能互补不足，满足一般教学需要。

四 写作训练设计

本文以中高级为例，探讨写作训练的设计以及网络工具的作用。中高级阶段的学生已基本熟悉中文的一般句式结构，汉字认读及打字有一定基础，对语句和段落组织的要求也容易理解，是加强写作训练的良机。因此，笔者以中高级说写课作为写作训练试点，尝试网记及 Quia 工具 的可行性和有效性。主要考查的是在非真实交流的写作活动中，网络工具如何起到促进语言技能的作用。

（一）教学条件及学生背景

课时：此教学尝试是在中高级班进行。中高级课时每周 2 次，各 75 分钟，一学期包括考试在内共 14 周（课时按 50 分钟算，共 42 课时）。

学生背景：学生共 20 人，大多数为非华裔背景的美国人，也有个别韩国学生。多数学生已学过约 350—400 课时的大学中文课程，也有暑期中国留学或旅游的经历。

设备条件：每个学生都自备笔记本电脑并可无线上网，教室与宿舍也大多具备上网条件。

汉语水平：从课程开始前的问卷调查和入学摸底考试（包括词汇测试及写作）看，大多数学生课程开始时表达能力大约在 ACTFL 要求的中级—中（Intermediate Mid）程度，个别学生达到中级—高（Intermediate High）。学生汉字认读水平高低不一，打字经验普遍不足（有的学生逐字认打），因此速度慢且偏误多。写作能力基本都低于口头表达能力。从问卷调查结果以及学生一般表现来看，词汇贫乏是造成表达不畅、偏误较多的主要原因。

（二）教学设计理念：技能系统训练模式

书写活动作为一种教学手段可根据教学需要灵活安排，而作为提高写作技能的训练，则需要一个系统的规划。纵观各种技能训练（球技、琴技等）都有三个显著特点：技能目标明确、先分后总、任务式检测验收。我们可暂且将这种训练方式称为"技能系统训练模式"，以便与其他教学模式（如汉语教学界中最常见的"精读模式"）相区别。本文中所探讨的教学设计（Zhang，2009b）在很大程度上是基于这种训练模式的理念。技能训练的核心为技能目标先行，这与近年来提倡的"逆向设计"（backward design）的教学理念相吻合。逆向设计（Wiggins 与 McTighe，2005）的三个基本步骤为：①确立所需要的结果（Identify desired results）；②确定能力表现（Determine acceptable evidence）以作为评估依据；③规划相应的教学活动（Plan learning experiences and instruction）。换句话说，所有的教学活动都服务于预期目标。所以只有在确立了目标（目的地）以后才能规划如何最快最有效地到达目的地的具体行程和步骤。

技能目标：按照以上设计理念，本教程确立的预期目标很大程度上基于美国外语教学学会对中高级说写技能的评测标准（ACTFL，1999；2001）：学习者基本能够以段落形式做描述、叙述、概括，并具有处理日常交际所需要的能力。教程参考 ACTFL 的具体评测要求拟出能力表现作为评估依据。明确了预期结果和评估标准，每一步教学活动则有的放矢，并可随时根据预期目标而跟进检测、调整。

先分后总：技能训练模式的另一特点是先分后总（点—线—面—体）的策略，即以循序渐进的方式先各个击破，然后由小渐大、组装整合。依照此训练路径，本说写教程采取主题—组件式的训练方式：将各主题分为小话题练习，然后再将各个"面"组合为"体"。也就是一个先分后总自下而上（bottom up）的训练程序。

检测验收：教程的每个阶段——即每课、每单元——都有具体技能目标。检测验收则在每单元结束时进行，根据预先确定的能力表现设计任务，如模拟真实生活情景中的书写交际任务，或针对主题完成描述写作任务。

（三）教学程序与内容

以 ACTFL 技能标准以及美国中高级阶段学生的能力来分析，要达到技能目标，学生首先需要突破的是词汇关。其次，汉字认读与打写准确率也与写作质量与效率直接相关。因此，教学内容须包括与技能目标相关的词汇，以及汉字认读及打字效率的练习活动。

如上所述，本教程的设计采用先分后总、点线面体的策略。从图 1 的示例中可以看出总训练框架（预期结果）为描述、比较、观点陈述类的介绍/报告技能，训练划分为数个主题（此处仅以物品、人物、地方主题为例），其中每个主题相对独立。主题之下分有不同的课别，为分话题各个击破的训练策略；而最后整合输出的是综合性的介绍，即达到预期目标的具体能力表现。这样的组件式的方式每个单元自成一体，单元内的各小课环环相扣，容易操作，也便于步步检测调整。

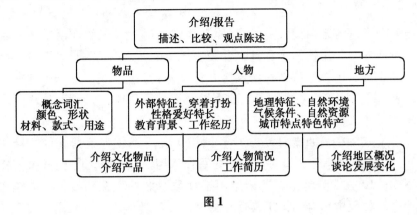

图1

（四）单元设计示例

下面以物品单元为例，具体说明此训练模式的单元目标（预期结果）、能力表现及写作任务。

单元主题	物　品
单元总目标	能够用段落方式及较为具体的词语描述物品外部特征、比较物品性能特点、介绍产品及相关信息，打字准确率达到至少95%
小课目标	每课结束时，学生应能够达到当课的预期结果（以下为各课目标）： 能够描述物体外部特征 能够用段落方式以及空间顺序描述静态空间、物品及布置 能够用段落方式比较物品性能功能 能够用多个段落描述、比较、评论产品特点及服务、推荐产品 能够用邮件方式进行交际沟通，解决问题
能力表现	学生能以打写的方式完成以下任务： 描述普通物品的颜色形状、形体特征，如国旗的图案 用空间顺序主题句、条理清楚地描述房间格局和布置、物品的放置或简单地说明画面内容 与人协商如何改变房间布置或更换物品 描述礼物，包括颜色形状、材料、体积、包装 与人协商退换订购的物品，说明物品的差异 介绍比较手机、电脑等产品：外观、款式、性能、功能、售后服务
写作活动	根据教学内容和进度安排，学生在物品主题的单元内有以下不同写作练习和任务： 写作练习：模拟与房东交涉改变房间装饰、布置、添置家具用品等 写作练习：模拟客户与客服中心写信，抱怨服务失误，比较订购物品与收到物品的不同，要求以免费快递方式退换 小作文（两段，叙述体）：讲述出国前后自己房间的变化，做比较 小作文（两段，叙述体）：描述一件文化物品或产品 阶段作文/报告：介绍产品或文化物品 定时命题写作测试（两段，20分钟）：模拟写信向朋友推荐产品，并与同类产品做比较

（五）如何利用网络工具

前面介绍过博客网记及 Quia 两种工具作为语言训练的辅助工具的不同优势。本教程即利用这两种工具配合表达技能训练，以达到最理想的训练效果。在教学尝试中，所有书写任务均以打写完成。选用的工具如下：

1. Word 文档：Word 文档不需要上网，而且便于文字处理和修改，所以适用于单元作文任务。

2. 网记工具：在此教学尝试中，网记工具用得较为频繁（约每周一次任务），主要目的是用于非真实交际的写作练习。较短的写作任务可直接在网上写作，10—15 分钟，但网记也用于登载写好的作文和报告，以作为作品集保存。教程中结合网记工具旨在将网记作为教学手段，利用其时序、频率及焦点三大特点，让学生熟悉网络写作的环境，适应写作的频率，养成高效率的写作习惯。在起步阶段，写作任务有相对较多的控制，而非自由式写作。

3. Quia：主要用于定时写作测试，偶尔作为收取作业的收件箱。

4. 配套网络课件：在教程中特别设计了语块练习，要求学生以看—念—打方式练习，在提高流利与准确度的同时，加强认读能力。打写可用一般电脑文档练习，也可用本教程配套的在线流利强化课件练习。在线课件可提供及时错误反馈和准确率，使学生能当即就注意到错误，并进行及时更正（见附录 1）。

值得注意的是，新时代的快节奏导致交际方式愈来愈向"短、频、快"方向发展，推特微博（Twitter）的普及即为最好的例证。因此本教程的书写任务设计以短小、频繁、限时为原则。以下表 1 中列出写作任务类别，注明各类写作任务的要求、工具及目的。

表1　　　　　　　　　　　　写作任务类别及目的

类别	写作内容及目的	字数	工具/形式
网记	建议 10—15 分钟完成；1—2 小段；每周例行书写练习；以当课的话题为主，练习当课的话题词汇	150—250	用博客网页打写，在 15—25 分钟内完成
小作文	建议 40—60 分钟完成；2—3 段；单元小作文，整合本单元的词汇及分话题；简单层次的描述、比较	400—500	用一般电脑文档打写、修改；上传博客网页

续表

类别	写作内容及目的	字数	工具/形式
小组报告	3—4 段；多层次描述、比较、介绍；阶段性组装整合，创意写作及综合应用能力；互动合作	650—800	用电脑文档打写；协调合作
定时命题模拟任务	简单看图描述：1 段（5 分钟） 模拟任务 1：1—2 段（15—20 分钟） 模拟任务 2：2 段（20—25 分钟） 阶段性写作技能测试，检查词语句式的活用以及即兴发挥的语段表达能力；老师命题并设计模拟情景；学生不得借助任何词表、词典或其他工具。	100—120 200—250 350—400	用电脑文档或电子邮件直接打写后上传 Quia 或电邮发给老师；或直接在 Quia 页面自动计时打写。

五　教学收效

第一个学期的初步尝试结果表明，网络工具的运用起到辅助写作练习的作用，下面以三个学生的表现为例，比较在描述方面的表达能力进步情况。这三个学生均为背景相似的美国人（非亚裔），程度可代表本班大多数人水平。

（一）测试评估

前测：学期开始时做了一次主题词汇及描述能力测试，其中包括看图描述人和物的外部特征，要求是用手写的方式写出相关的词汇，可用拼音。

中测：在期中时（物品单元学习 12 课时之后），做命题为"介绍产品"的阶段测试报告，要求打写完成，650—800 字。

后测：在期末时（物品单元结束约 9 周后、人物印象单元结束 5 周后、人物背景单元结束 1 周后）进行了课上限时命题写作测试，包括看图描述人物外部特征（与前测图片相同）、介绍产品特点、推荐人选三个命题，限时50 分钟内以打写方式完成，不能借助任何类型的字典或其他工具资源。

下面的表格显示三位学生在前测与后测中能力进步对比，其中前测是手写，后测为打写，所标的字数均含标点符号（见表 2）。表 3 为学生丙在后测中完成定时即兴写作的表现，表 4 则显示三位学生在后测中三个任务的总输出量和打字准确率。

表 2　　　　　　　　　　　　**看图描述人物外部特征**

	前测（学期开始时；手写）	后测（期末；该单元结束 5 周后；打写）
	 **图 2**	描述人物外部特征 How would you describe this person?（Hair, dress, shoes, carrying items, your impression/comment） 你怎么描述这个人（头发、穿着、鞋、携带物品及你的印象感觉）？
学生甲	［36 字］ heisi de，duan de toufa， shoushang you shoubiao， tazai chuan chuanzi，gao de xiezi ta hen piaoliang，yi fu ye hen piaoliang	［103 字；打字错误 = 2］ 那个年轻女性看长得相貌出众，身高比较矮，身材瘦瘦的，长着一头短发。她穿得很讲究、时髦，耳朵戴着一双耳环，身上穿着一条粉红色的纯［裙］子，脚上穿着一双高鞋子。她肩上戴着一个黑色的肩包。她给我的感觉是他［她］很讲究衣服。
学生乙	［19 字］ 她的 toufa 不 chang，她 chuan yige 白色和 hei 色的 qunzi	［133 字；打字错误 = 1］ 这位姑娘是一个年轻人，20 在上下，瘦高个，是一个亚洲人。她留短黑色的头发，皮肤很白。她戴着一对比较小的耳环。她长着苹果脸。她身上穿着一条很丰富的裙子，画着粉红色和黑色的图案。她背上拎着一个很大黑色的包。她脚上穿着比较高粉红色的高跟鞋。她看上去非常自信的人，长得很时髦。
学生丙	［22 字］ 这个女人很 piaoliang. 她的 tou 发很 du-an，她 na 一个红 bao。	［137 字；打字错误 = 0］ 这个姑娘长得眉清目秀，20 多岁的年轻人，长得瘦瘦高高的，身高 1 米 60 左右，身材比较苗条。她留着短发，长着一张鹅蛋脸和一双黑黑的眼睛，看上去像东方人。她穿着打扮美观大方，身上穿着短裙，脚上穿着一双高跟鞋，右手拎着一个小包。这个姑娘给人的感觉是她比较自信，但是别看她看上去有点严肃。

表3　　　　　　　　　　　**（期末后测）定时即兴写作任务**

试题：
你有一个中国朋友在一个中国公司工作，他/她请你帮忙找一个会说中文的美国人做公司的公关人员。你有两个朋友都很合适，所以准备推荐给你的中国朋友。你给这个中国朋友写一封邮件，介绍你的这两个朋友，并比较他们的不同特点。
提示：生理特征、穿着打扮、言谈举止、性格特点、兴趣爱好、特长、教育背景、工作经验
学生丙［字数＝767；打字错误＝5（0.7%）］
安娜好！
谢谢发给我邮件。我有两个朋友对你公司的职务很合适，请我介绍他们一下。
第一个人叫安娜。安娜是一个可爱的年轻姑娘，24岁，长得很眉清目秀，爱爱［矮矮］小小的，身高1米55左右，身材很苗条。她穿着打扮正式，身上穿着一条西装群［裙］，脚上穿着一双高跟鞋，背上背着一个书包。虽然她看上去比较严肃，但是说起话来很有礼貌，给人的印象是她特别有能力，教养，才干。很多人说安娜是一个比较外向的人，她很幽默，合群，等等，她给人的感觉是她是一个比较成熟的女性。其实她对外语特别感兴趣，她会说三个语言，汉语，德语，和西班牙语，但是最重要的是她对汉语很有能力。她2008年毕业于Harvard大学，获得过东亚学的学士学位，大学期间获得过中文的奖学金。她现在在乔治·华盛顿大学读二年级的汉语文学研究生，今年也获得过奖学金。安娜也有一些工作经验，看上去是一个很有能力，很有知识的女性。她2008年夏天时在一个美国高中学校当过汉语教师，教一年级和二年级的汉语水平。她2009年夏天时在一个大中国公司做过秘书，协助组织处理文件资料，因为她每天一定用汉语说话，所以她的汉语水品［平］提高了。其实安娜从事教育方面的工作，但是她今后可能想当公司的公关人员。
第二个人叫李白。李白是一个年轻小伙子，他26岁，中等个，长得相貌平平，身高1米70左右。他穿着比较俗气，头上戴着一顶黑帽子，身上穿着意见［一件］T恤衫，下身穿着一条牛仔裤，脚上穿着一双运动鞋，背上背着一个书包。虽然李白给人的印象是他没有什么能力，但他说起话来他很有见解。他是一个比较内向的男性，很文静，腼腆，等等。他对体育比较感兴趣，比如，爬山，打球，等等，其实他对汉语也有特长，虽然他在美国长大，但是他父母是中国人，所以他从小跟父母说汉语。李白2006年毕业于北京大学，他在北大是留学生，大学期间获得过奖学金，也获得汉语学士学位。他没有很多工作经验，现在在微软工作，他担任组织助理。

表4　　　　　　　　　**期末后测三项写作任务的总输出量与打字准确率**

	3项任务总输出量（字）	别字	打字准确率
学生甲	717	3	99.6%
学生乙	885	2	99.8%
学生丙	1163	6	99.5%

（二）能力进步评估

　　从上面的表中可看出学生在课程开始前的描述表达技能较低，用词简单笼统，输出量极少。而在总授课时间不到35课时的学练之后，学生对物品和人物的描述能力已经显著提高。从后测示例中可以看出，学生均能在规定的时间内不借助任何字典或资源，即兴发挥完成看图描述和模拟交际任务，而且输出的质与量上均有实质上的飞跃。

　　• 主题词汇：在前测中最突出的是学生的主题词汇极为贫乏，因此描述

的字数仅有 19—36 字（含标点符号）。而在中测的阶段报告时，输出字数已达到 650 以上（见附录 2）。在后测的即兴发挥测试中，学生不借助任何字典工具仍能用较为具体的词汇描述物品及人物特征特点（见表 2、表 3）。

● 交际功能：从交际有效性上看，三个学生在描述与介绍的技能上都达到预期目标

● 段落表达：高级水平的标志之一，段落表达能力。甲与丙两位学生在表达的连贯、语句的衔接上均达到预期结果，乙则不够自如稳定。

● 输出量：甲乙均在预期范围内（50 分钟内输出约 700—800 字，含标点），而丙却大大超出预期目标（1163 字）。

● 打字效率：输入的方式与准确率和效率直接相关。学期开始时，经验少的学生常用单字输入，效率低而错误多。而在期末的后测时，三个学生的认读能力及打字效率都已提高，准确率近乎 100%，超过预期的 95%。所犯的别字错误多为粗心所致（"一件"打成"意见"，"矮"打成"爱"）。

（三）电脑与网络工具的作用

在此教学尝试中，电脑与网络工具起到关键作用。总结如下：

1. 规律性写作：网记工具的时序、频率、焦点议题三大要素使其具有很强的条理性、规律性和目的性，有助于建立一种循序渐进、环环相扣的训练机制，使学生能够很快进入状态，适应规律写作任务。

2. 加速词汇积累：如前所述，词汇贫乏是中高级阶段表达能力的最大障碍，因此需要补充大量描述类的词汇。本教程词汇量较大，若沿用手写方式将无法在短期内达到以上教学效果。

3. 提高写作效率：传统的写作方式（作文、报告）通常需要时间思考准备，一般每学期 2—3 篇，频率低，收效有限。而本教程利用网记方式做"短频快"的例行限时写作练习（如 10—15 分钟写一个针对某话题的网记），有效地提高了学生的写作速度和交际技巧。限时命题的网记写作使学生逐渐适应了快速打写、集中思考的方式，因此在期末后测时能在限定的时间内顺利完成书面交际任务。

4. 强化认读能力：频繁的网记、作文等打写任务增加了学生认读汉字的机会，将语音、字形、词义联系在一起，在巩固新学词汇的同时也复习老词汇，有效地强化了汉字认读的能力。因此，在期末测试时打字准确率极高。

5. 作品资料集：按传统的做法，学生在完成写作后很容易丢失自己的作文。而网记工具将完成的各项写作都按时间顺序排列收集在一起，便于储

存管理，检索查找，也有助于复习。学期结束时，已积累了 10 多篇作品，给学生带来一种成就感。

6. 诊断与评估：网记自动生成的学生作文集还便于老师针对学生的写作问题进行诊断或对其语言进步进行评估。为教学方便，教师可用博客网页布置写作任务、建立典型错误数据库以便学生查阅，同时链接学生的博客网页（网记示例见附录 2）。

7. Quia 系统的测验工具使得网上定时写作、作业布置和收取、储存管理以及统一阅卷打印较网记和电邮更为便捷。从这一点上看，Quia 还可以更多地加以利用。

（四）学生反馈

期末问卷调查显示学生对用博客做规律性的写作反应良好，同时认为语块练习对表达流利度以及打字准确性也起到极大的促进作用。从以下学生评语中可看出对频繁写作任务的积极态度。

- "I was constantly writing so my typing and pinyin improved dramatically（由于不断地写，我的打字和拼音得到意想不到的提高）"

- "I especially liked the writing because writings，in my perspective，are a complex task that requiresvarious linguistic techniques/learnings（我特别喜欢教程的写作部分，因为在我看来，写作向来是一个需要语言技巧和知识的复杂任务）"

- "I really think my composition has improved greatly（我确实认为我的写作水平大有提高）"

- "I feel like I will be able to communicate more effectively now，because if I don't know what something is called，I can describe it（我觉得我能够更有效地与人沟通了，因为如果我不知道某物的名称时，那我也可以描述出来了）"

- "This course was more like learning the real life situations（这门课更像在学习实际生活情景）"

- "I like the blog entries. I just wish there was an easier way to have the teacher mark them up for the problems（我喜欢网记方式，只是希望有更容易的办法让老师能够将错处清楚标出）"

- "［I like］JOURNALS They forced me to really understand the grammar and how words were used. Really helpful！（我喜欢网记写作任务——因为可以迫使我真正认识语法结构以及词语的用法。确实很有帮助！）"

六　结语：教学总结提示

以上教学结果显示，打写为主、结合网络工具的技能训练模式可在较短的时间内有效地扩展学习者的主题词汇，使学习者的输出在质和量上迅速提升，在短期内达到甚至超过预期的结果。这说明用网络工具辅助技能训练模式的可行性和有效性，即使是非真实交流的网记写作仍然对学习者的技能起到积极推动作用。同时，学习者在输出上的突飞猛进也再次证明打写方式的成效大大优于传统手写方式（Zhang，1998；Xie，1999，2001；Kubler，2002；Xu，2005；He，2005）。有待进一步探讨的是，不同写作工具对输出质量和写作能力发展是否有不同影响。总之，中文书写技能的训练应与时代技术同步，不但能大大提高教学效率，也使训练更具针对性和实用性。

参考文献

ACTFL. （1999）. Preliminary Proficiency Guidelines-Speaking（Revised）.

ACTFL. （2001）. Preliminary Proficiency Guidelines-Writing（Revised）.

BBC News（2009）Children who use technology are 'better writers.' Available：http：//news. bbc. co. uk/2/hi/technology/8392653. stm.

Carla A. （2008）. Blogging in the language classroom：It doesn't "simply happen." TESL-EJ：The Electronic Journal for English as a Second Language. March 2008, 11 （4）. Available：http：//www. tesl-ej. org/wordpress/past-issues/volume11/ ej44/- ej44a3/.

Clark, C. &Dugdale, G. In collaboration with Booktrust （2009）. Young people's writing：Attitudes, behaviour and the role of technology. National Literacy Trust. Available：http：//www. literacytrust. org. uk/research/.

Edublogs. （2009）Blogging improves young people's confidence in their writing and reading. Available：http：//edu. blogs. com/edublogs/2009/12/.

Godwin-Jones, R. （2003）. Blogs and wikis：environments for on-line collaboration. Language Learning & Technology, 7 （2）, 12—16. Available：http：//llt. msu. edu/vol7num2/emerging/default. html.

He, W. （2005）Planning for the next generation Chinese language course：Construction and practice. Journal of Chinese Language Teaching and Research, 3, 57—60.

Jin, H （2009）Participatory learning in Internet Web Technology：A study of three web tools in the context of CFL learning. Journal of the Chinese Language Teachers Association, 44：1, Feb 2009.

Murray, L., &Hourigan T. (2006). Using micropublishing to facilitate writing in· the foreign language. In L. Ducate& N. Arnold (Eds.), Calling on CALL：From theory and research to new directions in foreign language teaching. CALICO Monograph Series, 5, 149—180.

Nagata, N. (1998). Input vs. output practice in educational software forsecond language acquisition. Language Learning & Technology, 1 (2), 23—40.

Nutta, J. (1998). Is computer-based grammar instruction as effective asteacher-directed grammar instruction for teaching L2 structures? CALICOJournal, 16 (1), 49—62.

Pew Internet. (2008) Writing, technology and teens. Pew Internet & American Life Project. Available：http：//www. pewinternet. org/Reports/2008/Writing-Technology-and-Teens. aspx.

Pinkman K. (2005). Using blogs in the foreign language classroom：encouraging learner independence. The JALT CALL Journal, 2005, 1, No. 1, 12—24.

Robb, T. (1996). The web as a tool for language learning. Journal of the Language Laboratory Association, Kansai Chapter, Vol. 6, pp. 1—11. Available：http：// www. cc. kyoto-su. ac. jp/—trobb/lla. html.

Soleimani, H, Ketabi, S. &Talebinejad, M. R. (2008). The noticing function of output in acquisition of rhetorical structure of contrast paragraphs of Iranian EFL university students. Linguistik Online, 34, 2. http：//www. linguistik-online. com/34 _ 08/soleimani. html.

Stone, B (2004). Who let the blogs out?：A hyperconnected peek at the world of weblogs. New York：St. Martin's Press.

Swain, M. (1985). Communicative competence：Some roles of comprehensible input and comprehensible output in its development. In S. Gass& C. Madden (Eds.), Input in second language acquisition (pp. 235—253). Rowley, MA：Newbury House.

Swain, M. (1995). Three functions of output in second language learning. In G. Cook, & B. Seidhofer (Eds.), Principles and practice in applied linguistics (pp. 125—144). Oxford：Oxford University Press.

Swain, M. (1998). Focus on form through conscious reflection. In C. Doughty & J. Williams (Eds.), Focus on form in classroom second language acquisition (pp. 64—81). Cambridge：Cambridge University Press.

Tan, Y., Teo, E. H., Wai L. A；& Lim, W. Y. (2005) Portfolio building in Chinese language learning using blogs. Singapore Ministry of Education.

Wang, D. (2010) 网络技术在高级汉语中的运用：VoiceThread, Voiceboard 和

Wiki. In D. Xu, J. Da& P. Zhang（Eds.）Proceedings of The 6th International Conference on Technology and Chinese Language Teaching（pp. 237—243）. National East Asian Languages Resource Center, The Ohio State University, Columbus.

Warschauer, M.（2010）. Invited commentary: New tools for teaching writing. Language Learning & Technology February 2010, Vol. 14, No. 1（pp. 3—8）, available at: http://llt. msu. edu/vol14num1/commentary. pdf.

Wiggins G. &McTighe J.（2005）Understanding by design. Alexandra, Virginia:? The Association for Supervision and Corriculum Development（ASCD）.

Wikiquote(2010). Crucible of Creativity(2005), http://en. wikiquote. org/wiki/Ward _ Cunningham.

Wilkins, D.（1972）? Linguistics in language teaching（p. 111）. London: Edward Arnold.

Xie, T.（1999）. Using computers in Chinese language teaching. In Madeline Chu（Ed.）, Mapping the Course of the Chinese Language Field, Chinese Language Teachers Association Monograph Series, 3. Kalamazoo, Michigan.

Xie, T.（2001）Digitizing for Chinese education: Using word processing software and the impact on pedagogy. Paper for the 2nd International Conference on Chinese Education and Technology, Taipei, Taiwan, December 2001.

Xie, T（2007a）Strategies and models of applying computer technology in Chinese language teaching. Proceedings of the 8th? International Symposium of Chinese Language Teaching. ? Beijing: Higher Education Press.

Xie, T.（2007b）. Blog, Wiki, Podcasting and Learning Chinese Language. Journal of Chinese Language Teachers Association, 42, No. 1.

Xu, D& Jin, H. G.（2009）网络参与式学习工具的评测. 2009 International Conference on Internet Chinese Education, Taipei（ICICE' 09）June 19, 2009.

Xu, P. & Jen, T. 2005. "Penless" Chinese language learning: A computer-assisted approach. Journal of the Chinese Lnaguage Teachers Association, 40, 25—42.

Zhang, D.（2009）Essay writing in a Mandarin Chinese WebCT discussion board. Foreign Language Annals, 42: 4, 721—741.

Zhang, P.（2009a）Video podcasting: Perspectives and prospects for Chinese mobile learning. Journal of the Chinese Language Teachers Association（JCLTA）, Feb. 2009, Vol. 44: 1, 51—67.

Zhang, P.（2009b）Developing Chinese fluency. Boston, Beijing, and Singapore: Cengage Learning.

Zhang, P.（2009c）Developing Chinese fluency-Online fluency enhancement program. Companion Website. http://biaoda. cengageasia. com, Boston, Beijing, and Singapore: Cengage Learning.

Zhang，P.（2010）Blogging as a tool for development of Chinese writing proficiency. In D. Xu，J. Da& P. Zhang（Eds.）Proceedings of The 6th International Conference on Technology and Chinese Language Teaching（pp. 273—281）. National East Asian Languages Resource Center，The Ohio State University，Columbus.

Zhang，Z.（1998）. CALL forChinese：Issues and practice. Journal of Chinese Language Teachers Association，33. 1，51—82.

附录1 《表达》网上流利强化练习课件： 语块练习及错字反馈（Zhang，2009c）

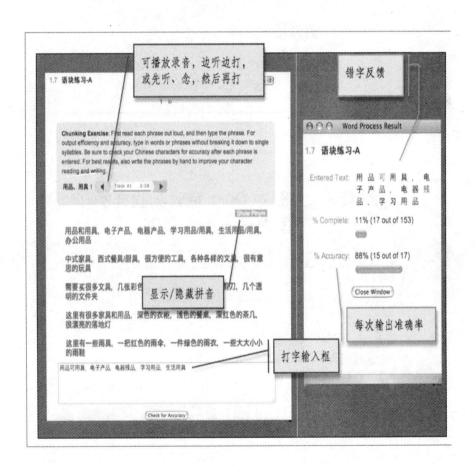

附录2　左图为教师博客网页示例
（含写作任务、学生网页链接）

右图为学生小作文样例（作者：Skye）。

附录3　上图为 Quia 定时测验样例，
下图为统一阅卷页面

U1-L2-miaoshu_fanglan

因为我现在只是一个大学生，所以我觉得现在的房间对大学生的生活水平来说已经不错了。不过我还是有一点不太满意，是得可以对房间做一些改变。现在的房间有一个卧室，一个客厅，和一个厨房。厨房又矮又小，放不下桌子，只可以在客厅里放一张桌子。客厅又宽又大，有两个小沙发，一个大沙发，一张圆形的桌子，有一张电脑桌子，还有一把椅子，可是，两个小沙发不太舒服，还有一点破旧。房间的墙不够明亮，太过阴了，都是米白色的。墙壁的颜色我也不太喜欢，是现金黄色的。房间也有一个小小卧室，卧室里放了放两张小的床。

首先，我希望把一间办公室。加了办公室以后，我就想把厨房变得更大一点。然后可以把那桌放置在卧室里。我还想把两张小沙发换成大的沙发，然后把墙壁换一些花花绿绿的颜色。对我一些简。我也希望把墙帘带换深色的，然后再把卧室加变一点。

Comments:

U1-L2-miaoshu_anna

这个房子又宽又大，墙的颜色都是米白色和灰色的，家具是房的或者米色的，沙发又宽又厚，颜色跟地板一模一样，地毯是太长方的，不够圆，感上有一种书架，可是里面只有一些花瓶，整个房子没有什么图案花纹，颜色也很沉闷，单调。

我想把墙帘或花花绿绿的。那样房子会变的很鲜艳，明快。我也想把书架换成新的有用的，把一些花儿在花瓶里。沙发和地毯应该变窄了，还得买一张小桌儿。

Comments:

U1-L2-miaoshu_吉丹妮

我对现在的客厅不太满意。我的客厅有一张橙色的桌儿，还有一个灰色的沙发，我认为沙发变得很好看，但是我不太喜欢桌儿的颜色，我的地毯又窄又短，我想改变一下，我的房间里的花纹很像子的，还有我的墙上有一张黑色的图画，在我的房间里还有一个米白色的衣柜，但是我认为我很想太矮了。因为我的客厅有那么多我不喜欢的东西，所以我想做改变一下。

我不太喜欢我的桌儿的颜色，所以我会把颜色变成黑色的，然后我会换我的沙发的沙发因为我现在太小了，我想把我的地毯变得更宽。我喜欢我的米黄得花枝，但是我不太喜欢床罩的颜色，所以我会把颜色变成灰绿的，我想把图画的颜色变更的，在我的房间里我的衣柜不够高，所以我想把这样子的衣柜换成高的。我认为这样作可能对我更满意。

Comments:

"中美文化交流咖啡室"：文化教学在网络平台上的实践与思考[*]

China-USA Culture Exchange Café: Practice and Reflections on Teaching Culture on the Web

姜　松　Jiang, Song　美国夏威夷大学

University of Hawaii at Mānoa United States sjiang@ hawaii. edu

近年来，文化的导入正在成为第二语言教学研究所关注的课题。有关第二语言文化教学的研究显示第二语言文化的导入对于学习者在目的语环境中能否成功地完成交际任务起着至关重要的作用。对于第二语言教育者来说，语言课程上文化导入的最大挑战在于如何为学习者在母语文化和目的语文化之间建立起沟通的桥梁，如何有效地突破第二语言交际中存在的文化屏障。网络语言教学的成熟和完善使传统的课堂得到了前所未有的延伸，也为第二语言的文化教学提供了新的可能。

本文通过对夏威夷大学研发的中美文化网络对话平台"中美文化交流咖啡室"的概括介绍和试用结果分析，展示"咖啡室"为文化教学设计的一系列中美学生网上互动任务，如文化词汇系联、完成句子、情境应对、真实语言材料的研习和反思、自由论坛等，阐明网络平台在文化教学中所发挥的搭建桥梁和突破屏障的作用，探讨试用过程中出现的问题和改进措施。

本文认为网络平台上的文化互动不仅能够使中美英汉两种语言的学习者通过网上任务的完成，分享、反思和深化对彼此文化的理解，提高目的语的表达与交际能力，而且能够实现语言及文字能力的共同提高。

---

[*] 本文初稿曾于2010年6月在"第六届国际汉语电脑教学研讨会"上报告，对与会者的反馈意见特此致谢。感谢匿名评审专家提出的建设性修改意见。感谢王海丹老师和唐润（Stephen Tschudi）老师为本文提供学生交流的原始资料，感谢他们通读本文初稿和修改稿并提出修改建议。

一　第二语言教学中文化的导入

文化的界定一直是学界富有争议的问题。早在19世纪末，英国人类学家 Edward B. Tylor（1871）就曾给文化做出了一个极为宽泛的定义："文化是一个复杂的整体，它包括知识、信仰、艺术、道德、法律、习俗以及作为一个社会成员的个人所获得的能力与习惯。"进入20世纪以来，关于文化的命题及其作用成为诸多社会科学关注的焦点。人类学家、社会学家、语言学家以及语言教育家都试图从各自学科的角度对文化及其作用做出适应于其需要的定义和解释。语言教育家 Brooks（1968）将宽泛的文化概念具体定位在下列五个方面：人的生长、人的完善、文学与艺术、生活模式和生命之道的总和。从语言教学的角度，Brooks 认为，作为生活模式的文化与语言教学有着最直接的关联。他把生活模式定义为在典型的生活情景中人们特有的符合社会团体所期许的思维、信仰、语言以及相应的一系列的行为方式。语言教育家 Kramsch（1998）进一步阐述了语言与文化密不可分的关联，她把语言与文化的关系表述为：语言表达文化现实；语言体现文化现实；语言象征文化现实。Lange（1998）从外语教学的角度更明确地提出文化是语言的一部分，语言也是文化的一部分。

基于语言与文化的密切关联，Krasner（1999）对语言能力进行了重新的界定，指出语法形式和它的实际应用反映了一个社会的文化价值。语法形式与结构上的能力并不代表语言的实际应用能力。实现成功的语言交际必须要与恰当的文化行为联系起来。90年代中期，美国外语教学协会（ACTFL）在其主持制定的外语教学国家标准中，提出在外语教学课程中增加文化导入的要求，并把文化教学（cultures）与语言的交流（communication）、联系（connections）、对比（comparisons）和团体运用（communities）并列为国家外语教育的五大目标。这一标准将语言课程中文化教学的目标确定为通过语言的学习，使学生掌握和理解这一语言所处的文化。这样的目标打破了以往以语法形式为主体的语言教学模式，将文化提升到了与语法形式同等重要的高度，并重新定义了衡量学习者是否掌握所学语言的标准，即语言学习者只有掌握语言所处的文化才能真正掌握这门语言（American Council on the Teaching of Foreign Languages，1996）。

在 ACTFL 外语教学国家标准的倡导下，语言教育者开始关注在语言教学中进行文化导入的问题，开始尝试将文化内容整合到语言教学的课程设计和活动安排之中。但在具体的教学实践中，作为一个新的教学目标，文化教学还存在着许多需要完善的地方。Yu（2009）对七种当前流行的初级汉语课本的文化部分进行了分析。分析结果表明尽管这些课本对文化都有不同程度的涉及，但总体上文化在课本中仍然处于附加的"注释"地位，还远没有成为教学的核心要素。这样的现状说明，文化教学依然是汉语教学中的一个薄弱环节。我们认为语言教学中文化导入的最大的挑战在于如何发现隐藏在语法形式背后的关乎交际成败的文化内容，以显性的形式将这些文化内容呈现给学生。这一挑战对于正值发展中的汉语教学来说更显得尤为突出。如何在语言教学中实现形式与文化的结合是文化教学成功与否的关键。Kramsch（1993）认为在进行文化导入的过程中，外语教育者不应将带有自己主观判断的目的语文化简单地输入给学生，而应将语言课堂变成由学习者自主感知、探索、发现、反思目的语与母语文化异同的开放的园地。网络技术在语言教学上的完善使传统的语言课堂得到了前所未有的延伸，也为实现Kramsch所倡导的文化教学原则提供了新的可能。

二　Cultura：网络文化教学的模式

在众多网络文化教学的研究与实践中，美国麻省理工学院和法国 L' I Institut National de Télécommunications 共同研发的 *Cultura* 跨文化交际项目（Furstenberg，G.，Levet，S.，English，K.，& Maillet，K.，2001）为网络平台上的文化教学提供了一个值得借鉴的样本。*Cultura* 是一个为在美国学习法语和在法国学习英语的学生建立的跨文化网络交际平台，目的是通过美国与法国学生完成网上任务型互动活动，发现、感受、理解和反思母语和所学目的语的异同，实现对目的语文化态度、思想信仰、交际方式和世界观的深入了解。借用 *Cultura* 大纲中的表述，"*Cultura* 旨在帮助学生获取另一双眼睛，通过这双别人的眼睛来看待宇宙世界。"在这一平台上，美国和法国学生主要通过张贴、阅读、评价、讨论等方式来完成由媒体文字、图片、电影、语言现象为基础而设计的文化教学任务。

文化对比是 *Cultura* 中各种任务的设计核心。*Cultura* 的研发者认为一种语法形式的文化含义只有在它与另一种文化发生碰撞时才能得到充分的彰显。对比是揭示文化内涵的有效方法。通过网络平台，*Cultura* 将来自于不同文化的同类资料，包括报纸广告、图片、系联词语等以对比排列的方式呈现给学生，从而突出隐性的文化内容，加速学习者对不同文化间异同的感知。

Cultura 另一个富有特色的设计是为学生搭建起一个各自用母语来充分

表达思想的平台，提供给学生一个直接接触交流对象用母语所作的张贴，即自己所学目的语的张贴的机会。也就是说，美国学生用英文，法国学生用法文来张贴，然后阅读彼此的张贴并进行讨论，讨论中依旧遵循各自使用母语的原则。这样设计的一个优势在于网络平台上出现的所有张贴的语言都处于母语水平，从而保证了作为真实阅读材料的张贴的语言质量，弥补了学生由目的语水平不足而造成的表达困难，也避免了以目的语交流的学习模式中常见的中介语误导问题。

此外，*Cultura* 还实现了 Kramsch 所提出的文化教学应该遵循由学习者自主发现和感知的教学原则。*Cultura* 中的交流任务是遵循构建教学法的原则而设计的。这些任务并不以单纯的文化输入为目的，而是通过对包含文化焦点的文字、图片、电影等材料的观察、比较和分析，启发学生自行发现、归纳、生成应该理解和掌握的文化现象，并通过对比、反思和讨论使之转化为目的语文化系统的一部分。这种教学方式避免了传统课堂上对外语文化的机械输入，使学生在完成以发现和领悟文化内涵为目的的网络任务过程中，自主生成和构建属于自己的目的语文化系统。

三 "中美文化交流咖啡室"的设计与试用

借鉴 *Cultura* 的成功经验，夏威夷大学于 2008 年初启动了"中美文化交流咖啡室"的项目开发，旨在推动汉语文化教学在网络上的实践。研发工作由本校东亚系王海丹、唐润（Stephen Tschudi）和笔者共同担当。建立这一网络咖啡室的目标是探索中文第二语言文化教学在网络平台的实践方法、使学生通过参与网站的任务型活动，在中美文化互动，母语文化反思及中英语言习得等方面取得成果。

（1）"中美文化交流咖啡室"的主体活动

"中美文化交流咖啡室"采纳 *Cultura* 的教学模式，立足于通过探索和发现实现跨文化学习的设计原则，把文化学习在网络平台上的实现过程具体划分为以下五个步骤：接触文化素材、张贴个人回应、观察与分析、交流与讨论以及自我反思。

"中美文化交流咖啡室"选用了由夏威夷大学国家外语资源中心（National Foreign Language Resource Center）开发的 BRIX 外语教学网络系统作为技术平台。在"咖啡室"主体内容的设计上，为配合通过探索发现文化的教学原则，结合实施效果和技术的可行性，我们选取了以下几种任务类型作为"咖啡室"的主体活动：①文化词语联想，②完成句子，③情境应对，

④真实语言材料的研习和反思，⑤语言诊所，以及⑥自由论坛。各项活动的设计思想和主要内容如下：

1. 文化词语联想

文化词汇联想是一种能迅速揭示文化差异的有效方法。不同文化背景的人为同一提示词所提供的不同的关联词能够反映出个人及其所处的文化社团对提示词所代表的概念在认知和理解上的差别。这一部分的任务是请学生先看由网站提供的提示词，然后在每个提示词下写出至少五个由提示词引发的、在学生头脑中即刻出现的系联词。这一任务有中文和英文两个版本。同一个提示词概念分别用中英两种文字表述。中国学生使用中文版本、美国学生使用英文版本。例如，中文版的提示词包括：关系、礼节、送礼、上司、上级、老板、同事、关系网、朋友、同学、地位；对应的英文版为：relationships, etiquette, gift-giving, supervisor, boss, colleague, network, friend, schoolmate, classmate, status. 网站对中国和美国学生提交的关联词按出现频率进行统计，并以列表形式提交给学生，作为下一步双方交流讨论的基础。

2. 完成句子

这一部分的任务是由"咖啡室"提供启发式的未完成的句子，要求学生为每个未完成的句子用三种不同的内容来补齐。每一种回答都需要学生根据自己的真实想法得出。这一任务同样也由中英文两个版本组成，分别服务于中国和美国学生。例如，中文版本的句子提示包括：（a）怎么样才算一个成功的人？我觉得……（b）一个理想的工作应该是……（c）我给礼物的目的是……（d）谈自己看法的时候，重要的是……对应的英文版本为：（a）A successful person is one who... （b）A good job is one that... （c）The reason I give gifts is... （d）When giving your own opinion, it is important to... 网站对中国和美国学生提交的回答进行统计和整理，并将结果反馈给学生，作为双方下一步交流讨论的材料。

3. 情景应对

这一部分的任务是以论坛讨论的形式进行的。教师给出一个情景任务，要求中美学生分别作出回应，提供解决问题的具体方法。这一任务也是由中英文两个版本组成。例如，在"送礼物"这一主题下，教师提出下面一个情景，要求学生按自己的想法提出应对。中英文版的情景提示如图1所示。

教师对中美学生的回答进行归纳和整理后交给学生进行下一步的分析，并要求学生就中美学生看法中有意思、有争议的地方展开开放式的互动讨论。

4. 真实语言材料的研习和反思

唐老师 UH Manoa 	2009-02-10 09:47:00.0 你是一个中型公司的办公室职员。春节快到了。请你说一说你会给谁准备礼物，准备什么样的礼物，给每个人礼物的时候说些什么话（或在每个人的卡片上写什么）。
王老师 University of Hawaii 	2009-01-26 10:28:00.0 You are an office worker in a medium-sized company in California. It's getting towards Christmastime. Tell us what gifts you have chosen to buy, to whom you are going to give them, and what you will say to each person when you present your gift (or maybe what you will write on the card).

图 1　中英文情景应对任务截图

这一部分的活动设计是首先选出能体现中美文化差异的图片、广告、电影片段作为讨论提示，要求中美双方的学生对所给材料进行对比学习，然后在论坛中用母语阐述自己的分析理解。接下来阅读其他同学的张贴，找出有争议、有分歧的地方并给予回应。例如，在这一部分中我们设计了一个比较中美招聘广告异同的任务。任务首先要求学生学习和比较两篇真实的中美工作招聘广告，然后按步骤在下面几个论坛中进行探讨。在"语言问题"专栏提出关于中英文招聘广告中的词语、语法、内容等方面的问题，由教师或同学给予解答。在"相似与分歧"专栏中，找出两个广告在格式、内容、招聘条件、语体风格等方面的相同和不同，然后与中美两方同学分享自己的观察和体会。在"讨论与交流"专栏中，中美同学一起讨论为什么这两个广告会存在异同，造成这种异同的深层原因是什么，这些异同反映了中国和美国怎样的社会心态和价值观。

5. 语言诊所

"语言诊所"部分主要是为了帮助中美学生克服在学习文化提示材料过程中遇到的语言难点和理解障碍。这一专栏实际上贯穿在所有的任务型活动之中，可以看成是文化教学中的语言教室。学生在这一专栏中提出语言方面的问题，教师针对学生的问题给予解答，并根据学生的需要提出语言学习的建议。

6. 自由论坛

自由论坛是一个开放式的、跨任务型活动的交际平台。它为中美学生提供了一个不局限于某一具体任务，自由交流的场所。在这里，中美学生可以就自己感兴趣的任何有关目的语的问题向目的语文化的"专家"，即自己的跨文化交流对象请教。同时这里也可以作为中美学生的一个交友平台，使学生将跨文化学习延伸到个人的生活之中。

（2）"中美文化交流咖啡室"的试用

完成了咖啡室的基础搭建后，于 2008 年夏季和 2009 年春季，我们分别进行了两次试用。在 2008 年夏季学期，7 名来自中国中山大学美国工商管理硕士课程、刚刚到达夏威夷大学的中国交换学生和 10 名夏威夷大学商学院攻读中国方向工商管理硕士学位的美国学生参加了试用。7 名中方交换学生的英文能力均通过夏威夷大学国际学生入学最低托福标准。10 名美方学生的中文水平，以 ACTFL 标准划分为三个等级，2 名为 Advanced，4 名为 Intermediate High/Mid，4 名为 Intermediate Low。在 2009 春季学期，有 18 名夏威夷大学中文班的同学作为美方学员参加了试用。18 名美方学员的中文水平，以 ACTFL 标准分为三个等级，5 名 Advanced to Intermediate High，3 名 Intermediate Mid，10 名 Intermediate Low。15 名中方学员为中国天津对外经贸职业学院的大学二年级学生。他们的专业包括国际贸易、物资流通以及商务英文。中方学员的英文水平均通过中国大学英语四级。

鉴于美方学员的中文水平存在不同等级，"咖啡室"在中文语言能力方面为美国学员设置了三个不同的学习目标。Intermediate Low 的学生需要在每个主题单元中学会使用至少 10 个新词汇，能利用这些新词语以完整句子的方式来比较中美文化之间的相同与不同。Intermediate High/Mid 水平的学生需要在每个主题单元中学会使用至少 20 个新词汇，并能利用新词语以段落方式表达自己对于中美文化异同的理解和思考。Advanced 阶段的学生需要根据自己在这个交流网站中的经验，以段落篇章的方式，对于中美文化现象的不同方面进行比较和分析，根据个人看法阐述导致这些差异的原因，说明自己对现象背后的深层思考。同时能够有意识地运用从"咖啡室"中学到的文化知识来矫正自己在目的语环境中的语言行为。

（3）词汇联想的试用结果

词汇联想是试用中相当成功的一项活动。从自己提供的系联词中，中美学生观察到大量的文化现象和观念。他们在对比分析和交流讨论中通过具体例证切实了解到同一词汇在不同文化中可能代表着完全不同的概念，表面对应的一个词可能在中英不同的文化中存在着不同的语义场，中英文母语使用者对同一个词可能会有不同的、甚至截然相反的解读。这些由学生自主发现的文化认知也赋予了他们进一步探究背后成因的动力。

例如在"gift-giving/送礼"的词语联想活动中，学生发掘和获取了中英文词语背后的文化内涵及形成的原因。活动开始，中美学生为每个提示词提交各自独立联想得到的系联词，教师对学生提交的系联词进行统计整理，并以图 2 的形式提供给学生作为分析的材料。

Word Association compiled results: China and US students Spring 2009
n=total number of replies received for the given query (each respondent gave a few replies)

Query 3: gift-giving n=74	Query 2: 送礼 n=85
birthday (7)	过年过节 (5)
Christmas (7)	过生日 (5)
caring (4)	礼尚往来 (5)
holiday (4)	办事 (4)
love (4)	谋求 (4)
generous (3)	朋友 (3)
thoughtful (3)	友好 (3)
celebration (2)	亲情 (3)
friendship (2)	婚姻财礼 (2)
fun (2)	贿赂 (2)
gratitude (2)	走后门 (2)
happy (2)	选择 (2)
kids (2)	钱 (2)
money (2)	串亲戚
obligation (2)	书
presents (2)	关爱

图 2　中美学生"gift-giving/送礼"词语联想统计结果

通过对系联词汇及其出现频率的研读，学生们能快速捕捉到中美双方对提示词理解的共同点和分歧，对形成这些异同的原因进行解读，进而形成新的文化认知。例如美国学生不仅注意到中美系联词的共同点："the top two words associated from the American students were 'Birthday' and 'Christmas'; the top two words associated from the Chinese students were 'Celebrating the New Year and Holidays' and 'Birthday'"，也注意到存在的分歧："The Chinese students made more associations with seeking help or favors, giving bribes, etc., while the American students made associations with emotion, responsibility, etc." "Chinese students used 办事 in response to gift giving. The association between gift giving and business seems to be stronger in China."

中国学生在注意到中美双方系联关系的差异的同时，进一步反思出现差异的原因，调整对自己文化和目的语文化的认知。例如："在'送礼'这个问题中，中国人更多的想到的是求人办事，贿赂等，而外国人更多的想到的是感情，责任等。""中国的学生有很多人写道'礼尚往来''贿赂''办事'等这些用钱或礼物的形式收买人内心或用钱来达到自己的目的的词语，而其他国家的学生根本就没有'贿赂'等这样的词语，都是些'happy''fun''thoughtful'这样的词语，这至少说明，起码在美国学生心中，贿赂在自己的国家是很少见的，而我们的同学却能轻而易举地想出这样的词语，证明这种现象在中国很常见！""这说明中美文化之间的差异往往也取决于社会现状和利益习惯等方面。中国人讲究'礼尚往来'，也就是说，付出是要有回报的。美国同学们则更注重感情，功利性较小。"

除了获取对词汇联想中提示词的深层理解外，学生们通过中美文化的对比，对目的语的普遍词汇特点也表现出新的认识。例如，在接触美国同学提出的英文系联词过程中，中国同学得出这样的印象："中文的词义比较单一明确，英文单词有许多都是一词多解。在不同的题中出现相同的单词。而且由于文化的不同，中国同学和美国同学对相同词的理解也不同。"虽然这一中国学生对中文词语同样具有多义性的认识有失偏颇，但可以看出词汇系联任务在启发学生对已经学过的英文词汇的意义进行深层次的探究、了解英文一词多义的现象方面还是发挥了积极的作用，并促使他们寻求进一步的解释。例如在分析"关系"的系联词中，中国同学注意到："美国同学用 nature。我不理解的是，这个词指的是人和自然的关系还是人与人之间很自然和谐的关系？这可能也体现了英文单词一词多解的一方面。"显然，前一位中国同学关于"中文的词义比较单一明确"的结论并不符合汉语词汇的事实，这种错觉的产生可能是因为对母语是中文的中国学生来说，他们对汉语的一词多义现象由于母语的原因本来就不那么敏感，而对由交流对象输入的作为新信息的目的语的一词多义现象则会有比较强的意识。这从一个侧面也说明互动对比对构建目的语的词汇意义系统具有一定的强化作用。另外，中国同学对英文特有的文化历史对美国同学选择系联词的影响也能有所注意："在'关系'的系联中，美国同学会联想到 church 和 God，这说明宗教在他们文化中的重要性。"

另一方面，中国同学提交的较为生僻的系联词也激发了美国同学学习新词语，探究相关文化背景的兴趣，从而起到增加中文词汇量，扩大知识面的效果。例如，"I saw a word'脑白金'in the 送礼 query. I asked my Chinese friend what was that. She told me that is a product which is made in China. It is very famous because of its Advertisement. May be the advertisement already influenced Chinese people. So, they think'送礼'='脑白金'. Interesting！"

（4）真实语言材料对比分析的试用结果

在真实语言材料的研习和反思部分，来自真实语料的中美招聘广告对比分析也为试用提供了一个成功的案例。

在这项任务中，中国和美国学生通过两份广告的初步对比，都能准确地捕捉到两份广告的不同。中国学生认识到："中文招聘中有性别、年龄、婚姻状况、身高的限制，而英文招聘中没有。""中国人要求的外表条件太多了，包括身高婚姻状况、形象好气质佳，而美国招聘广告没有如此的要求，足可见以貌取人这个缺点在中国广泛存在。""中国的公司大部分都只招收有相关工作经验的，而美国公司则不是，我很惊讶美国公司会给员工专门的培训。""外国的招聘却更注重个人掌握语言和工作的能力。"美国同学对两份广告的异同也表达了同样的体会："The first thing that struck me about the Chinese ad was that it was biased in wanting a female secretary, whereas, the USA ad wasn't as specific. I think the US company was trying to avoid being biased in order not to be blamed for 'sex discrimination,' since men can be secretaries too.""The Chinese ad was more concerned about personal qualities, rather than elaborating on the job description.""Although the USA ad wanted certain job skills, they were willing to train. However, the Chinese ad wanted a secretary with at least one year of experience."

在发现异同的基础上，中美同学对造成这些异同的原因展开了进一步的讨论，并认识到造成这种差异的社会基础。例如，中国同学写道："这种差异是跟各国的国情和传统文化有关的。相对于应聘者远远多于岗位的情况下，中国的招聘可以有挑剔的选择权。而外国的招聘广告明显更加开放。""在招聘广告上可以看出西方注重实际，而中方注重福利，而造成这种现象的深层原因就是人民的生活水平与上下级关系方面的种种情况。这种现象反映到了中国民众与企业更加注重福利来吸引员工工作，而西方则注重能力与技术来争取员工的加盟。中方更加注重金钱价值观，西方更加注重企业价值观。中方注重自己的实际生活，西方注重企业的发展。"

美国同学也基于自己的文化，提出自己的看法："I find it interesting that although the students in Tianjin noticed the differences between the job ads regarding personal appearance requirements, none of them mentioned one underlying reason for that difference: namely, that in the United States (and in other industrialized nations) it is illegal to make requirements for job positions that are not related to the job duties themselves. For example, in advertising for a secretary, "Selecting an individual based on outward appearances is foolish and inefficient. Height, appearance, marital status, and age have no correlation with the ability to produce in the workplace. Using such hiring practices is not only discriminatory but could produce disastrous results as choosing 'beauty' over 'brains' could directly affect the profit level of a company in a negative way. "

论坛的设置也为中美同学之间的直接对话提供了舞台，促使讨论的深入发展。例如，在回应中国同学认为中国众多的人口是造成招聘竞争激烈原因的观点，美国同学将讨论推进到企业自由与社会发展的关系，并对自己的母语文化进行了颇有深度的反思："I agree with your response that *Cultural* differences were apparent. I think it is interesting that Chinese companies have more freedom to require specific personality traits and physical appearances. It makes me question who is more free to do what. Where we have been restricted, Chinese companies have been given freedom. It seems the meaning of a 'free country' is more complex than I once thought. However, in business, sometimes what appears to be 'free' is really just a lack of oversight in the regulatory policies of the country. I wonder if this creates problems for different societal groups to find employment, such as older generations or less attractive persons. It would be a shame if all industries employed beautiful dummies (like Hollywood does) rather than a group of skilled workers with various physical characteristics. "

成功有效的跨文化交际不仅依赖于交流者对目的语文化的深刻理解，也在一定程度上取决于交流者对自己母语文化的认知程度，特别是经过对比和反思之后形成的对母语文化的新的认知更能使交流者攫取到那些通常不易察觉到的、蕴于深层的跨文化内涵（Wang, 2010）。真实语言材料论坛为实现这种跨文化的深层认知提供了可能。从前面所引的两段美国学生的张贴中，可以看出学生对论坛中所涉及的文化现象的认识经历了一个视角转换的过程：即从基于母语经验的对目的语文化的客观评价到基于目的语文化的对母语文化的主动的重新审视。对母语文化和目的语文化的深入认识甚至全新发现正是在这种视角转换的过程中得以实现的。因此，可以说论坛帮助学生获取了另一双"眼睛"，通过这双别人的"眼睛"他们不仅能够了解目的语文化，也能对自己的母语文化获取新的认识，并在两方面互动的过程中形成对文化的深入理解。

在与英文广告的对比中，中国学生对熟悉的中文应聘广告形成了具有批判性的新的认识，为实现 *Cultura* 模式所提倡的"通过另外一双眼重新认识自我"提供了又一个例证。例如，针对中文广告中的问题，中国学生反思道："外国的广告相对于求职者较人性化，能让求职者完全了解且明确自己是否合适此职位，非常详细。中国的广告简洁有的地方虽然只是几个字但却完全能表明达意，可有的地方不是很详细，让人觉得模糊。""美国职场更加重视能力和多国语言能力。在这一方面我觉得中国人应该向美国人学习，为了经济和社会的发展，我们不应该把目光只放在人们的外表，更应该重视一个人为公司创造财富的能力。""如果每个公司都要求有一年的工作经验，那么刚从大学毕业的大学生如何求职，这是一个很重大的问题，公司企业想着的只是用现成的人才，而不是去好好的培训新人让更多的人有经验起来，我认为这是缺乏社会责任感的表现。我国政府应该想办法改变这种现象。"

咖啡室中真实语料的使用也在弥补语言学习中课本知识的局限性方面发挥了很大的作用。例如，首次阅读英文广告后，很多中国学生根据自己课本中所学的英文语法得出了这是一篇有英文语法错误的广告，进而动手对英文广告中的用词和语言进行修改。例如"Date Listed：02-Jun-08 规范的写法应该是 June 8，2002"、"Skill requirements 应该是 Skills Required"、"Computer use 改为 Computer using"、"Significant of memory 改为 good memory""'Experience：Will train' 应该是 'Experience：Have or have not is ok'"针对这些误解，教师在语法诊所中对中国学生提出的英文语法问题进行解答，并对英文广告特有的语体风格给予了说明。从中国同学对教师讲解的反馈中，可以看到语法诊所的作用和教学效果："Thank you so much for letting us know the real ad，it's my first time ever to read the real one，i do benefit a lot from ur responses，it's a great opportunity for us to learn the native thing. ""我看到您说明所给出的英文招聘广告是真实准确无误的，感到很诧异，这体现我们缺乏对于书本的知识与实际生活的差异方面的学习。"

四 对网络平台上文化教学的思考

从前面对中美学生试用结果的分析中，我们可以看出"中美文化交流咖啡室"是引导中英文学习者通过网上互动跨入文化交际殿堂的一个有效平台，是实现 Kramsch 所倡导的"通过探索发现文化"的教学原则的可行途径。

传统课堂上文化的教学常常局限于教师的单一视角的文化输入，缺乏学习者母语文化与目的语文化之间的直接碰撞和交流，而跨文化网络交际平台则将每一个跨文化交际活动的参与者都赋予了文化教师的责任，为交流双方提供了一个从母语为目的语的交流对象身上了解多层次和多视角的目的语文化的机会。

在网络平台上的文化教学也颠覆了教师作为文化权威的传统定位，赋予教师文化交流辅助者的身份，使教师的注意力转移到保证学生顺利沟通、清除理解障碍、协调构建目的语文化系统，促进反思母语文化的任务上。这样的教师定位，给学生在学习中留下了发挥主导作用的空间，使学生不仅成为有效的目的语文化的吸取者，也使他们以母语文化专家的身份在文化交流的过程中承担起输出母语文化的责任。

从网络平台上文化教学的实际效果来看，有的放矢的任务型活动对实现第二语言文化教学的目的起着重要的作用。通过任务型互动活动的完成，中美双方学生的文化意识都得到了深化。学生们在探索、理解和掌握目的语文化知识的同时，也扩展了所学目的语的语言学知识，使得文化知识和语言技能得到同步提高。

中美学生深入的讨论和交流也说明以文化对比为特色的跨文化网络交际有助于揭示文化的差异，精确理解与目的语紧密交织的文化内涵，探索造成差异的社会与文化原因，有助于促进学习者文化解码能力的提高。

咖啡室的设计和试用在显示出潜力的同时，也反映出现存的困难和有待完善之处。

跨语言的母语交际对交流双方目的语的阅读水平具有较高的要求，目的语阅读理解能力的高低直接影响到交流的成败和质量。在我们进行的两次试用中，交流双方目的语水平的差异对交流效果都产生了一定的负面影响。美方学生从初级高到高级等至少三个不同级别的中文水平，造成美方同学在完成中文语言相关活动时无法做到步调一致，无法保证所有同学同时开始深层次的讨论交流。中国学生的英文水平虽然比较整齐，但明显高于美国学生的中文水平，使得中国学生能较好地理解美国学生，而美国学生则对中国学生的理解存在着较多的困难。这一现象给美国同学造成了一定的心理负担。初中级中文水平的美国学生对中国同学中文张贴的不完全理解，也限制了他们对讨论的参与。未来在组织类似的交流时，应当充分考虑参与者的目的语水平，挑选目的语水平相当的对象参加，以避免上述问题，获得更好的交流效果。值得注意的是，在原先的 *Cultura* 美法文化交流模式中，虽然交流双方学生的目的语水平也有所不同，但这一情况并没有对美法学生的交流和互动造成太大的困难，也没有让水平较低的同学感到明显的不胜任。相反交流双方因语言水平不对等而造成的互动与心理困难在中美文化咖啡室的试用中则表现得比较突出。导致这一差异的原因可能是由于法语和英文在类型学上比较接近，语言学上的差别比较小，双方在理解和沟通中遇到的障碍比较少。相反中英文在类型学上的距离比较远，语言学上的共同性相对美法文来说比较少，双方在交流与互动的过程中对阅读能力与汉字识别与书写的依赖性更强。因此在设计中美文化交流活动中必须考虑到中英文的语言特点和交流双方的实际目的语语言能力。

除目的语水平以外，交流双方的年龄、阅历、专业、年级等非语言因素对跨文化交际的深入与否也产生一定的影响。比如，在 2009 年春季学期的中美文化咖啡室的试用中，中国方面的学生均为大学本科二年级的学生，且没有人具有海外留学经历。而美方的参与者为大学四年级本科生和硕士研究生，其中很多人具有海外留学的经历，不少人还具有一定的工作经验。此外，双方所学的专业也有很大的不同。这种年龄、阅历与所学专业的不对等为双方的交流设置了一定的心理困难，在一定程度上阻碍了讨论的深入。对比中美双方学生的张贴，不难发现中国学生的张贴比较趋于对表面现象的对比、易于很快得出封闭式的结论，从而快速结束讨论；而美国学生的张贴则比较强于思辨、善于怀疑、长于得出开放式的结论，使讨论有意犹未尽之感。因此未来在挑选中美文化交流的参与者时，为获取最佳的交流效果，一定要充分考虑到交流双方的年龄、阅历以及专业年级的对等性。

中美双方不同的学期设置、时差等给寻求适合双方的最佳交流时间造成一定的困难。我们进行的这两次试用，都是在中美教师对这一项目的共同兴趣和个人互信基础上进行。而未来，如果将其作为正式的交流项目，则需要得到中美双方学院的积极支持和配合，也需要制定长期的项目规划。中美双方需要对各方面的协调组织，时间的配合、中方教师的培训、学生网站使用培训以及学生网上活动的质量监控等方面需要给予特别的关注，需要建立一系列具体的实施目标和可行的操作程序。

现有的"中美文化咖啡室"还不是一个能够完全独立的网络文化课程，目前仅仅作为一个文化教学的辅助性工具来使用。将这样一个平台正式课程化还有相当多的工作需要完成。特别是平台中现有的任务型活动的数量还不够多，不能满足一个学期正式课程的需要。未来，咖啡室需要补充更多实用有效的任务型网络活动，在可能的条件下，继续探索和扩充新的任务类型。

虽然本文报告的"中美文化咖啡室"的设计和运行是我们在网络平台上对文化教学进行的一次初步尝试，但试行中的实践经验无疑为进一步的改进提供了建设性的参考意见、为这一模式的完善积累了可资借鉴的材料。这一尝试也展示出了 *Cultura* 原型的推广前景，为这一模式在其他语言文化教学上的应用提供了一个具体的实例。此外，我们的尝试也表明网络平台上的跨文化交流可以为文化教学的研究积累丰富的原始材料，为进一步的理论探索奠定基础。

参考文献

American Council on the Teaching of Foreign Languages. (1996). *Standards for foreign language learning: preparing for the 21ˢᵗ century.* Lawrence, KS: Allen Press, Inc.

Brooks, N. (1968). Teaching culture in the foreign language classroom. *Foreign language Annuals*, Vol. 1, No. 3, 204—217.

Furstenberg, G., Levet, S., English, K., & Maillet, K. (2001). Giving a virtual voice to the silent language of culture: The *Cultura* Project. *Language Learning and Technology* 5. 1, 55—100.

Kramsch, C. (1993). *Context and culture in language teaching.* Oxford: Oxford University Press.

Kramsch, C. (1998). *Language and culture.* Oxford: Oxford University Press.

Krasner, I. (1999). The role of culture in language teaching. *Dialog on Language Instruction*, 13 (1-2), 79—88.

Lange, D. L. (1998). *The teaching of culture in foreign language courses.* Center for Applied Linguistics, Washington, D. C. ERIC document, ED 433 726 FL 025 983 Retrieved online.

http://www. eric. ed. gov/ERICDocs/data/ericdocs2sql/content_ storage_ 01/0000019b/80/15/db/94. pdf.

Yu, L. (2009) Where is culture?: Culture instruction and the foreign language textbook. *Journal of the Chinese Language Teachers Association*, Vol. 44: 3, 73—108.

Tylor, E. B. (1871). *Primitive culture: researches into the development of mythology, philosophy, religion, language, art, and custom.* London: John Murray. (reissued by Cambridge University Press, 2010)

Wang, H. (2010, March). *Enhancing literacy and deepening understanding: Forum discussion at Online Café.* Paper presented at the CIBER Business Language Conference, University of Pennsylvania, Philadelphia, Pennsylvania.

高班阅读课的网上课件：设计与应用
Online Components for Advanced Chinese Reading Classes: Design and Implementation

李兆麟　Lee, Siu Lun　香港中文大学

The Chinese University of Hong Kong slee@ cuhk. edu. hk

摘　要：很多学生在中文阅读课初期都充满信心，但高班时却有挫败感，甚至找不到学习方向。本文定位于香港的大学层面，集中讨论在对外汉语教学中，高班阅读课混合教学法任务型网上课件的设计与应用的实际经验。混合教学法结合网上语言输入，网上任务及真实课堂任务。真实任务是用语用框架，以真实或半真实的教学材料设计而成。本文讨论在香港一个对外汉语课程中进行的一项行动研究。调查结果显示混合教学方法的网上课件对学生成绩有正面影响。研究结果显示，混合教学法的任务型网上课件虽在汉字识别上没有直接影响，却提升了学生的阅读理解能力。

关键词：虚拟世界，网上工具，汉语教学，合作学习

Abstract： Many students find encouragement and satisfactions in the early stage of Chinese reading classes; however sometimes feel frustrated and disoriented in advanced levels (Hsueh, 2005; Lau, 2009; Mark & Lu, 2005). This paper discusses the empirical experience of designing and implementing a blended teaching and learning model in Advanced Chinese Reading classes in teaching Chinese as a foreign language (CFL) setting at university level in Hong Kong. The blended model combines online inputs and authentic tasks with classroom activities. Authentic tasks, using authentic or semi—authentic teaching materials, are designed based on a pragmatic framework. Action research has been done and investigates how the blended approach and the online components affect learning outcomes of the learners. The result suggests that the blended task—based approach, though does not show direct impact on character recognition, helps students increase their reading comprehension skills.

Keywords：Virtual World，Online tools，Teaching Chinese，Collaborative Learning

一　导论

网上学习和计算机辅助语言学习与教学（CALL[①]）是近年对外汉语（CFL）教学的主要课题。回顾以往文献，大多数 CALL 的论文都是以研究学生学习成绩与 CALL 相关技术的有效性为主，甚少讨论教学任务设计（O'Dowd & Waire，2009）。本文讨论在高班[②]中文阅读课中，一些与课堂活动相关的网上练习及阅读课件设计的真实经验。通过在香港中文大学雅礼中国语文研习所中进行的一项对外汉语教学行动研究，笔者得到了有关网上课件应用的调查结果。

汉语阅读课的初学者总是对他们的学习满怀信心和兴趣。从入门阶段到中级阶段，学生的进步是显著的。然而，受到汉字学习中边际效应递减现象的影响，他们往往容易感到灰心和丧气（Hsueh，2005；Lau，2009；Mark & Lu，2005）。"常识"告诉所有教中文阅读课的老师，他们应该增加学生的阅读量。但是，阅读数量的增加并没有自动地提升学生的学习成绩。另外的因素，例如阅读材料的真实性（Abanomey，2002；Bell 2005）以及任务的系统化设计则影响着学习者的成绩。我们知道使用搜索引擎随机地抽取网页来阅读，对第二语言教学是不合适的，因为网页上的内容在用词和句法上对学习者来说也许会过难（Murray & McPherson，2004）。这些见解反映了读得多并不代表与阅读技巧和策略的提升有直接关系。这并不仅是在计算机辅助语言教学中才会出现的问题，在传统的语言教学中也会碰到。以往，很少有研究是关于任务设计的。Shield 和 Kukulska—Hulme（2006：366）指出："……极少有研究是与语言学习网站的可用性有直接关系的，现有的研究总体上都是集中在技术方面。"既然，以网络为基础的材料和以书本为基础的材料是截然不同的，那么对两种媒介的不同学习成果进行预测就显得相当合理。本文就是讨论采用了混合教学法进行的高班阅读课，在网上课件方面的实际设计问题，并找出网上课件的使用与学生学习成果的关系。

---

① CALL 是 Computer Assisted Language Learning 的缩写。

② 高班是指在香港中文大学六个学期的课程中修毕四个学期的学生，高班学生已掌握 600—800 个汉字的运用。

二　高班阅读课

本文集中讨论的高班阅读课是以报刊阅读（课程代码：CCAN4633）为主。在大学两年制中文语言课程中，这是一门高级课程。表 1 列出在两年制中文课程中不同程度的阅读课。

CCAN4633 课程内的语言输入主要来自香港报章（中国大陆的报章亦一并使用）。在此课程中，老师教授学生这一类书面文章所使用的生词及句型，并且训练学生对这类文体的阅读理解能力。经过训练，学生能够复述他们所读的书面材料，且在不同语境中对问题进行讨论。以下是该课程的描述。

表 1　　　　　在两年制中文课程中不同程度的阅读及说话课

课程代码	课程名称	程度
CCAN2203	中文阅读 I	初级，200 个汉字
CCAN3303	中文阅读 II	中级 I，200 个汉字
CCAN4403	中文阅读 III	中级 II，200 个汉字
CCAN4503	高级阅读	高级 I，真实语料（200 个汉字）
CCAN4633	报刊阅读	高级 II，真实语料（200 个汉字）

表 2　　　　CCAN4633（高班中文阅读与说话课）课程描述

CCAN4633
报刊阅读 3 学分；每星期 3 小时
课程描述
这是一门通过阅读和讨论的方式，提高学生语言能力的高级课程。课程使用的教材均以标准书面汉语书写，从各大报刊摘录。课题包括国际关系、政治、罪案、经济、交通意外等等。
http：//www.cuhk.edu.hk/clc/curriculum_can.pdf.

（一）学习成果目标（learning outcomes）

研习所的课程设计者为报刊阅读班设置了两项学习成果目标[①]。包括：
1. 能够读出并理解汉字在真实语料及在专业环境中的意思。

---

① 学习成果目标（learning outcomes）是由香港中文大学雅礼中国语文研习所督导委员会订立，并获得香港中文大学根据质量标准审批。

2. 能够积极参与在正式或非正式情形下各种话题的讨论；能够以交际的方法，应付各式各样的说话任务；能在各种语境中有效地交际；能够满足学校及工作环境所需达到的中文要求。

Lee（2000）调查了 CFL 学习者的需求。调查数据证实了高班学生希望得到真实或半真实的语料，并以系统性设计的任务帮助他们提升阅读能力。学生希望这类材料能够在课堂或自学过程中使用。那么，老师在教中文高班阅读课的学生时，就应当尽量使用真实语料来训练学生的中文阅读能力。这些真实语料应当作学生阅读练习和口头任务的语言输入。而学生则期望能够获得以下两种阅读能力：

1. 精读能力——学生能够彻底地理解节选及重点的书面信息，并作口头报告。他们要能够逐字逐句地理解文章，并且完成需要高度准确性的语言任务。

2. 泛读能力——学生能够跳读并理解大量的文字输入，作出归纳总结。

除了阅读能力以外，本课程的目标还有提高学生识别和记忆汉字的能力，及理解由这些字组合而成的短语或句子的能力。

（二）阅读输入——建立阅读材料库（RMD）

在分析了学生学习需求的数据后，笔者确信需要综合真实语料，建立一个以语境为基础的教学大纲。笔者曾经在 2000 年做过一个叫做"报章数据库"的计划，这个计划稍后改名为"阅读材料库"。这个计划搜集了一系列报刊文章和真实语料，并将这些材料按学生的水平加以分类，例如香港新闻、国际新闻、政治新闻、经济新闻、罪案、休闲等等。Lee（2008a）搜集了逾千份的报刊文章并尝试在课堂中使用。这个计划用了将近两年时间完成。Lee（2008a）聘请了学生助手协助将报章分类，归档和输入计算机数据库。其中，主要工作是将搜集到的各种报章加以分类，编写读后练习和读后活动，方便老师在课堂上讲解或学生在课后作自学使用。除了大声朗读和反复练习以外，还有一些其他活动，例如概括文章大意，演讲等。目前，这个 RMD 数据库仍在不停地扩充，因为这个数据库是一个公开的资源，老师可以在数据库中添加材料。这个数据库对教师的备课工作（包括准备阅读课的教材）以及学术研究工作，例如词频分析、语料库语言学，甚至词典编写研究都特别有帮助。表 3 列举了 RMD 的内容和分类（Lee，2008a）。

表3	RMD 的内容与分类（2010 年 10 月更新）	
资源	分类	文章数量（份）
香港报刊	政治	237
	本地要闻	233
	经济	90
	国际	90
	罪案	70
	休闲	50
	意外	28

　　两年间，教师在课堂中使用这些数据库中的材料，并将这些材料用作传统面授式高班阅读课的阅读输入。

三　传统面授式阅读课

　　首先让我们回顾一下传统面授式阅读课中，教师是如何上课的。传统面授式教学包括了几个阶段。第一个阶段是对学生的"语言输入阶段"。在这个阶段，老师集中介绍教材的大纲和背景知识，学生需要在稍后的练习中使用这些内容。课堂上亦会介绍一些特定生词的含义和用法，句型句法以及与阅读课文相关的文化常识。这样，学生在日后的课堂上就可以运用这些知识。

　　第二个阶段是"练习阶段"。学生会被分派到一些练习，他们要使用在第一阶段学习到的知识来完成这些练习。在传统的课堂上，老师通常会让学生大声朗读课文，然后要学生用自己的话概括或复述故事内容。

　　第三个阶段是"提升与诊断阶段"。倘若学生的输出不太符合要求，教师可以帮助学生纠正和改进他们的用语。在传统阅读课上，教师会在这一阶段纠正学生的错误和巩固重点难点。教师会和学生进行问答，这样老师就可以检查学生对课文的理解程度。如果需要，老师还可以给学生整体的修改意见以及补充解释和练习。诊断结果可以帮助教师准备下一轮的"语言输入"和"练习"。图1展示了传统面授式课堂的教学流程。

四　高班阅读课网上课件的设计

　　现今，语言教师的主要角色是协助学习者提高语言熟练度，以及在现实生活或者工作中实际应用语言的能力。纵观历史，我们可以清楚看到对外汉语的教学法是从语法翻译法发展到回音法，从功能情景法发展到交际法的

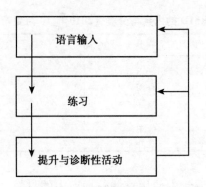

图 1　传统面授式课堂教学模式

（Munby，1978；Canale & Swain，1980；Lee，2005；吴伟平，2009）。

　　在 Sapir 和 Whorf（Sapir，1921；1929）对语言和文化的关系作了深入研究后，一些关于语言与文化的语言学理论，以及着重于研究真实语境与语言教学提高的教学议题都得到了一定发展。Hymes（1972）明确地指出独立于语用之外的语法规则是毫无意义的。他强调在学习一门外语时，社会文化的知识和获得能力是非常重要的。Hymes 认为想要了解语言是如何获得的，不仅要有一定语法基础，还要有能够自由运用语言的能力。

　　任务和任务型学习法被视为近年来外语教学法的核心元素（Nunan，2004；Pica，2005）。所谓的任务是指一种由意义主导的活动。这种活动是建立在学习者现实生活交际需要上的（Levy & Stockwell，2006：249）。在设计网上学习课件时，任务型学习框架也一并应用在内。以往，有的研究者高度重视电子阅读能力或超文本对学生表现的影响（Shetzer & Warschauer，2000）。然而，学者们却甚少研究语言教学中的网上任务设计。的确，想要弄清楚那些被广泛地运用在各种外语学习网络平台上的任务和任务设计办法是不容易的。网上的学习任务可以是以比较随意的形式出现，也可以是有比较严格的要求，需要学生交出一份完整的作业。有的网上学习任务着重练习语法或者某些文体，有的则关注外语中的文化点。因此，如何定位学习任务是相当重要的问题，透过网上交流平台，在决定需要集中培养哪种师生间、同学间或学生与内容间的互动外语能力的时候，尤其重要（Garrison & Anderson，2003）。可惜的是，这些任务是怎么设计的，网上学习的理论基础是什么，都在过去的研究中被忽略了。以下部分，笔者会介绍一些设计任务的经验以及高班阅读课的成果。

（一）在语用框架下设计任务

高班阅读课（CCAN4633）的老师设计了多个包含真实或半真实语料的学习任务（Tasks）。老师提前准备语言输入，然后传送上网。笔者选取了Moodle① 这个课程管理平台来进行网上输入和任务前的活动。

下列例子②包括了因工作需要学习汉语的高班学生的任务设计方法（Lee，2008a）。在任务开始之前，学生先上网查阅任务指引，如下：

阅读及演讲能力练习与活动指引

1. 阅读节选材料
2. 找出有用信息
3. 回答问题
4. 就特定话题作演讲。

在任务前阶段，下列材料（见表4）会被上载到网上平台。学习者需要事先读懂这些标题并且下载及阅读文章。

完成前置任务（pre-task）后，学生开始进行任务（task）。下面的任务A、B、C和D说明了所有分配给学习者的不同级别的任务是如何将读说能力融合起来的（Lee，2008a）。任务A、B、C、D从任务的正式度、长度和复杂度上反映了不同水平的能力。A是比较随意的（便饭后），D则是最正式的（在一个国际性会议上）。语言功能是粗体字部分，能力范围从描述到阐释，从阐释到劝说逐渐提升。

表4 上载至网上平台的阅读材料

代码	文章题目	日期	报章来源
N01	车辆废气 乃第二大污染源	28/08/06	文汇报
N02	尖旺不夜天 环保团体斥"光害"	12/03/07	都市日报
N03	污染物来源政府学者各不同	19/10/05	明报
N04	污染蔽蓝天六成美商或走人	28/08/06	AM730
N05	减少排放绿化香港	25/05/07	星岛日报
N06	空气清新剂损孕妇初生婴健康	20/10/04	明报

任务A：在一顿便饭后，你和你的朋友正在聊天，请描述以下情景。

---

① Moodle 是香港中文大学的网上学习平台。

② 本文以"环境保护"为例子介绍语用框架的任务。在真实材料中还有其他话题，如内地和香港经济关系、教育、道德、公共卫生、城市发展、交通、法律、国际关系和特别事件，例如：上海世博会等。

语境：非正式情景

语言功能：描述

任务 B：你被一所当地中学邀请作一个演讲（5 分钟）。请向来听你演讲的学生描述当前情景，并介绍自己的观点。

语境：较正式情景

语言功能：描述和介绍

任务 C：请对当前情形作一个演讲（10 分钟）。你现在被一家报社的记者采访。你是政府官员，请清楚地陈述和阐释你的部门的立场。

语境：正式情景

语言功能：陈述和阐释

任务 D：你现在参加一个国际性会议。请对当前情形作一个演讲（10 分钟）。清楚地发表你的意见和阐释你的立场并劝说参加者支持你的观点。

语境：非常正式的情景

语言功能：发表意见、阐释和劝说

通过上面展示的例子，学习者可以接受一连串系统性任务的训练。阅读练习并不是仅仅停留在传统的选择题或者对错题的阅读理解练习上，而是与真实任务有关。不同的任务可以根据不同的需要分配给学生，从而提高他们阅读课的学习动机。语境从随意逐步转变为到非常正式，而语言功能也从描述提升到劝说。表 5 中所列举的语言功能均是从美国的 ACTFL 说话能力等级分类发展出来的，是语用任务型框架的基础。

表 5　　　　　　　　　　语言应用系统中的语用点总结表

水平	任务类型
中级 Intermediate Level（I）	I1. 描述 I2. 解释（看图解释） I3. 指路 I4. 留言 I5. 介绍（日常生活） I6. 感谢 I7. 解释 I8. 说明 I9. 讨论 I10. 提供信息

续表

水平	任务类型
高级 Advanced Level（A）	A1. 投诉 A2. 分析 A3. 比较 A4. 阐释 A5. 陈述 A6. 建议 A7. 拒绝 A8. 推销 A9. 道歉 A10. 批评 A11. 介绍（半正式）
超高级 Superior Level（S）	S1. 发表意见 S2. 开会发言 S3. 公开致谢 S4. 劝说 S5. 反驳 S6. 祝贺 S7. 演讲 S8. 辩护 S9. 号召 S10. 介绍（正式）

在完成前置任务（pre—task）和任务（task）之后，老师会用后置任务（post—task）给学生反馈信息，通过回答问题或者改错练习的形式，同学也能在后置任务时进行审评，使老师和学生能对学习成果作出评估。后置任务阶段为汉语学习者提供了一个掌握重点难点和纠正错误的机会。

（二）影响语用任务型教学法难度的主要因素

从本文举例讨论的任务和练习，我们不难发现有些因素影响着语言课的难度。

1. 语言输入的难度，如语言形态、词汇密度（Halliday，1989）；

2. 课文结构和先验知识（Alexander，Kulikowich & Jetton，1994）；

3. 语言功能和技巧的难度；

4. 语境的正式度；

5. 任务的长度和复杂度。

设计真实任务和课程应该要贴近现实世界和工作环境，这样我们的学生才能够在完成学业后使用目的语。与说话任务的设计相结合的阅读输入是以语用框架为基础的，而语用框架是十分重视语境（说话者什么时候，什么地点和对什么人讲话）和语言功能的（吴伟平，2009）。

（三）计算机辅助任务型阅读课

以往有一些 CALL 的研究指出使用超文本能够提升学习者的动机和表现。Garcia 和 Arias（2000）比较了网上教学与书本教学对学生的影响。Liou（1997）研究了网络是如何直接影响语言学习的。有的研究（Biesenbach—Lucas & Weasenforth，2001；Hirata，2004）则关注计算机教学和学生表现之间的关系。有的研究对网络在社会和教学方面比较感兴趣。不同学者从其他角度研究网上阅读，发展出了"计算器素养（computer literacy）"（Corbel & Gruba，2004）、"数字素养（digital literacy）"（Glister，1997）等概念。此外，还有大量关于阅读者对网页理解程度的研究。究竟超文本是不是比书本优越是没有办法简单地判断出的。在第二语言或外语学习中，网络素养（internet literacy）的影响究竟有多大亦是很难断言（Murray & McPherson，2006）。

研究人员讨论了使用超文本和网上材料的优劣点。Morrison（2002）认为用超文本作为学习工具有四个优点：（1）可及性（accessibility）；（2）可再生性（renewability）；（3）适应性（adaptability）和（4）互动性（interactivity）。Garcia et al（2000）认为计算机主导型任务能更容易更快捷地找到所需材料和文献，以实现个性化的自学模式。

当然，技术性问题也有机会发生，有的学生有计算机，有的学生则没有；有的学生计算机水平较高，有的则较低。另外，学生对计算机的需求及使用能力也不尽相同（Morrison，2002）。Morkes 和 Nielsen（1997）认为在计算机上进行阅读比看书本更辛苦。这些方面都是网上阅读的不足。

（四）任务型混合式教学法模型

在网络科技的协助下，CCAN4633 课程的网上课件（输入，练习和任务）被设计和运用在辅助式任务型课堂教学当中。这些网上课件都是根据任务型混合式教学法模型组织和编排的。在混合型教学模型中，学生可以拿到网上课件，而且他们仍然需要上课。课程以 2 + 2 形式设立。这种模式包括了两节网上材料学习课和两节课堂学习课。每节课 50 分钟。大学会采用 Moodle 作为课程管理平台，将学习材料上载上去。与课程相关的网上材料包括了：

1. 语言输入：主要教材选自一份叫做 Newspaper Primer 的教材，教材内容连同音档会上载到网上，另外学生也可以购买印刷形式的教材。

2. 网上阅读练习：附加新闻（Additional Newspaper Articles）及附加句

子练习会作为朗读练习上载到网上。学生要大声朗读这些附件并且在线录音。

　　3. 真实任务：包括前置任务阅读，任务导读和课堂活动。学生要录下并且提交他们完成的任务。老师会在网上改正学生的错误并给予反馈信息。学生可以在收到这些反馈信息后，对他们的任务加以适当修改。然后，学生需要在上课时，当着老师和同学的面以口头方式作汇报。老师会在后置任务阶段为学生答疑和强化他们的语言能力。

　　图 2 是一个任务型混合式教学法模型的流程图。灰色部分代表面对面形式的课堂活动。它左边的方框是网上课件。网上课件从语言输入开始，或文字或音文件或视频输入。随后，学生要做网上练习，前置任务和任务。语言输入也好，网上练习也好，任务也好，都会为课堂活动提供必要数据和信息，例如哪些重点词汇，语法点和文化点是弱点，需要增强；哪些有误解，需要纠正。网上课件的应用能够协助课堂教学活动顺利进行，最终达到预期的学习目标。在最右边表示诊断性测验和期末考试评核课程的学习目标。

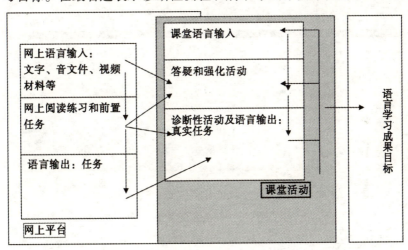

图 2　任务型混合式教学法模型的设计

　　图 3 展示的是 Moodle 主页的截屏。专为网上课程设计的网上课件有 3 种，分别是："网上语言输入"，"网上阅读练习"和"课堂活动前置任务及任务"。图 4 展示的是 Moodle "网上语言输入"的截屏。"网上语言输入"包括了阅读材料和课文录音，学生可以自由选择是否同时看和听文章或者像传统面授式教学那样，只看文字材料而已。

　　"网上阅读练习和前置任务"课件（见图 5）由阅读练习组成。学生要

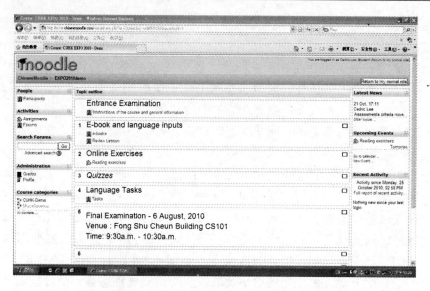

图3　CCAN4633 学生用 Moodle 时的主页的界面截屏

图4　CCAN4633 学生用 Moodle 做网上语言输入时的界面截屏

大声地朗读文章。有了 Audio Dropbox 的帮助，学生在完成阅读练习之后，音档就会被自动发送到老师的 Audio Dropbox 里，这样老师就可以在听到学生的作业然后给他们打分。这些练习让老师能够提前准备课堂强化和诊断活动。

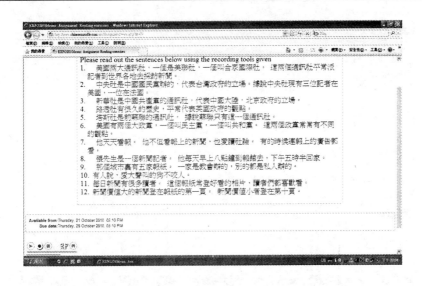

图5　CCAN4633 学生用 Moodle 做网上练习时的界面截屏

前置任务为网上任务（见图6、图7）和课堂任务作准备。前置任务提供了背景阅读材料或者一个小型数据库。学生也能够用这个课件看到一些内容情节，他们要大声朗读出这些背景阅读材料。另外，学生还要提前读完导读和语言情景介绍，这样他们才能够准备任务。之后，学生要用 Audio Dropbox 在网上提交他们完成的作业的音档文件，而老师会在网上给他们评语。在课堂上，老师就会集中在"答疑和诊断性活动"的部分。

五　行动研究

这部分讨论的是在融合了课堂教学与网上教学的高级汉语阅读课（课程代码：CCAN4633）中和任务型混合式网上教学模式的应用和实验的问题，而展示的材料至今全部在香港中文大学对外汉语课堂中使用了两年时间。

（一）方法论

从 2009 年至 2010 年间，一共有 4 个高班阅读班被选出来进行行动研究。4 个阅读班都由相同的老师任教，并且使用相同的教材。A 班有 4 个学生，D 班有 9 个。这两班都采用 2+2 混合式教学法。2+2 混合教学包括了两节网上练习和活动，以及两节课堂活动。B 班有 6 个学生，C 班有 6 个学生，采用传统的面授式教学法（见表6）。所有研究对象都参与了两年对外

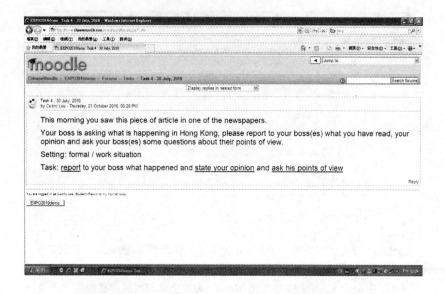

图6　CCAN4633 学生用 Moodle 看任务指示时的界面截屏

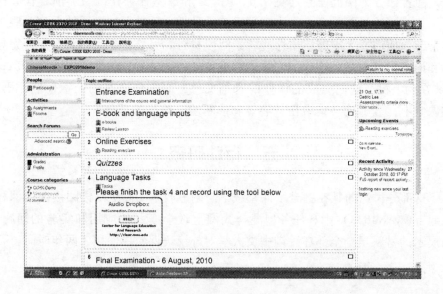

图7　CCAN4633 学生用 Moodle 做任务时的界面截屏

汉语学习，他们的广东话语言水平都不相上下（ACTFL 水平等级：IH）。一共有 13 个学生采用了混合式教学法，12 个学生采用了传统的面授式教学法。

表6 **行动研究的对象**

A 班	4 人	混合式课堂（任务型网上学习 + 面授型）
B 班	6 人	传统面授式学习
C 班	6 人	传统面授式学习
D 班	9 人	混合式课堂（任务型网上学习 + 面授型）

在这个研究里，一共设计了两种考试来对学生进行测试，分别是认字（20%）和阅读理解考试（80%），认字考试共有 10 个词组（长度由 2 个字到 6 个字不等），都是从学过的材料中抽出的。学生要能够大声读出这些词组，然后用这些词组造句。老师根据学生对汉字的熟悉度，包括读音，语法形式和词义来评分。

阅读理解考试有 5 段文章摘录。学生要看完这些内容，然后每篇都要口头回答 2 个问题（整个考试有 10 个问题）。这些文章都是从真实语料中摘录下来且没有在阅读练习及任务中做过，所有的答案都是以文章内容为基础的。答案的长度要有 4—5 句话，就像一个短的段落。这个考试的目的是检查学生能否从真实语料中提取正确信息。认字考试满分是 20 分，阅读理解考试满分是 80 分。两个考试总分是 100 分。

（二）数据分析

现在，让我们看看采用混合式教学法能否帮助学生达成学习目标。我们会用一些描述性统计工具，例如平均值（means）和频率（frequency counts）来分析数据。同时，我们会用交叉表（crosstabulation）和卡方（chi—square）来分析任务型混合式课程与学习者成绩间是否有依赖关系。我们还会用卡方（X^2）来分析零假设，即两组变量是否有独立性。如果它们之间并没有明显的独立性，那么就代表这些变量间可能存在一定依赖关系。

1. 比较不同班别的平均分

数据显示 A 班和 D 班的学生的平均分比 B 班和 C 班学生的平均分高。A 班平均分为 90.25 分，D 班为 91 分。然而，B 班平均分为 76.25 分，而 C 班仅仅有 69.83 分（见表7）。但是，4 个班在认字考试中的得分都差不多，大致在 17.2778 分到 18.5 分之间（见表8）。所以，平均分差别最大的就是阅读理解考试（见表9）。如果我们把 4 个班合成面授式班级和混合式班级两个大组，可以得到相似结果（见表10、表11、表12）。

表7 A、B、C、D班总分表

班级	平均分	个数	标准差	最小值	最大值
A班	90.2500	4	6.07591	85.00	99.00
B班	76.2500	6	8.06071	67.00	85.00
C班	69.8333	6	4.53505	65.00	78.00
D班	91.0000	9	5.68441	82.00	98.00
总计	82.2600	25	10.96027	65.00	99.00

表8 A、B、C、D班认字考试成绩表

班级	平均分	个数	标准差	最小值	最大值
A班	18.5000	4	1.29099	17.00	20.00
B班	17.5833	6	2.24537	15.00	20.00
C班	17.6667	6	1.63299	15.00	20.00
D班	17.2778	9	1.92209	15.00	20.00
总计	17.6400	25	1.79420	15.00	20.00

表9 A、B、C、D班阅读理解考试成绩表

班级	平均分	个数	标准差	最小值	最大值
A班	71.7500	4	4.92443	68.00	79.00
B班	58.3333	6	7.52773	50.00	65.00
C班	52.1667	6	3.12517	50.00	58.00
D班	73.7222	9	4.68449	67.00	79.00
总计	64.5400	25	10.60063	50.00	79.00

如果我们再看看下面的表10、表11、表12，混合式学习组学生的平均成绩（90.7692），比传统面对面学习组学生的成绩（73.0417）高。两组认字考试的成绩非常接近，17.625（面授式）对17.6538（混合式）。而阅读理解的成绩就是两组的区别所在，55.25（面授式）对73.1154（混合式）。

表10 两组（面授式和混合式）平均分比较表

组别	平均分	个数	标准差	最小值	最大值
面授式	73.0417	12	7.07896	65.00	85.00
混合式	90.7692	13	5.55883	82.00	99.00
总计	82.2600	25	10.96027	65.00	99.00

表 11　　　　　　两组（面授式和混合式）认字考试平均分比较表

组别	平均分	个数	标准差	最小值	最大值
面授式	17.6250	12	1.87235	15.00	20.00
混合式	17.6538	13	1.79565	15.00	20.00
总计	17.6400	25	1.79420	15.00	20.00

表 12　　　　　　两组（面授式和混合式）阅读理解考试平均分比较表

组别	平均分	个数	标准差	最小值	最大值
面授式	55.2500	12	6.36932	50.00	65.00
混合式	73.1154	13	4.64648	67.00	79.00
总计	64.5400	25	10.60063	50.00	79.00

2. 交叉表和卡方测试

从上面的数据，我们知道了混合式学习班的学生，阅读理解考试的成绩比较高，而且他们的总分也较高。我们用交叉表和卡方测试来检测学生的班别和成绩有没有关系。表 13 显示了大部分面授式学生（75%）的总分少于 80 分[①]，而所有混合式学生（100%）的总分则高于 80 分。这个结果是相当显著的 $[X^2 = 15.234, P < 0.000 (1df)]$。表 15 的结果相似。学生上的课和他们的阅读理解成绩之间有一定的关系。大部分面授式学生（83.3%）的阅读理解成绩达不到 80 分，然而所有混合式学生（100%）的阅读理解成绩则超过 80 分。这个结果也是非常显著的 $[X^2 = 18.056, P < 0.000 (1df)]$。我们再看表 14，结果发现学生上的课和认字没有直接关系 $[X^2 = 0.13, P < 0.910 (1df)]$。从平均值，交叉表和卡方测试的结果，我们可以作以下结论：任务型混合式教学法能够帮助学生的阅读理解能力。这也就能解释为何混合式学生的总分比较高了。但是，这两种模式对认字能力的影响都差别不大。

表 13　　　　　　　　　　两组总分交叉表

			总分		总分
			<80%	>80%	
	面授式	个数	9	3	12
		% 在面授式课堂中	75.0%	25.0%	100.0%
	混合式	个数	0	13	13
		% 在混合式课堂中	0%	100.0%	100.0%
总计		个数	9	16	25
		% 全体学生	36.0%	64.0%	100.0%

N = 25　$X^2 = 15.234$ P < 0.000（1df）

---

① 80 分是香港中文大学评分系统内 A - 的标准。

表 14 　　　　　　　　　　　**两组认字考试得分交叉表**

| | | | 得分 | | 得分 |
			<80%	>80%	
面授式		个数	3	9	12
		% 在面授式课堂中	25.0%	75.0%	100.0%
混合式		个数	3	10	13
		% 在混合式课堂中	23.1%	76.9%	100.0%
总计		个数	6	19	25
		% 全体学生	24.0%	76.0%	100.0%

$N = 25$ 　$X^2 = 0.13$ 　$P < 0.910$ 　(1df)

表 15 　　　　　　　　　　**两组阅读理解考试得分交叉表**

| | | | 得分 | | |
			<80%	>80%	
面授式		个数	10	2	12
		% 在面授式课堂中	83.3%	16.7%	100.0%
混合式		个数	0	13	13
		% 在混合式课堂中	.0%	100.0%	100.0%
总计		个数	10	15	25
		% 全体学生	40.0%	60.0%	100.0%

$N = 25$ 　$X^2 = 18.056$ 　$P < 0.0000$ 　(1df)

六　课程评估

　　学期末，我们向所有学生发出了总共 25 份调查问卷，询问学生对课程的评价，总共收回 25 份问卷。在下列的数据中（见表 16、表 17），第 7 项和第 16 项的平均分有所增加。传统的面授式的评分中，第 7 项的平均分是 4.583。混合式的评分（5.6154）增加了 20%。这表示采用混合式材料可以让学生觉得课程更加有启发性。第 16 项是关于科技服务和支持。很明显，混合式教学的得分（5.1538）比传统面授式教学的得分（2.5833）要高得多，至于其他项目的得分则相差不多。这说明网上练习和任务并没有让学生觉得加重了学习负担（第 12 项），也没有影响课程的组织和结构（第 9 项）。

表 16　　　　　　　　传统面授式课程评估（个数 = 12）

General comment of the course

item no	Statement	1	2	3	4	5	6	Mean	SD
item 6	The course was interesting	0	0	0	0	2	10	5.833	0.389
item 7	The course was stimulating	0	0	0	5	7	0	4.583	0.5149
item 9	The course was well—organized	0	0	0	0	2	10	5.833	0.389

Learning outcome

| item 10 | Learning outcomes of the course were clear | 0 | 0 | 0 | 0 | 2 | 10 | 5.833 | 0.389 |

IT resources and workload

| item 12 | The amount of workload required was appropriate | 0 | 0 | 0 | 0 | 1 | 11 | 5.9167 | 0.2887 |
| item 16 | The course was well supported by IT resources | 0 | 5 | 7 | 0 | 0 | 0 | 2.5833 | 0.5149 |

1—strong disagree, 2—disagree, 3—fairly disagree, 4—fairly agree, 5—agree, 6—strongly agree

表 17　　　　混合式课程评估（网上任务型 + 面授式课堂）（个数 = 13）

General comment of the course

item no	Statement	1	2	3	4	5	6	Mean	SD
item 6	The course was interesting	0	0	0	0	1	12	5.923	0.2774
item 7	The course was stimulating	0	0	0	0	5	7	5.6154	0.5064
item 9	The course was well—organized	0	0	0	0	3	10	5.7692	0.3755

Learning outcome

| item 10 | Learning outcomes of the course were clear | 0 | 0 | 0 | 0 | 2 | 11 | 5.8462 | 0.3755 |

IT resources and workload

| item 12 | The amount of workload required was appropriate | 0 | 0 | 0 | 0 | 2 | 11 | 5.8462 | 0.3755 |
| item 16 | The course was well supported by IT resources | 0 | 0 | 0 | 3 | 5 | 5 | 5.1538 | 0.8 |

1—strong disagree, 2—disagree, 3—fairly disagree, 4—fairly agree, 5—agree, 6—strongly agree

　　除了对问卷调查做定量分析以外，学生也给出了一些定性反馈（见下）。这些定性反馈反映了学生认为课程是"有用的"，并且能够将学生训练得"更加独立"和"有创意"。

　　"我认为这个课程十分有用。它能够帮我们更好地了解中文报纸。"

（学生#CCAN4633—014）

"我认为新的方法非常好。通过科技服务来学习是一个能让学生更加独立和有创意的新方法。"（学生#CCAN4633—017）

有的学生则认为，老师或者材料设计者还有更多提升空间，能更好地利用网上平台。

"可以用更多图表等，让学生能一看就知道材料是讲什么的。"

（学生#CCAN4633—016）

七　结论

本文集中在学习成果上讨论了高班阅读课的任务设计课题。文中列举了一些运用了真实语料的真实任务的例子。本文展示了对外汉语教学中，材料准备和教学法的新思维。教学材料和语言任务可以以电子化的形式出现，然后上载到网上并将课堂活动和任务型混合式教学相结合。网上课程可以采用任务型方法，实验证明，结果是积极的。这个实验性的研究反映了用混合式教学法和任务型网上课件学习的高班阅读课学生，阅读理解能力比用传统方式学习的学生高。然而，在认字能力上，两种模式的结果都差不多。

在传统的 CFL 教学理论里，老师和课程设计者将听说放在一起，读写放在一起。设计不同组合的任务可以训练学生不同的技巧。除了读、说（正如所举的例子），读、听、说以外，甚至可以是听、说、读、写一起。笔者在此想指出的是，在将来，读 + N，听 + N 的方法会得到发展。读和听可以在前置任务阶段给学生。在这个阶段，最重要的是培养接受性技能。真实任务可以集中在说和写上，并且以语用框架为基础，我们在前面的内容已经讨论过了。这种任务或者课程设计比较贴近真实生活和现实工作环境。这样就可以帮助我们的学生在完成学业之后使用目的语。后置任务在学生上完课或者做完网上作业之后，可以帮学生纠正错误和提升他们的语言能力。笔者认为这种任务型混合式教学模式可以在其他读 + N 和听 + N 的课程中应用。笔者相信，将会有更多关于混合式模型应用度的研究在不同背景的语言课程中展开。

参考文献

Abanomey, Abdulaziz A. (2002). The effect of texts' authenticity on reading—comprehension test—taking strategies used by adult Saudi learners of English as a foreign language. (Unpublished PhD thesis). Arizona State University, United State of America.

Alexander, P. A. , Kulikowich, J. M. , & Jetton, T. L. (1994). The role of subject—mattter knowledge and interest in the processing of linear and nonlinear texts. Review of Educational Research, 64 (2), 201—252.

Bell, F. L. (2005). Comprehension aids, internet technologies, and the reading of authentic materials by adult second language learners. (Unpublished PhD thesis). The Florida State University, United State of America.

Biesenbach—Lucas, S. , & Weasenforth, D. (2001). E—mail and word processing in the ESL classroom: How the medium affects the message. Language Learning and Technology, 5 (1), 135—165.

Byram, M. (1989). Cultural Studies in Foreign Language Education. Clevedon, UK, Multilingual Matters.

Canale, M. , & Swain, M. (1980). Theoretical Bases of Communicative Approaches to Second Language Teaching and Testing. Applied Linguistics, 1 (1), pp. 1—47.

Corbel, C. , & Gruba, P. (2004). Teaching computer literacy, Teaching with new technology. Sydney: NCELTR.

Garcia, M. R. , & Arias, F. V. (2000). A comparative study in motivation and learning through printoriented and computer—oriented tests. Computer Assisted Language Learning, 13 (4—5), 457— 465.

Glister, P. (1997). Digital literacy. John Wiley and Sons.

Halliday, M. A. K. (1989). Spoken and written language. Oxford: Oxford University Press.

Hirata, Y. (2004). Computer assisted pronunciation training for native English speakers learning Japanese pitch and durational contrasts. Computer Assisted Language Learning, 17 (3/4), 357—376.

Hsueh, Su—Ling. (2005). Design, Development and Evaluation of Chinese Radical and Character Tutorial by Hypermedia, Master of Science thesis, Brigham Young University.

Hymes, D. (1972), On Communicative Competence, in J. B. Pride & J. Holmes (eds), Sociolinguistics. Harmondsworth: Penguin.

LAU Fai Kim. (2009) Spoken vocabulary acquisition in students with autism in multimedia—facilitated learning context, PhD thesis, University of Hong Kong.

LEE, Siu—lun. (2008a). Use of movie and newspaper database in Chinese classrooms, CLaSIC 2008 conference organized by the Center of Language Studies of the National University of Singapore.

LEE, Siu—lun. (2008b). Task—based Curriculum Design in Teaching Chinese as a Foreign Language. The 11th Annual Conference of the National Organizations of Less Commonly Taught Languages, organized at University of Wisconsin, Madison, U. S. A.

LEE Siu—lun (2005). History and Current Trends of Teaching Cantonese as a Foreign Language: Investigatong approaches to teaching and learning Cantonese, EdD thesis, University of Leicester, U. K.

LEE Siu—lun. (2000). Needs of the learners learning Chinese as a foreign language in Hong Kong, Research report (Student campus work scheme), The Chinese University of Hong Kong.

Levy, M., & Stockwell, G. (2006). CALL dimensions. Options and issues in computer—assisted language learning. Mahwah, NJ: Lawrence Erlbaum.

Liou, H. C. (1997). The impact of WWW texts on EFL learning. Computer Assisted Language Learning, 10 (5), 455—478.

Mark Shiu Kee Shum and Lu De Zhang. (ed) (2005). Teaching Writing in Chinese as a Foreign Language. Mainland China. Springer Netherlands.

Morkes, J., & Nielsen, J. (1997). Concise, scannable, and objective: How to write for the Web. Available: http://www. useit. com/papers/webwriting/writing. html.

Morrison, S. (2002). Interactive language learning on the web. Available: http://www. cal. org/resources/digest/0212morrison. html.

Munby, John. (1978). Communicative Syllabus Design. Cambridge. Cambridge University Press.

Murray, D. E., & McPherson, P. (2004). Using the Web to support language learning. Sydney: NCELTR.

Murray, D. E., & McPherson, P. (2006). Scaffolding instruction for reading the web. Language Teaching Research, 10 (2), 131—156.

Nunan, D. (2004). Designing tasks for the communicative classroom. Cambridge: Cambridge University Press.

O'Dowd R. and Waire P (2009) Critical issues in telecollaborative task design, Computer Assisted Language Learning, Vol. 22, No. 2, April 2009, 173—188, Routledge.

Pica, T. (2005). Classroom learning, teaching, and research: A task—based perspective. Modern Language Journal, 89 (3), 339—352.

Shetzer, H., & Warschauer, M. (2000). An electronic literacy approach to network—based language teaching. In M. Warschauer & R. Kern (Eds.), Network—based language teaching: Concepts and practice (pp. 171—185). Cambridge:

Cambridge University Press.

Shield, L. , & Kukulska—Hulme, A. （2006）. Are language learning Websites special? Towards a research agenda for discipline—specific usability. Journal of Educational Multimedia and Hypermedia, 15 （3）, 349—369.

Snyder, I. （2002）. Silicon literacies. London：Routledge.

Sapir, E. （1921）. Language：an introduction to the study of speech. New York：Harcourt, Brace & World.

Sapir, E. （1929）：The Status of Linguistics as a Science. In E. Sapir （1958）, Culture, Language and Personality （ed. D. G. Mandelbaum）. Berkeley, CA：University of California Press.

吴伟平 （2009）:《语用框架与课程设置：从对外汉语教学到语言教学》，载吴伟平、李兆麟编辑:《语言学华语二语教学》，香港大学出版社 （Yu yan xue yu Hua yu er yu jiao xue／Wu Weiping, Lee Siulun bian zhu）。

述评：*ActiveChinese* 网络课程系列
Review of *ActiveChinese*

王海丹　Wang, Haidan　美国夏威夷大学
University of Hawaii at Mānoa United States haidan@ hawaii. edu

ActiveChinese （http：//www. activechinese. com/） is an internet-based Chinese teaching program that integrates all four areas of language skill instruction. It targets beginning and intermediate students in elementary, middle school, high school and college, as well as professionals who may need to use Chinese. *ActiveChinese* offers programs for children, schools, professionals and travelers that can be used as independent Chinese teaching programs or as supplements to existing ones.

The children's program caters to elementary and middle school students and the theme is "The Legend of the Sacred Forest." A magic wheel rotates through 12 units, each symbolized by one of the 12 animals of the Chinese Zodiac and containing three lessons. Each lesson is divided into three parts：Teaching points, drills and games. There is an ancient map in each unit that leads students through the 36 lessons. The children's program introduces 36 key sentences and phrases, 300 vocabulary words, 100 characters, basic Chinese pronunciation and radicals. A variety of games and exercises are incorporated into the program to create an active learning environment. There is a test at the end of each unit that is presented with graphics to keep learning fun.

The school program is for high school students. There are 31 lessons. Each lesson contains a dialogue, exercises, cultural and language points and an assessment. The dialogue is available in three modes：Immersion mode, extended dialogue mode and interactive mode. The immersion mode introduces a dialogue through an audio recording with Chinese subtitles. In the extended dialogue mode, each sentence in a dialogue is slowly pronounced, with subtitles color-coded according to tone, which helps students internalize this distinctive feature of Chinese and increase their awareness of the tones. *Pinyin* and tone marks are displayed right below each word and the English meaning is shown when the curser is pointed at the word. The interactive mode presents each sentence in a dialogue and allows students to record their pronunciation and compare it to that of a native speaker. There is also a button to turn the English or *pinyin* subtitles on and off.

The Exercise section drills pronunciation, vocabulary, listening comprehension, sentence patterns, communication skills and writing. Following the drills is a reading passage with a vocabulary list. The cultural and language points section is composed of facts and explanations related to linguistic and social features of China and the Chinese language. The last section of each lesson is an assessment, quizzing students on the material covered in the dialogue and language points.

The school program also has a 200-level version for students who have completed the first 31 lessons or whose Chinese proficiency is at the equivalent level. There are 15 lessons in this version, which are suitable for students preparing for an AP test or college level students. In addition to the school program features, it also incorporates a Chinese idiom into the dialogue of each lesson. Each idiom is illustrated with a slide consisting of four pictures, explanations and one example sentence.

The professional program has a virtual classroom and a live tutor, which is conducted through Skype. Its 42 lessons are stratified into beginner, beginner advanced, low intermediate and business. Like the school program, each lesson contains a dialogue, language points, drills and assessment. The dialogues in the professional edition are also available in three modes. The activity format in the drill section is similar to the school edition, too, but there is an additional character writing segment. This section features animated demonstrations of radicals and stroke order. Accompanying worksheets are downloadable to reinforce character exercises.

The travel program was created for people planning to visit a Chinese-speaking country. Unlike the other editions, this travel edition is much more compact than the other three editions in terms of content and format. It is only available in CD-ROM. Dialogues are relatively simple and followed by scripts with *pinyin* underneath the characters. The language points section introduces travel tips for traveling in China. Drills focus on practical sentences. The Cultural Shocker section lists many experiences a traveler may have during their stay in China.

The most unique feature of *ActiveChinese* is its animated, interactive themes. Most of the topics cover real-life situations and reflect recent changes in Chinese society, culture and economy. Topics specifically target school students in the U. S. and are particularly beneficial to learners who plan to visit China. For example, topics such as handling an emergency, hiring a maid and buying a bicycle are very practical for professionals living and working in China. Some small-talk in the school program is pseudo-authentic. For instance, words and expressions in the Comparing Cities lesson reveal the mindset of the young Chinese working class. Cultural knowledge in this lesson focuses on how young, white-color workers choose a place to work and how the Confucian ideal of filial piety still influences this tendency. In the Relationships lesson, the dialogue develops naturally. Expressions such as 帅呆了 (stunningly handsome), 百里挑一 (one in a hundred, cream of the crop) and 一见钟情 (fall in love at first sight) are included in a natural way. Other words introduced, such as 非诚勿扰 (if you are the one-literally, don't bother if you are not sincere) and 剩男剩女 (a single man or woman over 30 - literally a leftover man and woman) reflect up-to-date attitudes towards relationships of men and women of marrying age.

Two other unique features of *ActiveChinese* are its Chinese subtitles in the dialogues and animations of conversations. The value of textual support for listening has been supported by research comparing the effects of teaching a foreign language in visual form with or without text (Borras & Lafayete, 1994, cited by Chapelle, 2009). This type of pseudo-audio presentation of imitated authentic conversation of real life " provide (s) valuable modified input and resolves miscomprehension, as well as prompts noticing and deep processing. " (Chapelle, 2009, p. 631). The vivid animated scenes paired with conversations provide pragmatically useful, context-specific language input. This input offers more dynamic communications and thus provides a better and more feasible option for listening comprehension than regular classroom instruction. This approach also makes rote exercises and drills on a computer more engaging. This feature is also extended in the drills and exercises. While the dialogue is presented in the extended mode, learners are given opportunities to notice the details of language use. The interactive mode, in which students record their own speech and compare it to the pronunciation of native speakers, not only provides an opportunity for self-correction, but also generates repairing moves when feedback is provided.

Cultural Shockers, in the school program, professional program and travel program is unique. There are eight sets of vivid cartons with a total of 40 slides exposing learners to contemporary Chinese cultural issues in a fun way. After a brief introduction, an avatar narrates a series of scenarios that people from Western cultures may be surprised by when in China. Each scenario is illustrated by one slide consisted a set of four pictures and explanations. These pictures illustrate a variety of aspects of Chinese culture and a large portion focuses on Chinese dining culture. Other things that may surprise travelers are covered in the "city streets" related scenarios. This covers the potential scariness of crossing a city street and the frustration one may experience when asking for directions. The "friends" related topics deal with perceptions of friendship in China, and the theme shows things that a Chinese person may be quite accustomed to seeing but which may seem strange to outsiders. In addition, some uncommon social customs, such as the Chinese aversion to tanning, are covered.

ActiveChinese is available in online and offline formats, such as CD-ROM, software, textbooks and workbooks. There are also e-flash cards in both traditional and simplified characters. It also provides a complete set of teacher's resources, including textbooks, in-class PowerPoint slides for creative teaching activities, explanations of dialogues and language points and *pinyin* teaching guides. Other resources for teachers include written tests for each unit and lesson plans. There are also online resources for students, providing rich and engaging materials, such as *pinyin* and character help. Downloadable MP3 and MP4 files for dialogues and language points are also available. The flashcards can be personalized and allow students to review the vocabulary covered in each lesson.

It is worth pointing out that overall *Active Chinese* is a well-designed and self-contained Chinese language program. The animation dialogues are appealing to learners, interesting to watch and fun to listen to. The webpages of these dialogues are easy to navigate, repeat, rewind and skip. The dialogue design with three speeds pedagogically breaks down the learning process with respect to the principles of language acquisition. They successfully integrate sound introduction, tone demonstration, sentence intonation, character recognition and situational scenarios and create an effective platform for teaching and learning conversational Chinese for beginning learners. The explanations of language points are well constructed. They are easy to follow and it is easy to refer back to the text. The examples included are not only taken from the text, but also are expanded to general application. The recording feature is unique compared to other similar programs. The function of allowing learners to compare their pronunciations to the standard ones is attractive and impressive. The feedback on assessments is a desirable learning tool for students.

Today, Computer-Assisted Language Learning (CALL) offers multiple instances of exposure, negation and practice in a dynamic and multifaceted way outside the classroom (Chapelle, 2009). Effectively using multimedia materials to fill the motivation gap in language learning, *ActiveChinese* makes an important contribution to the field of teaching Chinese with technology. Its holistic design caters to the needs of a wide range of mainstream learners and related audiences such as educators, homeschool parents, and government agencies. Overcoming the limitations of traditional textbooks and time limits of classroom teaching, *ActiveChinese* provides its users with a vast database of texts, images and sounds and integrates its website, CD-ROM, downloadable e-textbook, e-workbook, PowerPoint slideshows, MP3 and MP4 files. This makes this program stand out in the area of meeting the diverse needs of users with different learning preferences.

Currently, *ActiveChinese* is widely used by private and public schools, as well as home-schooling families in the U. S. and many international schools and institutions. Testimonials from users show that innovation is the main attraction to all users. Kids especially enjoy the 12 animated chapters and the easy-to-use drag'n'drop formats. Teachers report that students enjoy learning outside of the classroom and make faster progress than when using only traditional methods of teaching. The technical support from the company is also highly acclaimed. The *ActiveChinese* website maintains a testimonial page (http: //www. activechinese. com/testimonials. jsp), providing potential users convincing evidence from participants.

Although student-centered communication and participation are a strength of this program, most of the communication in the program is between either the learner and the virtual tutor, or between the learner and automatically generated feedback. The provision of feedback has been one of the great challenges faced by CALL (Brett & Gonzalez-Lloret, 2009). An e-learning environment would have greater potential and be more effective if it promoted interaction between users during language acquisition. With the pedagogical trend towards live communication and peer learning, instant communicative forums between learners and teachers and live discussion boards among learners have been recognized as an effective tool in online teaching and learning. Research also proves the efficacy of oral and written communication among learners (Cpapelle, 2009). Since the language forms are more likely to be retained through interactional written and oral activities, *ActiveChinese* could be improved upon if it provided interactive connections such as a live communication forum, instant discussion board and collaborative tasks or activities requiring teamwork between learners from around the world. We expect to see tools such as blogs, wiki pages, live discussion boards and instant chat rooms that promote collaborative activities, participatory learning and real-time interactions not only with the teacher, but also with fellow students. Besides that, although the animations have provided pseudo-authentic scenarios, use of authentic online materials related to themes of lessons could further improve it.

This program is designed to be a comprehensive and integrated Chinese program, however, its attention to the four skills does not seem well-balanced. While oral production and Chinese character recognition skills are emphasized, writing and compositional skills are not addressed directly in any of the three main course programs. The coverage of all four skills would be more balanced if some characters and compositional writing tasks or activities could be added in the future. In addition, there is potential for the *ActiveChinese* designers to expand the exercise formats. So far there are only a limited number of exercise formats, such as multiple choice, fill-in-the-blank with given words and jig-saw puzzles, for all programs and all age learners. The e-learning package would be greatly enriched if some e-worksheet activities were also available online.

References

Borras, I. and Lafayette, R. C. (1994). Effects of multimedia courseware subtitling on the speaking performance of college students of French. The Modern Language Journal 78, 61—75.

Brett, D. and M. Gonzalez-Lloret. (2009). Technology-enhanced materials. In M. Long & C. Doughty (eds.) The Handbook of Language Teaching. Wiley and Blackwell, 351—369.

Chapelle, C. (2009). Computer-assisted teaching and testing. In M. Long & C. Doughty (eds.) The Handbook of Language Teaching. Wiley and Blackwell, 628—644.

移动学习——播客华语辅助教学初探
Mobile Learning-Podcasting for
Chinese Language Learning

陈桂月　林琼瑶　曾伟明　Haidan Wang　新加坡国立大学语言中心

clsckn@ nus. edu. sg；clslincy@ nus. edu. sg；clscwm@ nus. edu. sg

摘　要： 随着科技的发展，移动学习越来越受学习者的欢迎。播客作为一种移动学习的方式正逐渐受到语文教师的重视。新加坡国立大学语言中心也为学习华语作为外语的学生制定了一个播客辅助教材。本文就以参与学习的 200 个大学生为调查对象，探讨播客作为华语辅助教学的作用，以及学生的学习效果。通过问卷调查及定量定性分析，探讨播客在教学上的成效，为对外华语教学提出具体建议。

关键词： 播客，移动学习，华语

一　前言

科技发展日新月异，移动学习已成为许多现代人的学习方式。本论文尝试通过研究播客（podcast）作为一个辅助学习语文的平台，探讨其学习效果。播客（podcast）这个词是由苹果电脑的"iPod"与"广播"（broadcast）混合而成的。如果把博客（blog）称为网络日记的话，播客（podcast）就可以定义为网络音频加上视听文本的综合体。作为一个完整的播客，它必须要有一个传播与接收的过程，也就是所谓的制作方与订阅方。制作方制作或编辑视听文本内容，将它发布到网上，订阅方则利用播客捕捉器（podcatcher）及简易信息聚合阅读器（RSS）进行订阅，在网上收听、收看或接收 PDF 文件，又或者下载至 MP3 或 iPod 的随身播等移动通信设备上，这个过程才算完成。

移动通信设备近年来已成为许多人不可缺少的硬件。从 2001 年苹果公司推出第一台 iPod 开始，人们就不断追求更新的产品，iPod 自 2001 年推出至今已卖出了超过 2.2 亿台，从 2007 年至 2009 年的两年内，iPhone 及 iPod touch 触屏手机也卖出了 5000 万台（Siegler，2009）。根据市场分析机构 NPD 对 2011 年美国零售市场的统计，iPod，iPhone 及 iPod touch 第二季度在美国区的总销量超过 2000 万部，同比增长了 113%。① 接下来就是 iPad 的天下了，IDC 调查机构的统计数字显示，iPad 在 2011 年全球第一季的销售额就超过了 5000 万台。

移动学习在本文的定义是，学习者的学习场所从课室往外移动，能灵活地、不受时空限制地学习，边走边学也成为了一种选择。对于教学者来说，移动学习指出了新方法，将声像内容直接传送给学习者；对学习者而言，则能更快速与轻易地获取学习资料。无可否认的，播客语文学习在一些具体问题上还存在着局限，譬如学生是否能轻易通过电脑上网，或是否拥有移动通信设备等。从这个角度来看，那些经济较发达的国家及电脑和移动通信器材普及的国家，这个教学理念和方法的可行性要高一些。在这一点上，新加坡学生具有较大优势。据新加坡媒体发展局的最新统计，拥有个人电脑的家庭占了 83%，而拥有宽频网络的家庭则有 80%。② 而在新加坡所有政府设立的大学，学生都可以无线上网，学生以大学的优惠价购买电脑和手机并不是难事。

从 2007 年开始，新加坡国立大学语言中心的德文组就率先开始制作播客，利用播客教导德语，德文组也在这个实验计划推行一个学期后，进行了问卷调查，同时发表研究报告。随后在 2009 年，大学语言中心的华文、韩文、泰文和印尼文先后推出了自己的播客网站，华文和韩文则对学习者进行了调查，相继把初步的研究结果在不同的学术会议上发表（例如 Chan，2008；Chan，Chen & D？pel，2008；Chi & Chan，2009；陈桂月，2009）。

以上提及的播客研究有一个共同发现，那就是学生对于利用播客学习语文的经验相对薄弱。因此，如何制定适合学生要求的播客，如何提高学习效果，是制作播客作为语文教学的老师所特别关注的，在这方面进行的学术研究并不足够，而以华文为对外语文教学的播客更是少之又少。本文就希望通过这个研究，对这些问题作更深入的了解。华文组在 2009—2010 年第一学期推出华文播客，并于学期末进行了一个问卷调查，以求通过定量和定性数据分析，帮助制作者更好的了解播客教学的构想与学习效果，进一步了解播

---

① 资料来自 NPD 分析机构网站：http：//apple-laptop-store. com/2010/01/25/ipod-touch-sales-spike-55-mac-strong-in-education-overseas/。

② 新加坡媒体发展局 2009 年调查报告：http：//www. ida. gov. sg/doc/Publications/Publications_Level3/Survey2009/ENT2009ES. pdf。

客的设计是否达到学习目的，从播客使用者的角度反映出播客制作的质量，以便对将来的制作提供参考。

二 播客语言学习的文献综述

从 2005 年至今，越来越多语文教师尝试通过播客进行教学。日本名古屋财经大学在 2005 年就分发了 512 兆位的 iPod 给所有大学一年级的学生，英文老师利用播客让学生收听广播节目，以协助提高学生的听力水平（Monk，Ozawa & Thomas，2006）。问卷调查结果发现学生并不知道可以利用这个资源学习，有 65.6% 的学生没有或很少下载，只有 4.2% 的学生经常下载，有 45.3% 的学生觉得播客对他们的学习帮助不大或完全没用。

2007 年，英国的一组学者（Edirisingha，Rizzi，Nie & Rothwell，2007）在一个跨文化传播的课程里进行播客教学。他们制作了 6 个播客，在每个单元里加入课程介绍及学生访谈、讨论评估任务、演示方法及研究技巧等。结果却显示，有一半的学生并没有运用播客里的补充材料，理由是"太忙了"。在 35 个参与调查的学生当中，53% 觉得这些补充资料是有用的，因为它提供了课程信息，还有 40% 认为播客能激发他们对课程的兴趣，另外 40% 的学生则认为播客可以推动他们更专注于学习。

2009 年，美国大学的另一组研究人员（Abdous，Camarena & Facer，2009）在 8 个不同学科的课程里让学生利用播客学习，包括法文、德文、日文、西班牙文及文学，以及世界文学。参与调查的学生分成两组，一组 80 人强制利用播客学习（PIC），另一组 33 人无须强制收听（PSM）。结果显示，PIC 学生中有 72.5% 至少收听过一个单元，而 PSM 学生中却只有 45.5%。大多数学生认为播客的学习资料十分有用，65% 的 PIC 学生及 54.5% 的 PSM 学生认为他们会报读有播客的课程。总的来说，两组学生都认为播客可以提高他们的听说能力和增加词汇量。

新加坡国立大学语言中心的德文组从 2007 年开始积极投入资源制作播客教材，也从那时开始对学习效果进行有系统的研究（Chan et al，2008；Chan，2008）。最早的一个调查是给初学者收听的 14 个单元的播客，内容包括听力、口语、文法、词汇及学习技巧，以及德国文化和资讯等。德文老师进行了定量和定性分析，结果令人鼓舞。在 203 个学生中，有 97% 至少收听了 1 个单元，55.7% 的学生至少收听了 8 个单元。随后在 Chan 的另一个调查中，学生对于到德国或瑞士作短期交换生的预备课程播客更加投入，在 6 个单元中，有 66% 的学生收听了至少 4 个或以上，学生对德国文化和大学生活最感兴趣。

2009—2010 学年，新加坡国大语言中心韩文组也制作了 10 个单元的播客给 28 个中级班的学生收听。过后的调查显示，学生对以播客学韩文的意愿非常高，有 96.2% 的学生收听了，62.9% 的学生收听了全部单元，将近一半的学生（46.2%）是移动学习（大部分是在巴士和地铁上），还有 38.5% 的学生是在课室以外——校园、宿舍或图书馆里收听。（Chi & Chan，2009）比起之前德文组的调查，韩文组的学生更有意识地将播客学习融入日常生活中。

以播客教导华文的研究报告并不多，在新加坡和中国及中国香港、中国台湾四地，有一些语文教师利用播客教学，但并没有进行学习效果的研究。利用播客网站提供技术援助和鼓励播客教学的，有台湾的"华语 e 起来学习网"，中国国内的播客天下、土豆播客等也都内置了 RSS 阅读器，方便制作和学习者。然而在中国大陆，许多研究报告还停留在播客如何制作、播客有何功用等课题上。

三　播客单元之构思与设计

（一）过程

新加坡国大的华文播客取名《快乐播客》，以鼓励学习者快乐学习。制作过程分为构思，制作与播放三个阶段。

第一阶段确定播客内容、使用的语言、风格、单元及频率。为区别不同程度学生，《快乐播客》分六级，《快乐播客一》为零起点学生制作，目的在辅助课堂教学，作为课外补充和练习之用。为鼓励学生收听，播出后也在课堂上进行小测验和讨论活动。制作者仿效广播节目制作方式，轻松活泼地带出学习目标。单元的开头、中间及结束皆用音乐来区隔，第二和第三单元收录了两首华文歌曲。由于对象是初级学生，所以播客的语言乃华英语并用，但逐步增加华语的比重。在一个学期 13 周里，一共播出 4 个单元，大约每 3 周播出一个单元。

第二阶段是播客的制作。《快乐播客一》是配合华文一教材来构思的，四个单元的主题包括汉语拼音、打招呼、运动和团体作业。由课程专任教师负责撰稿与录音，录音及剪辑工作在校园录音室进行。

第三阶段是播放。华文组有一个互动教学网站《快乐 e-华文》，有关播客的单元信息和播出日期就公布在网页上①，学生可利用自动订阅（RSS）获取新的播客单元。同样的播客单元也放在新加坡国大的一个内联网平台 IVLE（Integrated Virtual Learning Environment）上，选读课程的学生都可以进入平台在线收听或下载。学期初老师会介绍播客教学的内容，指导学生如何下载收听，网页上附有详细说明。

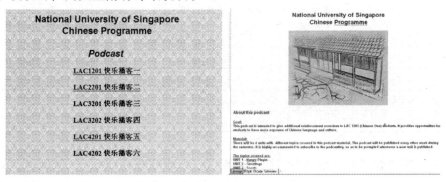

图1　华文互动学习网站

（二）播客单元内容

2009—2010 学年第一学期所制作的播客单元共有 4 个。每单元的平均长度是 3 分钟。表1 举例说明播客单元的基本架构。

表1　　　　单元内容架构《第一个单元：汉语拼音》长度：4 分 8 秒

时间	内容
0：00	开场音乐
0：06	华语开场问候
0：17	英语开场 + 介绍
0：43	插播音乐
0：47	单元主题 + 提问
1：07	插播音乐
1：13	练习指示—韵母
1：23	发音练习题目
1：41	插播音乐
1：45	练习指示—声母

① http：//courseware. nus. edu. sg/clu/.

续表

时间	内容
1：58	发音练习题目
2：31	插播音乐
2：36	练习指示—声母＋韵母
2：53	插播音乐
2：56	发音练习题目
3：16	插播音乐
3：18	练习题目解答
3：46	结束语
3：58	终场音乐

播客单元的基本设计包括四个要素：开、收场音乐、介绍、练习题目和结束语。首先授课老师先向学生打招呼，接着简介单元的内容与解释练习目标，然后要求学生进行口头练习，最后道别并邀请学生参与课堂讨论。为了增加学习乐趣，第二和第三单元也介绍了华文歌曲。此外，部分播客的文稿也放在网上供学生下载或列印。播客单元的播放日期在学期初就公布，届期授课老师也提醒学生收听。收听后一周在课堂上进行计分测验。测验问题也指出课堂讨论的方向。

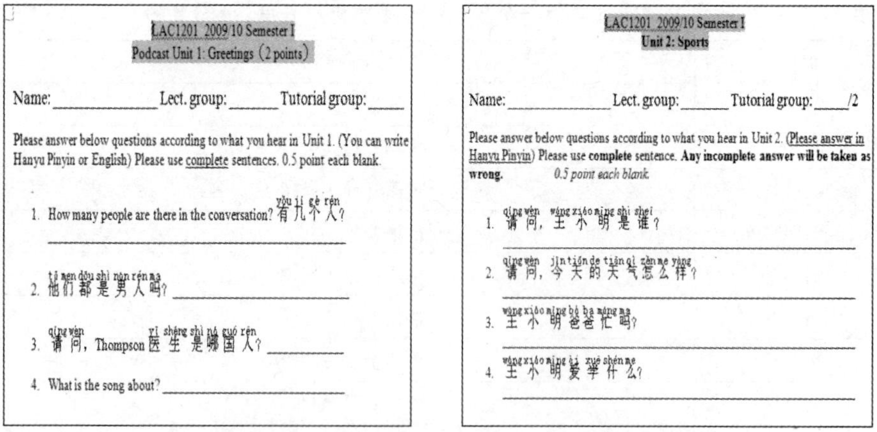
LAC1201 2009/10 Semester I
Podcast Unit 1: Greetings (2 points)

Name:______ Lect. group:______ Tutorial group:______

Please answer below questions according to what you hear in Unit 1. (You can write Hanyu Pinyin or English) Please use complete sentences. 0.5 point each blank.

1. How many people are there in the conversation? 有几个人？
2. 他们都是男人吗？
3. 请问，Thompson医生是哪国人？
4. What is the song about?

LAC1201 2009/10 Semester I
Unit 2: Sports

Name:______ Lect. group:______ Tutorial group:______/2

Please answer below questions according to what you hear in Unit 2. (Please answer in Hanyu Pinyin) Please use **complete** sentence. **Any incomplete answer will be taken as wrong.** *0.5 point each blank.*

1. 请问，王小明是谁？
2. 请问，今天的天气怎么样？
3. 王小明爸爸忙吗？
4. 王小明爱学什么？

图 2　测验题目《第二单元：打招呼》与《第三单元：运动》

四 调查研究

（一）研究目的

至今关于应用播客于外语教学的研究还相当有限，课堂应用经验作为研究是宝贵的，所收集的资料可作为未来使用播客教学和研究的参考。有关资料可细分为三个方面：

- 同播客有关的硬件、软件和网络资源的资料，以及学生使用播客的经验
- 学生使用《快乐播客一》的情况和使用模式
- 了解学生对播客学习华语的看法以及对播客的内容和制作等的意见

（二）问卷调查

资料的搜集通过问卷调查进行。问卷包括两大部分。第一部分是学生的背景资料，例如年龄、性别、国籍、居住地（校外或校内）、学院和年级，以及学生使用电脑硬件（个人电脑和/或 MP3 等）、软件（iTunes，Windows Media Player 等）和网络资源（宽频或调制解调器）的情况，还有学生过去使用播客的经验；第二部分针对《快乐播客一》的使用频率、时间、地点、动机，以及学生对播客设计的意见。题目包括封闭性（选择题）和开放性（问答题）两类。在选择题部分，我们采用李克特 5 点式量表（Likert-scale）。一共发出 193 份问卷，回收 166 份。

我们使用 SPSS 第 18 版来整理与分析数据，大部分采用描述统计学的方式，多选题则采用频率分析法。在李克特 5 点式量表，1 代表非常不同意（strongly disagree），而 5 则代表非常同意（strongly agree）。分析过程参考了个别题目之平均数（mean）和标准差（standard deviation）。

（三）调查结果

1. 硬件、软件和网络资源

多数学生拥有使用播客所需要之硬件和软件。超过七成（70.5%）的学生有 MP3，其中六成（59.4%）属于 Apple iPod 或是 iPhone。几乎每个学生都拥有笔记本电脑（97.5%），其中 65.6% 的学生还同时拥有台式电脑。此外，将近九成五（94.5%）的学生享有宽频网络服务，能够有效的在线收听或下载播客单元。少数学生（4.9%）虽仍然只有调制解调器，但他们

一旦进入校园，即可利用校园的宽频资源来收听。

2. 过去使用播客的经验

在《快乐播客一》之前，只有不到半数的学生（47.2%）使用过播客。其中25个学生（32.7%）曾经订阅，但大多数学生的订阅少于5个项目。曾经使用播客学习语文的学生只有11%。

3. 《快乐播客一》的使用情况

学生对于《快乐播客一》的收听气氛非常热烈，大多数学生听了所有单元。96.4%的学生听了3个以上的单元。没有听的原因，40%是因为没有时间，另外40%则是忘记了或认为没有必要。

大多数的学生（77.6%）重复收听单元内容，最常见的是2—3次（64.6%），有13%超过3次。绝大多数的学生（95.7%）使用个人电脑听取播客，其余学生偶尔使用MP3。有一部分或可归因于笔记本电脑的高普及率（97.5%）以及大学校园随处可取得的宽频网络服务。关于收听播客地点的调查结果也与此相符。几乎所有的学生（98.8%）都选择在家里（50.3%）或是宿舍里（48.5%）收听播客，24.5%在校园各处，2.5%是在走路或乘坐公共运输工具时收听。学生选择在家里或宿舍的理由是这些地点方便舒适，干扰也少，至于走路或乘车时收听则是节省时间，技术方便且有助于放松。多数学生表示他们只有在温习功课时才会听播客，而温习功课的地点通常是家里或宿舍。傍晚6点到夜间12点是最多人收听播客的时间（69.6%），中午12点到下午6点次之（33.5%）。校园范围内的其他收听地点包括图书馆、实验室、餐厅及朋友房间。

五　学生意见与建议

关于学生对《快乐播客一》的设计和内容的意见是以李克特5点式量表（1-非常不同意，2-不同意，3-没有意见，4-同意，5-非常同意）以及4个开放式问题来进行。

整体而言，学生对于播客的设计和主题的反映是正面的。包括主题（3.93）、长度（3.89）、播放频率（3.73）和单元数量（3.71），学生都认为是为恰当的。学生喜欢收听（3.61）且同意所选择的歌曲是有趣的（3.71）。

统计表格1　学生对于播客整体印象（设计与主题）

Item	Statement	Frequency of responses(percentages)					Mean	SD
		SD1	D2	N3	A4	SA5		
46	I would like to see more topics included.	0.6	9.0	23.5	48.8	15.1	3.71	0.863
47	I would like to see more language areas/skills included.	0	9.6	25.3	46.6	15.7	3.70	0.858
48	I find the overall technical quality to be good.	0.6	3.6	10.8	65.7	16.9	3.97	0.702
49	I find the audio to be sufficiently clear.	1.8	2.4	7.2	57.2	27.7	4.11	0.790

1—非常不同意，2—不同意，3—没有意见，4—同意，5—非常同意

学生在开放题的答案也呼应了这个结果：

I think it is helpful to have the vocabulary used in other ways than the actual lesson.

I enjoyed the music. I felt it was very helpful in understanding how things are supposed to sound, especially when studying on your own.

虽然大致的评价为正面，但学生也提出了一些改良建议。86%的学生认为播客单元可以更多。37%的学生提出播客的内容太困难，速度太快，所选择的歌曲不恰当。

More lessons with more frequency.

It is a bit too fast. Although the podcast can be played and stopped at any time.

Since songs are included, they should be more relevant to our age group, perhaps songs that are popular among the Chinese now.

把听说、发音、文法、词汇等学习重点拆开来看，学生普遍同意《快乐播客一》对于听力（3.88）、词汇（3.84）、发音（3.83）、文法知识（3.77）、文化知识（3.73）的加强是有用的，但是对于说（3.6）以及文法练习（3.6）的态度则比较保留。最负面的反映是使用播客来学习新句构的部分，学生不表赞同（3.43）。这很可能是因为当初的设计并没有特别强调文法练习。我们的教材主张语法的学习应该是隐性的，应透过多听多说潜移默化而不特别强调句构的分析。

统计表格 2　学生对个别学习成分的意见

Item	Statement	Frequency of responses (percentages)					Mean	SD
		SD1	D2	N3	A4	SA5		
37	I find the listening exercises to be useful.	2.4	4.8	14.5	56.6	19.9	3.88	0.871
38	I find the speaking exercises to be useful.	1.8	11.4	24.1	47.0	13.3	3.60	0.929
39	I find the pronunciation tips and exercises to be useful.	0.6	7.2	15.7	58.4	15.7	3.83	0.806
40	I find the grammar in formation and exercises to be useful.	1.2	4.2	21.7	58.4	11.4	3.77	0.760
41	The podcast lessons increase my grasp of new grammar structures.	2.5	14.1	30.1	44.8	8.6	3.43	0.923
42	I find the grammar exercises to be appropriate for a podcast.	0	9.6	25.9	55.4	6.0	3.60	0.753
43	I find the inrormation about Chinese culture and society to be useful	1.2	6.6	26.3	45.2	17.5	3.73	0.879
44	I find the vocabulary information and exercises to be useful.	0	4.2	17.5	64.5	10.2	3.84	0.662

1—非常不同意，2—不同意，3—没有意见，4—同意，5—非常同意

　　在技术层面，学生对播客的品质感到满意（3.97），尤其是清晰度（4.11）。学生也希望播课内容更丰富（3.71），包含更多语言技能的练习（3.7）。

统计表格 3　学生对技术面的意见及建议

Item	Statement	Frequency of responses (percentages)					Mean	SD
		SD1	D2	N3	A4	SA5		
33	I find the number of podcasts to be appropriate.	1.2	6.6	22.3	55.4	11.5	3.71	0.810
34	I find the frequency of the podcasts to be appropriate.	1.2	6.6	19.3	60.2	9.6	3.73	0.783
35	I find the length of the podcasts to be appropriate.	1.2	5.6	9.3	70.8	13.0	3.89	0.742
36	I enjoy listening to the podcasts.	2.5	10.5	26.3	44.4	16.0	3.61	0.960
45	I find the topics on the whole to be relevant to the course.	0	3.0	12.7	69.9	12.0	3.93	0.612
50	I find the songs very interesting. (Please tick this if you are in Chinese1.)	6.6	6.6	19.9	38.6	24.7	3.71	1.130

1—非常不同意，2—不同意，3—没有意见，4—同意，5—非常同意

　　学生也提出详细的意见：

I have been working at a radio station for 8 years and I can definitely say that the podcasts are produced professionally-from their content, structure and sound quality. Great work!

Keep on doing that, however make sure that it's relevant to the lesson and it's compatible with student's knowledge.

六 讨论

（一）移动学习

播客技术的出现让移动学习成为一个选择，也开启了语言学习的一个可能性。本研究的调查结果却显示，即便在软硬件具备的情况下，绝大多数的学生还是习惯利用电脑来收听，而非下载至 MP3 等。根据开放题的答案，主要原因有两点：（一）技术困难；（二）学习习惯。就技术的层面来说，一些学生反映他们不知道怎么去订阅或是下载；有的学生则觉得下载太花时间，而且由于《快乐播客一》同时放置在 IVLE 和网站上，上网收听对学生而言是最直接的办法。至于学习习惯，如前所述，学生习惯定点学习，家里和宿舍是最多人收听的场所。未来教师除了需要给予更多的技术指导，让播客的下载更为简易之外，也得帮助学生理解移动学习的好处。积极鼓励学生订阅。

It would be useful to include download link for downloading the MP3 for offline use. Current system doesn't necessarily work on all platforms and downloading the MP3 was sometimes difficult.

Podcasts are interesting, but it takes me long to download them.

（二）内容设计

1. 文化与生活

请学生针对播客的其他主题、语言技能或练习提出建议，结果发现生活（35%）和文化（32%）知识最受欢迎，其次是流行资讯、歌曲和新闻（30%）。这个结果同 Chan and et al（2008）和 Chi & Chan（2009）的发现一致。这显示语言学习者期望通过播客获取的是比较生活和日常的知识。基于这三个研究皆采用广播节目的轻松风格，可以推论播客更适合非正式、即时的学习，这也突出了播客教学有别于一般教学带的发展方向。就语言技能方面，将近半数（45%）的学生希望能够通过播客学习生活会话，其次是发音练习（19%），然后是更多词汇（16%）。

2. 困难度

如前所述，37%的学生认为播客内容对他们而言太难了。其中16%认为是语速的问题，12%认为是对内容或语音不熟悉，9%则认为是生词的关系。这指出未来播客教学的可以改进之处，包括减慢语速、慢速版本和正常速度版本并用、配合讲义以及加入填充或问答练习等等。

七　结语和未来研究方向

播客语言教学尚处于起步阶段，其可能性和应用方式皆值得进一步发掘。本研究的初步结果显示学生欢迎播客教学，也认为《快乐播客一》的设计是合宜的，他们肯定播客的制作品质及其有效性，也喜欢收听华语播客。本研究也发现播客教学更适合非正式、即时的学习，以及制作播客所需注意的重点，包括说话速度，文化和生活主题，给学生更充分的技术指导和鼓励，配合视觉材料和选择适合年龄层的歌曲等。

综合前人和本研究结果，华文组在新学期的播客教学已经作出了改进。制作者目前还在继续进行问卷调查，搜集更多资料以资未来播客教学的参考。至今关于播客教学的研究十分欠缺，还有许多值得进一步探讨的方面，包括播客内容的设计，学生使用播客的模式，播客教学在语言学习上的有效性，以及学生的动机等。这就有赖于未来同业的共同努力。

参考书目

Abdous, M., Camaraena, M. M., & Facer, B. R. 2009. MALL Technology: Use of Academic Podcasting in the Foreign Language Classroom. *ReCall*, 21 (1), 76—95.

Chan, W. M. 2008, August. *Der Einsatz vom Podcast in DaF-Unterricht: Ein Vehikel zur Landeskundevermittlung.* Paper presented at Asiatische Germanistentagung 2008, Seiryo University, Kanazawa, Japan.

Chan, W. M., Chen, I. R., & D? pel, M. 2008, December. Learning on the move: Applying podcasting technologies to foreign language learning. In W. M. Chan, K. N. Chin, P. Martin-Lau, M. Nagami, J. W. Sew & T. Suthiwan (Comp.), *Media in foreign language teaching and learning.* Proceedings of CLaSIC 2008 (pp. 36—69). Singapore: Centre for Language Studies.

Chi, S. W., & Chan, W. M. 2009, December. *Mobile Korean language learning. Podcasting as an educational medium.* Paper presented at the Korean Language International Symposium to Celebrate the 60th Anniversary of Kyung-Hee University, Seoul, South Korea.

Edirisingha, P. , Rizzi, C. , Nie, M. , & Rothwell, L. 2007. Podcasting to provide teaching and learning support for an undergraduate module on English Language and Communication, *Turkish Online Journal of Distance Education*, 8 (3), 87—107.

Monk, B. , Ozawa, K. , & Thomas, M. 2006. iPods in English Language Education: A case study of English listening and reading students. *NUCB journal of language culture and communication*, 8 (3), 85—102.

Siegler, M. G. 2009, September 9. Steve Jobs returns to the stage with some big numbers to share. *TechCrunch*. Retrieved on November 28, 2009, from http://www. techcrunch. com/2009/09/09/steve-jobs-returns-with-some-big-numbers-to-share/.

陈桂月 (2009):《移动学习——运用播客教导对外华语》, 发表于《第二届全球华语论坛》(2009), 中国暨南大学。

Integrating ChinesePod into Lower Intermediate Chinese Course

安世东　An, Irene Shidong　澳大利亚悉尼大学
The University of Sydney shidong. an@ sydney. edu. au

摘　要：本文简要介绍了初中级中文传统语言教学课堂引进网络中文教学平台——中文播客的成功经验，强调在运用电脑辅助教学使学生自主学习、移动学习成为可能的情况下教师所起的不可替代的作用。从课程设计、教学材料选择、教学活动、考评任务和测验设计，到执行各项课堂教学任务，监督并评估学习效果，整个过程需要以教学法原则作为指导。教师的首要任务是运用第二外语的习得与教学理论及教学法为学生创造适于第二外语习得的条件以促进学生的语言习得。

关键词：电脑辅助语言教学，播客，教师作用，理想的第二外语学习环境条件，自主学习

Abstract：This paper reports on the integration of a commercial Chinese learning podcasting service into the university Lower Intermediate Chinese course. It aims to highlight the role a teacher plays in a blended learning environment where mobile learning is enabled by adopting the new digital technology：podcast. From planning the curriculum，choosing relevant teaching/learning content，designing learning activities and assessment tasks，to monitoring and evaluating the effectiveness of the integration，this whole decision-making process should be driven by pedagogical principles. The critical teacher's role is to create and maintain conditions for optimal language learning environments with the help of technology. Even the successful application of technology will not be an end product itself but rather a new starting point because the teacher should always be on the way of adapting it to the new target cohort and environment.

Key words：CALL, podcast, teacher's role, conditions for optimal second language learning environments，autonomous learning

Introduction to ChinesePod

ChinesePod is an online language training service based in Shanghai China (www. ChinesePod. com). They publish lesson podcasts of different languages at different levels. Chinese lesson podcasts include different levels from newbie, elementary, intermediate, upper intermediate to advanced, and media lessons. The podcasts contain discussion of vocabulary and grammar, introduction to cultural knowledge, dialogues simulating real-life situations using colloquial language. They offer the learners abundant exposure to authentic target language use and culture information, which to a large extent, compensates for the insufficient target language input foreign language learners receive in a non-target-language learning environment. ChinesePod website also provides vocabulary lists, scripts of all dialogues, extended vocabulary usages, and discussion forums. With premium subscription, users can have access to all these features and download all the podcasts and other materials onto their computers or other mobile devices.

Background

In response to suggestions in the 2007 Departmental Review, our Chinese Department initiated projects to enrich the structure, accessibility and resource base of our language programs. Initially we had focused particularly on Lower Intermediate Chinese units of the Non-background Stream. These units were very 'content-heavy' with five contact hours each week devoted mainly to reading, writing and grammar; as such, there had always been a problem of finding sufficient time to properly incorporate listening and speaking components in these two units. In 2008, the department launched a strategic initiative to investigate ways of using online and multi-media resources to assist teaching and learning; especially to improve the students' listening and speaking skills. Based on recommendations from senior students a decision was made to trial the use of ChinesePod in the Lower Intermediate Chinese in the March semester.

The trial group has 47 enrolled students. They are all non-native Chinese speakers who have completed one year Chinese language study at the beginner's level at the same university or somewhere else. Their nationalities include Australians, New Zealanders, Koreans, Japanese and other Asian and European nationalities. The group has five face-to-face contact hours each week.

ChinesePod was fully integrated into the curriculum. The old textbook remained as the core textbook (Integrated Chinese Level 2) for grammar teaching and reading and writing training while ChinesePod materials were used mainly for listening and speaking training (for detailed descriptions please see Teacher's Role section below).

Results of the Integration

At the end of the trial period, the coordinator (author of the paper) conducted an independent survey to collect student feedback specifically on the integration of ChinesePod into the course. Out of the 47 students, 46 responded to the questionnaire. The following diagram shows the results:

As suggested in Figue 1, 31 (70.5%) stdents in the group either strongly agreed or agreed to the statement that they often listened to the ChinesePod lessons they downloaded onto their MP3/MP4/IPod or other devices. Students' responses to the statements regarding to the benefits of ChinesePod were generally very positive. A majority of students either strongly agreed or agreed that the ChinesePod podcasts provided them with many real life language items which they found very useful; that the implementation of ChinesePod into the course helped them improve their speaking skills and also helped them with their overall study in this unit. 38 (86.4%) students either strongly agreed or agreed that overall the implementation of ChinesePod into the course was a success and a similar proportion of students showed their agreement to the statement that the Department should continue to subscribe to ChinesePod in the following semester.

It should also be noted that only about 50% of the students thought

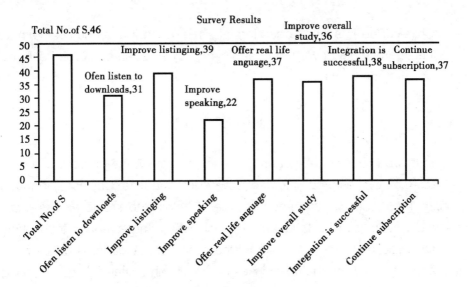

Figure1   Survey results (The far left column stands for the total number of students serveyed. The other culumns show the number of students who either strongly agree or agree with the statements in the survery)

that ChinesePod definitely helped them improve their speaking skills. However, most of the rest of the students felt uncertain about this item in the questionnaire while only two students declared that ChinesePod was not helpful for their speaking. This is not surprising considering that speaking skill is a productive skill which normally takes longer time to develop compared to listening skill. Therefore 13 weeks (one semester) maybe too short to show significant effects on speaking skill development.

In addition, the standard University survey showed marked increases in evaluations for several important aspects of this unit of study compared to the previous year. Overall the integration of ChinesePod into the course was a success from both the coordinator and the students' point of view. It improved the overall structure of this unit and partially rectified the perennial problem of shortfall in class time for developing listening and speaking skills, hence greatly enhanced the students' learning experience. The unit coordinator noticed a marked improvement in student performance and interest; observations which were clearly supported in student survey feedback.

ChinesePod has since been formally integrated in the courses. With its gradual improvement over the three years, it has been positively received by a majority of students.

Teacher's Role

In this paper, I will reflect on the teacher's role in the process of the integration of ChinesePod into the Lower Intermediate Chinese language course. I will focus on the teacher's role of helping to create and maintain desirable conditions for language learning when implementing technology into a language classroom. As far as the scope of this paper is concerned, the language learning mainly focuses on developing listening and speaking skills.

At the design stage

At the design stage, the teacher's initial role is to make sure that there is a pedagogical need for implementing technology into the classroom. As Sharma and Barrett (2007) put it, "we must ensure that the teaching is driven by the pedagogy and supported by the technology". The two major pedagogical issues with the previous mode of face to face teaching and learning in the lower intermediate course were: a) Students lacked exposure to the target language and opportunities to use the target language. b) Students had insufficient listening and speaking training in class. Thanks to mobile technology, learning is no longer confined to classrooms and homes. We are living in a "Mobile Age" characterised by mobility of people and knowledge (Sharples *et al.*, 2007; Rheingold, 2002). Podcasting technology has great potential in extending classroom teaching and learning beyond the traditional scope and making learning happen while learners are on the move.

As a web-based language learning platform, ChinesePod, with its professionally made and frequently updated podcast lessons, diverse and rich language resources, ease of navigation and other user-friendly features, are well received internationally. It's both convenient and reliable as a language learning tool. Their newbie to upper-intermediate level lessons focus on real life spoken language and have great potential in addressing the specific issues we were facing in the course and can at the same time motivate student interests in Chinese language. If adopted successfully, there is the possibility of extending student learning to outside the classroom.

Based on this initial evaluation of the ChinesePod program, a decision was made to bring it into the intermediate Chinese language units of study. However, good technology doesn't automatically ensure effective learning. Emphasizing on the importance of methodology in CALL (Computer Assisted Language Learning), the line from Jones (1986) some twenty years ago still holds much truth in today's digital age— "It's not so much the program, more what you do with it". Methodology in CALL is important and the teacher's role is to bring "methodological expertise" to the CALL classroom. Cameron (1999) also stated that "a CALL program or a Website in itself is but one element in the teaching/learning experience. It needs careful planning to fit it into the curriculum".

ChinesePod needs to be integrated into the curriculum to create a *blended learning* environment. According to Sharma & Barrett (2007), *Blended Learning* refers to "a language course which combines a F2F (face-to-face) classroom component with an appropriate use of technology". In the case of ChinesePod project, the "podcast" lessons are integrated into the traditional classroom teaching as listening and speaking components, to address the issues existed in the previous curriculum, while the original reading and writing components are remained and the old textbooks are still used.

The following logistic considerations are made during this design stage:

• One and half hours out of the five weekly face-to-face teaching will be devoted to listening and speaking with ChinesePod materials. The purpose is to ensure that the students receive proper teacher-led training and have opportunities to interact with 'authentic' audience and receive teacher feedback.

• Intermediate ChinesePod podcasts are chosen for this class. The lessons to be adopted are carefully chosen to make sure that the topics are closely related to the textbook lessons and the level of difficulty is equivalent to the textbook, and where possible, the vocabulary and grammar items learned in the textbook are recycled.

• Corresponding learning tasks and assessments are designed. Two listening tests (20%) are to replace one of the old reading and writing tests. A group project (15%), based on a series of ChinesePod lessons is designed and some weekly in-class speaking assessment tasks are also devised to encourage interaction and check the student speaking progress.

• A WebCT site, the CMS (Course Management System) commonly used across the university is used to provide the students with access to relevant teaching and learning materials such as answer keys to workbook exercises, which were previously discussed using class time. In this way, class time can be saved for more interactive activities based on Chinese-Pod. The WebCT site is also the platform for teachers to communicate with the students about the course in general, and especially about Chinese-Pod. Since ChinesePod study involves students' self study, the CMS plays a critical role in providing guidance and building up the sense of connectivity between the teachers and students.

At the implementation stage

The key role the teacher plays when implementing technology into the face to face teaching and learning is to enhance learning. According to Spolsky's general theory of second language learning (see Spolsky, 1989), both the learner factors (learners' language knowledge and skills, learner ability and affective factors) and environmental factors (in Spolsky's term "opportunity") are necessary conditions for second language acquisition. He argues that each of the components is important to the learning outcome, 'if any one is absent, there can be no learning, and the greater any one is, the greater the amount of learning' Spolsky (1989: p15). So it is reasonable to argue that in a formal classroom language learning setting, since the teacher has the power to influence the environmental factors, he/she plays a critical role in creating and maintaining a positive and constructive learning environment to enhance learning. Based on Spolsky's general theory of second language learning, Egbert *et al.* (2007) proposed eight conditions for optimal language learning environments as follows:

1. Learners have opportunities to interact and negotiate meaning.

2. Learners interact in the target language with an authentic audience.

3. Learners are involved in authentic tasks.

4. Learners are exposed to and encouraged to produce varied and creative language.

5. Learners have enough time and feedback.

6. Learners are guided to attend mindfully to the learning process.

7. Learners work in an atmosphere with an ideal stress/anxiety level.

8. Learner autonomy is supported.

The remaining part of this paper will focus on the teacher's role of creating and maintaining the eight conditions for optimal language learning environments in the ChinesePod integration project.

To ensure learner exposure to the target language

One important role the teacher plays in the ChinesePod project is to ensure the student exposure to the target language. This is realized by teaching and learning in both face to face mode and student self-study mode after the class.

The first half hour of the class time is usually teacher-led listening practice, when the students are exposed to the target language in the form of simulated real life audio dialogues from ChinesePod. During this time, the students are involved in various listening comprehension exercises focusing on different language items. This is usually followed by a 15-minute student self-study time on the computer after which the teacher conducts some on-spot tiny assessment tasks to reinforce some particular areas of learning on that day. Throughout this whole hour, the students are continuously exposed to the target language. The teacher's roles include designing tasks and worksheets, monitoring and helping to adjust the learning pace, explaining vocabulary, grammar and related culture knowledge, and providing feedback.

Class hour is limited and definitely cannot provide sufficient exposure to the target language. Web-based program like ChinesePod makes it possible and convenient to extend the classroom learning and keep the learners exposed to the target language after class hours. With the listening training provided in class as a guide and the two listening tests as external driving force, the students continue the learning by self-directed study in their own time and at their own pace. They have the opportunity to continue to immerse themselves in the target language input. They can study ChinesePod lessons via the web using the useful tools and resources provided or they can download materials onto PDAs (personal digital assistant) like smart phones, iPods, MP3/MP4 players to learn them whenever and wherever convenient for them.

To provide learner training and support autonomy

Exposure to the target language is a necessary but not sufficient condition for learning to happen. The teacher plays a critical role in guiding the students "to attend mindfully to the learning process and supporting student autonomy".

During in-class teacher-led listening, the students are guided through the learning process. Listening is categorised as both *bottom-up* and *top-down* processing. *Bottom-up* processing involves decoding of language into meaningful units from sound and *top-down* processing is making predictions and trying to match meaning with the sound. They are both necessary for developing listening comprehension (Healey, 2007; Peterson, 2001).

When faced with a listening task, the students are not necessarily aware of the listening strategies. Especially in a computer-assisted environment, they need training and guidance before they are able to mind their own learning effectively. As digital natives, many of the students may be "experts" to employ new technology for entertaining purposes; however, they are not necessarily experts in using computers to learn effectively. Therefore learner training in this regard is essential in implementing CALL (Arnold and Ducate, 2006; Hubbard, 2004).

As far as ChinesePod listening is concerned, the ChinesePod website provides all useful resources like vocabulary list, lesson dialogue scripts, and full lesson teaching etc, which are all available at the students' fingertips. Some students may start by reading the scripts or listen while reading the scripts. In this way, the *top-down* processing is completely missing and it will not benefit the students in dealing with listening in real life communication when no "scripts" are allowed. The teacher-led *top-down* listening training in class may provide learner training by demonstrating various listening strategies.

For example, the teacher usually leads a 3-minitue brainstorming exercise before each listening task to encourage the students to activate their *schemata*—their background knowledge about the topic and help them form expectations about the input information. After this warm-up activity, the teacher tries to engage the students in the listening task by providing various listening comprehension activities. The students listen with focus and specific goals and thus are guided to attend to the listening "mindfully". The listening strategies demonstrated in class may be adopted by the students while they do their self study.

A fairly large amount of the leaning with ChinesePod happens in learner-centred settings in or outside class, where the students learn independently. In the 15-minute in-class self-study time, the students work on the computers individually. They practice listening to the ChinesePod dialogue of that day, work on pronunciation and comprehension so as to get ready for the mini assessment tasks immediately followed. During this time, the students mainly have control over the learning process while working in a low-stress environment. The teacher takes a step back and acts as a supporter. She answers questions, corrects pronunciation errors, deals with technical problems, offers feedback to individual students, but she simultaneously exercises behind-the-scene authority of, for example, controlling the time or rectifying misbehaviour.

Apart from the ChinsePod lessons covered in class, the students are required to study a few lessons completely on their own. They need to complete this self-directed study to prepare for the listening tests and also for the in class speaking assessment tasks. In this process, the students have control over their study and are responsible for the learning outcomes. To support this autonomous learning and facilitate their sense of responsibility for their own learning, the teacher has critical roles to play. Many students are used to being fed by the teacher and may not necessarily be ready for self-directed learning nor do they really 'want' to take responsibility for their own learning (Healey, 2007; Oxford, 1990). The teacher should try to foster self-motivation by providing appropriate support and guidance (Chao, 2007).

In addition to the resources provided by the ChinesePod website and the in-class training which serves as a general guide to the self-study process, other measures are taken to offer further support to the student self-study. General guides (hard copy) to developing listening comprehension and to learning with ChinesePod podcasts are provided at the beginning of the semester, and the online copies are also available throughout the semester via WebCT site. Weekly speaking tasks are posted on WebCT together with specific requirements and marking criteria. Besides, guidelines for the two listening tests are also made known to the students in which sample questions and expectations are clearly stated.

Another major form of autonomous learning happens when the students are engaged in the assessment task: the Group Project. This is a semester-long *Project*, including several different yet related tasks based on a series of ChinesePod lessons, centring on the love story of six contemporary urban young people. The tasks include:

- Collaborating with their group members to study the scripts
- Conducting an online discussion to share understanding
- Writing the scripts for an episode of the play to continue the story
- Editing the scripts based on teachers' advice (on language errors) and rehearsing for the in-class performance
- Presenting part of the original play and their own creation of the play

Except, at the final stage, when the students present their performance in front of the class, the project is mainly completed by the students working in small groups after class without the teacher's presence. With its contemporary youth theme and colloquial language use, the play itself is intriguing. ChiesePod web site also offers accompanying resources to help their self-study, but to ensure the success of this student-centred learning project, the teacher's guide and support are necessary throughout.

Before the project is announced to the students, a detailed guideline is prepared, not only outlining the learning objectives, outcome and marking criteria, but also clarifying what exactly the students need to do at each stage and the deadline for each sub task. The teacher anticipates difficulties and problems and takes precautions to avoid or reduce them. For example, the students are reminded to type their discussion with Word software and make a back-up copy in case of loss of data due to technical problems. To avoid some less motivated students taking advantage of group work, the guideline makes it clear that if obviously unbalanced contributions to the discussion are detected, the student with limited contributions will be marked individually.

During the online discussion, the students are made aware that the teacher is monitoring their discussion, but the teacher seldom joins in unless errors or inappropriate behaviour are found. During the whole process, the students are in entire control over their interaction and collaboration, ways of clarifying and negotiating meaning. But the teacher does hold in-class discussion sessions in between the due dates of the sub-tasks to introduce related background information about the contemporary Chinese society and people and clarify misunderstandings in regard to grammar and vocabulary or misinterpretations of culture implications revealed from their work. In a word, the student autonomous learning is supported along the way by clear-cut guideline and teacher's appropriate feedback. This helps setting goals for their learning so they know where they are heading. They will feel assured because they know they will be directed back on track when they deviate from the path.

To create opportunities for interaction and encourage language output.

If the ultimate goal of language learning is language use then the essential task of classroom teaching is to create opportunities for the students to use the language in context. While implementing ChinesePod into the traditional classroom teaching, this has been given serious consideration. Various authentic speaking tasks resembling real life situations are designed to offer the students opportunities to use Chinese language in class. Engaging as many learners as possible is one major concern in designing the tasks. The students are usually assigned different roles as in real life and are required to interact in the target language with "authentic" audience—other students or occasionally the teacher. These tasks offer opportunities of negotiation and collaboration. For example, in one task, the students play smokers and non-smokers respectively and, they debate in groups about whether restaurants should ban smoking. The purpose of this speaking task is to practice stating one's opinion and providing supporting arguments, which are commonly used in real life situations. In doing the task, the students are required to not only state their own opinion but to respond to other students in the group either by supporting or opposing their view.

To cater for different students' learning styles, various types of tasks are designed. Some of them allow students time to prepare in or before class to help reduce affective anxiety; some require them to respond immediately to "authentic audience" (teacher or another student). Some allow them to interact in a small group setting with a low anxiety level; some require them to interact with the teacher to draw their attention to particular forms of the language or communication strategies. Various modes of interaction are adopted including individual student to teacher, whole class to teacher, pair work and group work. These different tasks may engage the students in a variety of situations they may find themselves in real life and encourage them to produce the target language to convey meaning, negotiate meaning and seek information.

However, the student's low language level may sometimes prevent them from achieving goals easily. The teacher's role here is to facilitate the process. His/her roles include monitoring and helping to adjust the learning pace, acting as "authentic audience", offering authentic language input, soliciting and demonstrating "varied and creative language" output, coming to the students' rescue when there is communication breakdown.

The group project is another task which offers the students opportunities to interact with each other and try to use the language in a meaningful way. Performing the original play may get the students familiar with the authentic way of real communication. The native speaker audio recordings introduce the students to the natural delivery of the Chinese language, adopting various tactics such as control of voice volume, using stress, rhythm and tone of voice to help convey meaning and emotion. In creating their own episode of the play, they actually have the opportunity to use the language they have learned in a creative way. The task is "authentic" to them because they are in the scene created by themselves using languages which make sense to themselves. When it comes to the final stage of performing the play, the teacher observes with pleasure that it is not just memorization of the "weird" lines. The students perform with their own understanding and interpretation of the story and characters. Watching different presentations of the same character after he is immerged in sadness after a break-up with his girlfriend—the emotionless face hidden underneath a hoody; a half drunk guy with a beer bottle in his hand, declaring to his friend that he does not care; a naive boy who still believes that their relationship can work out someday—I have to admit, I am both deeply amused and impressed. What impresses me most is the "real" communication. Not only the scenes and characters are authentic as they are all unique creations belonging to each individual group, but the language use is creative and authentic, because it carries each individual student's interpretation and understanding of the language in context. In this way Chinese language is made alive among this group of non native students.

Providing feedback

Providing timely feedback is another important role teacher plays in assisting learning. In the ChinesePod project, great effort is made to provide feedback on the student performance. The feedback mainly takes two forms: oral or written feedback and assessment.

Most of the oral feedback is provided in class while the students are completing different tasks. Depending on the learning situation, the feedback may be addressed to the whole class or given to individual student. For example, while the students are completing speaking tasks in class, the teacher's feedback includes offering encouragement, correcting language errors, fixing improper or ineffective communication, pointing out merits and areas for improvement. The feedback is best provided throughout the process instead of just in the end of the lesson, so that the students have a chance to reattempt using the correct form. Also, when providing feedback, care should be taken to the potential stress created by the feedback. Some students may feel frustrated by being corrected in front of the class. Therefore, the feedback should be given in an encouraging manner.

Written feedback to individual students is usually given on their written assignments. General written feedback on the class performance is usually sent out through emails or announcements on WebCT.

Major assessment tasks relating to the ChinesePod material include two listening tests, weekly in-class speaking tasks and the group project. Focusing on different areas of listening and speaking skill development, these assessments can collect information on student's progress in learning to allow the teacher to identify strengths and weaknesses in student leaning so as to adjust teaching plan accordingly. On the other hand, these assessments provide feedback to the students about their learning progress to help them discover areas for improvement and set goals for further learning. This is especially important for the student self-directed learning. Both guidance and feedback are necessary because they can help to keep the students on track and encourage them to move on.

The other forms of assessment used in class are short informal oral or listening assessments usually conducted right after each self-study session. Counting towards 10% class participation marks of this unit of study, it serves two purposes: one is to provide motivation for the students to complete their individual learning (this was especially important for those less motivated students); the other one is to provide opportunities for them to check their learning progress on the day and receive immediate on-site feedback from the teacher.

To perform on-going evaluation

Finally, the teacher's role is to perform syllabus evaluation. This evaluation should be on-going rather than one-off. Students should be included in the evaluation process. In the case of ChinesePod, survey and interview are used to collect student feedback. In addition, teacher's self-evaluation is equally important. It is done on a daily basis where the teacher constantly identifies issues based on the student performance as a reference for further task or lesson design. There is not a single teaching or learning method, approach or technique that works for all. A responsible teacher should always put him/herself in the position of changing and adjusting methodology to new environment.

Discussion

Successful as the integration of ChinesePod into the traditional course is, a number of issues are identified during and after the integration:

- In student-centred learning, the students should work freely but under guidance. To some students working individually in class means "class is over". They take advantage of this 'free' time to attend to their own business. Therefore, clear-cut ground rules and penalties when breaking the rules have to be negotiated and made clear before the start of a student-centred task. Also, a clear time line and expected learning outcome have to be made known to everyone. If time allows, an immediate formal or informal assessment may be followed to ensure learning happens to as many students as possible.

- More attention should be paid to the less motivated students and help offered to lower level students. The overall successful ChinesePod project was not without negative comments. Among those favourable comments on ChinesePod, the only one student who left the very emotional negative feedback "I hate ChinesePod!" left the teacher the deepest impression. Unfortunately, the survey was anonymous and there was no way to find out the reason why. But it does constantly alert the teacher of the different individual needs and learning styles the teacher should try to cater for when delivering teaching. More channels should be provided for students to offer on-going feedback so as to allow the teacher to adjust teaching constantly rather than only at the end of a program when it is too late to rectify. On the other hand, the teacher should be on alert to identify signs of "disengagement" as early as possible and offer assistance accordingly.

- It was taken for granted by the author that every single student living in this digital age is highly competent with computers and is comfortable working with computers. Actually this is not true. Johnston (2007) has pointed out, "It seems that, despite growing access to and use of computers, this anxiety (computer anxiety) remains a persistent factor in computer-assisted forms of learning". Most of student complaints about ChinesePod shown in the survey were concerned with technical issues of setting up the account, temporary failure of access to certain resources etc. In some cases, it was either because the students were not familiar with some basic computer operations such as downloading files or typing Chinese characters or because they didn't follow instructions. While some students showed a tolerance for these unavoidable problems associated with technology implementation, some other students were obviously frustrated by them. Therefore, it is necessary to keep the technical problems to a minimum. Actually, most of these issues can be avoided or at least reduced with better preparation. On the one hand the teacher needs to continuously update his/her knowledge about digital technology and try to get familiar with all the equipment and devices in use to be ready to tackle some common problems on spot. On the other hand, on-site training or a detailed guide with frequently asked questions should be made available to the students on day one and ongoing checking should be in place to make sure every student understands and follows instructions closely.

Conclusion

The teacher's role in creating and maintaining the conditions for optimal second language learning environments is unreplaceable when implementing CALL. It "takes more than just a blend of the learning resources available" (Yeh, 2007). The teacher should manipulate technology to serve the purpose of enhancing teaching and learning in a CALL program. Technology has great potential to enhance teaching and learning; people, both the teacher and the students should play active roles in unleashing its potential and the teacher should take the lead in this process.

References

Arnold, N., & Ducate, L. (2006). CALL: Where are we and where do we go from here? In L.

Ducate & N. Arnold (Eds.), Calling on CALL: From theory and research to new directions in foreign language teaching (pp. 1—20), CALICO, 2006.

Cameron, K. (1999). Introduction. In K. Cameron (Ed.), Computer assisted language learning (CALL): Media, design and applications (pp. 1—10), Seets & Zeitlinger, 1999.

Chao, C.-c. (2007). Theory and Research: New Emphases of Assessment. In J. Egbert & E. Hanson-Smith (Eds.), CALL environments: Research, practice, and critical issues (2nd ed., pp. 227—241). Alexandria, Victoria: Teachers of English to Speakers of Other Languages, Inc.

Egbert, J., & Hanson-Smith, E. (Eds.). (2007). CALL environments: Research, practice, and critical issues (2nd ed.). Alexandria, Virginia: Teachers of English to Speakers of Other Languages, Inc.

Egbert, J., Hanson-Smith, E., & Chao, C.-c. (2007). Introduction: Foundations for teaching and learning. In J. Egbert & E. Hanson-Smith (Eds.), CALL Environments: Research, Practice, and Critical Issues (Second ed., pp. 1—15), Teachers of English to Speakers of Other Languages, Inc., 2007.

Healey, D. (2007). Classroom practice: Language knowledge and skills acquisition. In J. Egbert & E. Hanson-Smith (Eds.), CALL environments: Research, practice, and critical issues (2nd ed., pp. 173—193). Alexandria, Victoria: Teachers of English to Speakers of Other Languages, Inc.

Hubbard, P. (2004). Learner training for effective use of CALL. In S. Fotos & C. Browne (Eds.), New perspectives on CALL for second language classrooms (pp. 45—68), Lawrence Erlbaum, 2004.

Johnston, B. (2007). Theory and Research: Classroom Atmosphere. In J. Egbert & E. Hanson-Smith (Eds.), CALL environments: Research, practice, and critical issues (2nd ed., pp. 333—348). Alexandria, Virginia: Teachers of English to Speakers of Other Languages, Inc.

Jones, C. (1986). It's not so much the program, more what you do with it: The importance of methodology in CALL. System, 14 (2), 171—178, 1986.

Oxford, R. (1990). Language learning strategies: What every teacher should know. Boston: Heinle & Heinle.

Peterson, P. W. (2001). Skills and strategies for proficient listening. In M. Celce-Murcia (Ed.), Teaching English as a second or foreign language (3rd ed., pp. 87—100). Boson: Heinle & Heinle.

Rheingold, H. (2002). Smart mobs: the next social revolution. Perseus Publishing, 2002.

Sharma, P., & Barrett, B. (2007). Blended learning: Using technology in and beyond the language classroom. Macmillan Publishers Limited, 2007.

Sharples, M. , Taylor, J. , & Vavoula, G. 2007. A theory of learning for the mobile age. In R. Andrews & C. Haythornthwaite (Eds.), The SAGE handbook of e-Learning research (pp. 221—247), SAGE Publications, 2007.

Spolsky, B. (1989). Conditions for second language learning: Introduction to a general theory. Oxford: Oxford University Press.

Yeh, A. 2007. Critical issues: Blended Learning. In J. Egbert & E. Hanson-Smith (Eds.), CALL environments: Research, practice, and critical issues (Second edition.), Teachers of English to Speakers of Other Languages, Inc. , 2007.

多媒体教学设计

对外汉语多媒体教学研究：
以 Scratch 自由软件进行创意课件设计
Multimedia Chinese Teaching and Research：
The Scratch Free Software for Creative
Design Courseware

陈亮光　Chen，Liang-Kuang　台湾国立台北教育大学

National Taipei University of Education Taiwan lkchen@ tea. ntue. edu. tw

摘　要：基于"学习者为中心"的设计原则，以产生有意义的学习课件下，本研究根据信息（视觉/图像和听觉/语言）加工双轨理论，透过学习认知的加工过程，将信息组织成一连贯的言语表征，融入对外汉语多媒体课件设计。采用 Scratch 自由软件建构适性化教学内容，易学且富逻辑思考的操作，将对外汉语教学与课件设计层次从 Work Hard 提升为 Think Hard 模式。

关键词：对外汉语多媒体教学，学习者为中心，信息加工，双轨理论

Abstract：Based on "learner-centered" design principle, to produce meaningful learning courseware, this study is using information（visual / images，and auditory / language）dual-coded processing theory, cognitive processes，and the information organized into a coherent verbal representation to make the foreign language multimedia courseware design. Using Scratch free software to build adaptive teaching content, the operation of logical thinking and the richness of the design will change the model of teaching Chinese as a second language（TCSL）from Work Hard to Think Hard mode.

Keywords：Teaching Chinese as a second language（TCSL），multimedia teaching，learner-centered，information processing，dual-track theory

一　前言

Scratch 是由美国麻省理工学院的 Lifelong Kindergarten group 所开发，它是一套可以运用多媒体来进行角色互动和自由编排的软件，用它来创造交互式的故事、动画、游戏、音乐和艺术都很合适。Scratch 软件图像的对象可以轻松地让教师设计出多元的情境问题，学习者在面对情境问题时，必须先去定义语言的情境问题为何，并且分析如何将语言情境转换成语言程序问题的困难度，将问题分为各个小问题，再去搜集相关的资料与回顾旧经验，经过分析、推理与归纳的历程后，写出解决问题的语言程序代码，最后立即加以验证结果，再不断地修正程序代码以真正完整解决问题。

Scratch 软件的直观式创作方式让语言转换历程进行得更为快速，而且作品创作的历程与问题解决的历程相似于语言的逻辑思考与运用，故 Scratch 软件在教学上应具有提升学生问题解决能力的潜在效应；同时，Scratch 软件又具有华语文的兼容性，也支持多媒体档案的汇入，应可为目前信息教师教学考量使用。其多媒体和互动功能强大，最大的特色，便是将程序变成堆积木的方式，而且采用符合语言文字架构，呈现有意义且完整的句子完成程序指令，让学习者就像说话、作文、组织故事等方式，逐一建构互动多媒体，除了有趣外，更免除了程序除错造成的困扰，只要合乎逻辑的语言堆砌，便能完成可视化接口，并可实时呈现执行结果，绝不会让学习者感到枯燥乏味。

在其官方网站上的一些文献数据提到，学习者在利用 Scratch 创作的过程中，能够学到包括语言、数学、计算机操作、流程设计、逻辑推理、问题解决，以及创造力等高层次思考能力。而且透过网络社群平台展示许多创作，其中多数相当有创意，令人对于 Scratch 对学习者的启发性有相当大的期待。

对外华语文学习者往往寻求有意义且富趣味的学习，不少教学者试图以创新方式提供教学内容。本研究利用互动多媒体程序设计时，以 Scratch 文字加图像的程序语言堆栈，一面进行完整华语文语句的学习，一面完成互动多媒体的程序执行，试图借有趣生动的多媒体设计，进而提升华语文学习者的动机和成效。当然，此教学形式是否能被学习者所接受？其喜好程度为何？其对对外华语文之学习有何帮助？以及此教学方式和内容是否可以成为一种创新的模式？有何启发？本研究即是针对此方面的课题加以探讨，希望能发现其中的影响，并能提供适切的教学建议给欲从事此教学设计模式的教师参考范例。

　　杨书铭（2008）在其硕士论文的实验研究中发现：Scratch 软件对于学习者之问题解决能力有显著的提升，但其研究中并未提及合适的 Scratch 软件教学行动方案以及软件教学上的困难与应改进的教学方法给信息教师参考，以及文献数据中，无有关 Scratch 运用于对外华语文教学的相关研究。因此，研究者希望经由行动研究法，规划发展并检讨 Scratch 软件融入对外华语文课程设计，以了解中级华语文学习者之语文学习，与运用目的语解决问题能力的状况，并且在实际教学现场和课程的实施中，进一步发现实际教学问题及尝试改进相关问题，以提供适当的信息教学计划，作为其他信息教育及对外华语文教学与课程设计者未来应用的参考。

二　文献探讨

（一）语言学习着重"问题解决能力"之培养

　　语言学习的重要目的在于沟通交际。而在交际的过程中，总会产生语言沟通的"问题"。在问题解决的研究中，最常见的定义便是指不能立即解决沟通目标和目前状况的差异，朱柏州（2002）认为个体在处于某种新的沟通情境中，为达成目标的状态，而必须使目前呈现的状态有所改变，而这两者之间的差异，即可定义为问题。学习者在生活中面对问题时，会使用先前认知到的旧知识解决问题，进而建构新认知。在问题解决之前，学习者必须要将若干已知的规则重新组织，以形成新的高级规则，以达到预定的目标状态。当问题被顺利解决后，学习者的知识、能力与经验也必然会提高（朱柏州，2002）和延伸运用。因此，问题解决是人类重要的心智活动，更是一个认知行为的过程。关于"问题解决"的定义整理如下表：

表1　　　　　　　　　　　"问题解决"的定义

学者	定义
Polya（1981）	认为"问题解决"是一种外显，或是认知的行为过程，这种过程是对问题的情境提出各种可能的解决方法，并且从这些可用的选择中，去选择出比较有效的方法，再加以执行。
Mayer（1992）	认为"问题解决"是从已知叙述到目标叙述的迁移过程，问题解决的思考是朝向达成某种目标的系列运作。

续表

学者	定义
王文科（1995）	认为广义的"问题解决"是指有机体获得情境问题的适当反应过程；狭义来说，是指有目的的指向活动或是一种形式的思维，而原有的知识、经验及当前情境问题必须重新改组、转换或聊合，才能达到既定的目标，也就是解决问题。
张春兴（1999）	认为"问题解决"是一个人运用各种知识，去达到解决问题的思维历程。
朱柏州（2002）	认为"问题解决"是一种去寻求对某项情境问题的可行解答或结果之过程，亦是一种思考组织和记忆事物的个人行为技术，也是对新的环境事物来做归纳，是个体必须响应对事物的各种记忆需求的结果。
李登隆（2003）	认为"问题解决"是运用学生旧有的经验和先备知识，去察觉问题、搜集问题并且加以思考的相关资料，再经由分析与推理，发展出新的解决方法，以获得解决问题的能力。
苏秀玲、谢秀月（2006）	认为个体在遭遇各式的问题时，会运用其先前认知的经验、知识、能力、个别技能和所获得的各种信息，来提出可能有效的解决方法，借此来减少所处问题情境与达成目标状态之间差异的过程。

综合各学者所提出的定义，在本研究中，将"问题解决"定义为学习者在面对生活中的语言沟通问题时，运用其先有语言知识、旧经验和思考能力，以获得运用目的语解决问题的解答，达成预定的目标，这种历程即是语言沟通的"问题解决能力"培养。

（二）信息工具应用于语言"问题解决"之探讨

语言学习时，常借由信息工具的辅助与融入来学习。近年来，信息工具如计算机、多媒体、网络平台，以及行动载具运用于语言学习，多数的学习者或多或少已接触并运用信息工具提高其动机及学习效能。然而，使用信息工具应用于语言"问题解决"之探讨并不多；利用语言程序设计语言学习工具虽不少，但是直接使用语言程序进行语言学习的研究并不多。

大部分的文献多探讨程序语言运用于训练学习者的逻辑、组织和问题解决能力。如赖健二（2002）指出，学习者应该学习程序语言，因为学习程序语言可以增进其逻辑思考能力、组织能力和问题解决能力；丰佳燕与陈明溥（2008）在学习计算机程序的研究上指出九成以上的学习者认为程序不是那样令人畏惧的；简易而功能强大的程序 Logo 发展者 Papert（1980）认为学习程序设计可以使思考更有条理，并提升逻辑判断能力。

又如，许铭津与刘明洲（1993）的研究指出一套计算机教学软件的发展，在教学法、教材的安排和人机接口的设计等过程都必须考量学习者本身的认知结构及心理成熟因素。因此，程序设计教学的教师，大多倾向使用简易、有趣且图像化的程序语言，像 Logo 语言（林裕云，2002；徐龙政，1995；崔梦萍，1999；黄文圣，2001）、计算机乐高（林智皓，2007；施能木，2007；蔡锦丰，2008）、Stagecast Creator（丰佳燕、陈明溥，2008）均有此特征，以及 Scratch 的开发，其软件语言工具更具有中文的兼容性，更是被积极地应用（杨书铭，2008）。

　　本研究以 Scratch 进行讨论与实验。Scratch 软件是美国麻省理工学院所发展的一套自由软件程序语言，可以用来创造交互式故事、动画、游戏、音乐和艺术，并且可以把具有创意的作品，发表在网络上与人共享。它更是设计来帮助数学学习、计算能力、语言逻辑思考，以及增加创意、有系统的推理和合作学习的整合性软件（麻省理工 Scratch 团队，2009）。

　　Scratch 是一个可视化的直观式积木组合式程序语言，它使用拖曳的方式将指令从程序指令区移进程序脚本区。这大大地减少了打字错误的机会，也不需要在初学之时苦于记诵指令的拼法。新版的 Scratch 已具有中文化的接口与指令名称，不再让语言的隔阂把初学者挡在门外。对外华语文学习者可以一边学习华语，试着以完整的句子，一边建构程序语言。

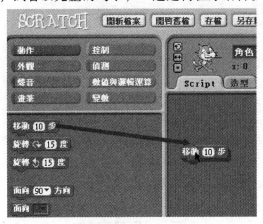

图1　Scratch 软件拖曳指令进入编写区

　　另外，积木组合的编写方式可帮助初学者在程序编写时更容易注意到指令程序的问题，哪一项指令该在哪一项指令的前面，都可以依积木组合的方式而不弄反，如此就不会在学习阶段时，因为不熟悉语法顺序或格式问题而出错，因而造成太多的失败经验而降低学习动机。而且，透过语言指令的堆栈，对外华语文学习者可以借由顺序和区块，检视华语文语块模块化的练习。可视化的直观式积木组合式和对外华语文学习时，语块的排列和组合，可以相互对照，以利于目的语的学习。

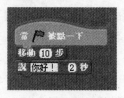

图 2　Scratch 可视化直观式积木组合程序代码

Scratch 软件的储存扩展名为 . sb，储存后的档案即可被装有可执行 java 的浏览器展示出来，官方网站亦有提供展示平台让全球学习者分享创意作品，提供评论。更重要的是这些作品都可以下载回去让学习者研究，不需转码或解码即可观看原始码，充分做到知识共享的精神。

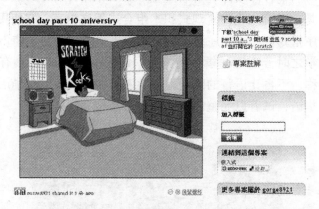

图 3　Scratch 官方网站展示之项目分享平台

Scratch 有这些从前程序设计软件所没有的优点，具有更容易被现在的学习者所接受的机会，因此，本研究用 Scratch 软件进行信息教学工具，以提升学生问题解决的能力，可为重要考虑因素之一。

三　研究方法

本研究采项目教学设计之研究方法，首先针对华语课程进行规划。研究对象是台湾北部某一华语教学单位，其中随机挑选一班中级程度华语学习者 8 位，进行课程活动设计。研究对象皆以完成 500 小时，具备 3000—3500 个之华语词汇量，能以听、说、读、写四项技能表达其完整的句子及沟通技巧。

课程的项目设计是以教材内容之词汇和语法句型，采任务型导向教学法，学习者透过 Scratch 软件语言程序设计搭配华语语言的认知型学习。预期将华语词汇和语法句型带入可视化的直观式积木程序组合，训练华语文语块模块化的练习。其流程图如下：

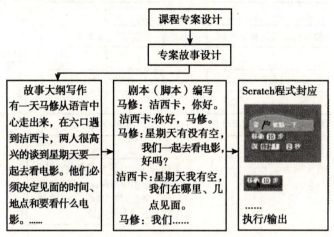

图4　课程项目设计流程图

本研究透过华语语言发展并实施 Scratch 软件课程，来加强学习者使用华语进行问题解决能力提升之成效。分析文献后，确立以行动研究来探讨 Scratch 软件融入的华语文课程设计，教学行动前依据理论基础拟立行动计划，并且实际进行教学；借着教学的观察与回馈来评鉴教学问题与修正计划，再进行第二步骤计划。以上所述简略画成下图所示（见图5）。

本研究将依研究历程与资料搜集，来探讨课程的设计、学生的学习现况、问题解决能力的影响及教师的专业成长。

四　分析讨论

（一）课程项目行动研究

Scratch 软件融入华语教学课程的设计发展历程，发展出问题导向学习教案设计，八个主要步骤依序是：（1）分析学习目标，（2）分析学习者，（3）决定可用的资源，（4）决定问题，（5）决定学习者角色与情境，（6）分析教材，（7）编写教案，（8）设计评量工具。

教学活动的设计分为十个单元，共十五节。前八单元为 Scratch 软件的基本能力的训练，让学习者具备相同的 Scratch 软件基本操作的先备知识，

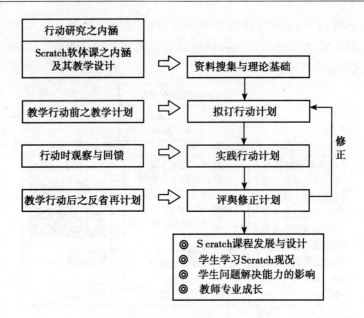

图5 课程项目设计行动研究架构图

教师在每一单元提出一个情境问题，并配合"问题解决辅助华语学习单"的学习，历经"界定问题、分析问题、搜集资料、提出解决方案、验证与改进"的问题解决过程，以培养学生提升华语问题解决的能力。这八单元再分为两个循环教学课程，以"Scratch 软件操作基本概念"为第一循环主要教学课程，以"Scratch 软件角色互动"为第二循环主要教学课程，第一循环课程教学时研究者亲身经验的发现和所得的结果，作为第二循环课程教学时研究者修改课程计划与课程行动的依据；后两单元则是进行小组合作学习，学生进行异质分组来解决语言情境问题，并且在完成后进行各小组发表作品与欣赏。

（二）Scratch 软件课程教学的实况与策略评估

1. 学习者对 Scratch 软件的满意度高

学习者在 Scratch 软件的科技接受模式量表中的"认知有用性"、"认知易用性"、"学习态度"和"行为意向"四个构面，以及"软件品质"和"教学品质"二项外部变项均属高分，显示学生对 Scratch 软件的满意度高。

2. 学习者满意利用 Scratch 软件融入华语文学习

依研究者教学日志的观察与学生质性问卷结果分析，Scratch 软件因支援多媒体汇入的功能，以及直观式积木组合式程序语言与实践华语文运用，受多数学习者喜爱。

3. 学习者有充分的信心完成 Scratch 作品

直观的拖曳指令让多数学习者表示在学习 Scratch 软件时感到很简单、比较没有学习困难；而且配合华语学习，将完整的语法结构与词汇组块，对照程序指令，有如堆积木有系统的堆栈起来，当完成华语句子的指令输入，拖曳对应程序区块，便能完成剧本中角色的动作，展现互动剧情。另外，Scratch 作品的同侪评论分享及程序代码分享，让学习者表现动机，也让学习者在制作 Scratch 作品上更有自信心。

4. 学习者课堂学习态度的表现是正向的

学习者上课表现出强烈的学习欲望，学习态度十分积极。在给予同侪作品评论时，也多能做出具体及友善的回馈，学习者均能把握任务导向原则，保持良好的学习态度。

5. 学习者在 Scratch 融入华语教学课程的学习历程表现优异

学习者的学习历程所完成的项目，其流程图如下：

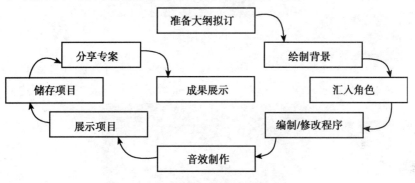

图6　项目学习历程流程

学习者在"了解问题、分析问题、撰写程序、检视结果与除错"的解题任务模型上，符合 Scratch 程序设计的过程；在整体表现上，学习者能将华语所学的经验与语言知识展现在"准备故事大纲"和"脚本编制"的环节上，这两个部分展现学习者华语词汇及语法的能力。学习者依脚本选取适当角色，并安排场景，语言使用的情境与合乎语用的规则呈现在"角色"与"情境"两层次。当进入程序编制与修改，华语学习者透过 Scratch 直观积木式的程序语言堆栈，转换华语剧本的情境对话，之后予以角色配音，将声音档案汇入角色扮演，此时，完全将剧本中的语言文字，转化成多媒体互动视觉呈现。经试验执行与反复修改验证，之后储存项目，并分享和展示其成果。

6. 学习者将语言学习惯连（connection）到其他学习领域

在学习应用层面，学习者透过项目学习到"理解"与"条件判断"的高层次思考模式。语言的训练，透过语言"听、说、读、写"技能转换成程序的编制，借由 Scratch 软件获得相当显著的成效，也展现创意的教学新模式，课程应用之"创作、分享、回馈、反思、再创作"的教学策略，亦达到预期的效果。

（三）专题制作范例

图 7　专题制作范例 1

专题制作：Cassy 的舞会（Cassy 邀请班上同学及好友参加舞会）

专题制作：Kevin 的沙滩旅行（Kevin 邀请班上同学及好友去海边）

图 8　专题制作范例 2

五　结论

Scratch 为美国麻省理工学院（MIT）的 Lifelong Kindergarten 原专为 8 岁以上儿童所开发的可视化程序语言，最大的特色是适用拖曳、组合的方式取代打字输入，免除程序语法除错的困扰。而且最新的版本（1.3alpha）已可以支持中文显示，有利于华语为母语或为目的语学习者学习。

　　有鉴于此，本研究将其融入华语文学习，其一引起学习动机，激发学习者的兴趣；其二透过直观式程序呈现，融入华语阅读和写作技能。除此之外，学习程序对学习者高层次思考能力有所帮助，并提高学习者使用目的语解决问题的能力，以及在人际沟通上的合作模式得以实践。

　　因此，本研究大胆研发一套适合华语学习者，利用语言学习并提升高层次思考能力的 Scratch 程序设计课程。试图将程序语言当成一个培养语言思考能力的工具（当然，非仅教导如何设计程序），在课程设计中融入华语语言知识与解题策略教学：了解问题、拟订计划、实行计划、回顾和分享，在一个没有恐惧、轻松自在的气氛下进行教学及训练。其课程架构如下：

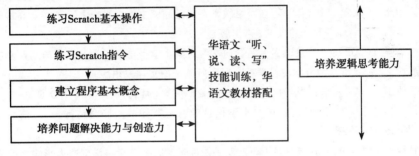

图 9　课程架构

　　鼓励学习者透过语言的学习，并发挥创意，由构想（扩散性思考）到实作（聚敛性思考），透过本研究设计得以实践。

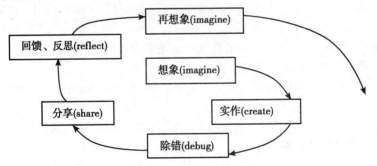

图 10　Scratch 程序语言创造过程螺旋状循环

参考文献

Agarwal, R., & Prasad, J. (1998). The antecedents and consequents of user perceptions in information technology adoption. Decision Support System, 22, 15—29.

Atweh, B., Kemmis, S., & Weeks, P. (Eds.) (1998). Action research in practive. New York: Routledge.

Busse, T. V. & Mansfield, R. S. (1980). Theory of the creative Process: A review and perspective. The Journal of Creative Behavior, 14 (2), 91—103.

Davis, F. D. (1989). Perceived usefulness, perceived ease of use, and user acceptance of information technology, MIS Quarterly, 13 (3), 319—340.

Mayer, R. E. (1992). Thinking, problem solving, cognition. New York: W. H. Freeman and Company.

Polya, G. (1985). How to solve it. Princeton, NJ: Princeton University Press.

王文华（2005）:《行动研究法在教育行政上的应用》,《学校行政双月刊》,第37、81—95页。

朱柏州（2002）:《合作学习在网络教学上对问题解决能力影响之研究》,（高雄师范大学工业科技教育学系硕士论文）（未出版）。

李登隆（2003）:《信息融入专题导向学习对国小学生自然科学习态度与问题解决能力之影响》,台北市立师范学院科学教育研究所硕士论文（未出版）。

吴清山（2002）:《问题导向学习》,《教育研究》（月刊）,第97、120页。

何荣桂、陈丽如（2001）:《中小学信息教育总蓝图的内涵与精神》,《信息与教育》,第85、22—28页。

林智皓（2007）:《乐高（LEGO）动手做教学对国小学童科学创造力影响之研究》,台东大学教育学所硕士论文（未出版）。

林裕云（2002）:《实施计算机Logo程序设计教学对台湾国小学生解题能力之影响》,屏东师范学院数理教育研究所硕士论文（未出版）。

周杏桦（2006）:《信息科技融入教学之相关问题探讨》,《中正学报》,第7、165—174页。

徐龙政（1995）:《LOGO作为国小信息课程初学者语言之适用性研究》,《台东师范学院学报》,第6、187—208页。

夏林清等译（1997）:《行动研究方法导论——教师动手做研究》,台北:远流出版社。

郭伯铨（2001）:《应用全球信息网培养国中生问题解决能力之实验研究》,高雄师范大学工业科技教育研究所硕士论文（未出版）。

崔梦萍（1999）:《计算机程序语言Logo和计算机多媒体教学对台湾省国小五年级学童的创造思考力之影响》,《台北市立师范学院学报》,第30、209—228页。

陈明溥（2003）:《网际网络与问题解决学习》,《台大教与学》2003年12月10日电子报专家专栏,第20期。

陈明溥（2007）:《程序语言课程之教学模式与学习工具对初学者学习成效与学习态度之影响》,《师大学报》,第52、1—21页。

张玉山（2006）:《创造力导向的网络化问题解决活动设计——国小生活科技课程的

实例》，《生活科技教育》月刊，39（5），45—64。

张志豪（2000）：《高中生活科技课程创造思考教学对学生学习成效之影响》，台湾师范大学工业教育研究所硕士论文（未出版）。

许铭津、刘明洲（1993）：《国小计算机教学软件开发策略之研究》，台东师范学院编印：《八十一学年国小数理科教育学术研讨会论文集》，第89—109页。

黄文圣（2001）：《国小学童在 LOGO 学习环境中数学学习与解题之研究》，新竹师范学院数理研究所硕士论文（未出版）。

温嘉荣、杨荣宗、许丽玲（2005）：《由科技接受理论看网络学习社群创新扩散因素》，国际科技教育课程改革与发展研讨会。

程慧娟（2006）：《PBL（Problem-Based Learning）问题导向学习法》，教学新知电子通讯。

杨书铭（2008）：《Scratch 程序设计对六年级学童逻辑推理能力、问题解决能力及创造力的影响》，台北市立教育大学数学信息教育教学硕士论文（未出版）。

蔡美华译（2003）：《行动研究法，Geoffrey E. Mills》，117，台北：学富。

蔡清田（2000）：《行动研究其在教育研究上的应用》，中正大学教育研究所（主编）《质的研究方法》，高雄市：丽文文化。

蔡锦丰（2008）：《LEGO MINDSTORMS 提升国小学童问题解决能力与科学态度之研究》，台东大学教育学所硕士论文（未出版）。

赖健二（2002）：《VB 程序设计进阶教材》，台北市：财团法人信息工业策进会。

谢铭珈（2008）：《国小学童网络媒体素养教育之行动研究——"以中年级网络媒体素养"为例的教学设计》，佛光大学传播学系硕士在职专班硕士论文（未出版）。

詹秀美、吴武典（2007）：《新编问题解决测验指导手册》，台北市：心理出版社。

丰佳燕、陈明溥．（2008）：《国小学生学习计算机程序之研究——以 Stagecast Creator 创作游戏为例》，GCCCE2008 第十二届全球华人计算器教育应用大会。

美国麻省理工学院多媒体实验室 Scratch 团队（2009），Scratch 简介．2009/3/12 参见 http://scratch.mit.edu/.

数位学习国家型科技计划办公室（2009）：《数位学习国家型科技计划——计划缘起》，2009/2/10。参见 http：//teldap.tw/.

活力教师：卡通与对外汉语教学

Animated Teaching：Using Cartoons in Teaching Chinese as a Foreign Language

连育仁　Lien, YuJen　台湾师范大学
National Taiwan Normal University lienyujen@ ntnu. edu. tw
林金锡　Lin, ChinHsi　加州大学尔湾分校
University of California, Irvine chinsil@ uci. edu
邱贵发　Chiu, Gueyfa　台湾师范大学
National Taiwan Normal University gueyfa@ ntnu. edu. tw

摘　要：在对外汉语教学中，卡通使用的研究相对较少，但因其兼具多媒体的特性，在语言教学中有许多的可能性。本研究旨在设计运用卡通于对外汉语的方式，并通过教学实施检验成效。受试者为 12 名在台湾一所大学读短期班的美国学生，程度为初级（上）左右。前、后测结果与学生问卷数据显示，此种教学方式能提高学生语言能力和兴趣。

关键词：对外汉语教学，卡通，语言能力和兴趣

Abstract：In teaching Chinese as a foreign language, little research has been done on the use of cartoons. Due to their multimedia features, cartoons have a great potential for use in language instruction. The current study describes the design of a curriculum using cartoons to teach Chinese as a foreign language and evaluates the effectiveness of the curriculum. Participants were twelve American adolescents who were enrolled in an exchange program at a university in Taiwan. Participants' Chinese proficiency was at the novice—high level. Pre— and post—test comparison and student surveys showed that this teaching approach improved students' performance and increased their interest in learning Chinese.

Keywords：Teaching Chinese as a foreign/second language, Cartoon, language learning interests and proficiency

一　前言

在语言教学里，目标语输入（input）占非常重要的地位（Ellis，1994），而获得这部分输入不外乎透过阅读与听力来完成。然而，在第二语言或外语教学的过程中，欲让学生透过阅读与听力学习并获得乐趣并非易事，因此，教学内容的趣味性与媒体的多样性扮演了非常重要的角色。教学内容的趣味性可透过故事来达成，而运用故事在语言教学中已有许多正面的研究成果，均认为故事有助于提升识字、词汇与听力理解（Dickinson，2001；Penno, et al.，2002；Verdugo & Belmonte, 2007）。媒体的多样性可通过网络多媒体等方式来呈现，从而引发学习者的动机，让学习者喜爱语言学习。媒体的多样性还可以呈现真实情境并与母语者沟通（Kramsch, A'Ness, & Lam, 2000；Warschauer, 1999）。此外，使用多媒体也可辅助学生较有效率地习得词汇（Al-Seghayer, 2001；Jin, 2004）。近年来由于科技进步，结合故事与多媒体的数位化说故事活动（digital storytelling）亦广泛应用于语言教学之中，研究结果显示此活动为有助于提高学生的听力、写作与沟通能力（Bull & Kajder, 2004；Verdugo & Belmonte, 2007），透过网络及多媒体的呈现与介接，学习者更可借由数位化说故事活动的成果向世界发声，与母语者进行直接沟通并表达自己的意见（Hull & Katz, 2006）。

为吸引学习者的学习兴趣，借助多媒体进行说故事教学活动常常会使用卡通（亦有人称为动态漫画）与漫画的使用。卡通与漫画因兼具图片与影片的优点，在语言教学中的运用可鼓励学生阅读，提高学生的学习动机（Derrick, 2008）。漫画使用的语体较为口语，包含了一些较不正式的用法，这些课本可能没教到的东西可借由阅读漫画来学习（Derrick, 2008）。此外，漫画通常比较幽默，在阅读中学习较容易得到乐趣，也可借此了解文化与双关语，更不会因为大量的阅读材料而退怯。然而，使用卡通与动画虽然理想，但实际上却会发生许多问题，如著作权问题、资源搜寻不易、现有资源不适切等问题，以往在这些方面老师处于被动，无法自行制作配合教学内容的理想教学材料。而这种情况因为多媒体方面的进步，现在老师可拥有创作卡通与漫画的权利，让教学更生动（林金锡、连育仁，2010a，2010b）。由于教师对教材内容的调整空间更大，卡通和漫画在教室的运用，也愈来愈具弹性，更能符合实际教学的需求。

综上所述，卡通与漫画拥有许多教学上的优势。因此，本研究期能透过将卡通导入以汉语作为第二语言学习场域的实际教学评估，研究及验证此教学设计方式的有效性。为了让学生练习语言并检视学习成果，在教学中除了观看动画与讨论外，学习者必须在课后依卡通的原样貌，创作自己的脚本，并利用网络工具自制动画，将听、说、读、写及汉字输入融合为课程的任务，让学生能透过课程任务练习各项语言能力。本研究所发展的教学模式在透过教师的试教及学习者成果的检验逐步修正，期能将此教学模式为对外汉语教学发展提供更多教学新意。

二　教学设计

本研究根据文献整理并设计卡通在对外汉语教学中的应用模式，并实际于青少年华语短期班及夏令营中实施。然后，再就学习者成效分析其可行性及需修正之处。

有效率的课堂教学背后必有良好的教学设计。教学设计的概念是根据心理学与信息处理等相关理论而发展出来的一门学科（Gagné, Wager, Golas, & Keller, 1974），而本研究采取在教学设计中广为使用的 ADDIE 模式（Gagné et al., 1974; Molenda, Pershing, & Reigeluth, 1996; Molenda, 2003）。ADDIE 是一个缩写字，代表五个教学设计中重要元素的首字母，分别是分析（analysis）、设计（design）、发展（development）、实施（implementation）与评估（evaluation）。以下部分则根据这五项教学元素分述之。

（一）分析

教学设计的第一个阶段是分析，此分析着重在两方面：学习者分析与教材分析。教材内容是寓言故事，并将原寓言故事以较简易的语言改写，以卡通的形式与较口语、较活泼的方式呈现出来，所以内容上会有一些初级程度学生尚未掌握的词汇与句型。

在学习者分析这方面，由于教学内容对初级学生有些难度，因此，本教学设计所针对的学习者，在听、说、读、写能力方面须达到美国外语教学委员会所制定的程度纲要（American Council on the Teaching of Foreign Language, 1985）的初级（上）水平（novice-high）或以上，学生要可以进行日常对话，并开始利用情境学习语言。

由于教学内容以多媒体的方式呈现故事为主，再加上教学内容较为活泼，因此本设计针对 K—12 之学习者。此阶段的学习者对卡通与故事有很高的兴趣，而兴趣往往会影响第二语言习得的结果（Gardner, 1985;

Krashen，1985；Wen，1997），所以将卡通利用在对外汉语教学中，并针对 K—12 初高级以上程度的学生的教学，应可结合学生的兴趣、动机，并配合各种活动，让学习者可以结合兴趣和听、说、读、写及中文输入等要素，在达成课程任务的过程中渐进完成语言能力的学习。

此外，由于此教学设计使用信息技术，在作学习者分析时亦须考虑学习者的信息素养与背景知识（Blyth，1999）。K—12 中文学习人数及教学课程在美国一直持续增加中（Wang，2009），从 K—12 学习者年纪来看，应多属于善用信息科技的天生数位人（digital natives）世代（Prensky，2001），而属天生数位人世代之学习者需要更多以信息融入的方式实施任务式教学法，供其于课中及课后运用信息科技，完成学习任务，以符合学习习惯（CDW，2010）。天生数位人由于生长在信息时代，多半有较高的信息素养，对使用新信息技术的接受程度较高，也较不会遇到技术问题。此外，数位化说故事活动能提供学习者更多探索语言表达的真实方式，并让学习者透过科技的辅助，亲身参与情境并达成语言学习的目标（Bull & Kajder，2004）。

（二）设计

在教学流程上，本研究参酌 Gagné（1985）所提出的教学九事件（nine events of instruction）来设计教学流程，各阶段教学内容及教学活动见表 1。

表 1　　　　　　　　　　　各阶段教学流程

教学事件	教学内容与活动
引起注意	教师以包含卡通、图片与声音信息之多媒体投影片教材显示课程主题，借此吸引学习者注意力并提升兴趣，使学习者进入学习的预备状态。
告知目标	教师先讲述故事名称与学习目标，让学习者对课程有初步认知。
提示回忆背景知识	由故事名称为触发点，教师引导学生回忆背景知识与相关词汇及句型。由于选材皆为学生已接触过之故事，因此在讲述过程中，教师会适时引导学生以中文说出故事关键内容用以回忆背景知识。
呈现教材	教师利用从故事动画中撷取之漫画图片置于投影片中口述故事。完成讲述后，即播放故事动画，让学习者借由动画的阅读与聆听加深学习印象。
提供学习指导	播放动画后，教师以投影片讲解动画中对话、旁白，并以超链接方式联结对话及旁白之生字词、语法说明页面。此外，教师亦提供纸本课文页面、生字练习、图卡等纸本辅助教材，作为学习与练习的参考依据。
引出作业	学习者有两项作业：学习单填写与卡通动漫故事创作，前一个活动是为后一个活动作准备。 教师在讲解完课程后即将学习者分组，并要求学生在学习单上的静态图片旁依自己对卡通的了解加入对话与旁白，自行创造属于自己的卡通故事。 学习者完成学习单后，以小组方式在无配音及字幕的卡通上录制旁白与对话，使其成为由学习者自制之卡通。详细步骤于表格后说明。

教学事件	教学内容与活动
提供回馈	教师于学习者填写学习单及创作动漫故事之过程给予指引和回馈，并在各组完成卡通配音之后，提供纠错性反馈（corrective feedback）以维持卡通内容的正确。
评估作业	学习者将成品上传至网络平台后，以成品之节奏性、合宜性、戏剧性、正确性及声音表情是否符合动画表现作为评量依据，评估学习成果。
促进记忆保留与迁移	在线展示并要求学习者讨论彼此创作的成品，以收复习及深度思考之成效。

Hull and Katz（2006）认为有效的数位化说故事活动设计应包含七点：a）观点，b）具戏剧性的主题，c）情感内容，d）经济性，e）合适的节奏，f）合适的声音旁白，g）适切的配乐。在学习者进行数位化说故事的创作阶段，教师应尽量导引学习者符合上列原则。据此，为使数位化说故事活动与课室环境有效率地结合，此阶段之课程内容皆预建置于 google sites 网站（参见：http：//sites. google. com/site/mtchuayu/）。将作业置于网站可让学习者在完成说故事任务的同时能依据网站的步骤及参考联结自行下载相关动画影片及录音工具，以便小组自行按照网站导引完成数位化说故事任务。结合 Hull and Katz 的数位化说故事设计观点，本活动流程如下：

a）以每组 3 人方式进行分组，要求学习者讨论各组对卡通故事的理解；

b）在课程网站上观看未包含配音及字幕之课程动画，依各组员所分配的不同卡通角色在学习单上填写脚本；

c）与教师讨论脚本内容的正确性和逻辑性；

d）运用计算机教室设备录制脚本内容，并将声音档案存成 mp3 格式；

e）在影片编辑器中导入未包含配音及字幕之动画原始档，并将自行录制之对话及旁白加入影片；

f）若时间允许，加入音乐声轨；

g）上传至 YouTube 网络空间，并为自己的影片档加入字幕；

h）要求各组分享并讨论彼此所创作之动漫故事，以练习说话及中文打字能力。

所有教学依上述流程完成后，学习者将产出各具巧思与创意之动漫作品，可作为课程成果检视之依据。

（三）发展

本教学设计以寓言故事为核心，由于课程时间所限，教学内容仅能以一个寓言故事为主，所以挑选了由陆锋科技五子登科网站所设计之"龟兔赛跑"动画故事为主要教学内容。作为教学用途，此卡通设计了两个版本：一个是包含配音与旁白，作为教材用（网址：http://www.youtube.com/watch?v=ZQ90IqguGlU）；一个是不包含配音与旁白，作为学生的任务（网址：http://www.youtube.com/watch?v=JUMjZq95t90）。若教师有兴趣采用这二段影片于教学上，可以上列网址参考运用。

图1   动漫教材动画

本研究所发展之教材着眼易于修改、播放、复制及应用，故采 Microsoft PowerPoint 为主要软件。为求未来推广或使用方便，本研究在发展时即以大多数学校既有之信息设备为主要考虑。硬件方面除教师授课所用之投影装置外，仅需具上网及录音功能之个人计算器或笔记本计算器数台及麦克风；在软件工具方面，本研究采用软件全部免费、容易取得的网络软件及服务为主，为让学生熟悉软件之运用，先于课中施以 1 小时软件运用教学。除教材投影片外，另加采用配音软件 Audacity 及剪辑动画软件 Windows Movie Maker，当学生在课堂完成配音及剪辑活动后，即要求学生将成品上传至提供讨论与评价功能之 YouTube，并于课程网站上提供为影片加上字幕的 CaptionTube（http://captiontube.appspot.com/）服务教学。期能以最简单的功能让学习者快速制作动画配音，并降低教师及学习者在软件学习上的负担。

（四）实施

为达到较好的教学效果，教师在课堂初始阶段透过图片及声音的展示，让学习者快速进入课堂的学习准备，融入学习氛围。在学习者已有相当准备后，授课教师始借动漫投影片，讲述课程主题故事，让学习者经图文及声光的辅助了解学习目标，据此建立后续课程内容的学习印象及线索（Paivio，1990）。教师在故事讲述过程中，除让学习者练习听力外，尚可透过提问方式，让学习者练习说话能力，并对后续课程建立更多可供提取之线索。授课教师完成故事内容的讲述后，立即播放课程动画，除能让学习者有更多的复习机会外，尚能借由动画及前述教师讲述故事内容的比较，增加对课程内容的印象。

在教室实施时，除多媒体卡通的讲述及展示外，卡通故事内容的深入讲解、语法练习的带领及词汇的说明亦是教学很重要的一环。在本教学设计中，教师所运用的语法及生字皆以超链接的方式在课程教材中呈现，教师能轻易依学习者的需求增加或减少原教材的生字/词与语法练习链接，使教学内容更符合教学现场的实际情况。学习者依教师导引完成课文内容的学习后，课程即进入练习及活动阶段，学习者将接受提问等活动确认对课程内容的了解程度，并分组以漫画学习单撰写小组成员讨论的故事或脚本，进入数位化说故事的创作阶段。

本课程创作阶段之教学实施流程皆建置于课程网站，依分组数据填写、影片选择、脚本撰写、配音、制作影片、上传影片及加字幕等阶段进行。在数位化说故事创作活动开始前，先于计算机教室给予学生 1 小时录音、声音与影片剪辑及中文打字训练。参与本研究之学生除中文输入法的切换较生疏之外，均已具备声音及影片剪辑能力，因此在数位化说故事活动的计算机操作上相当顺利。

（五）评估

本研究以数位化说故事之卡通创作成品为主要学习任务。因此，学习者为卡通配音所产出的作品是否符合数位化说故事活动设计七原则乃评估的重要依据。结合语言学习听、说、读、写等能力，课程成效之评估面向应包含：

a）故事内容是否与动画主题相符；

b）故事表达是否清楚、合宜，具体内容是否具逻辑性；

c）配音的声音表情是否与剧情设定相符，咬字发音是否清楚；

d）文法及词汇运用是否正确；

e）角色对白之节奏是否与动画影片确切结合；

f）对白及旁白是否与剧情设定相符；

g）是否融入合适的配乐或音效，字幕是否正确。

图 2　课程配音活动

图 3　由学习者自行设计之数字故事

除学习任务成品之评估外，本研究所设计之教材及教法将因不同设备、学习者需求及教学任务有相对应的修正空间。故于教学实施时，教师应根据学习者程度调整教材内容的难易度，发挥数位化教材之弹性特色。

三　研究问题

卡通在对外汉语教学中是一种较新的教学应用。从理论上来说，根据记忆双码理论（Paivio，1986）与先前数位化说故事的研究（如 Bull & Kajder，2004；Hull & Katz，2006）来看，将数位化说故事活动应用于对外汉语教学有其适用性与应用价值。从信息技术与课程整合和语言教学的角度来看，由于多媒体的声光效果及易于编辑性，数位化说故事可以在一定的范围内，让学习者有练习语言的机会，借由"说故事"的方式进行角色扮演，可让学习者学习不同语体，并从中学习文化。

本研究的研究问题如下：

1. 利用卡通于对外汉语教学之中，是否能提升学习者的语言能力？

2. 利用卡通于对外汉语教学之中，是否有助于提高学习者的动机和兴趣？

四　研究方法

本研究采取以设计为基础的研究法（design-based research methods）进行研究，借以了解学生的学习过程并建立教学理论（Wang & Hannafin，2005）。此种研究法主要实施于真实的教学情境下，借以了解学生如何学习，并建立教学理论，以及设计可以用来改善教学实务的产品。其目的是利用系统化但灵活性较高的方式来促进教学，在这过程中透过不断地分析、设计、发展与实施，并结合教师与研究人员来解决实际教学的问题，以设计可以用来改善教学实务的教学方法及教材（The Design-Based Research Collective，2003）。因此，本研究最终所发展之教材教法应由拟运用之教师依实际教学情况调整教学内容，以符合实际的教学需求，供其运用以改善教学实务。

（一）受测对象与课程时间

本研究于台湾台北某间公立大学的语言中心实施，受试者为 2010 年暑期来台参与短期游学班之美国学生，年纪为 12—13 岁。受试者在来台之前于美国中学学过一年中文。学生人数一共 12 人，男性 5 人，女性 7 人。每天授课时数为 6 个小时，为期 4 天，总时数共 24 个小时。

（二）研究资料

此研究的主要资料有二：前、后测与课程结束后的学生问卷。前、后测由华语测验推动委员会（Test of Chinese as a Foreign Language）所研制之儿童华语测验成长级试题中，各取 25 题而成，前测 IRT 难度参数为 -0.995，后测 IRT 难度参数为 -1.018，前、后测在难度上并没有显著差异。此测验所针对的对象为在非华语区学习 300 个小时以上，具有 700 个词汇量的学习者，符合这批学生的程度。学生在课前先接受前测，在课程完成后接受后测。

除施以测验外，在课程结束后要求学生填写课后问卷，以了解学生对各阶段课程内容的接受度，详细问卷内容请参见附录1。问卷为中文，但老师在发问卷时以英文解释，所以学生应该没有理解问题。

五 结果分析

（一）学习成效

前、后测各25题，每题1分。关于前、后测的叙述统计见表2。

表2   **前、后测之叙述统计**

	平均	标准偏差
前测	11.25	1.48
后测	13.92	2.53
样本数	12	

为了解预试之学习状况是否达到预期成效，由上表可知后测平均成绩高于前测成绩。前、后测成绩以成对样本 t 检定检验，二个平均值的差异达到显著水平，$t(11) = -2.79$，$p < 0.05$。换言之，经过短时间的密集训练，学习者的测试成绩有显著进步。

（二）动机与兴趣

根据学生问卷结果，所有问题的答案均是正面的，所有问题的平均值在3以上。学生认为利用卡通在对外汉语教学之中，能让他们对学中文更感兴趣（平均=3.83），而且与课本相比，学生更喜欢以卡通的形式学习中文（平均=4.08）。不仅如此，学生更期待中文教材里有多一点卡通动画（平均=4.16），并认为这样的学习方式符合他们的学习习惯（平均=4.16）。

学生的动机与兴趣可能来自三方面：更多的练习机会、成就感与对课程任务的喜爱。根据研究结果，学习者认为替卡通角色配音提供更多练习中文的机会（平均=3.67），而且这个活动让学生得到成就感（平均=3.67）。此外，学生喜欢这个为卡通配音的任务（平均=4.00）。

在所有问题中，平均最低的两个问题是第五题"我喜欢透过计算机学习中文"（平均＝3.33）和第七题"我认为这门课很容易"（平均＝3.33）。虽然学生认为这门课不是很容易，但学生表现出了高度兴趣并期待这样的学习模式，所以如果教材内容能更贴近学习者程度，学习者对课程与活动的喜爱程度应会提高。值得一提的是，后测成绩与第五题"我喜欢透过计算机学习中文"呈现高度相关，相关系数为0.61，$p < 0.05$，表示愈爱使用计算机学习语言的学习者，愈能在后测中得到较高的成绩。而爱使用计算机学习的学生，通常也喜欢为卡通角色配音（相关系数＝0.70，$p < 0.05$）。由此可见，当信息技术与课程整合时，学生的信息素养会影响到对任务的喜爱程度，进而影响到学习成果。

　　除了上述正面的结果，在开放性问题里，学生也提出了一些意见。学生于问卷中反映计算机技巧稍难、计算机教室过小，使其不易分组活动等问题（Computers were a little complicate, classroom was a little small. ）。另外，有部分学生表示这是个有趣的学习经验，使其享受甚于学校能给的学习乐趣（It was a fun, learning, experience. Usually I don't like school, but I had a wonderful learning experience here. Keep it up）。以上皆显示将卡通动漫融入对外汉语教学在设计及实际运行时间的成效都能让学生感到满意，符合天生数位人世代的学习需求。

六　结论与建议

　　本研究所设计之教学活动及课程由于学生人数有限，此结果可能不具备普及性。此外，由于课程实施的时间较短，尚不知此教学模式应用在一学期的课程中是否具备相同成效。虽然在研究实施及取样范围上有限制，但从本研究的结果来看，利用卡通于对外汉语教学中显著提升了学习者的学习效果，表示此种教学活动对学习成效有显著的帮助。此外，从问卷也能看出新世代的学生的确对结合卡通的教材有浓厚的兴趣，在课室里运用卡通及信息科技也能提升学生的学习动机，促其积极参与教学活动。从这次的实验研究中我们观察到新世代学习者对于信息科技的熟悉度高于预期，原先设定的数位能力训练课除中文输入外，录音、剪辑、档案上传等作业对受试学生来说几乎不需要教导，在简单练习后即能立即使用。因此，只要在教学设备允许下，对外汉语教学若能适时适度将卡通与数位化说故事导入课室，传统的中文教学即能从纸本跃上计算机及网络，师生能借着多媒体的声光协助及信息科技的易用性，完成与传统不同的学习成品，同时训练听、说、读、写及中文输入能力。

此外，将卡通动漫融入于数位化教材亦有很高的推广潜能。本研究所发展的数位化说故事教学活动教材除具有多媒体之声光效果特色外，更易于复制、修改、传递，对海外的中文教学来说，可省去纸本印刷、寄运的不便，也能让教师们针对学习者的需要或教学情境上的不同自行调整教材内容的难度与针对性，实为对外汉语教学可以继续发展的方向，建议后续研究可继续评估在对外汉语教学课堂中采用此种方式的教学及推广效果。

致谢：本文在撰写中得到许德宝博士的鼓励与支持，在此深表谢意。本文在实验过程中，感谢台湾师大国语中心同仁的协助，完成此实验。在技术方面，感谢陆锋科技授权使用该公司所制作的卡通动画并提供许多协助。此篇文章部分内容在第六届科技与中文教学研讨会上发表，并收录于会议论文集，亦感谢许多前辈在当时提供的宝贵建议。另外，亦感谢匿名评审的建议，让本文更加完善。

参考文献

American Council on the Teaching of Foreign Languages. （1985）. ACTFL profiency guidelines. Yonkers, NY：ACTFL.

Al-Seghayer, K. （2001）. The effect of multimedia annotation modes on L2 vocabulary acquisition：A comparative study. Language Learning & Technology, 5 （1）, 202—232.

Blyth, C. （1999）. Implementing technology in the foreign language curriculum：Redefining the boundaries between language and culture. Journal of Educational Computing Research, 20 （1）, 39—58.

Bull, G. , & Kajder, S. （2004）. Digital storytelling in the language arts classroom. Learning & Leading with Technology, 32 （4）, 46—49.

CDW （2010）. 21st—Century classroom report：Preparing students for the future or the past Available：http：//newsroom. cdw. com/features/feature— 06—28—10. html.

Derrick, J. （2008）. Using comics with ESL/EFL students. The Internet TESL Journal, 14 （7）. Available：http：//iteslj. org/Techniques/Derrick-UsingComics. html.

Dickinson, D. K. （2001）. Putting the pieces together：Impact of preschool on children's language and literacy development in kindergarten. In D. K. Dickinson & P. O. Tabors （Eds. ）, Beginning literacy with language：Young children learning at home and school （pp. 257—287）. Baltimore, MD：Paul H. Brookes.

Ellis, R. （1994）. The study of second language acquisition. New York：Oxford

University Press.

Gagné, R. M. , Wager, W. W. , Golas, K. , & Keller, J. M. (1974). Principles of instructional design (5th ed.). New York: Holt, Rinehart Winston.

Gardner, R. C. (1985). Social psychology and second language learning: The role of attitudes and motivation. London: Edward Arnold.

Gruba, P. (1997). The role of video media in listening assessment. System, 25 (3), 335—345.

Hull, G. A. , & Katz, M. -L. (2006). Crafting an agentive self: Case studies of digital storytelling. Research in the Teaching of English, 41 (1), 43—81.

Jin, H. G. (2004). Multimedia effects on Chinese character acquisition. Paper presented at the Conference on Chinese language teaching and Pedagogy, Chicago.

Kramsch, C. J. , A'Ness, F. , & Lam, W. S. E. (2000). Authenticity and authorship in the computer-mediated acquisition of L2 literacy. Language Learning & Technology, 4 (2).

Krashen, S. D. (1985). The input hypothesis. London: Longman.

Molenda, M. , Pershing, J. A. , & Reigeluth, C. M. (1996). Designing instructional systems. In R. L. Craig (Ed.), The astd training and development handbook (pp. 266—293). New York: McGraw-Hill.

Molenda, M. (2003). In search of the elusive ADDIE model. Performance Improvement, 42 (5), 34—36.

Paivio, A. (1986). Mental representations: A dual coding approach. New York: Oxford University Press.

Penno, J. F. , Wilkinson, I. A. G. , & Moore, D. W. (2002). Vocabulary acquisition from teacher explanation and repeated listening to stories: Do they overcome the Matthew Effect Journal of Educational Psychology, 94 (1), 23—33.

Prensky, M. (2001). Digital natives, digital immigrants. On the Horizon, 9 (5), 1—6.

Verdugo, D. R. , & Belmonte, I. A. (2007). Using digital stories to improve listening comprehension with Spanish young learners of English. Language Learning & Technology, 11 (1), 87—101.

Wang, F. , & Hannafin, M. J. (2005). Designed-based research and technology-enhanced learning environments. Educational Technology Research and Development, 53 (4), 5—23.

Warschauer, M. (1999). Electronic literacies: Language, culture and power in online education. Mahwah, NJ: Lawrence Erlbaum Associates.

Wen, X. (1997). Motivation and language learning with students of Chinese. Foreign Language Annals, 30 (2), 235—251.

林金锡、连育仁（2010a）:《卡通制作与语言教学》，论文发表于第六届国际汉语计算机教学研讨会，Columbus, OH.

林金锡、连育仁（2010b）:《华语文数位教学：理论与实务》，台北:《新学林》。

附录1　学生问卷

性别：□男　□女

1. 你认为卡通动漫能让你对中文的学习更感兴趣
2. 和课本相比，你比较喜欢以动漫的形式学习中文
3. 自己为卡通动漫的角色配音让我有更多的机会练习中文
4. 自己为卡通动漫的角色配音让我很有成就感
5. 我喜欢透过计算机学习中文
6. 我喜欢为动画配音再剪接的任务
7. 我认为这门课很容易
8. 我希望我的中文课本多些卡通动画
9. 这样的教学方式符合我的学习习惯

（以上问题均采用李克特五点量表，1代表非常不同意，5代表非常同意）

Integration of Technology into Day-to-day Classroom Teaching and Instructional Materials Design[*]

Henrietta Yang

Morehouse College United States hyang@ morehouse. edu

Abstract：The goals of this paper are twofold：first, to advocate the use of instructional technology in day-to-day classroom teaching to create an interactive and student-centered learning environment; second, to demonstrate how to apply instructional technology to help instructors develop interactive teaching materials efficiently. This paper consists of three sections：the first section discusses how students interact with the world nowadays and how they access information through technology. Students of this technological age grow up with technology devices such as smart phones, iPods, laptops, and iFlips. The way they interact with the world today is at their fingertips. Language educators need to grow with technology, refine teaching tools by integrating technology into classroom teaching and learning, and rethink how to utilize students' technology devices to help students to learn outside of class. The second section introduces three interactive activities and illustrates how to create them through SMART Notebook software step-by-step. The third section concludes the paper. The author stresses that instructional technology should be applied as a tool to increase students' classroom participation and that the classroom focus should always be on students and their learning process.

摘　要：本文的研究目的有二：其一，积极倡导在日常的汉语课堂教学

---

* Part of this article was presented at the Sixth International Conference and Workshops on Technology and Chinese Language Teaching in the 21st Century （TCLT 6） at the Ohio State University, June 12—14, 2010. I would like to thank the audience at the conference for their comments and input.

活动中使用现代教育技术，以形成生动活泼的教学环境和学习氛围，真正体现"以学生为中心"的教育主旨。其二，具体演示如何运用有关教育软件，进行交互式及有效的汉语教学内容设计，以适应信息化社会和"图像时代"学生对多媒体技术的需求，不断提高语言教学的质量。全文由三个部分所组成。第一部分为"导论"。根据近年来美国的有关研究报告和自己的研究心得，笔者较为详细地分析了当前信息化社会和"图像时代"，我们的教学对象——学生接触和使用高科技电子产品的情况，比如，当代大学生是伴随着高科技电子产品的不断涌现而长大的；他们目前最常用的产品有智能电话（smart phones）、苹果公司音乐播放器（ipods）、便携式电脑（laptops）和微型随身录像机（iFlips）等；他们探索外部世界和同外界的交往大部分是通过 Youtube、Skype 和 Facebook 完成的；他们每周花在娱乐媒体上的时间平均达到了 53 个小时。总之，这一代人就是在"指尖"（fingers）上生活着的。有鉴于此，本文作者将自己的研究目的特别"聚焦"于上述两个方面。第二部分是本文的重点，这是作者多年从事汉语作为"外语"的教学经验的总结。首先，本文作者从狭义的层面，对"课堂教育技术"（或曰"教学手段"）进行了界定，即：课堂教育技术指的是"在互联网接入下使用投影仪和计算机充分运用音频和视频文件进行互动式教学的技术"。作者特别推荐了"智能面板"（Smart Board）和"智能电脑软件"（Smart Notebook Software）这两种产品。与此同时，作者认为，这种"智能化"设备的有效使用，可以打造出一个"智能化课堂"（as a smart classroom）。随后，作者分别从三个角度，一步一步地演示了上述"智能工具"在汉语语句结构、数字练习和词汇复习等教学过程中的应用。在这些系列教学环节里，通过教学软件的使用，作者将句子结构的整合、语法规则的练习和数字词汇的记忆，巧妙地融入多媒体互动式教学之中，使整个教学过程避免了枯燥单调、机械重复，大大地提高了教学效果，并使学生在课外还"意犹未尽"，自己主动进行实践和练习。这就比较好地实现了一个"以学生为中心"的学习环境（create a student-centered learning environment）。作为本文的"结论"，文章第三部分辩证地指出：尽管本文提倡将现代教育技术应用于汉语课堂教学之中，但是必须看到，互联网、计算机和教学软件等，仅仅只是一个教学的"工具"（a tool）而已。作为汉语教师，我们课堂教学的重点，我们的"聚焦"，还是要放在学生的课堂参与及其学习的全过程之中。

Introduction

The goals of this paper are twofold: first, to advocate the use of instructional technology in day-to-day classroom teaching and learning; second, to demonstrate how to apply instructional technology to help instructors develop interactive teaching materials more efficiently. When instructors develop classroom teaching materials, several important elements need to be taken into consideration, including the learners' language proficiency level, language features, teaching objectives, and the learning outcomesthat instructors want to achieve. Advanced students who already have certain knowledge of sentence structures and vocabulary require different kinds of instructional activities and different types of instructional materials from beginners who have limited knowledge of sentence patterns and vocabulary. Chinese has a logographic writing system, and each character has its own unique shape. Therefore, learning Chinese characters demands more visual input than learning English words. Moreover, many different characters have the same pronunciation. Providing visual input of the characters in class will help learners to "picture" the characters. When instructors design classroom teaching materials, one important question that they need to ask themselves is what theywantto achieve through the materials designed. Is it designed to engage students and keep them interested in class Or, is it just to provide one-way information transmission from the instructor to students? If the goal is to design materialsthat canengage students in classroom learning, then anotherquestion that needs to be asked is how to achieve it. How to engage students, how to keep them interested, and how to interact with them are directly related to how students interact with information these days.

Students of this technological age grow up with technology devices such as smart phones, iPods, laptops, and iFlips. The kind of technology that students interact with nowadays differs greatly from the kind that students interacted with five to ten years ago. The way students interact with the world today is at their fingertips from exploring the worldwide web, sending out information through texting, watching videos on YouTube, or keeping in touch with friends through Facebook. Faculty in higher education or instructors in K-12havebeen modifying their pedagogical approaches in order to accommodate this new technological generation. Some examples of incorporating technology into pedagogy and curriculum are: online discussion forums outside of class, video conferencing via Skype, and online exercises. Different disciplines require different types of instructional technology. This paper focuses only on how instructional technology can help foreign language educators to create an interactive teaching and learning environment in the classroom and how it can be used to effectively develop day-to-day interactive teaching materials.

Like any educator, language educators too have to face a new generation who spend on average more than 53 hours a week on using entertainment media, a study released by the Kaiser Family Foundation on January 20, 2010 (Rideout et al., 2010). This shocking number, 53 hours a week, is even more than the working hours of a regular full time job (40 hours). This result is mainly driven by the popularity of mobile devices such as iPods and cell phones which already have ready access to multimedia games and songs. Language educators need togrow with technology, refine teaching tools by integrating technology into classroom teaching and learning, and rethink how to utilize students' technology devices to help them to learn outside of class.

Applying technology in languageand culture teaching is not new. Levy (2007) reports five projects which incorporate technologies for cultural learning: two e-mail projects (the Australia-Brazil-Collaboration project and the O'Dowd's 2003 study), online chat (Toyoda and Harrison, 2002), a discussion forum (Hanna and de Nooy, 2003), and a Web-based project (Furstenberg et al, 2001). One of Levy's findings is that the use of asynchronous technologies (e. g., e-mail) should precede synchronous technologies (e. g., online chat) in culture learning in order to achieve successful learning outcomes. Liaw (2006) reports a study designed to develop learners' intercultural competence through an online learning environment. With the help of computer technology, a group of students who studied English as a Foreign Language (EFL) in Taiwan were able to communicate with a group of American students in Texas about their own culture and cultural practices in the target language. Again, applying technology in language and culture teaching is not novel, and much literature has discussed applying technology in language teaching. This paper aims to contribute specific examples and practiceson how instructional technology, as a tool, can be utilized for instructional purposes in an effective manner and can be applied to create interactive materials in an efficient way.

Classroom Instructional Technologyand Its Application

Nowadays, classroom technology generally refers to a projector and a computer that has internet access ability and has CD ROM/DVD for playing audio and video files. This kind of classroom is mostly referred to as a smart classroom. However, another important piece of technology that is often found in a smart classroom today is a SMART Board™. [1] A SMART Board is a huge piece of interactive whiteboard, connected to a computer. This interactive whiteboard functions as a big touch panel. The company that produces SMART Boards also supplies SMART Notebook software. The combination of a SMART Board and SMART Notebook software is indeed a powerful educational tool for language educators. SMART Notebook software makes creating, delivering, and managing interactive teaching materials efficient and effective. If a classroom does not have a SMART Board, SMART Notebook software can still be downloaded as long as one's institution has purchased the hardware and has the licensed serial number.

When technology, as a tool, is applied appropriately, it can create a student-centered learning environment with authentic, meaningful, and contextualized materials. It can also engage students in classroom activities. One important note is that the classroom focus should always be on students and their learning process. Meskill et al (2002) report the conceptual and practical differences between novice and experienced teachers in terms of how they apply technology in teaching. Their findings show that experienced practitioners viewed technology such as computers as merely a tool, and all action for teaching and learning still resides in teachers and students. On the other hand, novice teachers see computers as being the locus of all action in the instructional process. Moreover, both Trotter (1999) and Meskill et al (2002) indicate that experienced teachers tend to carefully integrate technologies to complement and enhance existing curricula, while novice teachers employ technologies as a means of reward and punishment. For example, novice teachers would allow students to use computers as a form of reward for cooperative behavior. It is crucial to recognize that instructional technology should be applied as a tool to enhance students' classroom learning experiences and should not be used to overshadow students' learning process.

In the following sections, I will take Chinese examples forillustration to showhow to create interactive activitiesfor sentence structure exercises, number review, and vocabulary review within few steps.

Application 1: Sentence Structure Exercises

SMART Notebook software provides instructors a quick and easy way of creating interactive activities. For instance, sentence structure reconstruction. Words or phrases are in mixed up orders. Students can work alone or with a group to reconstruct the word order. As Warschauer and Meskill (2000) point out, this kind of activity can also be done through a pen on a piece of paper; however, the computer provides facilitative functions for both instructors and students. With the help of a SMART Board and its Notebook software, instructors can easily design activities that keep students engaged and increase students' classroom participation. Moreover, interactive activities provide students with visual input and keep them focused. To design an activity for sentence reconstruction is simple and quick. I will demonstrate how to create one step by step below.

Notebook software has a simple tool bar, similar to the tool bar in MSWord (as shown in Figure 1).

Step 1: Insert a table

There is an insert table function on the tool bar, circled in red. Click on the "table" button, and specify how many rows and columns you want in the table, just like how one would do in MSWord. However, the biggest difference between a table created by Notebook software and one created by MSWord is that the former is an interactive one.

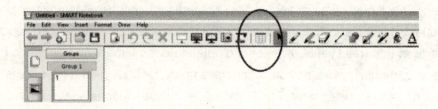

Figure 1

Step 2：Create texts

Type the characters or phrases that you would like students to recon-struct on a Notebook page. For example：今天几月几号？

Step 3：Duplicate the texts

Select what has just been created. A drop down button on the upper right corner will appear（where the red arrow points to）. After clicking on the drop down button，you will see a "Clone" function. "Clone" is a won-derful feature that quickly duplicates any materials（images，texts，or ta-bles）at once，which is really a time-saving feature for instructors. After clicking on the "Clone" function，another identical set of texts will be crea-ted.

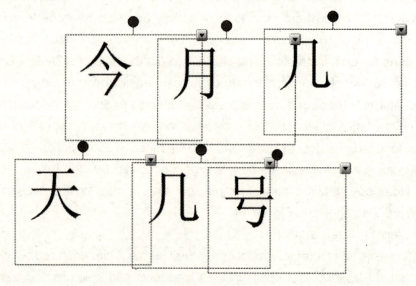

Figure 2

Step 4：Insert texts into the cells

Drag one set of the characters into the cells in the order you want as in Figure 3.

Figure 3

Step 5: Add Cell Shades

Cover up the cells by selecting those cells you want to cover. Then, right click on the mouse. A list of functions appears. Select " Add Cell Shade. " All the cells containing characters will be covered as shown in Figure 4. Students will not see the characters that are covered. The second set of the characters is what students will operate on the SMART Board.

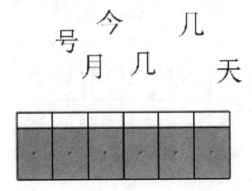

Figure 4

Now, an interactive activity for students to practice sentence recon-struction is created. If a SMART Board is available in the classroom, students will simply touch the characters on the board and drag them into the cells above the covered ones in the order they think is correct, as shown in Figure 5.

Once the characters are in place, students can check the answer on their own by simply touching the shades. The cell shades disappear when they are touched as in Figures 6 and 7.

This activity is simple and effective, especially for grammar re-

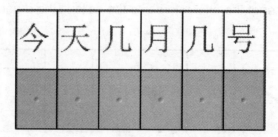

Figure 5

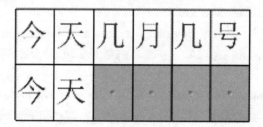

Figure 6

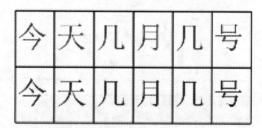

Figure 7

view. Every time when this activity was shown to students, students did not see this as a grammar drill, but as time to " have fun. " Even college students greatly enjoymoving characters around on the board and rearranging them into the order they believe is correct. They also enjoy checking the answer on their own. Based on my classroom observation, when one student was working on the .sentence reconstruction in front of the SMART Board, the rest of the students usually all focused on what he/she was doing. If he/she moved a character into a wrong cell, many students wouldraise their hands immediatelyand wanted to participateand go correct it. This really createsan enjoyable learning environment. For instructors, developing activities like the one above has many advantages. For example, it can be created in a very short time. Language instructors at college normally have to teach 10 to 15 hours per week. How to develop classroom teaching materials efficiently is crucial. Moreover, designing this kind of interactive activity does not require a lot of technological knowledge. If one knows how to use MSWord, one can easily learn how to do it with SMART Notebook software. Furthermore, instructors create a lively learning environment even when doing grammar drills.

Application 2

According to a Modern Language Association (MLA) report released in November 2007, students are nearly five times more likely to be enrolled in introductory (first- and second-year) language study than in advanced language classes (pp. 2-3). Students of Chinese at the introductory level have limited knowledge of vocabulary and sentence structures. Nevertheless, repetition is the mother of learning. How can instructors repeat the same information in class again and again but still make the class interesting? For instance, numbers, animals, and stationery are usually taught at the very beginning of Chineselanguage courses. What kind of interactive activities or teaching materials can instructors develop to engage students in classroom learning? In the following, I will demonstrate two activities designed through SMART Notebook software. The first one is designed to review numbers, and the second one is created to review vocabulary related to stationery.

Language educators are generally not technology specialists who do programming or operate complicated software. Language educators are usually users of technology. Whatever language educators create should be easy for them and easy for students to use. SMART Notebook software has another unique feature, i. e. , it has many ready-made interactive and multimedia lesson activities, stored under "Gallery Sampler" and "Lesson Activity Toolkit" as shown in Figures 8 and 9. Instructors only have to go to either folder, select the appropriate activity, drag the multimedia activity onto a blank Notebook page, and then modify/edit the activity content as needed. In few seconds, an interactive activity is created!

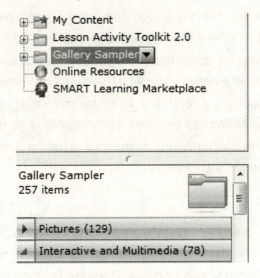

Figure 8

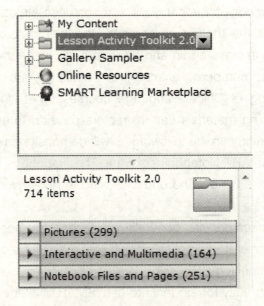

Figure 9

Number Review

When reviewing numbers, instructors can incorporate the dice from the ready-made lesson activities. Because the dice spins when it is clicked, it really creates an exciting and positive learning environment. Where the red arrow points to in Figure 10 is a color selection function. Instructors can create dices in different colors. Where the green arrow points to is a function that enables users to create multiple dices. For example, when reviewing numbers between 1 and 24, instructors or students can select 4 dices as shown in Figure 11. The change from one dice to four dices only takes one click. This kind of instant change not only draws students' attention but also saves time in class.

Figure 10

Figure 11

Vocabulary Review

Another excellent interactive multimedia activity that Notebook software provides is called "Image Match." Notebook software provides a ready-made interactive template, and what instructors, as users, have to do is simply entering information into the template. For instance, Figure 12 is a blue Image Match. The blank squares are for images; the blue oval-shaped spots are for texts; and the blank oval-shaped places are for the texts that match the images above. Figure 13 shows the four different functions above the big squares. When instructors are ready to enter texts and images, then click "Edit" to insert the teaching materials into the template. The "Check" button is for students or instructors to check the result after students match texts to the images. The "Reset" button will shuffle the texts and images and create another new interactive activity in one click. If students are not able to solve the matching exercise, they can simply click "Solve", then the interactive activity itself will solve the matching and show the correct answers.

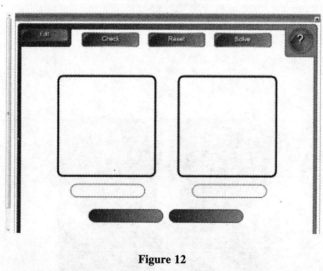

Figure 12

Figure 13

Figure 14 is an example of vocabulary review activity. After students learned the Chinese names for those stationary items, the instructor could engage students in this activity to check their comprehension. Students would come to the board and drag the characters to match the images. After moving the characters to the spots they believe matching the images, students couldclick on the "Check" button toverify the answer themselves as shown in Figure 15. This activity can be applied multiple times in class. By simply clicking on the "Reset" button, a new arrangement will be created as shown in Figure 16 (cf. Figure 14). This activity can assess if students can recognize the characters and if they know their meanings. Of course, this can also be done through pens and paper. However, providing students an interactive learning environment can increase students' interest and involvement.

Figure 14

In section 2, three interactive activities were presented, and step-by-step illustrations were listed. Incorporating interactive and multimedia activities into day-to-day classroom teaching not only can create a positive learning environment, which can easily engage students into the learning process, but also can increase students' motivation and interests.

Conclusion

This paper demonstrates that creating interactive activities can be quick and easy if the right tools are applied. In thisera of technological prevalence, language educators need to learn how to apply technology wisely in order to make teaching material development efficient and effec-

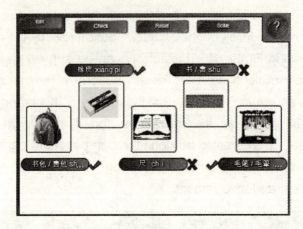

Figure 15

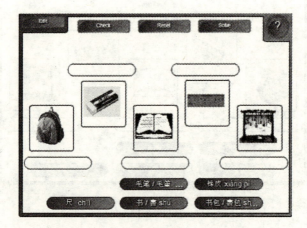

Figure 16

tive. Although one of the goals of this paper is to advocate the use of instructional technology in day-to-day classroom teaching and learning, it should be made clear that technology should only work as a tool to enhance students' learning process and to increase their classroom participation. The classroom focus is still on students and their whole learning process.

References

Furstenbert, Gilberte, Sabine Levet, Kathryn English, and Katherine Maillet.

(2001). Giving a virtual voice to the silent language of culture: the *Cultura*project. Language Learning & Technology, 5 (1), 55—102.

Hanna, Barbara, and Juliana Nooy. (2003). A funny thing happened on the way to the forum: Electronic discussion and foreign language learning. Language Learning & Technology, 7 (1), 71—85.

Levy, Mike. (2007). Culture, culture learning and new technologies: Toward a pedagogical framework. Language Learning & Technology, 11 (2), 104—127.

Liaw, Meei-ling. (2006). E-learning and the development of intercultural competence. Language Learning & Technology, 10 (3), 49—64.

Meskill, Carla, Jonathan Mossop, Stephen DiAngelo, and Rosalie Pasquale. (2002). Expert and novice teachers talking technology: Precepts, concepts, and misconcepts. Language Learning & Technology, 6 (3), 46—57.

Modern Language Association. 2007, 13 Nov. Modern Language Association Newsletter. Accessed 16 Mar. 2009.

    <http://www. mla. org/pdf/release11207_ ma_ feb_ update. pdf>

O'Dowd, Robert. (2003). Understanding the "other side": Intercultural Learning in a Spanish-English E-mail Exchange. Language Learning & Technology, 7 (2), 118—144.

Rideout, Victoria, Ulla Foehr, and Donald Roberts. (2010). Generation M①: Media in the lives of 8- to 18-Year olds. Henry J. Kaiser Foundation, Menlo Park, California.

Toyoda, Etsuko, and Richard Harrison. (2002). Categorization of text chat communication between learners and native speakers of Japan. Language Learning & Technology, 6 (1), 82—99.

Trotter, Andrew. (1999). Preparing teachers for the digital age. Education Week, 19 (4), 37—42.

Warschauer, Mark, and Carla Meskill. (2000). Technology and second language teaching and learning. In Rosenthal (ed) Handbook of Undergraduate Second Language Education. Mahwah, NJ: Lawrence Erlbaum.

---

① SMART Technologies Inc. does not sponsor, affiliate, or endorse the information presented in this paper. The content presented in this paper is solely a personal contribution to the foreign language education field.

云平台软件 VoiceThread 试用

利用 VoiceThread 提升语言技能
——注重能力表现的活动设计
Using VoiceThread to Boost Proficiency Development:
Performance—Based Activity Design

张 霓 Phyllis Zhang 美国乔治·华盛顿大学

The George Washington University, United States zhang@gwu.edu

摘 要：本文介绍利用 VoiceThread（VT）来为中高级/高级程度学习者进行语言技能训练的多种方式。与 PowerPoint 及 Prezi 等用于介绍演示的工具相比较，VT 所具有的异步（asynchronous）及分享互动功能有利于课外合作参与式学习活动，无论是由教师主导还是学生自己掌控。为获得最佳效果，VT 活动设计应与技能目标紧密联系，注重语言形式和结构的提升，并利用视觉及语音功能来强化语言的输入与输出，促进习得过程。作者提出四种技能为纲的活动类别，10 种不同侧重面的学练活动，以及基本的能力表现评估标准样例。文章认为语言教师应对 VT 加以充分利用，并结合 PPT 的功能，以使活动设计更加有效。

关键词：网络 2.0，VoiceThread，PPT，语言技能，语言能力，演练任务，异步练习活动

Abstract：This article introduces various ways to use VoiceThread (VT) for upper level proficiency development. Compared with popular presentation tools such as PowerPoint and Prezi, VT has asynchronous and sharing features that promote collaborative learning outside of class through teacher-and student-led activities. To achieve optimal results, VT activities should align with level-appropriate performance goals. The activity design should also attend to form for accuracy and proficiency development. The use of available visual and audio features can effectively enhance the language input and output, facilitating the acquisition process. The author proposes four categories of proficiency-oriented activities with ten types of performance-based learning tasks/exercises, and a sample rubric for general performance assessment. The article concludes that language instructors should fully utilize VT and incorporate PPT features to achieve better design results.

Keywords：Web 2. 0，VoiceThread，PowerPoint，language proficiency，performance-based，tasks，asynchronous activities

一　引言：多媒体工具新秀 VoiceThread

近年来网络 2.0 工具的分享、互动、合作的概念和操作方式逐渐影响和深入教育领域，Voice-Thread（VT）就是一个很好的例证。VT 是一个 2007 年推出的网络产品，提供多媒体呈现、多人评论的平台，使参与者以异步（asynchronous）方式进行网上讨论和交流。此程序的内容呈现演示方式多样，不仅可用图片及视频，亦可用文字档案。参与讨论或评讲的方式包括五种：录音、打字、电话拨打、视频或上传音档。此外，分享 VoiceThread 的方式也很灵活，可直接通过电子邮件发送参与者，也可将 VT 嵌入可自控的网页上，将链接提供参与者。VT 在 2007 年推出后立即受到教育及商务人士的青睐，并且至今用户热情仍在持续。

VT 之所以受教育人士欢迎的一个主要原因是 VT 有利于网络合作参与式的学习方式（collaborative learning），能够有效地推动学生的社交及互动技能，对学习者的学习、动力及解决问题的能力都起到积极作用（Faculty Focus，2010），可使课上的内容在课后得到延伸、扩展和深化。有人提出，异步讨论比课堂讨论更有质量，因为学生可不受时间的限制，能在参与讨论之前对课上的内容进行整理消化，并对自己的发言多加思考（Orlando，2010）。在外语学习方面，VT 的利用也为学习者开拓了更广阔的学练空间。杜克（Duke）大学的一项阿拉伯语课程的调查显示，多数学生对 VT 的反映比较积极。在调查中，59% 的被访者认为用 VT 进行口头技能练习甚至比面对面的谈话更有帮助，78% 的学生认为语言课应该对 VT 加以利用，65% 的认为 VT 练习活动促进了他们口头表达能力（Kennedy，2010）。VT 在中文作为外语的教学尝试中也初见成效，如让学生看图自编故事、录音上传分享的办法来起到巩固新学词语、提高表达能力的作用（Chen，2010），或利用 VT 做视频杂志报道及观点讨论，以增加学生课外语言练习与实践的机会，并为教学增添趣味性（Wang，2010）。可以看出，VT 的活动方式有助于建构式（constructivist）教学设计，注重培养、发挥学习者的学习兴趣，解决问题的能力，使其在合作参与中有更多机会独立思考、培养高层次的技能

（Bruenner，2011）。

　　从 VT 目前的使用情况看，在语言教学上的利用还不够充分。从 VT 的多媒体演示＋互动评说功能来看，其对语言技能训练的用途仍大有潜力可挖。但无论工具如何，若要加以充分利用，首先需要明确三方面的问题。其一，此工具与其他工具有何重要区别，即它的优势主要在哪些方面？其二，教程的目的为何，即所教课程有哪些预期目标、如何能利用此工具来更好更快地实现预期目标？其三，如何评估学生的表现。有鉴于此，本文先对 VT 的特点做简略介绍，并与其他大众化的工具做一个比较。笔者将以中高级教程为例，就怎样利用 VT 来辅助表达技能的训练进行探讨，并针对中高级/高级技能训练提出几种任务设计方案及评估标准。

二　VT 的特点和使用步骤

　　作为幻灯式（slides）内容呈现演示的一种多媒体工具，我们首先想了解的是 VT 的优势何在，特别是与其他用于演示介绍的应用程序 PowerPoint（PPT）及 Prezi 有何主要区别。在做比较之前，我们须对 VT 的主要功能有所了解。在三种工具中，VT 的制作步骤算最直接透明的。只需上网开户，稍微浏览演示短片后即可开始试做。每种主要功能演示片仅 1—2 分钟，十分简洁明了，约 10 分钟之内就能掌握基本步骤。即使用户不看演示短片，边玩边学，也可以无师自通。

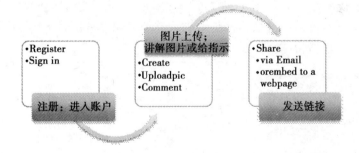

　　具体流程如下：

　　1）注册开户（Register）：进入 VT 网站（http：//voicethread. com），选择注册开户，程序简单，只需要录入电子邮件信箱（email address），设定登录密码即可。账户类型很多，K-12、高等院校、商务用户等，个人或集体账户都有，价格不等。但若不做选择，注册后即自动拥有免费账户。一般来说，以下两种用户类型足以满足一般语言教师的需要：

a. 免费用户（Free VT Account）：含 75MB 用户档案储存空间，以及基本的用户使用权限，如三条会话线（threads），30 分钟的视频评讲时间，每个上传文档上限为 25MB。此用户类型适合大多数语言教师的一般需要。另外，教师自己可开数个免费户头，需要时学生也可自行开免费户，来解决空间不够的问题。当确实感到需要增加空间时，可再考虑购买专业用户权。

b. 专业用户（VT Pro Account）：年费 59 美元，含 10G 的储存空间，其他用户使用权限也较高。此用户类型适合使用频率较高、学生较多、需要储存空间更大的教师。

2）幻灯片准备（Slides preparation）：若只用图片做简单的评讲，可直接上传图片（见下一步）。但 VT 界面不像在 PPT 里那样可以随意排版，添加文字说明，所以最好是利用 PPT 来进行幻灯片版面设计，益处良多：

- 可以在画面上加上练习要求和语言提示
- 便于保存设计档案，以便日后修改更新
- PPT 的各种模版、图表等都可加以利用，也可对图片做简单处理，如在上面加字、标记，或进行裁剪、调整色调等
- 上传图片大小一致，有统一的风格、背景及色调
- 幻灯片做好后，存为图档格式（PNG 或 JPEG），便于上传后保持字体及格式显示正确（笔者建议最好不用 PDF 和 WORD，虽然 VT 兼容这两种格式，但中文显示可能会发生错码或空白的情况。）

3）上传图片（Upload）：进入账户（sign in），选择"制作"（Create）、"上传"（Upload），即可从自己的电脑或其他来源点选图片上传（图 1）；可批量上传（多张同时点选）。

右边的两张图片为上传的图片。

若想更换某图，点选该图，然后点击左下方图片的顶端"replace"处，即可重选图片。此更换功能极为方便，甚至可在日后加上评论内容之后更改。点击左图下方可为该图加上标题。

图 1　VT 制作界面

4）解说评讲（Comment）：图片上传后，作者即可为图片做基本解说介

绍。点选第一张图片，然后选"Comment"，即跳出整个图片框。点击图片下方"Comment"，然后选择录音、打字、视频或其他评讲方式（图2）。点击某种方式，即可开始录音或打字，若不满意，可删除重来。

图2　VT 评讲方式选择

此为整张图片的下部，点击"Comment"之后，即显示评讲方式，通常用录音和打字的较为普通，视频会占用户较多的储存空间。
录音或打字都可随时删除或重做。

5）随机勾画标注（Doodle）：开始评讲解说时，还可以做随机勾画标注（图3）。点击"Comment"后，图片右下方会出现一个调色板，点击调色板即可在图上做勾画标注。

图3　VT 视频播放/解说—评讲界面
（图片来源：http://voicethread.com）

本图片为上传后正在播放、解说的视频内容，周围的小图各自代表作者或其他受邀的或自动来访的参与者。VT 按顺序自动播放每人的音像或文字评语。
左上方第一人为该作品的作者，采用视频方式进行解说/评讲。此画面为播放录制的评讲。
左下方人头图片代表当前参与者。
可点击下方的 Comment 处，即显示评论方式，如录音、打字、视频等方式评讲时可选用勾画标注功能。

6）利用"添加身份"功能（Add identity）：笔者将其称为"分身术"，因为此功能可以将作者一人变成多人，以不同头像或其他图形代表。点击图片左下方代表评讲人自己的人头图片（见图3），即可启动此功能（图4），这样便于设计多个解说人身份，增加互动层面，如"多对一"的采访问答方式。

教师一人可变成多重身份，即每个身份都可做解说、评讲、提问等等，可从不同角度来丰富会话和互动方式。

图 4　VT"增添身份"功能

7）更换图片而保存评语（Replace）：若制作完成后想更换图片，但又想保留已经录制的音频或文字，只需在编辑（Edit）状态下点击需要更换的图片，然后选择图片上方的"replace"即可。

8）发布分享（Share）：录音或打字的解说/评讲制作完毕后，就可点选"share"来发布分享了。VT 提供便捷的电子邮件方式发送，只要作者登记上收件人的信箱邮址即可当即发送。收件人收到的邮件里含有一张图片加说明，点击图片即可上网对图片进行评讲或听读别人的点评。其他发布的方式是将 VT 嵌入自己可掌控的网页，将网页链接提供给对方。

9）其他功能：VT 网站为用户提供所有 VT 用法步骤及动画短片演示，帮助初学者很快进入使用状况，详见 VT 网站（http：//voicethread.com），此处不另作说明。

三　利用 VT 促进语言技能：可行性

从一般美国大学课程设置来看，中高级/高级程度班级的课时较少，多数学校每周只有 3 个课时。学生课上练习机会较少，课后作业集中于词汇、课文读写、语法练习为多，互动式的练习较难进行。VT 的多媒体功能可提供互动学练活动，正好可以填充这个空白，将传统的单一孤立的纸笔练习转变为一种丰富、多元、多样化的、群体的互动分享，为外语学习提供更多的可能性以及练习实践机会。基于 VT 的特点，以下四大类课外活动有极高的可行性：

1）讨论问题、交流看法（Discussion of issues）：就某课文或专题进行深入讨论，以互动方式促进高层次的理解和思考，增加练习机会，提升语言表达技能。

2）跟进练习（Daily tasks）：根据教学单元的要求，按部就班地直接以语音或文字输入方式完成各项练习，磨炼口头及书面的实用技能；这种练习的特点是短频快，每次任务并不需要很长时间，但需要经常性、有规律地进行，已达到练习、复习、巩固的目的。

3）技能整合、创意演示（Integration/Creative projects）：阶段整合，完成个人或小组的模拟演练或演示报告；需要学生事先做复习准备、选择题目、内容；查阅资料、检索图片等，并整合单元的词汇、结构等；可用于阶段性或期末评估。

4）结构与形式练习（Form-focused tasks）：除用图片视频外，也可用文字作为讨论内容的主体，增强学生对文字的理解以及对语句及段落结构形式的注意。VT 的随机标注勾画功能为此类活动提供了极大的方便。

此外，可将两种掌控方式相结合，充分利用其优势：

a. 教师掌控（Instructor-led）：有利于完成由教师 VT 账户发出的任务，提供内容范围和要求（如图片、视频及文字提示），全班学生按照要求在同一界面上以口头或打字方式完成任务。利弊：教师只需进入自己的账户即可看到整班学生的任务完成情况，便于教师检查、点评，但不利于较长、较复杂的任务，也对学生的创意发挥有所限制。

b. 学生掌控（Student-led）：每个学生自己开设自己的免费 VT 账户（或以小组设立集体账户），完成课程中布置的各项活动，期末即积累为个人/小组作品集（digital portfolio）。利弊：便于学生的创意发挥，也有助于教师检查评估个人或小组的进步表现，适用于阶段性的评测任务，如演示报告或技能测试。教师检查作业时需要逐一打开学生的网页查看，不便收集保存、比较每个学生的评讲。

四　VT 活动设计尝试

活动的设计应基于教学目的和课程目标，练习活动则较为系统化，针对性和目的性也更强，这样能使 VT 的功用发挥得比较充分。

（一）教学设计理念

1）技能标准为目标（Performance-based goals）：从美国的标准测试要求看，中高级/高级阶段者须有成段表达的能力，除人际沟通能力外，还须具有描述介绍、讲述事件、陈述观点、访谈对答的基本能力（ACTFL，1999）。因此，任务和练习的设计可以这些技能要求为目标。

2）注重语言结构与形式（Focus on form）：第二语言习得研究显示，有效的语言输出不仅要注重内容（meaning），也要重视交际中语言结构及形式的恰当准确（attention to form）（Long，1991），而后者常可通过直接/显性的讲解呈现来实现。因此，在各种活动设计中，也需要设法提升学生的语言表达层次和准确性，即活动应含有适当的语言要求，提示学生应用这些目标结构。这不仅包括使用恰当的词语句式，也包括有效的表达形式和段落组织结构，使交际沟通或演示介绍顺畅、得体、有效。

3）视觉强化效应（Input enhancement）：在呈现方式上也须注重视觉强化效应，即通过颜色、字体、提示等直接的显性方式增强内容呈现的凸显性，使学生能注意（noticing）目标结构要求，在演练过程中对其加以应用，从而有效地促进内化与习得（Gascoigne 2006，Jin 2005，Schmidt 1995，Sharwood 1993）。

4）检查评估（Performance checks and assessment）：检查评估不是简单地为了对学生的作业做一个优劣鉴定（evaluation），而是对学习活动进行验收、总结和调整的过程。此过程的重点在于找出学生能力表现的具体证据，检查评量其达到预期目标的程度，并给予适当的评语反馈（Wiggins & McTighe，2005）。因此，检查评估注重的是教学效果和进步情况。检查评估二者各有侧重：检查通常为短频快或小结性的评量方式（formative assessment），而评估则为阶段性或终结性的评量方式（summative assessment）（Sandrock，2010）。

（二）VT 活动设计及侧重点

基于以上理念及 VT 的特点，笔者设计了以下 10 种 VT 任务/练习侧重点，以辅助中高级/高级教程的技能训练和评测（详见第 76 页表 1）：

1）描述特征 Describing physical features

2）比较异同 Comparing and contrasting

3）描述过程 Describing a process/sequence

4）介绍特色 Introducing characteristics

5）解说图表 Interpreting charts/diagrams

6）讲述故事 Telling/retelling a story

7）表达看法 Expressing views and opinions

8）访谈问答 Interviewing and receiving an interview

9）段落结构 Paragraph structure/organization

10）准确表达 Focusing on accuracy：words and expressions

五　示例及操作说明

为了便于说明和举例，以下设计和举例基于笔者编著的中高级教程《表达》（Zhang，2009，2010）。示例中的活动设计均可作为演练或阶段整合评测任务。

示例 1　（图 5、图 6）描述外部特征：现在是什么样子，可以做什么改变

技能	口头及书面交际，成段表达；描述外部特征、形容感觉、描述物体、按照空间顺序有条理地描述空间；做行动方案建议
结构	处所 + V 着短语、V 在处所、在处所 V、把 X 改成……
方式	由教师选择方式（教师掌控或学生掌控），规定图片或让学生自选图片，并明确语言要求，规定完成的日期 用 PPT 制作两张幻灯片，一张为说明，一张为图片 + 语言提示 （详见图右边的说明）

表 1　　　　　　　　　10 种 VT 任务/活动侧重点设计

技能表现	目的/目标	适用范围	活动方式	VT 呈现方式
1—描述特征（口头/打字）	详细具体的特征描述；以主题句、空间关系及顺序、方位词语等组织段落	物体、美术、人物外部特征；室内/室外空间；自然风景、城市外观等	学生看图，并根据文字提示和要求描述图片内容	单张或多张图片，可含文字提示及描述要求
2—比较异同（口头/打字）	用比较方式加强段落描述的层次和力度；有条理地比较特点	物体、产品、人选、工作、气候/环境问题、地理特点、城市特色	学生看图，并根据文字提示和要求做描述、比较	同类图片数张（如两个城市），含描述要求及比较用语提示
3—描述过程（口头）	用表达顺序的词语作为连接过渡，清楚地说明过程的每一步	某物制作过程；申请工作；办理手续；指路等	学生看图，根据文字提示和要求描述过程或步骤；	系列组图；单张地图或社区图；演示过程的视频
4—介绍特色（口头）	主题句明确，语句连接及段落组织有条理	风俗习惯（如过年）、某地风光、城市特色等	学生解说一组文化或地方特色的图片	内容与某主题相关的图片或视频
5—解说图表（口头）	用适当的专门词语，如数据表达、方位等，有条理地对内容加以说明	含数据的各种图表，地区社区地图	学生根据文字提示和要求解说图表、地图	图表、地图；适当加文字提示和要求

续表

技能表现	目的/目标	适用范围	活动方式	VT 呈现方式
6—讲述故事（口头/打字）	叙事方式和连接性词语句式，使叙述连贯，并掌握各时间段的动词形式	简单故事、个人经历、事件经过、旅游过程等	学生解说自己的一组图片，或根据提供的图片和要求解说或概述、复述内容	视频短片或图片故事，文字提示，问题提示
7—表达看法（口头/打字）	掌握讨论辩论常用词语	谈论产品、人物、地方、环境、城市、经济等各类话题	学生看图或视频后表达自己的看法	单幅或多幅图片，视频短片；可含文字提示、要求
8—访谈问答（口头）	即兴对答，用适当的访谈用语，如开头、结尾套语以及惯用回答方式	工作面试、问题咨询、特点介绍等	就某话题或图片提问，学生逐一回答	单张或多张图片；可利用 VT 的多重身份功能营造"多对一"谈话方式
9—段落结构（打字）	段落的条理清楚、层次分明；主题明确、衔接连贯、自然流畅	描述、比较、叙述或陈述看法	学生看一段有组织缺陷的文字，建议如何重组；或加上开头和结尾；老师点评	一张或多张文字为主的幻灯片，描述类可适当配图
10—准确表达（口头/打字）	用词准确、成语恰当、词语搭配恰当	描述、比较、叙述或陈述看法	类似游戏竞猜活动：学生看图或文字提示后，说出/写出适当的词语、表达法或句子；老师点评并公布正确答案	多张幻灯片，可含文字和图片提示

用 PPT 或 Word 准备好文字说明，上传到 VT。
若不需要长段的说明，也可用 Comment 的方式添加语音或文字指示，如左边显示。
语音或文字输入随时可删除修改。

图 5　情景和任务说明（教师掌控方式）

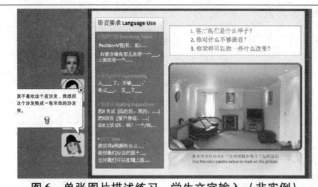

图6　单张图片描述练习，学生文字输入（非实例）

老师将图片和语言要求用
PPT 准备好，上传到 VT。
　　学生以语音或打字方
式完成描述（可规定一种
方式）。
　　学生描述时可用勾画
标注方式。

示例2　　（图7）　比较利弊，表达看法：应该用哪种替代/再生能源

技能	口头/书面交际，成段表达；同意或反对意见，陈述观点、举例说明、比较利弊
结构	主题句；概括句＋具体说明句；比较用语、陈述观点常用句式及表达法
方式	● 教师掌控，明确语言要求，规定完成日期。若作为评测，可不提供词语提示 ● 此练习可为课上辩论做前期准备（第一轮），即由个人发表看法（1—2 段），第二轮可在课上进行，老师在课前公布 VT 上的观点，学生各自做准备，就某人的看法提出不同意见，并深入讨论，提出具体论据（辩论，1—2 段）

图7　单张图片讨论辩论任务，学生语音输入（非实例）

老师将图片和语言要求用
PPT 准备好，上传到 VT。
学生可在规定的时间范围
内各自完成讨论任务。若
录音时不满意，可删除
重录。
第一次讨论老师可选择关
闭式，即每个学生在做评
论时看不到别人的意见；
第二轮在课上进行有针对
性的辩论，课前可在网上
看到所有人的意见，各自
按要求做辩论准备。

示例 3　　　　　　　　**（图 8）描述方位，说明过程步骤：怎么走**

技能	口头交际，连贯表达；准确描述方位，说明步骤、顺序
结构	方位词语句式；处所＋有/是个……；处所＋就是……
方式	• 由教师掌控，明确语言要求，规定完成日期 • 可先在课上做社区描述（空间关系、方位等），熟悉社区布局及常用词语 • 在课后的 VT 练习之后，老师可检查个人表现后，找出典型错误，在课上统一纠正；然后选择个别学生在课上做角色扮演，再次检测

图 8　单张图片描述，学生语音输入，颜色标出路线（非实例）（操作时可点击图片放大或移动画面）

若作为测试任务，可选择不提供词语提示。

老师可用"分身法"假设一个马克和丽丽，营造一个对话情景。如假设的马克说："我现在在阳光南路的酒吧，请告诉我到天天来小吃怎么走。"学生即用语音输入法回答，并标出路线。作答时若不满意可随时删除重录。

示例 4　（图 9、图 10）介绍特色（系列活动）：采访、解说、概述地方特色

技能	理解诠释；采访式答问；表达演示，以解说或概述方式介绍地方特色
结构	话题常用句型及表达法；采访客套话语，提问方式、答问方式 段落主题句、转折过渡句、语句连接
方式	• 连环系列任务，讨论；一对一或多对一采访式答问；一对多表达演示 • 由教师掌控，统一内容；明确语言要求，规定完成日期 • 第一环：课上先做第一轮讨论及视听，导入主题 • 第二环：课外学生做模拟采访（一对一或多对一）；图片解说、书面概述 • 第三环：课上做真实信息互访交流（一对一或多对一）；之后可作个人演示报告（一对多在课外异步进行，以便同学互动点评）

系列活动示例：介绍地方特色《我的家乡》

课上 >> 信息输入	课外 >> 输出技能演练	课上+课外 输出技能运用
• 主题导入 • 视听理解	• VT模拟采访 • VT解说图片 • VT概述写作	• 真实信息交流 • 个人演示报告

在课堂初步视听练习之后，再在课后跟进，用 VT 播放视频短片作为复习，接着做下面的采访问答。

图 9　视频短片导入话题，学生完成视听练习，准备回答问题

一对一采访：教师自己充当采访者，提问；学生为被采访者，逐一回答。
多对一采访：教师可利用"分身法"制造多个提问者轮流提问；学生逐一回答。
图片解说：学生按要求的词语句式（略）逐一解说图片，每张图片可点击放大；用语音输入。
概述特色：学生按段落结构要求（略）概述地方特色，用打字输入。

图 10　选视频中的图片作为提示，辅助学生完成
采访及解说或概述练习

六　检查评估的评分标准

　　为了确保 VT 活动达到预期的收效，还应设计一套基于能力表现的评分标准（rubrics）。设计这样的评分标准可有效地增加评比量的透明度，不仅方便教师在评分上的统一性，同时应事先公布给学生，以增强学生对学习目标和具体要求的意识，从而有效地提高语言输出的质量。例如对中高级程度

的目标而言，在总体上可列出以下一般标准（表2），其他具体标准可据当课具体 VT 任务而定。

表2 **VT 活动的一般评分标准示例**

（部分参考 ACTFL 口语水平评测标准）

	超过预期结果 Exceeds Expectations	达到预期结果 Meets the Expectations	未达到预期结果 Does not Meet the Expectations
内容 Content	Relevant to the subject; has general statements and supporting details; content is challenging or interesting to the reader; shows clarity and a depth of thinking	Relevant to the subject; has some details to support general statements; shows evidence of effort in the work; generally has clarity in conveying meaning	Irrelevant to the subject or missing details or both; demonstrate simple thinking and/or casualness; repeat ideas already shared.
话语/文字 Text Type	Uses paragraphs and connected sentences with cohesive devices.	Uses strings of sentences and sometimes connected discourse of paragraph—length.	Uses simple sentences and some strings of sentences.
句子结构 Sentence Structures	Uses longer and complex sentences; uses general statements with supporting details; includes various sentence structures and patterns	Has emerging complex sentences; uses general statements with some supporting details; applies sentence patterns	Mostly uses simple sentence; uses general comments/ statements without enough supporting details; sometimes applies structures and patterns
词汇 Vocabulary	Uses a wide range of vocabulary, including specialized and precise vocabulary, and appropriate idiomatic expressions and stock phrases; applies key sentence structures and expressions.	Consistently uses a range of general and specific vocabulary, including some specialized and precise vocabulary such as idiomatic expressions or stock phrases.	Uses a range of general vocabulary and limited specific words; seldom uses idiomatic expressions and/or stock phrases
任务要求 Required Elements	Includes all required elements plus additional information.	Includes all required elements with or without additional information	Includes some but not all required elements

七　三种工具比较：VT 、PPT 及 Prezi

介绍了 VT 的功能用途之后，可以将 VT 与 PPT 及 Prezi 两种常用的工具在报告演示功能上做一个简单的分析比较，以便明确哪种工具适合我们的日常需要。三者各有长短利弊，很难一概而论。

（一）PPT 与 Prezi 的异同

PPT 是大家较为熟悉的报告演示工具，Prezi 为近年来网络呈现演示工具中的佼佼者，两者各有所长。简言之，在呈现功能上，PPT 具有更多的处理方式和灵活性，如调整字体颜色、动画、自动播放、图片呈现方式、背景音乐插入等等；局限是需要安装程序，在网络上运用较受限制。另外，PPT 在演示模式下不能任意跳动、来回点评，也不能随意放大移动画面。而 Prezi 恰好弥补了 PPT 的欠缺。Prezi 正如一张空间无限的大白板供你任意布局图文音像，并可在报告演示时放大、缩小，或着眼局部或纵观全局；来回跳跃、上下移动也较为自如。此外，Prezi 是网上应用程序，不需要安装，免费版基本能满足一般需要。显而易见，二者的区别在于 PPT 为规律整齐、有条不紊地呈现模式，而 Prezi 则为动感、变幻式的呈现模式，二者功能互补，各有其用。例如，在呈现文字内容或播放影像资料时，PPT 便捷灵活，而在呈现地图、地区概况、地理环境时，Prezi 的优势及演示力度显而易见。

（二）VT 的特点和优势

从前面的介绍可以看出，VT 与前二者相比有很多方便之处，总结如下：

1）VT 综合了 PPT 与 Prezi 的部分优势，如：

a. 各类档案兼容性强，文字档、图档、音档、影档

b. 画面放大移动较 PPT 灵活

2）VT 具有前二者所欠缺的分享互动功能：

c. VT 提供异步参与互动、分享的功能，使课堂教学在课文得以延伸和补充；

d. 可用语音、视频、文字等输入方式直接参与交流，提供多种形式的练习方式；

e. 在语音评论输入的同时，说话者可在画面上随机勾画标注（doodling），起到视觉辅助或强化的效果；

f. 作者的"分身法"功能（add/change identity）可使教师随意变换身份，丰富了介绍演示的方式与效果（如：一对一提问方式可以转化为多对一的方式）。

综上所述，三种工具各有所长，应酌情选用（详见表3）。

表 3 三种应用程序功能及特点比较

	PPT	Prezi	VT
处理文字颜色、字体、图片 Manipulate colors，fonts，images	+ + +	−	−
演示内容局部放大、画面移动 Zoom and pan	−	+ + +	+ +
来回跳动选择 Jump back and forth	+	+ + +	+ +
插入图档、音档、影档 Insert picture，audio，video	+ + +	+	+ + +
插入音频视频链接 Insert hyperlink to audio or video	+ + +	+ + +	
线上播放演示（音频及视频） Online presentation	−	+ + +	+ + +
线下播放演示 Offline presentation	+ + +	+ + +	fee—based
异步、分享、评论 Asynchrony，shareability，comment	−	−	+ + +
打印 Printability	+ + +	+	−
画面设计 Presentation design	+ + +	+ + +	
安装程序 Software installation	需安装 Yes	不需安装 No	不需安装 No
程序费用 Application cost	需办公软件 Install MS Office	教师与学生免费 Free for education	基本版免费 专业版 59 美元/年

注：表中加号或减号（+/−）代表该工具是否具有此项功能；多个加号代表功能强。

八　结束语

本文对 VoiceThread 作为语言教学的课外辅助工具进行了探讨，并将其与 PPT 和 Prezi 的功能做了分析比较。三种工具在内容介绍演示方面各有利弊，可以互补（见表3）。如 VT 有诸多优势可以利用，而且相对来说步骤比较简单。但 VT 并非完美无缺，有些方面有待改进。如 VT 的界面除了评讲时可以输入文字外，其他地方却不能直接打字，这给老师造成不便。因此在目前状态下，设计 VT 任务时最好结合 PPT 做版面设计，以便在文字、画面处理上获得最佳效果。若 VT 今后能加上插入字框功能（insert text box），而且能简单处理颜色、字体、字号，那么 VT 在语言教学上将会有更多发挥利用的空间。

从教学设计上看，VT 演练活动不应限于热门话题评讲讨论，而应利用 VT 的优势扩大语言功能和技能练习范围。同时，仅仅用图片为主导、让学生自由发挥式的评讲对技能的提高是极为有限的。笔者建议在设计任务时针对技能要求补充语言要求和提示，用视觉强化效果增加语言输入的有效性，以引导学生对目标结构有意识地应用，从而逐渐提升表达层次，促进习得。为了让 VT 活动获得最佳收效，应该让学生明确具体的评分标准，使学生有意识地去接近并达到目标。

可以预见，随着科技的快速发展和人们交际方式的改变，以及网络资源的日益丰富，相当一部分的语言学练活动将逐渐移到课后网上进行。因此，适应时代需要、利用网络资源进行教学规划设计，也将成为今后语言教师们一项长期持久的任务。

致谢：笪骏、刘世娟、卫立等老师对本文进行了审读并提出了宝贵的修改意见。作者特此表示由衷的感谢。

注释 Notes

1. 本文的大部分 VT 设计基于作者编著的中级—高级教材《表达》（*Developing Chinese Fluency*），Cengage Learning，2009/2010。

2. 本文中的部分 VT 设计基于作者为以下教师讲习班做培训演示时所做的设计：

- 2010 *STARTALK Chinese Teacher Professional Program*，Houston and Dallas，Texas May 1—2.

- 2010 Chinese Pedagogy Workshop，organized by Confucius Institute at George Mason University，Chinese Language Teachers Association of Virginia，and Asia Institute and East Asia-Center at the University of Virginia，at George Mason University，May 8.

- Technology Workshops—Session 4，The 6th International Conference on Technology and Chinese Language Teaching（TCLT6）. The Ohio State University，Columbus，June 14.

参考文献

ACTFL（1999）. Proficiency Guidelines—Speaking（Revised）. American Council on the Teaching of Foreign Languages.

Bruenner，I.（2011）. Using VoiceThread for Language Learning. Abstract for conference，International Association for Language Learning Technology（IALLT），Irvine. Available：http：//www. iallt. org/event/iallt_ s_ biennial_ conference_ at_ uc_ irvine_ june_ 21_ 25_ 2011/proposal/using_ voice_ thread_ for_ langu.

Chen，T.（2010）VoiceThread：An effective tool for speaking practice. In Xu，D. ，J. Da，& P. Zhang（Eds. ），Proceedings of the 6th International Conference on Technology and Chinese Language Teaching（pp. 63— 67）. Columbus：National East Asian Languages Resource Center，The Ohio State University.

Faculty Focus（2010）. Asynchronous Learning and Trends. Available：http：// www. facultyfocus. com/topic/articles/asynchronous-learning-and-trends/

Gascoigne, C. （2006）. Toward an understanding of input enhancement in computerized L2 environments. CALICO Journal, pp. 147—162.

Jin, H. （2005）. Form-focused instruction and second language learning：Some pedagogical considerations and teaching techniques. Journal of the Chinese Language Teachers Association, 40（2）, pp. 31—54.

Kennedy, M. （2010）Students react positively to VoiceThread in an Arabic class. Center for Instructional Technology （CIT）, Duke University. Available：http：// cit. duke. edu/2010/05/lo-language-fellows/.

Long, M. H. （1991）. Focus on form：A design feature in language teaching methodology. In K. de Bot, R. Ginsberg, & C. Kramsch （Eds. ）, Foreign language research in cross-cultural perspective （pp. 39—52）. Amsterdam：John Benjamins.

Orlando, J. （2010）. Using VoiceThread to Build Student Engagement. Asynchronous Learning and Trends, Faculty Focus. Available：http：// www. facultyfocus. com/articles/asynchronous-learning-and-trends/using-voicethread-to-build-student-engagement/.

Sandrock, P. （2010）. The keys to assessing language performance：A teacher's manual for measuring student progress. Alexandra, VA：ACTFL.

Sharwood S. （1993）. Input enhancement in instructed SLA：Theoretical bases. Studies in Second Language Acquisition, 15, 165—179.

Schmidt, R. （1995）. Attention and awareness in foreign language learning. Honolulu：University of Hawaii at Manoa.

Wang, D. （2010）. 网络技术在高级汉语中的运用：VoiceThread, Voiceboard 和 Wiki. In Xu D. , J. Da, & P. Zhang （Eds. ）, Proceedings of the 6th International Conference on Technology and Chinese Language Teaching （pp. 237—243）. Columbus：National East Asian Languages Resource Center, The Ohio State University.

Wiggins, G. & McTighe, J. （2005）. Understanding by design. Expanded 2nd edition. Alexandra, Virginia：Association for Supervision and Curriculum Development （ASCD）.

Zhang, P. （2009, 2010）. Developing Chinese fluency （表达）（Textbook and Workbook）. Singapore, Boston, and Beijing：Cengage Learning.

Zhang, P. （2010）. Blogging as a tool for development of Chinese writing proficiency. In Xu, D. , J. Da, & P. Zhang （Eds. ）Proceedings of the 6th international conference on technology and Chinese language teaching （pp. 273—281）. National East Asian Languages Resource Center, The Ohio State University, Columbus.

VoiceThread 应用于中文教学的几个例子
Application of VoiceThread in Chinese Teaching and Learning: Some Examples

苏芳仪　Joanne Chen　美国南加州尔湾谷学院

Irvine Valley College United States jchen@ ivc. edu

摘　要：课堂时数有限，学生听和说的时间常常不足，针对学习需求来设计口语练习作业，使每位学生都有练习听说的机会，是笔者起初使用 VoiceThread 来设计教学练习的动机。文章第一个部分介绍什么是 VoiceThread 及其技术上的使用，包括 VoiceThread 的呈现方式，如何注册一个账号和 VoiceThread 三个主要区域的功能。第二个部分主要介绍笔者应用 VoiceThread 于中文教学的实际例子。第三部分比较 VoiceThread 与其他录音工具，以及运用 VoiceThread 的优点。文章最后为有意将 VoiceThread 运用于中文教学的教师提出实施 VoiceThread 教学时的几项要点与建议。

关键词：中文教学，VoiceThread，录音工具，语言教学，听说练习

Abstract：VoiceThread, an interactive collaboration online tool, allows people to collect and share group conversations in multimedia formats at one place from anywhere in the world. It can be used as a powerful tool in language teaching and learning to improve student listening and speaking skills. This article first introduces what VoiceThread is, including its presentation methods, registration information, and its three major working areas. In the second section, the author shares how she used VoiceThread in the Chinese teaching and learning, such as for lesson reviews, culture reports, group work, discussion, and exams. In the third section, the article compares VoiceThread with other online voice recording tools (e. g. , Wimba, Voki); and discusses the advantages of using VoiceThread, such as encouraging student participation and making language learning more engaging; helping to promote creative critical thinking and collaborative skills. In the last section, the article provides suggestions for instructors and researchers interested in using VoiceThread in Chinese language teaching and learning.

Keywords：Chinese language teaching，VoiceThread，Recording tools，language instruction，listening and speaking practice

一　VoiceThread 简介及在技术上的使用

VoiceThread（http：//VoiceThread. com/）是一种在网络上集合文字、影像、声音、影片呈现的多媒体，并能让用户通过电子邮件发送，崁入 blog、Moodle、Blackboard 等教学平台网站，让留言者直接在在线留言的工具。将 VoiceThread 打开时，仿佛在看一个有声音的幻灯影片（Slide Show）。对着屏幕中的图片主题留言以后，留言者的照片就会出现在框框两边，而其声音文件会出现在屏幕下方。想听哪位讨论者的留言只要点他的照片就可以听到了①。

图 1　VoiceThread 范例：看图说故事——莉莉的男朋友

集合了多位参与者的声音后，屏幕下面便形成了一条声音线，所以称之为 VoiceThread。参与讨论留言的人不需要聚集在一处，但彼此又听得到对方意见，类似一个网上语音留言板。申请一个 VoiceThread. com 的使用者账号一开始是免费的，有了账号以后就可以开始制作 VoiceThread。免费账号能制作三个作品。想要制作更多作品的话，VoiceThread. com 也提供 Pro，

---

① http://voicethread.com/about/features/.

K-12、Higher Education、Business 等收费等级不一的付费账号给学校团体及社会人士①。

　　注册完账号，登录之后，会看到屏幕上方三个区域：Browse、Create、MyVoice。

图 2　VoiceThread 的三个主要区域

　　Browse：Browse 的功能为让用户浏览，及搜寻有关的 VoiceThread。

　　比如：打入关键词搜寻 Chinese，会出现 26 页五百多个 VoiceThread 作品②。

图 3　搜寻"Chinese"的作品

　　MyVoice：MyVoice 是持账号者的作品存放区，相当于我们的档案文件夹点入 MyVoice 以后，可见到制作好的作品按完成时间顺序排列，图 4 中的三个作品的中间作品，右上角的黄色说话框框代表这个作品有新的留言。

---

① 　http://voicethread.com/products/.

② 　http://voicethread.com/?#q + Chinese. 2011 年 6 月 22 日搜寻的结果。

图 4   MyVoice 作品档案区

Create：Create 是制作 VoiceThread 的工作区。

点 Upload 上传档案，可上传的档案类别很多，如 PDF、Word Doc、PPT、PPTX、JPG、PNG、Video、Flash 等①。档案上传之后，标明作品名称，回到 MyVoice 就会看到刚制作好的 VoiceThread 了。

图 5   Create 制作作品的工作区

点一下刚上传的 VoiceThread，打开作品，在下方点 Comment 就可以开始发表意见了。方式有录音、录像、文字留言、电话留言、上传音档、影片档，一共六种②。

留言完成后，最后的步骤是决定如何分享给学生，邀请学生参与作答或留言。点下一 VoiceThread 右下角的 Menu 功能选项表。

a. 点 Delete 去掉此作品。

b. 点 Make a copy 可以复制另外一个 VoiceThread 作品。

c. 点 Share 能用 Email 寄 VoiceThread Link 给已经设定好的群体③。

---

① http://voicethread. com/about/features/media/.

② http://voicethread. com/about/features/commenting/.

③ http://voicethread. com/about/features/sharing/.

图 6　以 Web-cam 录像的留言方式　　　**图 7　打字留言方式**

　　d. 点 Edit 会回到 Create page。Create page 下面有设定功能区。按照我们的需求可做不同的设定。Embed 提供 HTML Code 以及 URL link。Export 提供下载 VoiceThread 为无须网络的影片之功能。Playback Options 可以设定是否愿意让他人下载 VoiceThread。

图 8　Menu 的　　　**图 9　Create Page 下方的设定区**
**　　功能选项表**

　　Publishing Options：

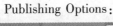

图 10　Publishing Option A　　　**图 11　Publishing Option B**

　　Publishing Options 的四种选择决定作品的公开程度。制作者可以按照需求预先设定好其作品私密性程度。勾选 Moderate Comments 的话，留言者的留言不会被其他留言者听到，除非制作人打开档案。而不勾选 Moderate comments 的话，留言者能马上相互听到他人的留言 ①。

二　应用 VoiceThread 于中文教学的几个例子

笔者使用 VoiceThread 的最初动机出于加强学生听力与口语的能力。笔者任教的 Irvine Valley College 中文班每班人数皆在四十人左右，以下情况经常出现在各级语言课：

（1）学生背景及语言程度参差不齐。

（2）一个班级人数过多，教师很难跟学生一一进行口语练习。

（3）学生的反应速度不一，年龄差距太大。

（4）上课时数有限，无法顾及全部学生的需求，学生口语练习不足。

（5）课外缺乏对象练习，学生口语练习不足，而降低学习的动机。

（6）课室中的听力练习，重复的次数不够而效果不彰，或流于枯燥乏味。

（7）为顾及学生学习语言的自信心和心理压力，教师很难重复纠正发音太多次。

由上面几点来思考学习者需求，制作课外辅助教材是有其必要性的。制作听说辅助教材的目的是使背景不一的学生都能从辅助教材中受益，鼓励学生在自主性参与过程中，提高学习兴趣，增加练习听说中文的机会。除此以外，提升学生的语言组织能力，团队合作技巧，创造性思惟能力，也是笔者在设计 VoiceThread 教学活动时所期望见到的 ②。

以下介绍几个实际例子

（1）教学课程：作为课程的辅导教材，笔者将课程的 PPT 上传到 Voice-Thread，配上录音，放在 Blog、Moodle、Blackboard 等教学平台提供学生听力练习。学生能一边听老师的录音，一边录音，然后听自己的录音练习来比较发音的准确度。这类 VoiceThread 有文字声音影像的教学课程，目的是帮助学生课前准备课后复习。教师如果能使用 Webcam 录制影像声音，学生可以更清楚地看到教师发音的嘴形。这里举的例子是中文三第五课课文句型练习③。

---

① http://voicethread.com/about/features/moderation/.

② http://voicethread.com/?#q + ivc + chinese + lesson.

③ http://voicethread.com/?#u348538.b1529429.i8062010.

图12　中文三第五课课文句型练习①

（2）录音作业：配合课文内容的录音功课练习，笔者建议设计 VoiceThread 作业时，幻灯片页数最好不要超过两张。如果第一题请学生念课文，偏向复习式的发音练习，第二题就可以设计可以自由发挥的练习。比如本例中文一第十课的课后作业②，第一页请学生叙述图片，第二页请学生回答问题。

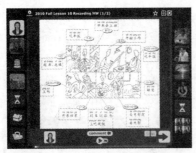

图13　配合中文以第十课课文的录音作业

（3）照片故事：学生练习叙述自己的照片故事。例子是中文三的"分享我的照片"。做法的第一步是先请每位学生传照片给笔者，笔者把全班的照片都上传到同一个 VoiceThread 作品，嵌入 Blackboard 教学平台。上课的时候打开 VoiceThread，学生谈一谈照片里的故事；下课以后，请学生到 VoiceThread 录音再叙述一次照片的内容。本例是一个延伸练习，虽然课堂上学生们已经谈过他们的照片，但是可能没有达到教师预期的流利程度，回家再练

---

① 作为课程类型的 VoiceThread 作者并没有要求学生一定要录音，学生可以自行练习。

② http://voicethread.com/#q.b1429680.i7560305.

习一次是有必要的①。一个 VoiceThread 可以最多上传五十张图片或幻灯片，很适合利用作为全班共同参与的 Project。

图 14　中文三学生的照片故事

（4）文化报告：做法与照片故事类似，笔者请学生搜集一个文化主题数据，如一位有名的中国人、一个中国的城市等，做成一张幻灯片后传给老师。笔者收集好学生的幻灯片后，上传到 VoiceThread，嵌入 Blackboard 教学平台上，请学生到自己的幻灯片那页作录音报告，报告时间长度为三到五分钟。录完音以后，最少拜访两位以上同学的作品去看去听，一定要作 Comment，可以用录音、录像、打字等方式，若打字留言请打中文字。到这里才算完成文化报告。老师也到每位学生的作品去打字、留言、回响，给予鼓励建议。这里举的例子是中文二的文化报告《一位有名的中国人》②。

图 15　中文二的文化报告

---

① http://voicethread.com/#q.b1345906.i7159892.

② http://voicethread.com/#u348538.b1850405.i9731869.

（5）合作学习（小组 Project）：这个"在餐厅里"例子中的两位学生编了一段有关爱吃什么菜的有趣的对话①。这个例子的做法是将学生分成小组，请学生以"约会"为主题编写一段对话，之后用多媒体呈现。有的学生选择拍摄 Video 影片，有的选择使用照片上传到 VoiceThread，然后录音。让学生以"制作者"身份做 Project 时，教师需要先带领学生学习 VoiceThread 的技术，过程当中也要提醒他们做好 Publishing Options 设定，如此才能分享给他人。

图16　中文一的学生作品：在餐厅里

（6）叙述练习：这是一种使用图片，配合课程的语法练习，目标为加强学生的语法与发音。这里举的例子是中文二第十五课语法练习，教学目标是能够叙述东西的位置与方向②。请学生听了老师的问题以后再作答，题目的难易程度可以在教师的题目中调整。

（7）话题讨论：邀请全班学生对同一个话题发表意见。做法的第一个步骤是教师先在课堂中提出话题，全班分成小组讨论，之后进行辩论或作小组报告，请学生课后再到 VoiceThread 发表自己个人的意见③。

（8）考试前的听力与说话练习：笔者把题目录音录好，先让学生考口语之前在家练习，目的为降低学生考口语时紧张的情绪。正式考试口语时，老师可以从中间挑选几个题目来考④。

（9）听力与口语测验：笔者在 2011 年春季班中文二期末口语考试，第一次尝试使用 VoiceThread 让学生在家里录音回答。做法是给学生三天的时

---

① http://voicethread.com/#q. b1132655. i6076412.

② http://voicethread.com/?#u348538. b451349. i2401760.

③ http://voicethread.com/#u348538. b1989920. i10504736.

④ http://voicethread.com/#u348538. b769472. i4082462.

图 17 中文二第十五课练习叙述东西的位置与方向

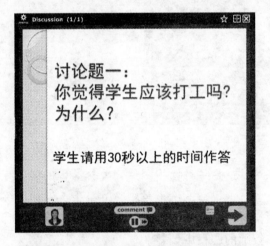

图 18 讨论题例子——学生应该打工吗？

图 19 Chinese IA Practice

间，请学生先仔细听题目，再以中文回答，考题一共十题，每一题要用30秒的时间作答，且一定要在期限内完成。学生可以按照本身的程度尽情发挥作答。对于人数多的大班，在线口语作答节省了很多课堂的时间，学生不必等待别人，也减轻了面对面口语作答的紧张程度①。因为是考试性质的VoiceThread，考试期间在 Publishing Options 设定上，笔者勾选 Moderate Comments，这样学生在作答时就无法听到看到其他同学的回答了②。

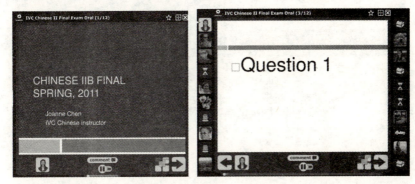

图 20　中文二期末口语考试

（10）听力档案夹：笔者将听力练习或测验录制好存放于 VoiceThread，除节省了笔者的计算机空间，还有其他好处：

a. 档案容易整理：Worksheet、Power point、PDF 等档案都能加上录音档，上传 MP3，或插入影片③。

b. 档案修改容易：可以在 VoiceThread 修改部分题目，重新录音，调整前后题目，无须全部重新制作，音档分段的地方也容易辨认④。

c. 本校每一间教室都有计算机和网络，可以随时利用。

这里所举两个例子都可以重新录音，或更改录音档，下方的声音线很容易辨认是哪一段题目，以方便需要时重复播放。

比较 VoiceThread 与其他录音工具

---

① http://voicethread.com/#u348538.b1973714.i10415005.

② http://voicethread.com/about/features/moderation/.

③ http://voicethread.com/about/features/media/.

④ http://voicethread.com/support/howto/VoiceThreads/Editing/.

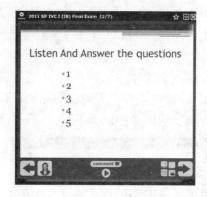 

图 21　教师的听力档案夹

表 1　　　　　　　　　比较 VoiceThread 与其他录音学习工具表格①

Tools	Allow student record online	Allow interactive activity	Online storage
Audio Drop Box (Free account)	Yes	No	Yes / MP3 files
Audacity (Free Download)	No / need to download first	No	No / MP3 files
Voicethread	Yes	Yes	Yes
Wimba Wimba pronto	Yes	No / Yes	Yes
Voki Voki.com	Yes Creating a talking Avatar	No	Yes
GoAnimate http://goanimate.com/	Yes Creating a cartoon story	No Yes with group work	Yes

　　对现代语言教师来说，选择并灵活运用录音工具于教学，已是一项必备的技能了②。上图为笔者于 2011 年 4 月 30 日在 CLTA_ SC 研讨会的报告③中提出适用于语言课的几个录音的工具，并作了简单比较。

---

①　http://www. slideshare. net/sulaoshi/developing-speaking-activities-7760810.

②　http://novastartalk. nvcc. edu/unit2.

③　http://blog. huayuworld. org/ivclaoshi/13774/2011/04/29/89902.

（1）Audio Drop Box 是 Center for Language Education And Research 提供的免费工具，容易使用，可以嵌入教师的教学平台①，方便学生录音。只有教师一人能听到所有学生的录音，但是学生之间无法听到他人的意见②，教师也无法做对应的回答。

（2）Audacity 是一个实用的录音工具。但是学生送出 MP3 音档以后，教师要一个一个档案打开来听，时间上不经济，跟 Audio Drop Box 一样，教师无法在教学平台上做相对的响应③。

（3）Wimba 是付费的工具，通常附在 Blackboard 平台中，教师同样要将录音档案一个个打开。Wimba Pronto 现在有实时响应的功能，教师能在线与学生同步谈话④。

（4）Voki 的特色是让使用者选择制作一个会说话的虚拟化身（Avatar），加上录音以后，Voki 的造型千变万化可爱讨喜，但是 Voki 只有单向的输出，没有让观者响应的功能⑤。

（5）GoAnimate 提供制作动漫的场景，使用者可以自由选择人物，制作一段有情节的动漫，配上声音后趣味性高，非常适合利用于语言课中。但是与 Voki 同样，没有让观者响应的功能⑥。

简单比较之下，除了没有如 Skype⑦、MSN、Wimba Pronto 的实时性对话功能，VoiceThread 具备了以上录音工具所有特点并加上⑧：

（1）容易使用；只要有计算机上简单的麦克风、Webcam，就能制作。

（2）在线工具：不需要下载或占用计算机储存空间。

（3）容易分享：在线分享，不需要用 Email 寄录音档案。

（4）协同合作：多人能够在同一个 Project 作品中协同合作，并以录音、录像、打字等多种方式参与。

（5）响应功能：参与者之间都能留下意见，得到多向回馈。

---

① http://web. cortland. edu/flteach/mm-course/audiodropbox/index. html.

② http://blog. huayuworld. org/ivclaoshi/13774/2011/04/29/89425.

③ http://gofree. com/download/Audio/Sounds/audacity. php? gclid = CPaCl6DbyakCFQFsgwod 4nidPQ.

④ http://www. wimba. com/.

⑤ http://www. voki. com/.

⑥ http://goanimate. com/.

⑦ http://www. skype. com/intl/en-us/home.

⑧ http://sites. google. com/site/voicethreadsclassroom/Home.

（6）容易编辑：能够上传图片、影片、文本文件，并加上录音。

（7）保留私密性：可以调整 project 作品的公开程度。

（8）创造性：挑战参与者的语言、图片、影片、音效的组织能力①。

集合 VoiceThread 教学的实际经历与 VoiceThread 的特点，笔者简单归纳出运用 VoiceThread 在教学上的三大优点②：

- 鼓励了学生主动性参与的意愿。
- 加强了学生学习语言的结构性与功能性的听说练习。
- 提升了学生的创造性思惟能力。

三　实施 VoiceThread 的几项要点

本文首先介绍了什么是 VoiceThread，如何申请账号及三个主要功能区域，然后介绍了笔者应用 VoiceThread 于尔湾谷学院中文课程中的一些例子。此后把 VoiceThread 与其他四个影音工具作了简单比较。最后笔者想对有意使用 VoiceThread 作为教学工具的中文教师们提出一些实施的建议。

实施之前请教师们充分了解本身的教学需求与明确之教学目标，再针对这个具体目标设计教学活动。利用 VoiceThread 设计有创意性的教学活动有上百种③，但请教师们首先考虑：

a. 制作这份教材的目标是什么？

b. 对学生的产出（Student Learning Outcomes），教师的预期是什么？

c. 对使用 VoiceThread 的过程中出现的技术问题④，教师如何解决⑤？

要充分了解 VoiceThread 技术与应用，笔者建议教师先使用免费账号练习（一个 Email 可以申请一个账号），来回实验，充分了解 VoiceThread 各项功能，掌握 VoiceThread 制作技巧之后，再考虑加入付费会员。教师们如果已经使用 Blog、Moodle、Blackboard、Wikispaces、Google-site 等教学平台，嵌入 VoiceThread Project，方便学生直接操作录音，是最有效率的方式。

---

① http://thinkingmachine. pbworks. com/w/page/22187721/Think-VoiceThreads.

② http://www. facultyfocus. com/articles/asynchronous-learning-and-trends/using-voicethread-to-build-student-engagement/.

③ http://www. ideastoinspire. co. uk/voicethread. htm.

④ http://voicethread. com/support/howto/Troubleshooting/.

⑤ http://somenovelideas. typepad. com/some-novel-ideas/2011/01/using-voicethread-in-your-class-room. html.

　　倘若学生计算机知识不足，技术方面需老师协助，建议教师们先做好以下准备：

　　a. 因每一位参与录音的学生都需要申请一个 VoiceThread 账号，为节省时间，教师可预先制作如何申请 VoiceThread 账号，如何录音的 PPT 档案或教学影片供学生参考，比如：For first time VoiceThread user ①，并在课堂上详细示范如何录音的步骤。

　　b. 在教学平台上预先将 VoiceThread 作业准备好，并说明作业的内容与评分要求，作业截止日期等注意事项。督促学生，确实检查功课，发现没有完成的，找出问题所在，是技术性方面还是个人的因素，然后提醒学生完成。

　　最后，笔者想提醒有兴趣使用 VoiceThread 于教学上的教师们在开始制作 VoiceThread 教材之前，从"参与者"，也就是从学习者的角度去了解 VoiceThread。先到 VoiceThread Browse② 参观不同科目不同类型的 VoiceThread，尝试 Comment 的留言、录像、录音、打字等各项方式，感受一下学习者的心理。多欣赏 VoiceThread 网站上教师们的教学设计，体验学习活动的效果，参考他人的成功经验，如此将能节省自身的摸索过程，达到事半功倍之效。

　　致谢：本文在撰写过程中得到刘士娟博士和张霓博士的鼓励，并认真阅读全文，提出诸多修改建议，在此深表谢意。另外，对尔湾谷学院 Professor Susan Fesler 帮忙修改英文题要，表示衷心感谢。

附　录

文章中提到的网站

1. VoiceThread

* http：//voicethread. com/

2. 笔者的 VoiceThread 课程例子链接

* IVC Chinese Lesson：http：//voicethread. com/？ # q + ivc + chinese + lesson

* 教学课程：http：//voicethread. com/?#u348538. b1529429. i8062010

---

① http：//www. slideshare. net/sulaoshi/first-time-user-of-voicethread.

② http：//voicethread. com/?#q.

- 录音作业：http://voicethread.com/#q.b1429680.i7560305
- 照片故事：http://voicethread.com/#q.b1345906.i7159892
- 文化报告：http://voicethread.com/#u348538.b1850405.i9731869
- 小组合作：http://voicethread.com/#q.b1132655.i6076412
- 叙述练习：http://voicethread.com/?#u348538.b451349.i2401760
- 话题讨论：http://voicethread.com/#u348538.b1989920.i10504736
- 考前复习：http://voicethread.com/#u348538.b769472.i4082462
- 听力与口语测验：http://voicethread.com/#u348538.b1973714.i10415005
- 教师档案夹：http：//voicethread.com/share/489445/

3. 教学平台

- Blackboard：http：//www.blackboard.com/
- Moodle：http：//moodle.org/
- Wikispaces：http：//www.wikispaces.com/
- Google-site：http：//sites.google.com
- Blog（e.g.Blogger）www.blogger.com

4. 录音工具

- Audio Drop Box：http：//clear.msu.edu/teaching/online/ria/audioDrop-box/
- Audacity：http：//audacity.sourceforge.net/
- Wimba：http：//www.wimba.com/
- Voki：http：//www.voki.com/
- GoAnimate：http：//goanimate.com/

5. 实时性对话工具

- Skype：www.skype.com
- MSN Messenger：http：//explore.live.com/windows-live-messenger?os = other

汉语语料库开发

成语的语料统计分析
A Corpus and Statistical Study of Idioms

张正生　Zheng-sheng Zhang　美国圣地亚哥州立大学
San Diego State University United States zzhang@ mail. sdsu. edu

摘　要：汉语成语丰富，但难学难用；从本体研究的角度来看，目前对成语的语法和语体特征还所知甚少。本文报告一项利用平衡语料库和文本分析软件所作的统计研究。使用这些工具能让我们发现一些不易观察到的现象，如频次、词条—词次比、成语用字情况以及成语在不同语境和语体中的分布，不仅能从宏观的角度观察成语的通性，也便于微观地进行个例分析。且省时省力，较依赖语感更具系统性。初步研究结果显示，虽然汉语中成语非常丰富，但它们的重复度并不高；在用字上，四字成语各音节的重复率不同，以第三音节为最高，而第四音节为最低，可诠释为第三音节虚字多，而第四音节实字多。从内部结构来看，四字成语中，二二型为最多，交叉型为次，外包型和内揳型最少。成语有多种语法功能，但在不同语境中的分布并不均匀，作为谓语和定状语的成语频率较高；由于同形的成语不一定有相同的语法功能，语法功能也不容易预测。成语在不同的语体中分布也不尽均匀；公文性/技术性强、感情/修辞/本土色彩/主观成分少的语体中出现频率甚低。成语的低重复率、句法功能的限制和低预测性也许与其习得的困难有关。此调查应该对成语的教与学有一定的指导作用。

关键词：成语，语料，文本分析，统计方法，语体研究

Abstract：Idioms pose special difficulties to learners of Chinese；their grammatical and stylistic characteristics also have not been sufficiently studied. This article describes a study of idioms using corpus and concordance resources. These tools allow us to discover facts about idioms that are otherwise not apparent，including their frequency of occurrence，type-to-ken ratio，pattern of character use and grammatical and stylistic distribution. They allow us to gain both macro view of idioms as a category as well as micro view of individual cases，efficiently and systematically. Preliminary results from the study show that although Chinese has a large number of idioms, their rate of repetition is rather low. In terms of the use of characters, the repetition rate of the four characters in four character idioms is not the same, with the third character being the highest and the fourth character the lowest, suggesting greater number of functional elements for the third position and content elements for the fourth position. In terms of their internal structure, among the four character idioms, the "2 + 2" ($1^{st} + 2^{nd}$; $3^{rd} + 4^{th}$) types predominate, followed by the interweaving types ($1^{st} + 3^{rd}$; $2^{nd} + 4^{th}$), the circum-fix and infix types being the least common ($1^{st} + 4^{th}$; $2^{nd} + 3^{rd}$). Idioms exhibit a wide range of syntactic functions, but their syntactic distribution is skewed, with predominantly predicative and attributive uses. Due to the lack of one-to-one form-function correspondence, it is also not straightforward to predict the grammatical functions of idioms. The distribution of idioms in different genres is also uneven, with few occurrences in official/technical genres that are characteristically free of emotional/rhetorical/subjective nuances. The difficulty in learning and studying idioms may be attributed to their low repetition rate, the restriction and unpredictability of syntactic functions. This study should be of pedagogical value to the teaching and learning of idioms.

Keywords: idioms, corpus, text analysis, statistical method, genre studies

一　引言

在高年级对外汉语教学中，怎样对待成语一向是个相当棘手的问题。能否使用成语无疑是衡量汉语水平的一个指标，多数学习者虽对成语不无兴趣，但用起来却要么不敢用，要么用得不得体，不免产生望洋兴叹的挫折感。对成语的掌握应该提出什么样的要求，怎样教才能使学生敢于使用，少出语病，都是一些亟待解决的问题。

笔者认为，成语教学上的问题应该寻源于成语本体研究上的不足。与一般词汇相比，我们对成语的语法和语体特征都还了解甚少。一般教科书与参考辞书也都局限于成语的释义而缺少关于语法功能和语体特征方面的讲解，更缺少语体方面的指导。成语习得和研究的困难还可能与其较高的词条—词次比（Type-Token Ratio）①有关。汉语中的成语非常丰富，可是重复率比一般词语低得多。研究、使用和学习这种重复率低而又特性各异的词语自然困难度大一些。

本文利用几种新近研发的平衡语料库和文本分析软件，对于成语的基本频率、语法特征和语体分布作一个描述性的分析。文本分析软件能让我们统计成语在不同句法环境中的频率，而平衡语料库则可以告诉我们成语在不同语体中的分布情况。使用这两种电脑技术，能统计大量语料，既能做宏观的观察，又便于个例的分析；不仅省力省时，还有比较强的系统性。

二 语料

本研究使用的语料均免费取自互联网。主要为英国 Lancaster 大学 2005 年肖中华等人研发的 Lancaster Corpus of Mandarin Chinese（简称 LCMC）。LCMC 包括一百万词次，语料选自 1991 年前后，来自中国大陆的各种出版物。在 LCMC 问世后不久，肖中华与 UCLA 的陶红印又合建了 UCLA Corpus of Written Chinese（简称 UCLA），与 LCMC 结构相同，但语料却取自 2000—2005 年间中国大陆网上的出版物。

虽然规模不算大，LCMC/ UCLA 却包含了 15 种书面语体。且分类甚细，仅新闻体就又分新闻报道、新闻评论和新闻综述三个次类；小说体又分言情、普通、武打、科幻、侦探五个次类。

LCMC/UCLA 内所有的词条都具有详细的语法标记。采用的标记为北京大学计算语言学研究所研发的 PKU Tagset。因为 LCMC/UCLA 有词性标记，因此除了可以查询单独词语的词频并显示其上下文之外，还可以查询整个词类的出现频率，以及一个多词性词的某一种用法的频率。PKU Tagset 将成语单独分类作出标记（=i），因此对我们的研究提供了极大的便利。

LCMC/UCLA 的另一个优点是配有网上查询界面，可免费使用。LCMC 网上界面的链接为：http://score. crpp. nie. edu. sg/cgi-bin/lcmc/conc. pl（UCLA 网上界面的链接为：http://score. crpp. nie. edu. sg/cgi-bin/ucla/UCLAconc. pl）。查询结果例句后还列出统计数字。除了原始频次以外，为

---

① 词条指不同的词，不包括重复的词；词次指词出现的频次，包括重复的词。词条—词次比反映词汇使用的重复程度。词条—词次比越高，重复度就越低。

了便于数量不等的不同语料之间的比较，还提供了归一化（normalized）[①]后每万词次的相对频度。但 LCMC/UCLA 的界面对于文本研究来说有一定的局限性，主要是搜索项不能超过一个。好在搜寻结果可以存档为 txt 文件，以作进一步统计分析之用。此外，只能搜索整个词，而不能搜索不成词的字。另外，这两种语料库只包括书面语体，因此本研究也只限于成语在书面语中的情况。

除了 LCMC/UCLA 以外，本研究还参考了网上下载的 1998 年 1 月和 2000 年 1 月的《人民日报》，也均带词性标记。

鉴于本研究的重点以及所用语料库的限制，本文将不讨论与成语的定义相关的问题。语料库中标为成语（即标记为"i"的），即作成语处理。关于成语的定义和划界问题，读者可参阅刘叔新（2001）、徐耀民（2004）等学者的论著。

但本文假定以下为共识：虽然成语多为四字格，但成语可以多于或少于四个字，而四个字的也不都是成语。这跟 PKU Tagset 的处理方法是一致的。除了成语以外，还有一类四字格的词，标为"l"（fixed expression）。这些四字格的词语便不在本调查范围之内。

三　成语的一些基本统计数据

（一）基本频率

表 1 为四种语料的总词次以及成语的词次：

表 1　　　　　　　　　　　　四种语料中的成语总数

	LCMC	《人民日报》	《人民日报》	UCLA
时间	1991 年	1998 年 1 月	2000 年 1 月	2000—2005 年
总词次	1000000	1120000	1284466	687025
成语词次	4767	5033	5215	2711

为确保语料库之间的可比度，图 1 显示每万词次中的相对频次：

从上图可以看出：

[①] 归一化将绝对频率转变为相对频率，公式为：原始频率÷总词次数×10000。归一化确保不同数量语料之间的可比性。

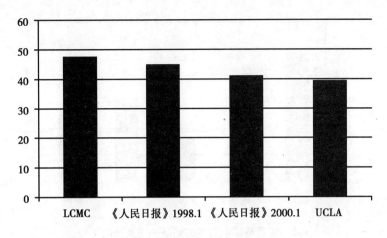

图 1　四个语料库中成语的相对频次

1. 作为一个类，成语的频率相当高，均在每万词 45（±5）词次左右，即将近 0.5%。这比"地"类副词还略高（0.35%）。

2. 四个语料库中成语的相对频率（每万词次）惊人地相似。

3. 仅从这些语料库来看，最近十几年成语数量似乎有减少的倾向。这是否偶然，还有待进一步研究。

（二）词条—词次比（Type-Token Ratio，即词条重复率）

在 LCMC 的 4767 个成语词次中，有 2313 个不同的成语词条，词条—词次比为 0.4852。换言之，成语的重复率相当低，平均每个成语只重复两次左右。相比之下，副词、形容词，甚至名词和动词的重复率都较之为高。下页图 2 显示成语和四个主要词类的重复率比较。

虽然平均下来每个成语词条出现两次左右，实际上大部分词条只出现一次，如图 3 所示。

大量的成语词条（多于两千），加上极低的重复率，是成语难学的原因之一。

（三）最高频成语

LCMC 中频率最高的 20 个成语为（按频率排列）：

艰苦奋斗　无可奈何　全心全意　解放思想　小心翼翼
千方百计　坚定不移　引人注目　建功立业　彪形大汉
众所周知　理直气壮　自力更生　因地制宜　无私奉献

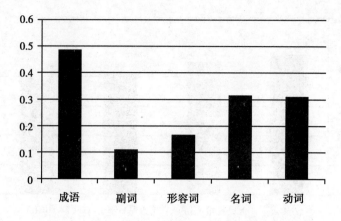

图 2　成语与四个词类的词条—词次比的比较

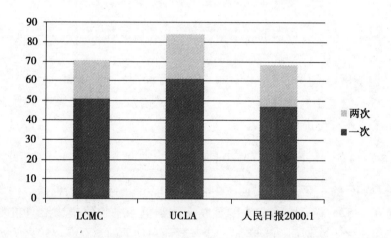

图 3　三种语料中出现一次与两次的成语数比例

实事求是　莫名其妙　成千上万　不知所措　讨价还价
UCLA 中频率最高的 20 个成语为（按频率排列）：
莫名其妙　不知不觉　不知所措　小心翼翼　此时此刻
众志成城　无能为力　牛郎织女　一模一样　突如其来
弄虚作假　乱七八糟　徇私舞弊　一无所知　一动不动
玩忽职守　前所未有　哭笑不得　不可思议　一如既往
成语重复度低也许还可以从另一个角度看出，即这两个语料库中频率最高的成语几乎不重叠。只有三个成语（小心翼翼、莫名其妙、不知所措）同时出现在两组成语中。

（四）用字情况

1. 高频字

图 4 显示 LCMC 中最高频成语用字：

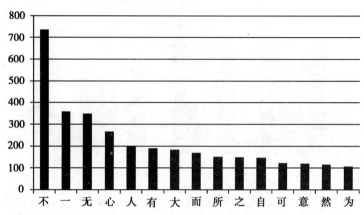

图 4　LCMC 中 15 个最高频成语用字

表 2 为四字成语中各音节的 15 个最高频字：

表 2　　　　　　　四字成语中各音节的 15 个最高频字

	第一	频次	第二	频次	第三	频次	第四	频次
1	不	257	心	141	不	346	意	70
2	一	189	不	132	无	152	色	49
3	无	136	然	80	一	142	心	44
4	大	82	人	71	而	122	生	42
5	自	78	所	71	之	93	知	42
6	有	67	可	61	大	78	目	41
7	心	62	言	59	其	72	人	36
8	千	56	无	57	自	68	然	35
9	人	49	而	46	为	66	事	31
10	风	41	头	45	所	66	地	31
11	相	33	之	42	有	60	行	31
12	五	31	目	41	相	48	力	30
13	坚	30	有	40	如	47	下	29
14	天	28	以	36	可	44	想	28
15	艰	27	口	35	人	42	业	27

2. 字条—字次比（Type-token Ratio，即字的重复率）

以下为三种语料中四字成语各音节字条—字次比。

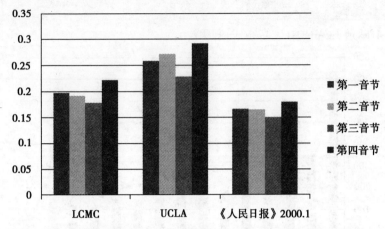

图 5　三种语料中四字成语各音节字条—字次比（Type-token）

值得注意的是，三种语料中，第三个音节字条—字次比均为最低，而第四个音节字条—字次比均为最高，意味着第三字重复率最高，而第四字重复率最低。这可能跟第三、四音节的功能不同有关。从表 2 可看出，第三个音节的虚字较多，而第四个音节的实字较多。

3. 成语内部结构

成语内部结构五花八门。仅从不同音节组合能否成词，四字成语可分以下几类：

二二型：

1＋2：训练有素

3＋4：一本正经

交叉型：

1＋3：今非昔比

2＋4：千辛万苦

外包型：

1＋4：乱七八糟

内搋型：

2＋3：不以为然

图 6 显示了这几种类型的相对频度（成词率＝某类组合成词数÷某类组合总数）：

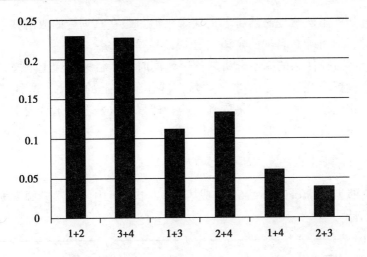

图6　LCMC中四字成语不同音节组合的成词率

从图6可看出，二二型（一二、三四）的成词率最高；外包型和内揳型（一四、二三）的成词率最低；交叉型（一三、二四）的居中；交叉型中二四又高于一三。

四　成语的语境和句法功能

以上的统计未考虑语境和语体的因素。本节调查成语的语境分布，并以此推测其句法功能。首先讨论一下语境标记（即搜索项）的选择。

（一）语境标记的选择

有些关键字，如"的"、"地"、"得"，基本上能明确显示定语、状语和补语的句法功能，自然为语境标记的首选。这类字还包括体态助词"了"、"着"、"过"等。这类语境的查寻和诠释都最直截了当。

然而，有些语境标记只能帮助我们间接地推测出句法功能。比如，起断句作用的主要标点符号比较容易搜索，但标点符号并不能直接告诉我们成语的句法功能。例如，句首的成语除了可以是主语之外，还可以是定语、整句的状语或倒装句中的谓语；而句尾的成语则可能单独作谓语，也可能被副词等其他成分修饰。但如果能同时包括上下文，那得到的信息就清楚得多。如成语前后均为逗号或句号时，其单独作谓语甚至成句的可能性就相当大。

成语周边的主要词类也可以帮我们推测成语的句法功能。但因本研究使用的文本分析软件只能提供表层共现的信息，因此用其推断句法功能时必须谨慎。例如，虽然量词必然跟名词共现，但紧跟在量词后的成语并不一定本身是名词，而可能是名词的定语（如成语后是"的"时）。

由于本研究使用的文本分析软件不能同时搜索目标项和上下文，最容易使用的语境标记往往只是"半"语境。除了诠释上的不便，这种"半"语境往往互相叠加，使统计结果受到影响，即累计次数会大于总词次，累计百分比也会超过百分之百等。

（二）不同语境中成语的频次

图 7 即为 LCMC 中的 4767 个成语在 12 个语境中的频次。频率太低的语境忽略不计。

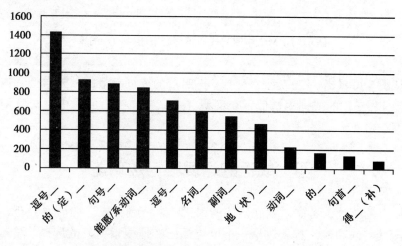

图 7   LCMC 中的成语在 12 个语境中的频次

图 7 应该说有一定的代表性。根据 1998 年 1 月《人民日报》所作的统计（未显示）几乎完全与此相同。成语最常出现的语境是逗号及句号前，即子句与全句结尾，分别占第一和第三位。亦可能出现于句尾的补语和宾语的频率较低（见下文），成语最常见的语法功能当为谓语的主要部分。至于为何在子句尾的频率高于全句尾，还有待进一步研究。这也许是因为子句的频率本来就高于全句（在 LCMC 中，逗号出现次数 = 120410；句号 = 42423）。

在定语标记"的"前出现的成语频次占第二位，因此成语第二常用的句法功能为定语应当无疑。

其次为动词后的成语。但观察具体的例句，这里的成语大多数并非宾语，因为这些动词并非及物动词，而是各种主动词前的修饰成分，如能愿动词要、会、可能，以及系动词（就）是、为、可谓、觉得等。这就从另一角度显示了成语的谓语性。

逗号后成语出现的频次也相当高。但这不能说明什么问题，因为这个语境中的成语可以有几种不同的功能，如主语、定语、状语、谓语等。

名词和副词后的成语也多为谓语。

在状语标记"地"前出现的成语不如"的"前，但仍有相当数目。

在动词前出现的成语可以有不同功能，如主语、无"地"标记的状语，或与成语呈并列关系的谓语。

定语"的"后的成语为主语或宾语，远低于"的"前的成语数。

句首的成语可以作主语、定语、谓语等。

补语标记"得"后的成语当为补语，比"的"、"地"前数量少得多。

根据与"的"、"地"、"得"共现频次的排行，作为定＞状＞补＞的成语的排行明显是：定＞状＞补。

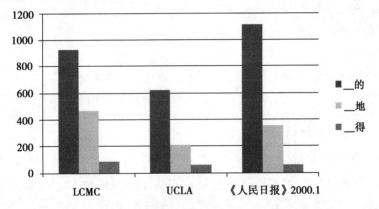

图8　三种语料中成语作为定、状、补三种句法成分的频次

这可能反映了这三种句法成分本身的频率。

综合上述观察，成语作为谓语的频率应当为最高：谓＞定＞状＞补。至于作为主语和宾语的成语，我们假设以下的排行：谓＞定＞状＞主语/宾语＞补值得注意的是一些成语分布上的不对称：

作谓语多于作主语（在句尾多于在句首）

作定语多于被定语修饰（在"的"前多于在"的"后）

作状语多于被状语修饰（在"地"前多于在"地"后）

作补语多于被补语修饰（在"得"后多于在"得"前）

在名词/动词/副词后多于在其之前

这种不对称可能是因为成语多用于描述和修饰而不是被描述和被修饰。

最后需要指出的是，同形的成语功能不一定相同。完全同形的"一言一行"和"一心一意"只能分别作名词和副词，而"三心二意"则又不同。但带"之"的成语似乎都是名词性的，而带"以"的如"以礼相待"、"以讹传讹"、"以身作则"、"以身殉职"、"以退为进"则似乎都是谓语。

（三）成语句法功能的特殊性

如上所述，跟一般词类相同，成语在句子中也有多种句法功能。但由于成语的来源和特殊的形成过程，与一般词类相比又有些特殊的句法特点。一般来说，成语自成整体的特点比较突出。以谓词类成语为例。该类成语虽然在句法功能上与动词和形容词类似，却有以下几个不同之处：

无重叠形式

不带体态助词"了/着/过"（成语后"了"均为句尾语气词）

不带宾语（把字句除外）

一般不被状态副词修饰（"地"类）

不带补语

这种种限制都反映了成语形式固定，自成一体的特殊性。

成语的特殊性在较长的、复合式的成语中看得更明显。虽然四字格的成语为绝大多数，多于四字的成语也不是没有，如"青出于蓝而胜于蓝"，"车到山前必有路"等。还有在结构上明显由两部分组成的，如"一不做，二不休"；"成事不足，败事有余"；"耳闻是虚，眼观为实"等等。虽占少数，这些成语却为我们了解成语的特性提供了很好的线索。这些多于四字/复合式成语的分布最受限制，可以看做一种极端类型。例如，以上这些成语一般最常见于以下这些语境：

真是/确实是＿ ＿ ＿ ＿ ＿ ＿ ＿

所谓/可谓＿ ＿ ＿ ＿ ＿ ＿ ＿

俗话说/道＿ ＿ ＿ ＿ ＿ ＿ ＿

（并列/同位子句），＿ ＿ ＿ ＿ ＿ ＿ ＿

句首＿ ＿ ＿ ＿ ＿ ＿ ＿ 并列/同位子句。

这类语境可以归结为系词宾语、引语和同位语。为什么较长的、复合类成语更容易出现于此类语境呢？这跟它们表达的意思有关。这类较长的成语，一般都单独包含一个完整的命题。运用这类成语，就是将这些完整的命题整合在句子里。最简便的整合方式莫过于将它们作为系词宾语、引语和同位语。使用四字格的成语当然也多多少少有整合的问题。因此，大多数谓语性的四字格成语都能用于上面这些语境。

（四）个案分析

以上的分析是把成语作为一个整类来处理的。因为词次较多，这样可以让我们从一个宏观的角度来观察成语的分布倾向。但如果只停留在这一层面，我们就不能回答以下这些问题：

a. 成语内部有无次类

b. 同一成语的句法功能是单一的还是多样的

c. 造成成语分布频率差异的是不同的成语还是同一成语的不同功能

这些问题都必须通过详细的个案分析来回答。用文本分析软件可以穷尽地搜索到某语料库中某一词语的所有的用法。这样做显然比依赖语感有系统性。以下即为 LCMC 中随意抽取的 48 个成语的用法。这些成语的取样法如下。先将 4767 个成语按笔画排行，然后每 100 个成语中取头一个。

表3 LCMC 中 48 个成语的个案分析

	谓语	定语	状语	主/宾语	补语
一不做，二不休	1				
一无所知	7	1			
七嘴八舌	1		6		
不可多得		1			
不由分说			3		
不顾一切	1		5		
争先恐后	1		3		
人所共知		4			
低三下四	1				
全心全意			19		
初露锋芒	1				
十全十美	3				
原原本本			1		1
同舟共济	1				
善男信女				1	
坐立不安	3				
大声疾呼	4				
夺眶而出	3				
安居乐业	8	3			

	谓语	定语	状语	主/宾语	补语
小题大做	1				
庞然大物				3	
当机立断	6		3		
心惊胆战	1				
思绪万千	2				
想入非非	1	3			
扬长避短	3	1			
推三阻四	1				
旗帜鲜明	2		3		
无济于事	5				
春风满面			1		
望而却步	1				
横冲直撞	1				
气喘吁吁			2		
浴血奋战	2			2	
灯红酒绿	1	1		1	
理直气壮	3		10		
目瞪口呆	2				1
破天荒	1		1		
紧锣密鼓	2		1		
老实巴交		1	1		
自告奋勇	4		1		
花天酒地	2	1			
血雨腥风	1				
议论纷纷	6	1		1	
跋山涉水	1				
适得其反	4	1			
长治久安				4	
面目全非	4				
高不可攀		1			
总计	92	19	60	12	2

根据上表，我们可以作出以下这些观察：

a. 成语的确有次类。

b. 同一成语的句法功能可以是多样的。少数成语只有单一的功能。如"小题大做"只作谓语；"善男信女"只作名词；"全心全意"只作状语；"不可多得"只作定语等。多数成语可以有多种句法功能，不同功能的频率也有差异。例如，"七嘴八舌"作状语的频率大于谓语。而"当机立断"主要作谓语，但有时也作状语等等。

最后一行的总计，除了状语高于定语外，基本与前面根据宏观数据所作的排行相符，即：谓语＞定语＞状语＞主/宾语＞补语。至于状语和定语之间排行的例外情况，还有待进一步研究。也许可以归咎于取样太小，以至于个别成语的比重过大。例如，"全心全意"和"理直气壮"分别出现19次和10次之多，使得状语的频率不合比例地增高。

五　成语的语体分布及其语义/语用特征

（一）不同语体中频次的排行

除了语境和句法功能之外，同样值得探讨的是成语的语义和语用特征。但做这方面的研究却不那么直截了当。以下我们通过间接的手段做一些推断，那就是成语的语体分布。

由于 LCMC 可以将不同语体分别统计，因此我们能够比较成语在不同语体中的分布情况。以下为成语在 LCMC 15 种语体中的词次以及每万词中相对频度的排行。

从上面的排行，我们可以作出以下这些初步的观察：

成语最多的语体为：新闻综述＞新闻评论＞言情小说＞传记/散文

成语最少的语体为：官方文件＜科技＜技能/爱好＜宗教

语体次类之间的排行也有所不同：

新闻综述＞新闻评论＞新闻报道

言情小说＞武打小说＞侦探小说＞普通小说＞科幻小说

由于 UCLA 与 LCMC 有相同的结构，我们可以很容易地做一个对比。成语在 UCLA 各语体中频次的排行如下（见图9）。

我们可以看出，UCLA 的排行与 LCMC 有相同处，也有不同之处（见图10）。

成语最多的语体为：大众知识＞侦探小说＞武打小说＞普通小说

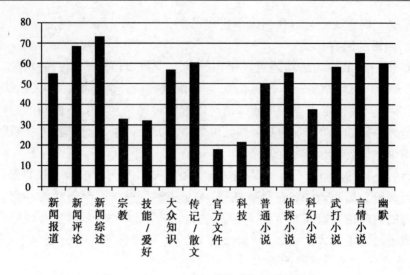

图9　LCMC 15 个语体中成语频次的排行

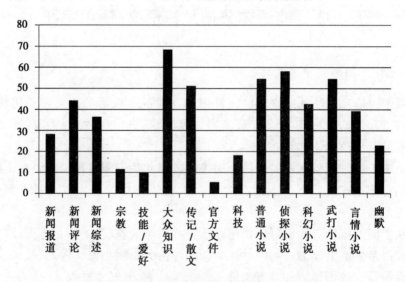

图10　UCLA 15 个语体中成语频次的排行

成语最少的语体为：官方文件＜技能/爱好＜宗教＜科技

UCLA 中成语最多的以小说类为主，但 LCMC 却以新闻类为主。虽然两个语料库中成语最多的语体不同，而成语最少的语体却完全相同，即均为官方文件、技能/爱好、宗教和科技语体。

在次类排行方面，UCLA 也跟 LCMC 有所不同：

新闻评论＞新闻综述＞新闻报道

侦探小说＞武打小说＞普通小说＞科幻小说＞言情小说

尤其是言情小说，从频次最高变为最少。但两个语料库也有相同之处，即：

新闻评论/新闻综述 > 新闻报道

武打小说 > 普通小说 > 科幻小说

两个语料库为何有这样的差别还有待于进一步研究。但从以上数据，我们至少可以看出一些成语语体特征的端倪，即：

成语与公文性/技术性强、感情/修辞/本土色彩/主观成分少的语体相抵触。

这就可以解释官方文件、技能/爱好、宗教、科技文献中的低频次，而新闻报道中成语少于新闻评论和新闻综述也就同样可以理解了。这种推断有以下两个佐证：

《现代汉语频率词典 》（1986）统计了四种语体，即政论、小说、科技和口语。其中前三类为书面语体。附录 3 （p. 1489）中列出了各类语料中不同音节词的统计数据。其中最接近成语的为四字词语。而在三类书面语体中四字词语频率排行恰恰为 ： 政论 > 小说 > 科技。这不能说只是一种巧合。

郑岳超 （2005） 在 "小学语文教材中的成语" 中对小学课本中的成语作了一些统计 （http：//www. jhyx. net/Article/ShowArticle. asp？ ArticleID = 5），并对成语不均匀的分布作了一些讨论。他的观察跟我们的完全吻合：

散文、革命/历史题材 > 外国文学、应用文

前两类恰好是 "感情/修辞/本土色彩/主观成分" 多，而后两类则相反。

（二） 不同语体中成语的词条—词次比

前文提到，成语作为一个类，词条—词次比相当高，也就是说重复率比较低。那么不同语体中的词条—词次比如何？图 11 为 LCMC 15 个语体中的词条和词次数。

图 12 为 15 种语体中词条—词次的比率。应当指出，由于不同语体中的词次不同，它们之间没有完全的可比性。一般来说，词次越高，词条—词次比越低，因为词条重复的机会越多。因此图 12 仅作参考之用。

比率最低的为官方文件及报告。这可能反映了在此类文体中，有重复使用少数成语的倾向。与官方文件类似的是新闻综述类。虽然传记/散文文体中的词次最高，但词条—词次比却较低，说明此类文体中重复的成语较多。反过来，在小说类中，无论词次多寡（科幻小说低而言情小说多），词条—词次的比率都普遍偏高，这与《现代汉语频率词典》中关于文学作品用词分散的观察是相吻合的。

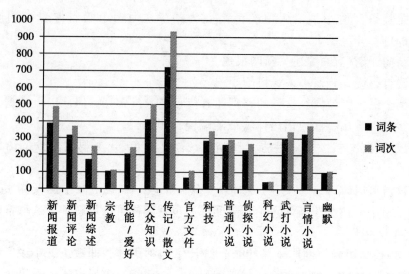

图 11　LCMC 中 15 种语体的词条—词次数

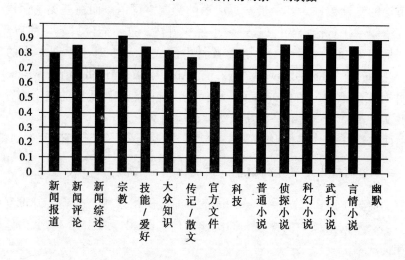

图 12　LCMC 中 15 种语体的词条—词次比

（三）语体分布和句法功能的关系

　　以上关于语体分布的观察是把成语作为一个整类来处理的，未考虑句法功能。但如前所说，大多数成语不只有一种句法功能，而且同一成语的不同功能可能有不同的出现频率。因而在作进一步语体分布的研究时，有必要考虑句法功能这个因素。图 13、图 14 以 LCMC 中作为定语、状语和补语的成语在各种语体中的频次（每万词次）举例：

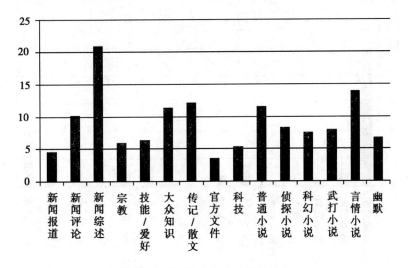

图 13　LCMC 中作为定语的成语

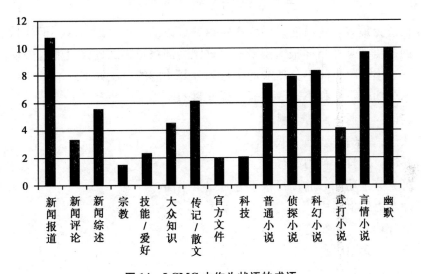

图 14　LCMC 中作为状语的成语

　　值得注意的是，分开功能后的排行显然有别于不分功能时的排行。当然，官方文件、宗教、科技、技能/爱好依然为成语较少的语体，而小说类，尤其是言情小说，仍名列前茅。但新闻次类间的排行却很不同（见图 15）。

　　不分功能：新闻综述 > 新闻评论 > 新闻报道

　　定语：新闻综述 > 新闻评论 > 新闻报道

　　状语：新闻报道 > 新闻综述 > 新闻评论

　　补语：新闻报道 > 新闻评论 > 新闻综述

　　作定语的成语的排行跟不分功能时的排行是一致的，以新闻综述为首而

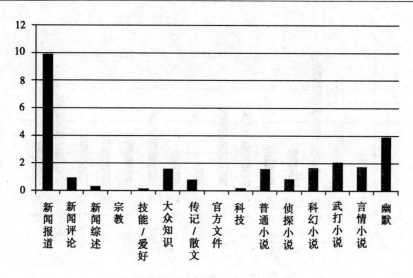

图 15　LCMC 中作为补语的成语

新闻报道为最末。这可能是因为作定语的成语的比重大的缘故。但作状语和补语的成语却是在新闻报道中最多。这跟新闻报道描述性强可能有关系。

三个小说次类间不分功能的排行和分开功能的对比如下：

不分功能：武打小说＞普通小说＞科幻小说

定语：普通＞武打＞科幻

状语：科幻＞普通＞武打

补语：武打＞科幻＞普通

可见分开功能后的排行跟不分时完全不同。

幽默语体也同样：

不分功能：第 5 位

定语：第 10 位

状语：第 2 位

补语：第 2 位

这是否因为状语和补语性的成语在幽默这种叙事语体中更重要？语境和语体的关系显然有待于进一步的研究。

（四）语境与语体的变异系数

有了语境和语体两个变量的数据，就可以做一些其他宏观的统计，如变异系数，即语境和语体内部的差异程度（变异系数 "coefficient of variance" ＝ Standard Deviation ÷ Mean × 100，为 Excel 统计功能之一）。

1. 不同语境中语体的变异系数

首先，在特定语境中，不同语体之间的差异程度似有不同。以下即为
LCMC 的成语频次在 5 种语境中语体变异系数的排行。

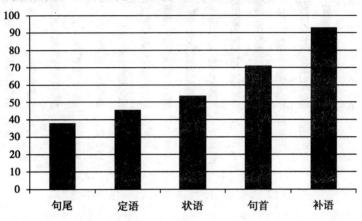

图 16　LCMC 5 种语境中的语体变异系数

如果假设句尾和句首分别代表谓语和主语的句法环境，那么以上排行就
完全吻合上文所述"谓语 > 定语 > 状语 > 主/宾语 > 补语"的排行。可见语
体变异系数跟某语境的频次成反比，即成语越多的语境，语体之间的差异
越小。

2. 不同语体中语境的变异系数

反过来，在特定语体中，不同句法环境之间的差异程度也似乎有所不
同。以下为 LCMC 的成语频次在 15 种语体中语境变异系数的排行（12 种语
境：的＿＿，得＿＿，名＿＿，动＿＿，副＿＿，逗＿＿，句＿＿，＿＿
的，＿＿地，＿＿句，＿＿逗，＿＿动）：

可见语境变异系数跟语体的频次也呈一定的反比关系，即成语少的几种
语体，如官方文件，句法环境之间的差异也较大。

比较两种变异系数，我们可以看出语境之间的差别（43.4 : 62.73947—
106.1966）似乎大于语体之间的差别（55 : 37.89844—92.9183），也就是
说，同一语境中语体之间的差别小于同一语体中语境之间的差别。在图 17
的排行中，还有一个值得注意的现象，就是新闻和小说两大类次类间的亲疏
关系。新闻语体的三个次类完全排在一起。而小说语体中，只有武打小说独
树一帜，其他四个次类的数值均很接近。

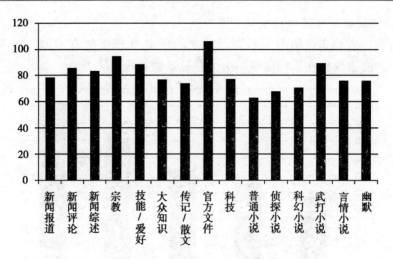

图 17　LCMC 15 种语体中的语境变异系数

六　语体之间的亲疏关系

有了成语在语体和语境中分布的数据，我们还可以用统计软件（如 Excel）得出语体之间的关联度，以此推出语体间的亲疏关系。表 4 显示了小说类次类间的关联度。除了跟侦探小说较接近以外，武打小说似乎跟其他次类都很疏远。这跟武打小说在其他方面的分布数据似乎是吻合的。

表 4　　　　　　　　　　LCMC 中 5 个小说次类之间的关联度

	普通小说	科幻小说	侦探小说	武打小说	言情小说
普通小说	1				
科幻小说	0.927623	1			
侦探小说	0.886647	0.849973	1		
武打小说	0.779607	0.767623	0.911543	1	
言情小说	0.949721	0.909193	0.916473	0.858326	1

几个次类之间的亲疏关系是否能用以下的排列表示（一维的表达显然有缺陷，如言情与侦探小说的关系其实近于科幻小说）：

普通小说——言情小说——科幻小说——侦探小说——武打小说

七　结语

本文利用平衡语料库和文本分析软件，对成语的句法功能和语体分布作了一个初步调查。调查结果显示，成语的出现频率相当高，但每个成语的重复使用度并不高。在用字上，四字成语各音节的重复率不同，以第三音节为最高，而第四音节为最低，可诠释为第三音节虚字多，而第四音节实字多。从内部结构来看，四字成语中，二二型为最多，交叉型为次，外包型和内揳型最少。成语有多种语法功能，但在不同语境中的分布并不均匀，作为谓语和定、状语的成语频率较高。少数成语只有单一的句法功能，而多数成语同时具有多种功能。不同的句法功能出现的频率有所不同，基本排行为谓语＞定语＞状语＞主/宾语＞补语。由于同形的成语不一定有相同的语法功能，语法功能也不容易预测；成语在不同的语体中分布也不尽均匀；公文性/技术性强、感情/修辞/本土色彩/主观成分少的语体中出现频率甚低。不同的语境中，语体的排行也有所不同。成语的低重复率、句法功能的限制和低预测性也许与其习得的困难有关。

这些研究结果对于成语教学应该有一定的指导作用。例如，应按照成语的频次、类型、句法功能、分布情况在课程设计、选材和教学上做出相应的取舍。并应培养学习者的语体意识，避免成语运用不得体的现象。

还有很多问题有待进一步研究。在句法功能方面，我们只调查了成语的句法功能，而尚未细究成语内部结构与其句法功能的关系。在语义分析方面，如何更系统地研究成语的语义和语用特征，也同样是一个重要的课题。本研究所用的语料均来自中国大陆。如能对两岸三地的成语使用做一个比较，将会是饶有兴味的。另外，本文的统计数据仅为描述性的，尚未给予统计意义上的诠释。

参考文献

刘叔新（2001）:《习用语辞典与成语惯用语问题》，李如龙、苏新春编《词汇学理论与实践》，商务印书馆。

徐耀民（2004）:《成语的划界、定型和释义问题》，周荐编《二十世纪现代汉语词汇论文精选》，商务印书馆。

王还等（1986）:《现代汉语频率词典》。

郑岳超（2005）:　《小学语文教材中的成语》，http：//www. jhyx. net/Article/

ShowArticle. asp？ArticleID =5.

McEnery，Tony and Richard Xiao（2005）The Lancaster Corpus of Mandarin Chinese, Lancaster University，http：//www. lancs. ac. uk/fass/projects/corpus/LC-MC/.

Tao，Hongyin and Richard Xiao（2007）The UCLA Chinese Corpus. UCREL，Lancaster. http：//www. lancs. ac. uk/fass/projects/corpus/UCLA/default. htm.

语料库建设与汉语作为第二语言教学
Construction of Chinese Corpus and Its Application
of Teaching Chinese as a Second Language

王　惠　Wang Hui　香港中文大学

The Chinese University of Hong Kong City University of Hong Kong

朱纯深　Zhu Chunshen　香港城市大学

wanghui@ arts. cuhk. edu. hk ctzhu@ cityu. edu. hk

摘　要：本文着重介绍利用英、汉双语平行语料库进行汉语作为第二语言的教学。该平行语料库以信息结构为理论基础，对语篇实施双层标注（即背景知识和以信息结构为理论基础的语言现象），通过双语对比，突出汉语的语言特征。通过对本语料库的学习，学生不仅可获得对汉文语篇从细节到整体布局的把握，而且可以通过英、汉语篇的对比，更深入地学习中文语篇的构成。

关键词：英、汉平行语料库，双层标注，汉语教学

Abstract：This paper describes the application of an English-Chinese parallel corpus to the teaching of Chinese as a second language. Drawing on theories of information structure, the corpus is annotated in a dual mode, i. e., annotations on background knowledge and textual phenomena, with a view to highlighting Chinese linguistic features through English-Chinese comparative analysis. Through studying and comparing English and Chinese on different text levels, the corpus is designed to help students achieve a better understanding of the organization of Chinese texts.

Keywords：English-Chinese parallel corpus, dual-mode annotation, Chinese language teaching

一 引言

20 世纪 90 年代语料库语言学的兴起给语言教学提供了很多新的思路和途径。大批语料经过加工制作成语料库应用于教学资源的开发、课堂语料分析和学习者语料库的研究（Aijmer，2009；Gavioli，2006；Hidalgo et al.，2007；Scott & Tribble，2006）。语料库在语言教学的应用由语料库的功能决定，而语料库的功能与语料库的加工程度（主要指语料标注）直接相关。审视过往的研究，我们发现有关语料库与汉语教学的研究集中表现在汉语口语语料库（杨翼等，2006），汉语学习者语料库和中介语语料库（储诚志、陈小荷，1993；陈小荷，1996）方面，如对外汉语教学界已建立的语料库有"汉语中介语语料库"，是以在中国就读的外国留学生汉语作文或练习材料为样本收集对象，抽取了 740 个学生的 1731 篇书面语，共计 1041274 字的语料作为样本加工入库（储诚志、陈小荷，1993）；而"现代汉语研究语料库"主要是以国内汉语出版物（小说、散文、报告文学、话剧脚本、相声、演讲词、故事等）为原始材料，从中抽取 2000 万字粗语料，在此基础上建立了一个文本属性库，再从粗语料中抽取 200 万字的精语料，建立了语料库检索系统（孙宏林等，1996）。在已建成的语料库中，对语料库的标注局限在标注词性、计算词频、词语检索、排序上。在对 2003—2009 年发表在中文核心期刊《世界汉语教学》和《汉语学习》的文章统计之后，笔者发现，对语料库进行深层次加工，将其直接应用于汉语教学的研究以及相关语料库的建设还很少见。用郑艳群（2006，p. 103）的话说，当前"语料库的建设基本上还停留在大规模低水平的重复劳动上"。

鉴于此，本研究力图在语料库建设，特别是语料加工方面有所突破，以期加深并拓宽教学语料库的应用。研究之初的目的是开发一个能帮助学生自主学习翻译技巧的平行语料库。在研发过程中，我们发现学生在利用语料库学习翻译技巧的同时，也培养了语言学习（包括对外汉语学习）的能力。研究所开发的平行语料库致力于帮助学生通过英、汉对比深入了解汉语语法，适用于汉语作为第二语言的中、高级阶段的教学。利用平行语料库学习语言，一是可以打破人们对传统的利用语法翻译法学习语言的认识，建立新的借助翻译学习语言的视角；二是可以帮助学生利用双语对照提高自己对双语（汉语和英语）的认识。这一切都要通过语料标注系统的建立来完成。

二　双语平行语料库与语料的挑选

平行语料库有两种含义：一是指在一种语言中语料上的平行（语料选取的时间、对象、比例、文本长度等）；二是两种或多种语言间的平行采样或加工（郑艳群，2006，p. 90—91）。本文研究的是第二种意义上的平行语料库。双语平行语料库在20世纪90年代以后开始得到开发，如英国曼彻斯特大学科技学院翻译研究中心的"翻译英语语料库（Translational English Corpus）"（参见Kenny，1998），北京外国语大学王克非教授的"双语平行语料库"，北京大学詹卫东、柏晓静（2003）等开发的"BABEL汉英平行语料库"等等。但是，已建成的双语语料库大多用于词典编纂（张柏然，2008）、翻译研究和翻译教学（秦洪武，2007；王克非，2004；王克非等，2007），用于汉语教学的双语语料库建设以及相关研究还很少见。本研究开发的英汉双语平行语料库，对语料库采取双层标注，既可用于翻译教学也可用于语言教学，因而拓宽并加深了对平行语料库的应用。

本语料库中的语料来自英国《金融时报》（*Financial Times*）中文网站的*Daily English Lesson*栏目，包括30篇英中对照的财经类语篇，大约23000个汉字、12000个单词（此后称为"FT语料库"）。其中，英语语篇为源语语篇，汉语语篇为目的语语篇。使用这些语料，缘于以下几点原因：

（1）《金融时报》是著名的英国国际商业和财经类报纸，它所刊登的文本具有较高的质量保证。本研究已得到《金融时报》的授权，可以无偿使用其双语财经文本，从事以香港城市大学为基地的研究和教学；

（2）《金融时报》*Daily English Lesson*栏目中的作品是由不同作者写作，不同译者翻译的。这在一定程度上使得本教学语料所涉及到的语言现象更加多样化。

本研究所选30篇语料是在2004年写作并翻译的，内容都与当时的热点财经问题有关。每一对平行语篇均以段落为单位，英、汉语小句对齐排列。

三　研究框架

如上所述，过往研究对语料库的加工多停留在词性标注、词频计算、词语检索和排序上，这使得语料库对于语言教学的作用大多局限于通过对标注字/词/句的检索和统计为教学和研究提供数据上。这样一来，语料库的大小，而不是语料的加工深度，直接影响到语料库的应用。这一点限制了语料库应用于语言教学的深度。FT 语料库设计的关注点不在于其包括语料的多少，而在于其对语料进行深加工的理论基础和对文本现象的系统分类上，以拓宽语料库在汉语作为第二语言教学的应用。

本研究以 Lambrecht 的主题—焦点结构和 Halliday（1994，p. 37—9）的主位结构理论为理论基础，从信息结构和语篇功能的关系出发，探讨文本是如何通过信息分布及管理，换句话说，也就是文本如何通过各种语法和修辞手段凸显信息，组织文本进而发挥作用的。这在本文作者的其他论述中都有论及（参看 Zhu & Yip，2010；Zhu & Wang，即将出版），为清楚起见，本小节将本研究的理论基础加以概括总结，以期读者对 FT 语料库的建设及应用有完整的认识。Lambrecht（1994，p. 338）认为，"语篇功能 …… 是形式系统中固有的。没有信息结构，就没有句子"（本文作者译）。由此可见信息结构与语篇功能的关系及其在语篇中的重要作用：信息结构的构成直接影响其所在语篇功能的发挥。Halliday 认为在无标记的主位—述位序列中，主位是已知信息，述位是新信息；而在 Lambrecht（1994，p. 15，342）的信息结构中，在主位表明语用关系时，主位就成了主题。综合来看，主位就是语用主题，焦点占据了句末位置（即尾焦点），在语用关系上就成为述位中最突出的部分。但事实上，除了尾焦点之外，一个句子成分还可以通过其他突出方式如被动态、强调句、修饰关系成为焦点（见 Zhu，1996a，1996b）。换句话说，主题化和焦点化都可以突出信息，从而对信息接受者产生一定的影响，文本也因而带有某种语用功能。我们进行的文本标注，从根本上来说，也就是要对比、解释跨语言文本信息突出方式的异同。通过比较，学习者更清楚对同一信息，不同文本是如何进行分配、组织、管理以达到希望的语用效果的。

这样一来，以信息结构为基础的标注可以帮助学习者意识到文本中各种信息凸显的方式，并通过对比英、汉文本，更好地掌握两种语言的信息组织模式。语料库中所出现的信息凸显方式可以大致分为七类（参看 Zhu &Yip，2010）：

（1）信息组织：按照主位—述位，主题—焦点组织信息的各种文本现象；

（2）信息分配：在文本架构中，把信息分配到焦点/非焦点位置的各种方式；

（3）信息实现：信息实现的各种方式；

（4）信息表现：语篇特有的信息表现方式；

（5）信息清晰化：目的文本中将原文信息表述清晰化的趋势；

（6）信息和辅助信息：特定语言形式负载的信息；

（7）信息重组：目的文本重组源语文本的信息结构。

标注词的设计是以这七类信息凸显方式为基础的，每一类标注词都针对一种信息凸显现象。例如，信息组织方式包括标注词"尾焦点、'是'字结构、主位—述位顺序不变"等；信息实现方式包括标注词"替代、同义词、重复、缩写、主语省略"等；信息和辅助信息包括标注词"对称、平行、对比、双关、递进、首字母缩略、韵律"等。到目前为止，我们已经发现并总结了90个相关语言现象（标注词）。所有标注词按字母顺序组成标注词单，词单是开放式的，研究者可以根据语料添加和删减，以满足不同语料的需要。

四　双层标注

本研究的标注有两大类构成：一类是文化知识标注；一类是上面提到的有关信息结构的语言现象的标注。第一类主要是对于英、汉特有的文化现象进行标注，以帮助学习者理解原文；语言知识的标注主要对"标记性"信息结构，即突出信息的特殊语言现象进行标注。通过这些标注，学习者可以增强自己对平时未注意到的汉语中的语言现象的认识，也可以通过英、汉对比加深对中文信息结构的理解。文化现象标注以［文本序号＋段落序号＋标注序列号］表示。例如［10.5.2］，表示第十个语篇第五段中的第二个文化现象；语言知识的标注以［文本序号＋段落序号＋字母］表示。例如［24.9a］，表示第二十四个语篇第九段中的第一个语言知识点。下面我们通过对 unmarked 的标注［2.3a］来具体看看关于语言现象的标注是如何进行的。

以［2.3a］为例：

［2.3］The 15—20 per cent increase, amounting to about 190, 000 cars, is also well below the year-on-year increase in May 2003, which was more than 60 per cent[2.3a].

［2.3］15％—20％的增长约等于19万辆汽车，也远低于2003年5月，比2002年同期有高达60％以上的增长[2.3a]。

关于［2.3a］的标注如下，其中括号中的部分是标注词：

［2.3a］根据上下文（context），译文将 year-on-year 译为"比2002年同期"，这使得信息表达清楚明确（clarity）。根据常式（unmarked），信息量小的英文定语从句（relative clause）在汉语中可以译成前置定语，这种方法

使信息分布更紧凑。

[2.3a] 的标注显示，根据上下文，汉文将英文中的 year-on-year 的意思中"上一年"这一信息具体化为"2002 年"，这使得中文表达更加清晰化，有利于读者的理解；另外，对于英文中定语从句，标注中介绍了汉文中的通常表达方式，并说明这种表达对于信息传递的效果。

关于文化现象，由于本语料库主要由财经语料构成，标注的文化现象主要与财经领域相关，这对商务汉语的学习尤其有利。以 [27.8.1] 和 [27.8.2] 为例，其原始语料如下：

[27.8] While the results were helped by a tax credit[27.8.1]，Wal-Mart said an increase in expenses，led by wages，energy and accident costs，along with healthcare costs，put pressure on net profit margins[27.8.2].

沃尔玛表示，虽然财报结果受益于税收抵免[27.8.1]，但以薪资、能源、事故成本和保健成本为主的支出增加，给净利润率[27.8.2]带来压力。

关于 [27.8.1] 和 [27.8.2] 的标注如下：

[27.8.1] 税收抵免（a tax credit）：一项所得税减免，可用来抵消其他所得税项目以直接减少应付所得税额。

[27.8.2] 净利润率（net profit margins）通常以百分比表示，是公司有效控制成本的指标。净利润率越高，证明公司越有能力将收入转化成实际利润。净利润率可用于同一行业的公司比较，也可用于不同行业的公司比较，测出哪个行业利润高（摘自 inverstorwords. com）。

五　语料提取

学习者打开语料库所在文件夹，双击 index 文件，即进入开始页面，再点击"开启（open）"，进入语料库界面，如下页图 1 所示。界面中英、汉语料以段落为单位平行排列，英文语料在左，汉文语料在右。所有经标注的英文语料以浅蓝为底色、以黑体凸显被标注部分，汉文语料则以浅蓝底色凸显。界面右侧是"标注词（glossary）"和"帮助（help）"按键。按"标注词"键可显示所有标注词，而按"帮助"键，界面就会出现帮助菜单，帮助用户学习如何使用语料库，如图 1 所示。

要提取关于文化现象的标注，学习者可将光标停在 [文本数＋段落数＋序列号] 标注的语料上，然后左击鼠标，关于此语料中出现的文化现象的标注就会在语料下方出现，如图 1 所示。

学习者可通过两种方式提取语言现象的标注，一是通过点击被标注小句

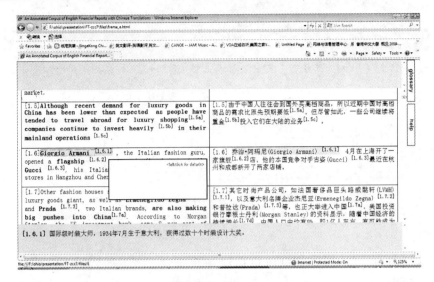

图 1   语料库界面及文化现象标注

进入。光标落到任何一个标注过的小句，光标右侧就会出现一个标注词列单。此列单所列的是在此小句中被标注过的标注词。学习者只需左击鼠标，关于此小句中出现的语言现象的标注就会在语料上方出现，如下页图 2 所示。一是通过"标注词（glossary）"按键。单击界面右上方的 glossary，就会出现一个标注词列单。单击任意一个标注词，例如［tense］，学习者就会看到一个列表，此列表中标明语料库共有 7 个此类标注，并一一列出语料库中出现与此 tense 相关的所有的小句标注，如［1.1a］、［1.7a］。此时如单击［1.7a］，界面立刻就会出现此小句出现的上下文，小句以黄色为底色凸显，如图 3 所示。

六   讨论：FT 语料库在汉语教学中的应用

传统的翻译教学法，又称语法翻译法、阅读法或古典法，是一种传统的外语教学法。它以母语为教学工具，通过让学生进行翻译或造句，来教授和练习语言的语法知识。这种教学法的缺陷之一在于，它主要采取讲解和分析句子类型、句子的语法结构、词汇意义和用法，忽略了语言在实际生活中的语用功能（Huang，2001，p. 88）。具体地说，翻译教学法常常割裂了词/词组、小句与语篇的关系，脱离语言环境，使学习者往往只注意到词/词组/小句的语法规则，而忽略了该词/词组/小句与语篇之间相互

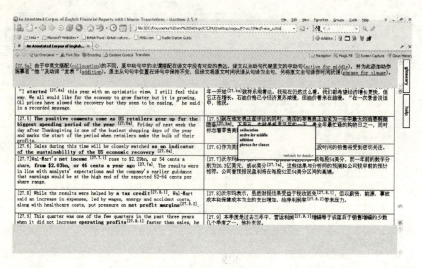

图 2　语言现象标注

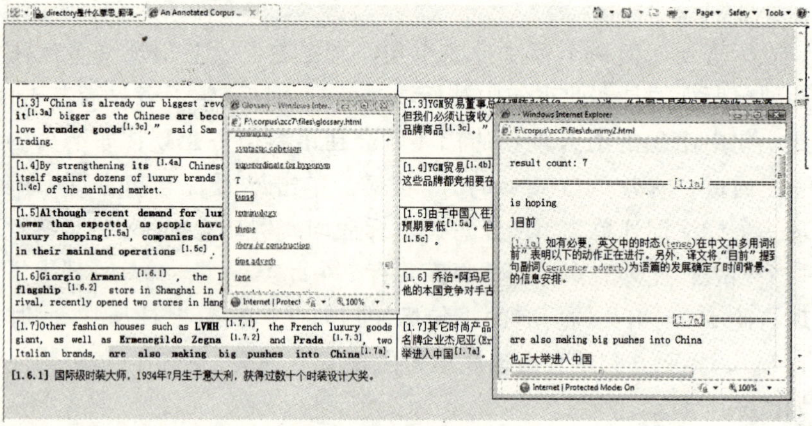

图 3　语料提取

制约的关系。FT 语料库打破了这种传统翻译教学法的限制，创造出更有利的学习环境。具体而言，运用 FT 语料库学习中文的优势有两个：第一，它有助于提高学习者对语言细节的意识，加深对学习细节的学习；另一方面，它将对语言细节的讨论置于一定的语篇当中，注重语言细节与语篇整体的互动关系，有利于学习者从整体到细节全面掌握汉语言的用法。第二，通过英、汉对比，它有助于学习者加深对汉语言的认识。

（一）细节学习和整体把握

本研究将词/词组、小句置于语篇之中，在标注中，将其用法与整个语篇结合起来，目的是使学习者了解某一中/英文表达方式/语法规则如何与小句及语篇联系起来发挥语用功能。

以［2.1a］为例，以下是［2.1a］的语料：

［2.1］The rate of growth in car sales in China slowed substantially in May, executives, dealers and analysts said[2.1a], hit by the central government's new restrictions on car loans[2.1b].

［2.1］汽车业经营主管、经销商和分析师表示[2.1a]，中国汽车销售增长率5月份显著放缓，原因是中央政府对汽车贷款设定了新限制，汽车销售由此遭到打击[2.1b]。

［2.1a］的标注如下：

［2.1a］按照常式（unmarked），"某某人说/表示/认为……"句式在英文中通常放在句中或句末，以句末居多，而在中文中通常置于句首。但是，此处如以"经营主管、经销商和分析师"直接开头，句子节奏可能会显得突兀，因此需要根据上下文添加修饰词/词组。注意添加部分的信息要准确。例如，如添加"中国的/驻中国的"，添加信息对原文实质信息的适用范围做出限定或扩充，使得译文改变了原文信息，因为根据原文上下文推断不出这些人来自哪里；而此处添加的"汽车业"是循文章主题而得（context），与语篇内容一致。

学习者如在学习unmarked的过程中，不明白其中讲到的context，或想更多了解，可通过点击括号中的标注词context，进入关于context的标注集合。在所列出的所有关于context的标注中，学习者可任意点击其中一句的标注，即可看到此句所在的语篇。这种由点及面的方式不仅表现在具体的标注上，而且表现在语料库标注的整体编排上：学习者既可学习每一标注的具体内容，还可通过点击标注词看到语料库中与此标注词相关的被标注过的例子及标注（如上述图1所示）。通过它们，学习者就可较为全面地了解此标注词的用法。如果学习者想看看某一例所处的具体语篇，可点击标记图标（如［1.7a］），该小句及其所在语篇就会呈现在学习者面前。

（二）英、汉对比的标注内容让语言学习更深入

语料库在标注时要注意比较英、汉两种语言在表达时的各自特色，以帮助学习者清楚认识到在英、汉转化时要注意的地方。这种比较的标注方式可

以清楚地展示英语在何种情况下用何种方式来表达，与之相比，同样的情况在汉语中的表达方式是什么，为什么，预期的效果是什么等。这对于汉语学习是非常重要的。

以［9.4a］为例，原文如下：

［9.4］But after the party comes the hangover and the bill [9.4a].

［9.4］但是，盛筵结束了，沉醉犹存，还有账单[9.4a]。

［9.4a］的标注内容是：

［9.4a］英文的倒装句型（inverted construction）有强调突出信息的作用（emphasis），但是它在中文中很少有对应表达式。英译汉时，中文通常的做法是将它们处理成正常语序。中文使用四字格（quadrisyllabic idiom）来翻译hangover and the bill，因为四字格内涵丰富，富有节奏感。

上述的标注指出英文的倒装句型在中文中通常的表达方式，并且对汉语中四字格的使用做了说明。如果学习者想进而了解更多英文倒装句在中文中的表达方式，可通过点击括号中的标注词 inverted construction 获取。这样一来，通过实例，学习者就可比较全面地了解中文是如何处理英文中的倒装句了。

七　结论和改进

本研究力图突破以往语料库在教学研究上的局限，通过标注系统帮助学习者全面了解和掌握汉语语篇的构成。但是，由于时间的局限，本语料库在许多方面还需改进：如设计界面过于单一，语料体裁不够丰富，缺乏练习等等。为了弥补这些不足，我们正在开发另一个研究项目："展示性语篇和英中双语文化展示（Presentational Discourse and Bilingual Presentation of Culture in Chinese and English：A Systemic-Functional Linguistic Approach）"（香港城市大学项目编号：7002057，2007-)。① 此项目语料在财经领域之外，涉及

———————————

① 该项目现已并入一个更大型的综合双语写作与翻译在线教学平台的建设项目中（城市大学项目编号：6000304）。鸣谢：本文受香港城市大学研究项目"展示性语篇和英中双语文化展示（Presentational Discourse and Bilingual Presentation of Culture in Chinese and English：A Systemic-Functional Linguistic Approach）"（项目编号：7002057，2007—）及"英汉财经翻译机器辅助教学（Machine-Aided Teaching of English-Chinese Financial Translation）"（项目编号：6980030，2004）的资助，特此鸣谢。作者也对《金融时报》允许将其英中文本用于以城市大学为基地的教学及科研活动表示衷心的感谢。

不同主题和体裁，不仅包括双语语料，还包括中文单语语料，这使得语料所包含的文化/语言现象更加多样。中文单语语料的加入是考虑到双语语料库中的中文语料，其用词、句法结构、语篇组织会不同程度地受到源语的影响。纯粹在中文环境中的创作的中文就可弥补这方面的不足，使学习者了解到在双语语料中出现的语言信息凸显方式在中文单语料中的表现形式是否一样，如有不同，那么中文系统中惯用的模式是什么；另一方面，在 FT 语料库以信息结构为基础做标注的基础上，新的研究项目对标注系统进行了更深更广的扩展：同一个语篇在从词到句到段落的不同层面上得到立体的标注，学生因而得以从不同侧面学习语言，进而加深对双语（中文与英文）语篇谋篇布局的理解及掌握。新语料库为提高学习效率，还增加了学习者自我测试的界面。假以时日，我们深信在 FT 语料库基础上建设的新的语料库会更全面、更系统、更有效地帮助语言（比如对外汉语）教学。

参考文献

陈小荷（1997）：《"汉语中介语语料库系统"介绍》，胡明扬主编《第五届国际汉语教学讨论会论文选》，北京大学出版社。

储诚志、陈小荷（1993）：《建立"汉语中介语语料库系统"的基本设想》，《世界汉语教学》，第 3 期。

秦洪武、王克非（2007）：《对应语料库在翻译教学中的应用：理论依据和实施原则》，《中国翻译》，第 5 期。

孙宏林、孙德金等（1997）：《"现代汉语研究语料库系统"概述》，胡明扬主编《第五届国际汉语教学讨论会论文选》，北京大学出版社。

王克非、秦洪武、王海霞（2007）：《双语对应语料库翻译教学平台的应用初探》，《外语电化教学》，第 118 期。

王克非（2004）：《双语平行语料库在翻译教学上的用途》，《外语电化教学》，第 100 期，第 27—32 页。

杨翼、李绍林（2006）：《建立汉语学习者口语语料库的基本设想》，《汉语学习》，第 3 期。

张柏然（2008）：《平行语料库与积极型汉英词典的研编》，上海译文出版社。

郑艳群（2006）：《对外汉语计算机辅助教学的理论研究》，商务印书馆。

Aijmer, K. (2009). *Corpora and Language Teaching*. Amsterdam：John Benjamins.

Gavioli, L. (2006). *Exploring Corpora for ESP Learning*. Amsterdam：John Benjamins.

Halliday, M. A. K. (1994). *An Introduction to Functional Grammar*. London：Arnold.

Hidalgo, E. , Quereda, L. & Santana, J. (2007). *Corpora in the Foreign Language Classroom*: *Selected Papers from the Sixth International Conference on Teaching and Language Corpora* (*TaLC* 6). Amsterdam: Rodopi.

Huang, Hui-ling. (2001). *Current Teaching Approaches in Taiwanese English Classroom and Recommendations for the Future.* Unpublished Phd thesis. Claremont, UMI.

Lambrecht, Knud. (1994). *Information Structure and Sentence Form*: *Topic, Focus, and the Mental Representations of Discourse Referents.* Cambridge, New York and Melbourne: Cambridge University Press.

Scott, M. & Tribble, C. (2006). *Textual Patterns*: *Key Words and Corpus Analysis in Language Education.* Amsterdam: John Benjamins.

Zhu, C. & Hui Wang. (forthcoming). "Feasibility and Acceptability of a Corpus-based, Machine-Aided Mode of Translator Training: ClinkNotes and beyond" . *The Interpreter and Translator Trainer.*

Zhu, C. & Po-ching Yip. (2010). "ClinkNotes: Towards a Corpus-based, Machine-aided Programme of Translation Teaching" . *Meta*, 55 (2).

Zhu, C. (1996a) "Syntactic status of the agent and information presentation in translating the passive between Chinese and English", *Multilingua*: *Journal of Cross-cultural and Interlanguage Communication*, 15 (4).

Zhu, C. (1996b) "Translation of modifications: about information, intention and effect", *Target*: *International Journal of Translation Studies*, 8 (2).

CALL 与传统教法之比较研究

CALL 和传统教学法对汉语初学者影响的定量研究

CALL and Traditional Instructions for Chinese Beginners：A Quantitative Research

王大亮　Daliang Wang

Mercyhurst College United States dwang@ mercyhurst. edu

摘　要：通过对比两组汉语初学者的学习成绩，此项研究致力于调查 CALL（电脑辅助语言教学）教学法和传统教学法对于汉语学习的影响。具体地说，此项研究调查 CALL 教学法是否会更有效地提高学生的学习成绩。此项研究详细解释了 CALL 和传统教学法的不同，对两个对比组的学习成绩进行了比较。研究结果表明，利用 CALL 教学法的一组学生的成绩和传统组的学生稍微不同，但从统计学角度看，差异很小。文章最后力图解释研究结果的原因，教学上的意义，以及运用科技教学须注意的事项。

Abstract：By comparing the learning results from two groups of Chinese learners，this research project aimed to investigate the different effects on learning by using CALL and traditional instructions. Specifically，this research studied whether CALL brought better learning results for students. Two different classroom instructional methods were described in this research. The learning outcomes of the two comparing groups were analyzed and the results indicated that the differences on test scores between two groups were not statistically significant. Possible explanations for the results were also discussed，and concerns in using technologies in a classroom were also presented.

一　简述

电脑辅助语言教学（CALL：Computer-Assisted Language Learning）作为外语教学法的一种，在过去的几十年内影响深远。很多中文教师用电脑辅助教学取得成效，有关的研究著述也很多。但是，总的来说，有关 CALL 的量化研究很少，尤其是 CALL 在实际语言教学中的有效性及可靠性缺乏研究数据作为支持。如 Leloup and Ponterio（2003）指出，目前多数关于电脑和外语教学的研究集中在电脑的具体应用上，这些应用早就被假定会辅助或者提高学生的学习效果，但很少有研究测量 CALL 应用后的具体学习效果。CALL 和传统汉语教学法所带来的不同学习效果需要进一步研究。

此项研究旨在对比 CALL 和传统教学法对于学汉语的学生成绩的影响，调查CALL 能否帮助学生取得更好的学习成绩。此文论述对比了两种不同的教学环境和方法，比较了这两种教学环境所产生的教学效果，并进一步解释其中的原因。最后，文章讨论了运用电脑进行外语教学时需要注意的事项。

二　文献综述

（一）CALL 在教学中的积极作用

电脑是现代外语教学中重要的教学工具。外语教师和研究者早已认识到CALL 在外语教育中的积极作用。有句谚语叫"科技不会替代教师，可是会运用科技的教师会取代那些不会运用科技的教师"。这是很多外语教师积极运用电脑科技的动力之一。这一部分的文献综述重点介绍运用电脑进行外语教学的种种优势。

- 提高学生的学习兴趣和学习动机

外语学习需要大量的重复与操练，有时不免烦琐枯燥。没有学习兴趣，学习难以进步。而研究表明，通过电脑所能提供的语言交流、游戏、动画、图片，以及其他影音学习材料，电脑辅助教学可以提高学生的学习兴趣和动机（Harmer，2007；Ilter，2009；Ravichandran，2000）。

- 增强学生信心

电脑可以帮助那些害羞或是学得慢的学生自由表达，而不必害怕当众讲话的压力。一项研究表明有些学生更喜欢先同电脑练习语言，再和其他人交流（Kataoka，2000）。另一项研究（Wang，2004）认为学生在使用电脑学习外语时觉得自由度高，得到更多鼓励，从而能更好地提高语言能力。

●鼓励自主学习

电脑及互联网使学生能够随时随地接触到学习材料。这样学生就能按照自己的进度学习。这种学习的灵活性可以满足学生的不同需要，使得学习个人化，从而更好地提高学习效果（Borras 1993；Gong, 2002）。

●提供实用的学习材料和理想的语言环境

课本上的语言材料具有滞后性，总是和真实语境中的材料不同。学生如果能够随时得到真实语境中的学习材料，学习就更有针对性和实用性。同时，用真实语言材料学习，学生在同说目标语的人交流时更有自信（Domingo, 2004）。比如，网络上的多媒体学习材料就能随时给学生提供真实的语言环境。学生也可以利用网络空间交朋友，同说母语的人交流。

真实语境中的学习材料不仅能缩短课本知识和实际运用语言之间的距离，更能为学生提供理想的学习环境，因为外语学习本身就应是一个真实和自然的过程。

●促进文化学习

目标语文化的学习是外语学习中重要的部分。利用网络和电脑科技，学生可以轻易地接触到真实的文化场景，通过图片，音频和视频来学习正确的语言运用。网络的虚拟社区也可以将学生置于这样的文化环境中，学生觉得自己是其中一员，也就更容易感受和理解目标文化（Stepp-Greany, 2002）。

●减轻教师的责任

一旦很好地运用，CALL 可以极大地减轻教师的教学责任。学生如果能够独立地用网络及学习软件完成学习任务，教师就能腾出时间来做一些电脑所不能提供的教学任务。如安排口语测试，修改文章，或者设计课程（Lai, 2006）。

●教师可以更好地监督学生的学习进程

监督学生的学习进程并及时提供反馈对外语教学来说至关重要。许多外语教学软件或者网站可以协助教师监督学生的学习进程，并将学生学习过程数据化。教师就能及时检查学生的学习进度，从而更有针对性地教学（Chapelle, 2010）。

（二）CALL 在外语教学中的问题

虽然 CALL 在外语教学中有很多优势，但是问题依然存在，基于文献综述，所列如下：

●较高的教育成本

高质量的语言项目对电脑、网络、软件的设备自然要求较高。利用电脑教学必然带来教育成本的增加，这对不富裕的学生和学区来说不利。Gips、DiMattia、& Gips（2004）等人认为在语言教学中使用电脑科技会提高成本降低教学质量，一个原因就是贫穷的学区或学生负担不起，就无法从中受益。另外一些学校也会觉得这样会带来经济压力，因为他们要买硬件，更新软件，培训人员（Wang，2005）。

- 对电脑技术的要求较高

成功的利用 CALL 教学需要老师和学生都有较高的电脑技术素养。没有一定的运用电脑、网络的能力，尤其是如果老师缺乏这方面的素养，CALL 的优势就无法凸显。研究表明美国老师在运用教育技术教学这方面准备非常不足（Wang，2005）。对不少老师来说，用电脑科技教课需要适应一个新的教学模式，这是个不小的挑战。许多老师因为缺乏运用电脑的能力，就根本不愿在教学中使用科技（Vu，2005）。

- 没有完善的语言教学软件或程序

由于语言本身的复杂性决定了一个完美的语言学习软件及电脑程序是不存在的，不断地升级电脑软件或程序必然会影响 CALL 教学的有效性（Lai，2006）。

- 无法处理突发情况

许多教师认为电脑不过是人工智能，无法解答学生在学习中随时遇到的问题。Indrawati（2008）认为，学习外语时，一个学生碰到的问题复杂多变，没有电脑能像老师那样随时准确地答疑解惑。现在科技在人机交互方面的发展还相当有限。

- 减少师生交流

教师在外语教学中的作用至关重要。科技和电脑永远都不能取代语言学习中人的因素。Son（2002）的研究强调了电脑只是教学工具而非结果，任何时候，师生交流都是学习中的主要因素。

三　研究方法

这一部分研究项目中使用的研究方法，其中包括研究对象，研究采用的不同教学环境及教学方法，收集研究数据的工具，研究过程，对研究数据的统计分析，以及数据解读。

- 研究对象

研究对象是宾州 Mercyhurst 学院汉语初级班的学生。这是个混合型的班级，学生以本科生为主，也有几个研究生。上午班有 24 个学生，下午班有

11 个学生。没有一个学生有汉语言文化背景和语言知识。我们每周有 3 次课，一共 4 个小时上课时间，课程持续 10 周。

● 研究环境设置

汉语 101 是专为没有背景知识的汉语初学者设置。此课程为学生提供汉语听说读写（汉字）4 个方面的基础知识和训练。两个汉语班使用一样的课本和其他教学材料。上午班 24 个学生在一个普通教室学习，这个教室有一台电脑和相连的投影仪。授课方法包括老师直接授课，运用 PowerPoint 授课，及用录像作为辅助。这个教室小而拥挤，所以互动式的学习活动有限。但是，师生之间的互动，尤其是问答，较为频繁。

另外一组 11 个学生在语言教室上课，这个专门的语言教室有 18 台电脑和一个教师主控台。每台电脑都配有耳机和话筒。每个学生有一台自己的电脑并且教师鼓励学生使用，所以学生的学习较为个人化。学生学习方式包括学生在电脑上打汉字，用电脑练习听说，用网上语言游戏学习，用专门的汉字学习网站练习汉字书写，用网上的视频及其他多媒体材料学习。每堂课教师通常先教授汉语知识，然后布置练习让学生在电脑上学习，教师一直监督学生学习并随时提供反馈。

这两个教学环境大不相同。显然语言教室能够提供一个更理想化的学习环境，从而学生具有更多的学习优势。首先，小班教学可以增加师生及学生之间的交流互动。其次，电脑辅助提供的不同的教学活动可以持续保持学生的兴趣。最后，学生能够得到教师更多的关注和学习反馈，这在第二语言教学中至关重要。而在普通教室，师生间的互动多是以个别回答或集体回答的方式进行的。教师也无法给予每个学生个人化的关注和反馈。

● 数据收集和处理

数据主要通过考试取得。学习测评方式包括每周测验，文化课题，小组作业，口语考试，以及期中、期末考试。针对此研究，研究数据只从期中期末考试中收集。试卷考项包括多选题，问答题，翻译和写汉字。口语考试单独进行。考试期间不使用电脑。通过试卷，教师收集两组考分作为数据，并将每组数据细分为听说读写 4 个方面的分数。

然后，教师运用统计软件 SPSS 进行分析数据。这些分析包括描述性分析和独立 T-test，以研究在两个不同教室中学生的不同学习效果。

四　结果

此项研究探索两组不同学生在不同学习环境下的学习结果。一个主要研究问题是：CALL 教学会影响学生的汉语学习成绩吗？如果有影响，具体在听说读写的哪个方面影响显著？基于文献综述，一个可能的研究假设应该是这两个不同的学习环境会产生不同的学习效果，在语言教室学习的学生应该比在普通教室的学生学得更好。但是，研究结果并不支持这一假设，总的来说，两组学生并没有明显的学习差异。

期中考试在学期第五周进行，主要测试学生听，读和书写汉字的能力。数据分析表明普通教室的学生考得比语言教室的学生稍微好一些（M = 34.2/40）。但是分析显示统计差异并不明显，t（33）= 1.16。期末考试和其中考试的形式一样，只是题目更多并且有一个独立进行的口语测试。数据分析表明两组学生期末考试的成绩几乎没有差别（M = 39.0/50 vs. M = 38.5/50），仅有的细微差别也没有统计意义上的差异 t（33）= 0.23。分析结果见表1。

表1   **两组学生的期中期末考试成绩**

期中考试

教室	人数	平均分	SD.	t
传统教室	24	34.1875	5.62373	1.16
语音室	11	32.0000	4.98498	

期末考试

教室	人数	平均分	SD.	t
传统教室	24	39.0417	7.05093	0.23
语音室	11	38.5000	6.24099	

在具体分析两组学生在听说读写每个方面的差异时，分析结果显示同样的模式。分析显示在各项语言能力中，普通教室的学生成绩略高于语言教室的学生，但是，这一差异同样没有统计上的差别。数据分析结果见表2。

表2   **四项语言能力中的成绩差别**

阅读

教室	人数	平均分	SD.	t
传统教室	24	9.3958	.70679	.77
语音室	11	9.0909	1.22103	

t（33）= 0.77, p > 0.05

写汉字

教室	人数	平均分	SD.	t
传统教室	24	17. 8958	1. 53211	1. 24
语音室	11	16. 7727	2. 83164	

t (33) = 0. 1. 24，p > 0. 05

口语

教室	人数	平均分	SD.	t
传统教室	24	8. 2292	. 92053	. 75
语音室	11	7. 9091	1. 28098	

t (33) = 0. 75，p > 0. 05

听力

教室	人数	平均分	SD.	t
传统教室	24	25. 1875	3. 93096	1. 22
语音室	11	23. 7273	2. 93567	

t (33) = 1. 22，p > 0. 05

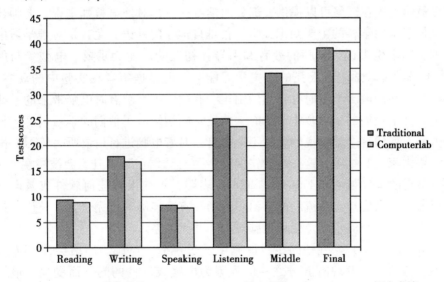

Traditional：传统教室；**Computer lab**：语音教室；**Test scores**：考试成绩

五　讨论

　　此项研究的数据分析表明，CALL 教学并没有带来太大的学习优势。普通教室的学生和语言教室的学生在考试成绩上几乎一样。这一研究结果和此前的不少研究大相径庭。当然，此研究学生人数、时间以及测量方法规模不大，有一定局限性。但这一结果还是值得进一步探讨。这些探讨基于教师的自我解释、学生的交流，以及文献综述。

（一）教师在教学准备（运用电脑），监督及评价学生学习中的作用至关重要

在外语教学中，教师的作用至关重要。在教室中运用电脑科技对教师来说是新的挑战。当学习从普通教室转到语言教室，教学方法也随之改变。相应的，教师的角色也从一个知识拥有者变成了一个学习促进者。而学生则对学习有更多的主动权。CALL 的运用要求教师要有充足的教育技术，在备课时要做更多有针对性的准备。对于这样一个教学模式的转变，不经过大量的实践和教学，教师很难完全胜任。相对于一个传统教师而言，CALL 教学中教师要做更多的准备，这些都会影响 CALL 的效果。

（二）学生独立学习的能力可能被高估

虽然说现在网络可以提供大部分的学习材料，对外语教师来说，老师还是掌握了本门学科的主要知识，学生很难自学一门外语。尤其是对于学习中文的美国学生来说，教师的教育和引导在初级阶段尤为重要。电脑参与的CALL 教学要求学生有很强的自主学习能力，但是据笔者在实验中的观察，有些学生在用电脑学习时有相当的困难。有的学生反映有时电脑带来的一些问题打乱了他们的学习步骤，有时一些技术问题影响了他们的学习进度。另一方面，就像有个学生说的，她不愿意自己对着电脑进行口语听力练习，她宁肯跟大家一起练习，这样她的错误就会"自动纠正"并且不会被注意到。

最近的一项研究（Falsgraf, 2009）表明，目前没有任何软件或是电脑可以教会一个成年人说流利的外语。因为没有人能够通过完全自学外语，达到成人阶段的交流水平。使用电脑与否，并无关系。

Kotter's（2001）在他的在线课堂中通过视频、电邮、网络会议等方式授课，他的研究发现有五分之一的人因为电脑或软件的问题而受挫，最终退课。

（三）学生的科技水平层次不齐

今天的大学生是随着网络和数字技术长大的，因而通常被认为精于电脑科技。但对于用电脑学习外语而言，不少学生还是有困难。我的班里有几个学生觉得用电脑学习使他们有挫折感，因为他们没有做好准备。学生的电脑网络知识是保证 CALL 教学成功的一个先决条件，但在此项研究中，至少有三个学生觉得他们的电脑水平有限，用电脑学习很不适应。作为教师，笔者也的确在实验过程中花了不少时间来解决一些技术问题，像如何用电脑打中文，如何用软件交流，或是处理一些电脑及软件故障。这些宝贵的课堂时间本该用于实质性的学习，有时候确实打乱了课堂教学的流畅性。在 Lee（2004）的一项研究中，学生电脑知识的不足几乎导致一个网络合作学习实验完全失败。

（四）人类的直接交流在外语学习中无法被替代

大脑专家 Patricia Kuhl（2008）博士，华盛顿大学脑科学研究中心主任最近重新研究了电视对婴儿学习语言的影响。她再次发现，婴儿无法通过电视或声音学会外语。她进一步指出人际的、社会的交流是外语学习中的关键，而不是电视或电脑。对于学习外语的成年人来说，人的因素依然最主要的。CALL 为学生提供了个性化的学习，但不可避免地影响了师生之间和学生之间的直接交流。

Conrad（1999）发现在学习外语的第一个学期中，学生更喜欢简单的重复练习或是控制性的学习，而不是通过电脑或网络进行创作性的语言交流。许多外语学习者可能更适应以教师为中心的传统外语学习，就是学生作为集体和老师交流（Vu，2005）。

这一点对于英语为母语的汉语学习者来说更是如此。因为没有任何的语言文化背景，我的很多学生更愿意直接或是集体和我交流。

Jones（1996）指出老师和学生应该牢记任何 CALL 带来的只是"虚拟"而非"真实"。另外一个教育者进一步阐释说："在外语学习中，没有任何可以替代人与人的交流，一个电脑软件，不管多么先进复杂，都不能真实直接地展现一个不同语言文化。"（Gong，2002，p. 9）

六　结语

对老师和学生来说，用 CALL 学习具有很多优势。但是用电脑科技教学的一些问题也不容忽视。教师需要进行更多的定量研究来确定电脑科技到底在怎样的程度上促进外语学习，如何最有效地利用科技学习。这样才能结合 CALL 与传统教学的长处来优化教学方法。同时，在一个"网络化"的教室中，老师和学生也应该做好充分的准备来应对新的变化，使学习成功。CALL 必须与好的教学理论，教学设计结合，才能发挥最大作用。同时，只有电脑辅助学习满足了学生的学习兴趣和需求，最大限度地提高了学生的成绩，学生才能真正从中受益。

虽然此项研究受限于时间和人数，但此定量研究的结果对于准备或是已经在用电脑科技辅助教学的老师来提供了一些有用的信息。更重要的是，此项研究对于负责教育预算的学校管理层提供了可资借鉴的信息。在经济不好，教育经费不足的时候，外语教学项目总是首先在学校的缩减名单上。因为在美国，不少人相信学生只要用好的学习软件就能学会一门外语，无需教师。但迄今没有研究表明学生可以通过软件及电脑学会外语。至少此研究再次印证了那句老话：科技不会替代教师，可是会运用科技的教师会取代那些不会运用科技的教师。

参考文献

Chapelle, C (2010). The spread of Computer-Assisted Language Learning, *Language Teaching*, 43 (1).

Conrad, D. (1999). The student view on effective practices in the college elementary and intermediate foreign language classroom, *Foreign Language Annals*, 32 (4).

Domingo, N. (2004). Computer assisted language learning：Increase of freedom or submission to Machines Retrieved January 25, 2010, from http：//www. terra. es/personal/nostat/

Falsgraf, C. (2009). Do-it-yourself products won' t make you fluent. Retrieved October 11, 2009, from http：//www. registerguard. com/csp/cms/sites/web/news/sevendays/21178549-35/story. csp.

Gips, A. , DiMattia, P. , & Gips, J. (2004). The effect of assistive technology on educational costs：Two case studies. In K. Miesenberger, J. Klaus, W. Zagler, D. Burger (eds.), Computers Helping People with Special Needs, Springer, 2004.

Gong, J. (2002). The employment of CALL in teaching foreign/second language speaking skills. *Post-Script*, 3 (1). University of Melbourne, Australia. Retrieved December 29, 2009, from http：//www. edfac. unimelb. edu. au/research/resources/student_ res/postscriptfiles/vol3/vol3_ 1_ gong1. pdf.

Harmer, J. (2007). The practice of English language teaching. NY：Pearson ESL.

Huang, S. & Liu, H. (2000). Communicative language teaching in a multimedia language lab, *The Internet TESL Journal*, 6 (2). Retrieved January 20, 2010, from http：//iteslj. org/Techniques/Huang-CompLab. htm.

Ilter, G. B. (2009). Effect of technology on motivation on EFL classrooms. *Turkish Online Journal of Distance Education*, 10 (4).

Jones, R. G. (1996). Creating Language Learning Materials for the World Wide Web. in. Warschauer M. (ed), Telecollaboration in foreign language learning: proceedings of the. Hawaii Symposium. Honolulu, Hawaii: Second Language Teaching & Curriculum Center, University of Hawaii at Manoa.

Kataoka, K. (2000). Computers for English Language Learning in Japanese Schools. (ERICDocument Reproduction Service ED439600)

Kennedy, C., & Levy, M. (2009). sustainability and Computer-Assisted Language Learning: factors for success in a context of change, *Computer Assisted Language Learning*, 22 (5).

Kotter, M. (2001). Developing distance language learners' interactive competence-can synchronous.

Kuhl, P. (2008). Childhood development: early Learning, the brain and society, Retrieved January 25, 2010, from http://www.youtube.com/watch?v = Fcb8nT0QC6o&feature = player_ embedded audio do the trick *International Journal of Educational Telecommunication*, 7 (4).

Lee, K. W. (2000). English teachers' barriers to the use of computer assisted language learning. *The Internet TESL Journal.* Retrieved January 22, 2010, from http://iteslj.org/Articles/Lee-CALLbarriers. html Lee, L. (2004). Learners' perspectives on networked collaborative interaction with native speakers of Spanish in the US, *Language Learning and Technology*, 8 (1).

Leloup, J., & Ponterio, R. (2003). Second language acquisition and technology: a review of research. Eric Digest. Retrieved January 25, 2010, from http://www.cal.org/resources/digest/0311leloup.html National Center for Educational Statistics (2000a). Teachers' tools for the 21st century: A report on teachers' use of technology. Washington, DC: Author.

Ravichandran, T. (2000). *Computer-assisted language learning (CALL) in the perspective of the interactive approach: advantages and apprehensions*. Paper presented and published in the Proceedings: National Seminar on CALL, Anna University, Chennai. Retrieved January 20, 2010, from http://members.rediff.com/eximsankar/call.htm.

Son, J. B. (2002). Computers, learners and teachers: Teamwork in the CALL classroom. *English Language Teaching*, 14 (2).

Stepp-Greany, J. (2002). Students perceptions on language learning in a technological environment: implications for the new millennium. *Language Learning and Technology.* 6 (1).

Vu, T. V. (2005). Advantages and disadvantages of using computer network technology in language teaching. *Journal of Science*，*Foreign Languages*. Retrieved January 25，2010，from http：//faculty. ksu. edu. sa/saad/Documents/advant% 20and%20disadvant%20of%20CALL. pdf.

Wang，D. ，& Piper，D. （2005）. Secondary students：new resources for technical support. *Pennsylvania Educational Leadership*. 24 （1）.

Wang，L. （2000）. The advantages of using technology in second language education：technology integration in foreign language teaching demonstrates the shift from a behavioral to a constructivist learning approach，*T. H. E. Journal*，32 （10）.

Wang，Y. （2004）. English magazines，motivation + improved EFL writing skill. *English Teaching Forum*. 42 （1）.

Warschauer，M. （2005）. Social cultural perspectives on CALL. In J. Egbert， G. M. Petrie （Eds. ） CALL research perspectives. Mahwah，NJ：Lawrence Earlbaum.

对外汉语网络课程教学实例分析
Online Chinese Teaching and Learning: Case Studies

程朝晖　Zhaohui Cheng　佐治亚州肯尼索州立大学

Kennesaw State University United States zcheng1@kennesaw.edu

摘　要: 本文基于 4 个学期的汉语网络语言课程的实际教学实例, 对汉语网络语言课程的学习与教学做一个纵向的分析、研究, 为汉语的网络教学提供一些实际的经验、教训。研究的材料、方法包括对课程和学习者的语言测试、观察分析以及问卷调查和数据统计分析。本人的这份研究结果有以下几点启示: 1. 如果网络课程设置得当, 则听说读写各方面的教学结果与课堂教学相当, 但在效率上不及课堂教学。2. 对于汉语语言课程的学习, 学习者可能更喜欢选用面对面的课堂学习方式, 而非网络课程。汉语水平越低的学生越是如此。因此, 网络课程的设计如何更人性化、更加强调学习者之间的相互交流和互动、更及时有效的反馈将是网络语言课程设计所要注意的方面。3. 汉语网络课程可以提高学习者的汉字识字水平。4. 即使是网络教学课程, 教师的作用仍然非常重要, 不可忽视。网络语言课程的效果离不开学习者严格的自律和教师的严格要求与监督。

关键词: 中文教学, 网络语言课程, 汉语网络教学, 网络语言教学效果

Abstract: This study is based on my four-semester online Chinese teaching experience, focusing on comparative analysis of learning outcomes from the teaching models of both face-to-face and online instructions. My study suggests that online Chinese instruction may obtain similar learning outcomes if it is carefully designed and well executed, but the efficiency isn't as good as the one of classroom instruction. Learners may still prefer face-to-face class if both types of instructions are available, especially for those at the lower or beginner's levels. This study also suggests that the design of online language instruction should pay a close attention to students' interactivities as well as other communicative modes in order to create a native or near native language learning environment. Online Chinese instruction may help learners gain their abilities to recognize Chinese characters due to more readily available online readings materials. Finally, the instructor's supervising and the learner's self-discipline are equally important to ensure the effectiveness of online learning.

Keywords：Chinese language teaching, online language class, Chinese online language teaching and learning, results of online language teaching and learning

一　导言

随着高科技的发展，计算机辅助语言学习（CALL）以及远程网络语言课程（Web-based Distance Language Learning, DLL）的研究正方兴未艾，对外汉语教学方面也是如此，尤其是在北美地区。不仅是计算机辅助汉语教学，一些完全在网络上进行的汉语教学课程也在很多大学开设，以适应汉语学习者的需求。随着网络科技的不断进步，中文教学软件和网站也越来越多样化。这其中有免费或收费的汉语网络教学网站，通过网络的电脑视频汉语课程，汉语教学博客，一些大学自行设计的汉语网络课程，以及汉语的网上测试等等（Yao 2009）。然而，正如 David Barr 等所指出的，大多数的计算机辅助课程和网络课程都主要注重于非口语化的阅读、写作、听力或者填空一类的练习。口语对话课程、成对的和成组的角色表演练习与讨论都还大多是在通常的课堂教学中进行（Barr et al. 2005, p. 56）。相关的研究内容也主要着重于把电脑、网络作为媒介的书面语言交流和学习方面的研究（Stepp-Greany, 2002, p. 165）。完全的包括听说读写各个方面的网络语言教学，尤其是汉语的网络语言教学效果究竟如何？是否能与面对面课堂语言教学的效果在听说读写各方面都能相同或一致？这一方面的研究目前还不是很多。虽然已有研究显示，网络语言课程在口语教学方面与课堂语言教学的教学效果一致（Blake et al. 2008），但汉语是否也一样？汉语的网络教学有哪些问题？今后的发展有哪些需要重视之处？Felix（2001）曾列出学生所反映的网络语言课程的一些缺陷，如"缺乏口语练习"、"没有与同伴的互动"、"没有足够的反馈"、"教师不在现场"等问题（p. 47）如何解决？这一切都需要在实践中逐步总结。本文在四个学期的汉语网络课程实际教学的基础上，对汉语网络课程作一些研究、分析，为今后汉语网络课程的设计、研究与发展提供一些经验和参考。

二 课程设计与设置

Georgia Perimeter College 是一所环绕亚特兰大城，有五个校区两万多学生的社区大学，笔者曾在这所大学任教 4 年（2005—2009），帮助这所学校建立、发展中文项目。因为只有笔者所在的校区开有正式的中文课程，所有中文课程皆由笔者一人负责，为了给其他校区的学生提供中文课程以及增加选修中文课程的学生人数，从 2006 年秋季开始，笔者独立设计、开设了中文网络课程，以适应不同地点、不同学习时间的学生需要。考虑到中文学习的特殊性，即汉字学习和打字问题，中文的网络课程是二年级的初—中级汉语语言课程和高级班以华裔学生为主的中文读写课程。本文所用的研究材料主要基于 2007 年秋季至 2009 年春季四个学期的实际教学。

Volle（2005）指出，远程的外语教学必须包括语言教学的各个方面，即：阅读、词汇、语法、写作、听力、文化以及口语表达（p. 146）。笔者的二年级网络汉语课程设计便是如此。课程所选用的教材为《中文听说读写》第二册（*Integrated Chinese*，Level I Part 2，Cheng & Tsui Publish Company）。这套教材共三册，分初、中、高不同水平，每册包括课本、练习本、汉字练习本和一套 CD 盘。这套教材在北美很多院校广泛使用，笔者的一年级初级汉语课程也是使用这套教材，而 GPC 的学生在学完两年社区大学的基础课程转入其他大学以后大多也会继续使用这套教材。考虑到教材使用的实用性、广泛性和连续性，笔者所开设的汉语网络课程也就同样使用这套教材。如前所述，此网络课程设计的目的主要是让完成了一年级中文课程学习的学生能够继续二年级的初、中水平的中文课程学习，不因上课时间和地点的限制而有所中断，所以二年级的中文网络课程是一年级课堂教学课程的继续。教学理念、程序都与一年级的课堂教学相同，要求学生在语言内容和难度提高的情况下，仍然能够根据教学大纲较好地完成听说读写各个方面的学习任务，达到语言运用的更高水平，在各方面的平均成绩力求达到 B（80分）以上。网络课程的教学程序如下：

1. 学生使用教材预习生词、课文，提出问题。

2. 教师通过网络回答问题，讲解新课的生词，并根据新词引出有关的语法问题或文化问题，或根据词素作词汇扩展，讲解同一词素的不同词及用法和例句。

3. 学生做简单的口语练习，主要是朗读每一课教师给出的一些例句与课文，学习使用新词、新句型。学生可以用录音、与教师面对面或通过电话进行。每人 5—10 分钟。

4. 学生使用教材和网络上的增补材料做有关的词汇、句型练习，并阅读理解课文。

5. 学生使用教材做听力和阅读理解的练习，包括对课文的阅读理解练习。

6. 学生做翻译练习，强化对生词、句式的掌握。

7. 根据课文内容，教师给出相应的题目或要求，学生做综合性的口语对话或表述练习。对话要与教师和其他同学用电话或面对面方式进行，表述则增加了录音方式。总共每人 20—30 分钟。

8. 单元测验。

中文网络课程使用佐治亚州各大学共用的 WebCT Vista（又名 iCollege）Blackboard 网络课程平台。每一课课文、生词、语法以及有关文化背景方面的所有讲解都用 Camtasia 软件将讲解内容（Word 或 PowerPoint 文件）制成文字录像（包括讲解的文字内容和教师的动态讲解声音、光标指示同时出现，请见附录一样本），置于课程网页。学生可用现今电脑皆备的 Flash Player 或 Windows Media Player 打开这些录像文件，边看边听教师的讲解，除看不见教师本人外，与正式的课堂讲解无异，而且可以随时暂停或反复播放。除文化知识背景外，所有的讲解也都附有纯文字版本，学生可以打印下来作为复习材料，不需要另做笔记。选修此网络中文课程，学生也不需要购买或准备其他任何软件设备，以减轻学生负担。学习语言是为了使用语言，学生除了要掌握相应的语言知识以外，还必须掌握语言技能，即将语言应用到实际的交际中去。这就需要大量的各种语言练习，尤其是口语交际的练习。本网络课程所有的练习和作业除了课本中的以外，教师也适量增加了一些。所有的作业与练习要求也都放置在每一课的文档中，学生必须根据课程进度和安排在指定的时间内完成。网络平台中的"日历（Calendar）"有每项任务必须完成的时间提示，教师也会在单元测试与考试之前用 email 和网络 Announcement 提醒学生提前准备。由于在初级汉语课中学生已经学完汉字的基本部件知识和汉语拼音打字，所以在二年级的网络课程中，听力、阅读、语法句型、翻译练习必须靠打汉字完成，在规定期限内 email 给老师或交给老师。听力练习以教材所配置的 CD 为主，尤其是练习课本中的听力部分为学生必须完成的听力作业。为了解决通常的网络语言课程口语练习缺乏的问题，以及避免在其他研究中出现的因技术设备的问题所造成的对口语练习效果的影响（Barr et al.，2005），口语练习的方法尽量考虑简单易用，采用了以下三种选择方式：（1）学生根据每课教师所给的口语练习要求制成个人单独的、表述性的（非对话）口语练习录音文件，email 给教师。
（2）用多方同时通话的电话会议的方式，在指定时间内与教师和其他同一时段的学生通过电话完成对话形式的口语练习。（3）面对面交谈：若干学生在指定的时间与教师会面，当面完成一对一或一对多的对话或表述。每个学生根据需要任选两种或多种方式做口语练习。但结果是几乎所有的学生都是选用第二种或第三种口语练习方式，第一种基本无人选用，尽管有很多口语练习只是要求学生讲述一段故事、观点或者经历，并不需要口语对话。原因将在下文做分析。每周的口语练习时间每人不少于半小时。所有的测验和考试的笔试部分都在网上进行，听力测试由于当时使用的网络平台中做测试的部分无法在文本文件中加入声音并控制学生的播放次数，便和口语测试一样单独分开进行，通过电话或面对面方式让学生听测试材料，但听力的问题回答写在网上的试题答卷中，在规定的时间内完成。

针对华裔学生的高年级网络中文读写课程是笔者对"如何运用信息科技教授语言"，以及"如何让学习者有效地使用信息科技来学习语言"（Shetzer and Warschauer，2000，p. 172）的电子文学课程尝试。读写课以会说中文的华裔学生为主，也有少数曾经在中国长期学习过中文，中文水平达到较高水平的美国学生。这些学生在汉语听说方面都已经没有问题，主要是在中文读写方面作些提高。阅读文章为笔者自编，包括时事新闻消息、网络文章、中国古典文学和现、当代文学名篇选读等。各类体裁均有涉及，类似于中国的大学语文。写作练习包括应用文写作、中文翻译和其他各类体裁、题材的写作。每两周都有一个不同的阅读、写作专题。阅读写作都通过网络完成，所有的阅读作业也都需要学生自己在网络上查询、总结，教师与学生通过email 联系，完成答疑和指导。学生的作业也是用 email 递交，教师修改、点评后用 email 返回给学生，有的放在课程网络上供全班讨论、参考。

本文主要研究汉语语言课的网络教学问题，比较在课堂（面对面）与网络两种不同的教学环境下，中文语言课程的教学结果（outcome）是否能够相同，学生是否同样能够较好地完成学习任务，达到教学目标，以及网络语言课程的设计与教学有什么需要注意的方面。因此，本文主要研究对象为二年级的语言课程，高级班的阅读和写作课程在此不作讨论。教学结果的比较是通过学生在不同教学环境下的各种测试成绩对比来分析，其他方面则通过对参与汉语网络课程学习的学生的问卷调查结果和教师的观测来完成。

三　测试结果

（一）测试成绩比较

受报名选修的学生人数限制，每个学期开设二年级中文网络课程以后，就没有了二年级的中文课堂教学课程，所以无法对网络和课堂教学作横向的比较。但笔者负责 GPC 所有的中文课程，大部分学习中文网络课程的学生都是从上一个学期的一年级初级班升上来的，笔者对他们的学习进程都很了解，可以对他们作纵向的比较，即在教材、教师的教学理念和教学方式、测试的题型与标准尽量保持一致的条件下，比较他们在课堂教学和网络课程不同学习环境下的学习进度和效果。比较的内容包括他们在听说读写各个方面的成绩。比较的方式是看学生们在两种不同的教学环境下，他们的平时测验平均成绩，期末考试成绩和期末口语测试成绩。平时测验是每学完一课，就进行的听力、语法和阅读笔试测验，每学期五次。期末考试包括对一学期所有课程的听力、语法、阅读的笔试。期末口语测试主要考察学生汉语口语的表达程度，主要从以下几个方面来考察：发音、口语语法、表达的连贯性和用词、语法的正确性以及对所学内容的表述程度。每个学生的口试又包括两个部分：（1）学生自己的成段表达。内容由学生自定，但必须与本学期的学习内容有关，必须要用上本学期所学的主要语法点和词汇。（2）教师根据所学内容，随机提问十个问题，学生必须听懂问题，并回答正确。为了比较结果尽可能准确，所选的学生测试结果都是在紧邻的两个学期分别在不同的教学环境下所得的成绩，即上一个学期在课堂教学环境下学习，而下一个学期就在网络教学的环境下学习。中间有学习间隔的学生一概排除。所有的测试方式和标准都尽量一致，只是测试内容的难易程度根据所学习的内容而有不同。

下面是十四位学生分别在不同的教学环境下的测试成绩示意图（见下页）。

1. 平时测验平均成绩
2. 期末考试成绩
3. 口语测试

由于是同组人在不同的教学环境下的测试结果，我们用对应的 t-Test（Paired t-test）来检验两种环境下的成绩是否有不同。下页表格即是 t-Test 的结果和无区别可能性数值"p value"。

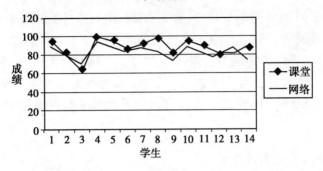

平时测验

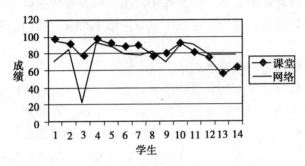

期末考试

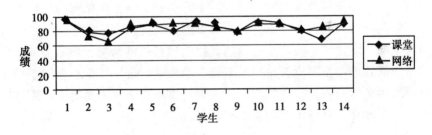

口语测试成绩

课堂和网络教学成绩对比的 t-test 数据表

	测验成绩		期末成绩		口试成绩	
	课堂	网络	课堂	网络	课堂	网络
总数 N	14	14	14	14	14	14
平均成绩	88.4	82.7	83.7	78.7	85.4	85.4
误差标准 sd 值	5.77	18.9	6.5			
平均值 Mean	5.64	5.0	0			
t 值	3.66	0.987	0			
可能性 p 值	0.003	0.341	1			

从上面的图示和表格可以看出：平时测验成绩，网络课程要比课堂教学略低。二者相同的可能性 p 值只有 0.003，即只有 3% 的可能性为二者相同，不同的可能性达 97%。期末考试成绩除个别学生以外，二者基本接近，p 值为 0.341，即二者相同的可能性为 34%，不同的可能性为 66%，不同的可能性大于相同的可能性，但难以作结论。口语测试二者完全相同，p 值为1，可能性达 100%。即在汉语口语方面，课堂教学与网络教学的教学结果没有区别。

（二）测试结果原因分析

上面测试统计数据显示，学生在听、读、写方面的笔试成绩网络课程要低于课堂教学的成绩。如果单纯从测试数据结果来看，我们似乎可以得出这样的结论：

网络教学的结果不及课堂教学。

然而以上数据由于人数有限，误差会较大。而且影响测试结果的原因也较多，需要做具体分析。首先，课程难易程度不同。尽管测试的对象、问题方式和评分标准一致，但由于是作纵向比较，网络课程是二年级内容，比课堂教学的一年级课程程度高。其次，面对面课堂教学的测试都是用手写的形式，而网络课程中的测试都是打字。学生尽管在一年级学了中文打字，但还不熟练，还不太会用连拼方法，速度较手写要慢。网上测试有时间限制，尤其是平时测验的时间是个半小时，与课堂测试时间相同，打字速度慢可能会影响学生的正常发挥。因此，这里的数据结果只能供参考，却不能就此断定网络教学的效果不及课堂教学。对于所有的测试结果还需要结合对学生的观察来做一些具体分析，找出其原因。下表是将所有笔试中的听力、阅读、语法三部分各换算成百分制后的所有平均分数：

	听力	阅读	语法句型
课堂教学平均分数	84.3	89.3	84.6
网络教学平均分数	84.7	90.2	67.2

根据表中的各项平均成绩，我们再来对网络课程的听力、阅读、语法和口语等方面作一些具体分析。

1）听力理解部分　分析所有的测试试卷，发现以下现象：在网络课程的所有笔试中，大部分学生的听力都失分较少。平均分与课堂教学的听力测试平均成绩基本相同，甚至略高。一年级的课堂教学课程，听力测试以单句话为主，比较容易听懂。而二年级的网络课程中，听力测试的难度大大加强了，所听的内容都是一段话或一个小故事，但学生在这一部分的测试平均成绩却并没有下降。通过与学生的交谈发现，在网络课程中，学生们听教材配套 CD 的时间要大大多于他们以前在课堂教学课程中的时间。除了听力内容难易差别所引起的练习时间多少不同外，也有一些其他的原因。在一年级的课堂教学课程中，虽然教师也要求学生课后听 CD，并作为作业完成，但由于在一年级很大一部分学生选修中文课程只是尝试性质，有的甚至只是为了完成学分，所以学习态度不是非常积极，有的学生即使没有完全听懂，听力作业有错误，也不复习、改正，浑水摸鱼现象在所难免。为了不"吓跑"学生，教师在教学上的要求也不是十分严格。在网络课程教学中，学生人数相对较少，每个学生每周都必须在指定时间内做口语会话练习，其中就包括朗读句型与课文、与教师的会话等；而每一课的听力练习部分也同样作为学生的指定作业，必须交给教师批改。选修高一级网络中文课程的学生，多是愿意继续学习中文的学习者，学习态度也比一年级时积极，大多数学生都能够认真完成作业，课后听力练习所花的时间也比较多，相应的，其听力理解水平也有很大提高。要是一年级面对面的课堂教学也能对学生如此严格要求，而学生的学习态度也同样积极的话，其听力理解水平应当也会更好。所以如果两种类型的课程对听力都能有相同的设置和要求，学生学习态度一致，那么教学结果应当也会相似。若有不同，应当是与教学内容的难易、学生的学习态度与练习时间有关，不在于采用何种形式的教学环境。

2）阅读理解部分　网络测试的所有笔试中，阅读理解部分的失分也较少。单只这一部分的平均成绩甚至比面对面的课堂教学阅读测试部分要高 1 分左右。这还是包括了其中一位因各种原因成绩下降至极低的学生的平均成绩，若将这位学生的成绩排除在外，其他 13 位学生在阅读方面的平均成绩比课堂教学要高近 4 分。这说明，在网络教学中，尽管阅读的词汇、内容难度增加了，但学生的阅读水平保持了与课堂教学同样的、甚至更多的进步。分析原因，发现是由于本网络课程的特点和要求所致。首先，教师对生词、语法等的讲解都是文字和声音同时显现的，所有例句和讲解内容都有文字出现。学生在看教师讲解的过程中，无形中提高了汉语字、词、句式的阅读量。其次，在学生每周的口语练习中，每个学生都必须朗读正在学习的课文或句型，这也要求每个学生都必须认识课文中的每个汉字。面对面的课堂教学虽然也如此要求，但朗读课文时由于班级人数较多（26—28 个），是分组进行，教师无法关注到每一个学生。而网络课程的朗读练习虽然也是根据学生的时间来分组，但人数要少得多，教师很容易就能够发现每个学生的问题，这就迫使每个学生都要好好多加练习。练习量的无形增加，自然也带来汉语阅读能力的提高。这也从一方面证明了认知语言学的研究结果，即更多的语言运用可以增强语言习得的效果。

还有一点需要提到的是网络课程中的汉字学习问题。笔者的观察发现，随着汉语阅读能力的提高，学生的汉字识字能力要比一年级大大加强。尤其是所有的书面作业都要求汉字打字或手写汉字完成，这样就促进了学生的汉字辨识能力。但这也带来另外一个问题：由于大多数学生都是用电脑打字完成书面作业，学生们手写汉字的能力或停滞不前，或有所下降。若让他们手写汉字，则很多字只记得某个部分，写出来常常缺笔少画，而且笔顺也不对。对于对外汉语教学中的汉字学习问题，学者们有着不同的观点。有的认为，随着科技的进步，汉字打字的机会要大大多于手写的机会，所以，对于学习汉语的学生只要求会认汉字、会打汉字即可。但另一部分学者则认为，会正确的笔画笔顺，会正确地书写汉字也是学习汉语的必需。认识汉字不等于会写汉字，这也是汉语与其他拼音文字语言的区别。如果手写汉字也作为要求的话，如何设计手写汉字的练习将是汉语网络教学的一个难点所在。现今 SmartBoard 中的一些软件可以通过 iPad，让学生用手指或笔端触屏的方式练习笔画与写汉字，但与汉字教学配套的练习软件目前还没有或极少。随着科技的进步，这一难题也许会很快得到解决。

3）语法句型部分　这一部分的测试包括新的句型结构测试和句子翻译。这一部分大多数学生的失分较多，平均成绩比课堂教学中的语法部分成绩低了 17 分，没有达到较好的学习结果和教学要求。在语法学习方面，二年级的教材中语法难度比较大，象方位表述、结果补语、趋向补语、可能性补语以及"把"字句等都是美国学生比较难以掌握的中文语法难点。除了教材每课附有说明外，教师也把每课的语法要点重新作总结概括，使之简明易懂。所有讲解也都做成了文字录像放在网页的每课之中，有的是与生词同时讲解，有的是单独的文件。然而，通过与学生的交流和问卷调查，教师发现，对语法和句式的学习，很多学生并不重视。很多学生只是看一看教材上的说明，并不去看教师的解说，结果似懂非懂。做口语句型练习时，学生们都是将句型记住，但没有真正理解。也有一些学生自律性较差，对教师指定的需要打字或手写完成的书面作业，特别是句型、翻译方面的练习常常拖欠，不能及时完成。这也造成在测验的时候这一部分失分较多。这说明：（1）对于网络课程，语法方面的学习可能不及面对面教学那样可以在教师的引导下有针对性地练习有效。（2）学习者必须要有较强的自律和自觉学习能力，而教师的严格监督和要求也必不可少。

因此，网络教学在设置时要考虑到如何针对较难的语法点，让学生能够如同在课堂教学中一样有反复练习与使用的机会，尽量多设计一些有针对性的语法练习任务，比如增加包含某一特定语法形式的阅读和口语练习，否则学习效果会不理想。

4）口语表达部分　口语方面的测试是与笔试分开的。如上图 3 所示，课堂教学和网络教学的平均成绩完全一样，t-Test 的数据结果是 100%，完全一致。这似乎证实了其他有关的研究结果（Blake et al，2008）。其实这也与在本网络课程设置时对口语练习的重视和安排分不开。网络课程中每人每周半个小时与教师的口语练习要求，使得每个学生不得不对口语练习相当重视，而且练习的时间也大大超出了课堂教学中的口语练习机会。口语练习除了对话以外，还有成段表达的练习。课堂教学的课程每周总共才 3 小时，而且每班的学生人数也要大大高于网络课程的人数（26—28 人），虽然教师在教课的过程中尽量使用汉语，并设计了各种活动或任务来让学生尽可能地练习说汉语，但每个学生能在课堂上单独练习口语的时间还是十分有限，课后的练习时间和机会也是因人而异，完全靠学生本人的安排和自觉。所以课堂教学中的口语练习反而不及网络教学，这也是为什么在本网络教学中，课程的内容难度提高了，但学生的口语表达能力也能随之提高没有下降的原因。这也说明，在设计网络课程时，若能够重视口语练习的设计，对学生进行口语练习量化的要求，采用多样化的口语练习和语言活动形式，是可以避免网络课程口语练习机会的不足的。

以上各项分析表明，虽然在笔试测试方面网络课程要比课堂教学课程的成绩低，但原因主要是网络课程设计时，语法和句型教学方面的练习机会与要求不足，需要有针对性地多设计一些相关的练习。其他听说读写方面，受测试的学生都满足了教学要求，取得了与课堂教学同样的进步，在阅读与辨认汉字方面甚至有所超出。因此，如果网络课程能够设置得当，对学生在听说读写各个方面都能安排充分的学习、练习和使用的机会，对每一部分的练习都作出量化的要求和标准，那么网络汉语语言课程的教学结果（outcome）若不能超出也应当不会低于课堂教学的结果。

四　问卷调查

网络汉语课程的教学结果虽然能够做到与课堂教学相当，但是是否与课堂教学一样有效率？学生们对此的看法又是如何？为什么？有什么必须重视的问题？作为教师，我们也有必要从学习者的立场、观点来分析网络教学课程。笔者在每个学期结束，都会给学生发一份问卷调查，以了解学生对网络课程的各种看法，如网络课程是否与课堂课程一样便于学习，有哪些问题和困难，有什么建议等等。现收回 24 份回复，其中学语言的学生 18 份，高级班中文读写的学生 6 份。下面对问卷调查的结果与原因分别作分析、研究。

（一）课堂学习还是网络学习

所有学习中文读写的华裔学生都对中文网络课程持赞赏和支持态度，认为网络课程不但提供了学习时间和地点上的便利，而且课程的读写练习对他们的中文水平提高很有帮助，尤其是很多练习需要学生自己上网查询资料，学习效果比单纯的教师课堂讲授要好，学到的内容更多。附近其他的大学还没有类似的中文课程，希望这类中文课程还能够继续开设。这也从一方面证实了其他的一些研究结论：计算机辅助教学和网络教学有助于语言读写方面的练习和提高（Sullivan，1998），对学生阅读的及时、详细的修改和评论对阅读的进步也很重要（Murphy，2007）。由此也可以看出，语言的读写课程似乎更适用于运用网络进行。

但因为本文主要是分析汉语语言的网络课程教学问题，对中文读写这一部分的网络课程就不作探讨。下面主要对二年级学习网络语言课程的学生的问卷调查结果作些分析、研究。

问题	回答数量	答案
课程设置和教材选用是否合适？	18	很合适
	0	不合适
教师的文字录像讲解是否有用？	18	非常有帮助
	0	没有太大帮助
网页上教师的讲解是否每课都看？	11	每课都看
	7	有的看，有的不看
网络课程更适合哪方面的学习（可选多项）？	2	都适合
	14	阅读
	12	书写
	6	听力
	2	口语

问题	回答数量	答案
学习网络汉语课程最困难的是	4	语法
	4	书写
	6	口语练习
	3	不懒惰，保持进度
	1	无困难
如果同时有汉语网络课程和课堂课程，你选哪种？	14	选课堂教学课程
	4	选网络课程
选课堂课程或者网络课程的原因		选课堂课程是因为：更容易学；可以在课堂上随时跟教师和同学交流；听老师的课堂讲授更清楚；有更多的听说机会。 选网络课程的原因：时间上很有弹性，适合自己的时间安排；老师对每个人单独的辅导和练习比对整个班的讲课要好；教师与学生能经常通过网络联系，提供帮助。

选课堂课程或者网络课程的原因是因为：更容易学；可以在课堂上随时跟教师和同学交流；听老师的课堂讲授更清楚；有更多的听说机会。

选网络课程的原因：时间上很有弹性，适合自己的时间安排；老师对每个人单独的辅导和练习比对整个班的讲课要好；教师与学生能经常通过网络联系，提供帮助。18 位二年级网络语言课程的学生问卷回答如表中所列。从表内的问卷回答可以看出，尽管汉语网络课程的教学能够做到与课堂教学结果相当，可是大部分的学生还是更喜欢课堂教学。在问卷调查所收回的答案中，有 78%（14 位）的学生表示更愿意选课堂教学课程。大部分的学生认为，网络课程适合读写方面的学习，而不适合其他，尤其是语言口语方面的学习。这证实了其他相关的研究。Jin（2009）对三种不同网络教学工具的汉语教学、学习研究也指出："面对面的课堂交流仍然是学习者所最喜欢的方式。"（p. 41）那么造成这一现象的原因又是什么？今后的网络语言课程设计又有哪些应该注意的方面？

（二）问卷结果分析

针对问卷调查的结果，我们有必要作更进一步的分析，找出问题和原因所在。对学生们的各项回答，也需要做具体讨论，发现值得重视的问题。

1）语言的特点所致　语言是交际的工具。任何语言的使用与交流都需要及时的回应与信息反馈，尤其是口语交流方面。语言的理解、交流和沟通不仅仅是声音的问题，还牵涉到交流者之间的视线交流、表情、手势、体态等等。越是语言水平低的学生越需要依赖这些非声音元素的帮助和提示来理解和表达目标语言。问卷调查的结果说明，对语言课程来说，学习者更倾向于选择自然的学习环境，不习惯于机械模式。问卷调查中，有近一半（6位）的学生认为，网络课程不适合语言口语的练习。在本网络课程中一个很有意思的现象就是前面所提到的学生们选择口语练习的方式。尽管教师给出了三种口语练习方式，即录音方式、电话会议方式和面对面交谈方式，让学生任选，可是录音方式却几乎无人选用，只有一位学生因为旅行去了国外，不方便用其他方式而用了一次。其原因不仅仅是信息设备和技术问题（录音需要配备话筒，制成声音文档）。在我们所使用的网络课程平台 WebCT 中配有 Winbar 这一网络对话软件装置，教师也曾让学生学习使用，但是学生们都不愿意用，而且由于当时的软件版本较低，使用效果也不理想。即使是用电话和面对面的口语练习方式，更多的学生还是尽可能用后一种，电话方式也只有口语水平较高的学生和受距离、时间限制的学生使用，大部分的学生都表示更愿意跟教师做面对面交谈，即使口语练习的主题是以学生表述为主，对话较少也是如此。学生们认为自然的、面对面的交流更容易懂，谈话更自然，更有利于他们的口语表达。语言本身的特点决定了语言教学和学习需要一个轻松、活泼的语言环境。课堂教学可以让教师随时了解学生的反应，掌握和调整课程进度，调整讲述内容和方式，以帮助学生理解、掌握。学生也可以随时提问，学生和学生之间也便于交流和互相帮助，而且教师还可以随时插入其他话题来调节课堂气氛，使之有张有弛。而这一切都是目前的网络教学所难以做到的。尤其是当学习者在目标语言掌握还很不够的情况下，很难让他们相互之间用目标语言进行网络上的练习和沟通。这也是学生们觉得网络汉语课程中语法、书写和口语学习是难点，而课堂学习更容易的缘故。

2）学习的效率问题　很多学生也反映他们花在网络课程上的时间要比课堂教学课程多，因为很多在课堂教学中可以集体完成的练习，在网络课程中每个学生都必须单独完成。这也是很多学生更愿意选择面对面课堂学习的原因。Stepp-Greany（2002）的研究也发现了这一点。另外，课堂教学可以让学生随时与同学、老师交流，随时解决问题，不需要等候。这一点也是网络教学所不及。而且从教师这一方面来说，花在网络教学上的时间也比单纯的面对面课堂教学要多得多。从网络课程的设计到教学，教师要花费比课堂教学多 2—3 倍的时间来完成。同样的练习，由于学生们的学习时间不同，不得不分开重复进行；对学生们的问题解答也常常因为不同的对象会重复多次，更何况教师有时候还要花费时间帮助学生解决某些设备和技术性的问题。这说明，网络教学虽然在最终能够取得与课堂教学一样的教学结果，达到教学目的，但这是建立在多花教学时间的基础上的，不如课堂教学有效率。

3）学习的自觉性问题　网络课程设置的目的是为学习者提供时间和地点上的便利。然而这种便利并不一定就会带来有效的学习结果。有研究表明，远程的网络语言教学要求学生有高度的自觉性和独立的学习能力，否则很容易半途而废，导致中途退学（Carr，2000；Dreyer，Bangeni & Nel，2005）。这一现象在笔者的汉语网络课程中也有体现。每个学期都有学生不能按时完成作业和学习内容，从而造成跟不上进度，最后不得不中断课程学习。在问卷调查中，有三位学生表示，避免懒惰，准时学习，跟上课程安排进度也是他们在网络课程学习时的难点所在。因此，网络教学虽然是由学习者自己来安排学习时间，但也还必须对学生有严格的监督和要求，并能给学生提供随时的帮助和指导。在本网络课程学习的过程中，学生们之间的互动与交流非常不够。虽然教师每个学期都把学生们的 email 公布在课程网页上，便于学生们的互相帮助和交流，学生们也可以利用 WebCT Vista 中的 Discussion Board 讨论板作交流，然而在没有教师督促的情况下，几乎没有学生去做。Beauvois（1998）所发现的在网络课程中，学生们相互之间的互动（interaction）要比课堂教学课程多这一现象并没有在笔者的网络课程中出现。这一方面可能是由于学生受汉语水平和时间限制所造成，另一方面也需要教师更进一步的督促和引导，比如将其加入教学大纲（syllabus）的要求之中，给以一定的评分，不能仅仅是让学生自主决定参与与否。

4）教师的作用　问卷调查中，要求学生解释为何会更愿意选择课堂或网络课程学习。这是一个开放型问题，问卷中没有选项，学生可以根据自己所想，自由写下答案。然而，学生们在解释时，都把教师的作用作为原因之一或主要原因。学生选择课堂教学是因为可以更好地与教师交流，可以更清楚地明白教师的讲解。而选择网络课程的学生也把教师的作用列为其选择的原因：教师可以与学生经常性地保持联系，可以有针对性地帮助每一个学生解决问题。这都说明，无论是课堂教学还是网络教学，教师都起着极为重要的作用。这不仅仅是在口语练习方面。正如 Zähner 等文中所指出的，教师在帮助完成语言型、任务型以及技术方面的活动中都极为重要（Zähner et al.，2000）。其他一些相关的研究（Glisan et al.，1998；McGrath，1998；Stepp-Greany，2002）也都证实了教师在科技环境下的教学中的重要性。只有教师的参与，才能对每个学生的学习状况作充分的了解，才能随时根据学生的状况对课程内容和进度随时作调整，才能在学生遇到困难的时候对学生提供帮助和鼓励，才能对学生随时监督使之能够按时完成学习任务，也才能使得网络课程人性化和自然化。甚至在学生遇到技术问题的时候，也需要教师来帮助解决。这不仅牵涉到教师有关课程的知识问题，还涉及了教师本身对最新的科技设备软件的了解和使用能力。

Ehrman（1998）、Price（1991）等人的研究还指出了教师与学生之间的关系在语言学习中的重要性。教师和学生之间建立相互信赖的朋友式关系，能够激发学生学习的热情，乐于学习，也会更努力地去学习（Ehrman 1998）。而教师朋友式的帮助比权威性的指令更能减少学习者的焦虑感，从而学习效果也更加有效（Price 1991）。在网络教学中，如果教师能够通过网络经常性地与学生保持联系，反而比课堂教学更容易建立一种朋友式的关系。Jiang & Ramsay（2005）的研究证明了这一点，而这也在笔者的网络汉语课程中表现出来。作为教师，笔者与学习网络课程的每个学生的沟通与联系要比与学习课堂课程的学生多得多，几乎每天都要用 email 回复学生的各类问题。每周的口语练习由于学生们的时间不同，大多也是与一个学生或若干个学生进行。这就无形中拉近了与学生们的距离。很多时候，教师与学生不仅是交流学习问题，也会作为朋友谈谈其他话题。有的学生因为距离较远，平时不会跟教师见面，但都会主动找一个机会专程来教师的办公室与教师见面、交谈；有的学生做口语练习时，常常把他们的男（女）朋友也带来，希望通过教师的影响，得到他们的朋友对学习中文的支持。有 Facebook 的学生都把教师作为邀请对象，希望教师能够加入他们的网上交流。这也从学生们的角度反映出他们对与教师的关系的重视。因此，网络课程虽然是作为一种远程教学的手段，却反而能够拉近与学生们之间的关系。而网络课程教学，教师的角色和积极参与仍必不可少。

五　总结

本文在若干学期实际的汉语网络教学基础上，对汉语的网络语言课程作了研究、分析和总结。研究表明，汉语课程若能设置得当，兼顾语言的听说读写各个方面的教学与练习，那么网络课程的教学结果（outcome）应当能与课堂教学相同，并达到预期的教学目标，然而效率却不及面对面的课堂教学，学生的学习时间和教师的教学时间都要比课堂教学多。网络教学由于主要是面对电脑由学生自主进行，语言教学又有其特殊性，口语练习需要有轻松、自然的交流环境，而不是只对着机器进行；汉字的书写练习也是电脑打字所不能替代。这一切都造成了网络汉语教学的局限性。就如同 Simonson 等所指出的，远程的网络语言教学不是对所有学习者在所有的环境下都合适（Simonson et al.，2000）。也正因为如此，很多汉语学习者更倾向于选择课堂教学课程，而不是网络教学课程，尤其是在语言学习的初、中级阶段。正如 Yao（2009）所指出的，汉语网络教学需要设计更多训练表述（写和说）与相互交流（包括所有的听、说、读、写）技能的活动与练习，以及能够给予学习者有效的、指导性的反馈功能（p. 19）。相信今后电脑、网络科技的发展能够解决这些问题。正如 Hutchby（2001）一书中所指出的，科技产生不了人类，但人类却能产生将技术产品与人类会话结合的科技（p. 206）。当今的网络和软件技术的发展，已经可以将任务型教学法运用到汉语网络课程中。例如，可以运用 Skype 来做远程一对一或成组的口语对话练习，甚至可以让汉语学习者与远在中国的中国朋友或学生作面对面交流；使用 Voice-Thread 网站可以做口语或书面讨论，做口语音像演示；运用 SmartBoard 中的软件可以设计汉语的智力游戏与互动练习等。现在，为网络教育课程所设计的软件和网站也越来越多。再说，网络教学不受时间、距离的限制，网络交流也比其他方式便捷。更进一步，网络教学使教学从以教师为主导的教学方式转向由学习者为主导的主动学习方式，从而能够更好地适应学习者的不同需求，更好地达到学习目的。这些也都是网络课程的优点所在，也是网络语言教学会进一步往前发展的大势所趋。尤其是在北美对外汉语的中学、高中课程教学中，由于教师的匮乏与学生的分散，展开网络与课堂相结合的教学方式不失为一个有效的解决办法。因此，汉语的网络教学需要更多学者的参与、研究和探索，尤其是在汉字教学、练习，句型教学以及口语练习方面。归纳而言，本文对本人的汉语网络教学的研究可以给出以下几个方面的总结：

1. 如果网络课程设置得当，能充分包括各方面的练习需要，则听说读写各方面的教学结果（outcome）与课堂教学相当，然而在效率上有所不如。

2. 对于汉语语言课程的学习，初、中阶段的学习者可能更喜欢选用课堂学习方式，而非网络课程。将来的汉语网络课程要更多地考虑语言人性化、自然化的设计和互动、交流问题以及如何及时反馈的问题。

3. 汉语网络课程可以提高学习者的汉字识字水平。

4. 即使是网络教学课程，教师的作用仍然非常重要，不可替代。网络语言课程的效果离不开学习者严格的自律和教师的严格监督与要求。

本文的研究虽然有若干学期的实际教学为基础，但由于受到选修中文课程的学生人数的限制，能用于研究的材料还不够充分，一些观点也不能作为结论。而且本网络课程的设计与教学也存在一些缺陷与片面化，所得的结果也不能够作用于所有的网络课程，更多更深入系统的相关研究还是必须的。这里只是抛砖引玉，提供若干经验与教训，以期待将来同行之间有更进一步的探讨。

附录一　网络课程文字声音共显讲解样本示意

1. 词汇讲解（用 Flasher player 的文字、声音显示）

2. 语法讲解（用 Windows Media Player 的文字、声音显示，PowerPoint file）

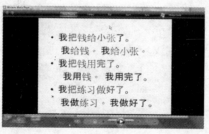

附录二　口语练习题样本

第十二课　在饭馆
口语练习题：
I. 对话 Dialogue
Ask each other:

1. 你喜欢吃什么饭菜？

2. 你常常在哪儿吃饭？

3. Read the menu in the Lesson 12 folder, do role play, ask and tell what the dishes you want to order. The "client" must at least pick one dish, one soup and one drink. The "waiter/waitress" should give more suggestions.

II. 表述 Narrative stories

Tell the experience that you ate at a Chinese restaurant last time. In your story, please tell：

1. 你是跟谁去的？是去吃中饭还是吃晚饭？

2. 饭馆在哪儿？叫什么名字？

3. 你点了什么菜？

4. 一共多少钱？贵不贵？

5. 你喜欢这家饭馆的饭菜吗？

6. 你会不会再去这家饭馆？

参考文献

Barr, D., Leakey, J. & Ranchoux A. (2005). Told Like It Is! An Evaluation of Anintegrated Oral Development Pilot Project. *Language Learning* & *Technology*, 9 (3).

Beauvois, M. (1998). Conversations in Slow Motion：Computer-Mediated.

Communication in the Foreign Language Classroom. *The Canadian Modern Language Review*, 54 (2).

Blake, R., Wilson, N. L., Cetto, M. & Pardo-Ballester, C. (2008). Measuring Oral.

Proficiency in Distance, Face-to-face, and Blended Classrooms. *Language Learning* & *Technology*, 12 (3).

Carr, S. (2000). As Distance Education Comes of Age, the Challenge Is Keeping Up with the Students. *The Chronicle of Higher Education*, 46 (23), A39-A41. From http：//chronicle. com/free/v46/i23/23a00101. htm.

Chapelle, C. A. (1998). Multimedia CALL：Lessons to Be Learned from Research on Instructed SLA. *Language Learning* & *Technology*, 2 (1).

Chapelle, C. A. (2001). *Computer Applications in Second Language Acquisition：Foundations for Teaching, Testing and Research*. Cambridge：Cambridge University Press.

Dreyer, C. , Bangeni, N. , & Nel, C. （2005）. A Framework for Supporting Students Studying English Via a Mixed-mode Delivery System. *Distance Education and Languages*: *Evolution and Change*, B. Homberg, M. Shelley and C. White （Eds.）. Clevedon, U. K. : Multilingual Matters.

Edbert, J. L. & Petrie, G. M. （2005）. *CALL Research Perspectives*. Mahwah, NJ, USA: Lawrence Erlbaum Associates, Inc. Ehrman, M. （1998）. The Learning Alliance: Conscious and Unconscious Aspects of the Second Language Teacher's Role. *System*, 26 （1）.

Felix, U. （2001）. The Web's Potential for Language Learning: The Student's Perspective. *ReCALL*, 13 （1）.

Fotos, S. & Browne, C. M. （2004）. *New Perspectives on CALL for Second Language Classrooms*. Mahwah, NJ, USA: Lawrence Erlbaum Associates, Inc.

Glisan, G. , Dudt, K. , & Howe, M. （1998）. Teaching Spanish Through Distance Education: Implications of a Pilot Study. *Foreign Language Annals*.

Hutchby, I. （2001）. *Conversation and Technology*. Cambridge, England: Polity Press. Jiang, W. & Ramsay, G. （2005）. Rapport-Building Through CALL in the Teaching Chinese as a Foreign Language: An Exploratory Study. *Language Learning* & *Technology*, 9 （2）.

Jin, Hong Gang （2009） Participatory Learning in Internet Web Technology: A Study of Three Web Tools in the Context of CFL Learning. Journal of the Chinese Language Teachers Association, 44.

Levy, M. & Stockwell, G. （2006）. *CALL Dimensions*: *Options and Issues in Computer-Assisted Language Learning*. Mahwah, NJ, USA: Lawrence Erlbaum Associates, Inc.

McGrath, B. （1998）. Partners in Learning: Twelve Ways Technology Changes the Teacher-Student Relationship. *Technological Horizon in Education*, 25 （9）.

Murphy, P. （2007）. Reading Comprehension Exercises Online: The Effects of Feedback, Proficiency and Interaction. *Language Learning* & *Technology*, 11 （3）.

Price, M. L. （1991）. The Subjective Experience of Foreign Language Anxiety: Interviews with Highly Anxious Students. *Language Anxiety*: *From Theory and Research to Classroom Implications*. E. K. Horwitz and D. J. Young （Eds.）. Englewood Cliffs, NJ: Prentice Hall.

Shetzer, H & Warschauer, M. （2000）. An Electronic Literacy Approach to Network-Based Language Teaching. *Network-Based Language Teaching*: *Concepts and Practice*. Mark Warschauer and Richard Kern （Eds.）, Cambridge University Press.

Simonson, M. , Smaldino, S. , Albright, M. , & Zvacek, S. （2000）. *Teaching and Learning at a Distance*: *Foundations of Distance Education*. Upper Saddle river,

NJ：Merrill/Prentice Hall.

Stepp-Greany, J. (2002). Student Perceptions on Language Learning in a Technological Environment：Implications for the New Millennium. *Language Learning & Technology*, 6 (1).

Sullivan, N. (1998). Developing Critical Reading and Writing Skills. *Language Learning Online：Theory and Practice in the ESL and L2 Computer Classroom*, Janet Swaffar, Susan Romano, Philip Markley & Katherine Arens (Eds.). Austin, TX, USA：Labyrinth Publications.

Volle, L. M. (2005). Analyzing Oral Skills in Voice E-mail and Online Interviews. *Language Learning & Technology*, 9 (3).

Yao, Tao-chung (2009). The Current Status of Chinese CALL in the United States. *Journal of the Chinese Language Teachers Association*, 44.

Zähner, C., Fauverge, A. & Wong, J. (2000). Task-Based Language Learning Via Audiovisual Networks：The LEVERAGE Project. *Network-Based Language Teaching：Concepts and Practice*. Mark Warschauer and Richard Kern (Eds.), Cambridge University Press.

自然语言处理文献述评

《中文自然语言处理导论》书评
Review of *Introduction to Chinese Natural Language Processing*

姜　松　Jiang, Song　美国夏威夷大学

University of Hawaii at Mānoa United States sjiang@ hawaii. edu

Kam Fai Wong, Wenjie Li, Ruifeng Xu, Zheng-sheng Zhang (2010). Introduction to Chinese Natural Language Processing. In Hirst Graeme (Series editor), Synthesis Lectures on Human Language Technologies. Morgan & Claypool Publishers. x + 148 pp. Paperback ISBN：978 – 1 – 59829 – 932 – 8. e-book ISBN：978 – 1 – 59829 – 933 – 5.

Introduction to Chinese Natural Language Processing (《中文自然语言处理导论》) 是由 Morgan & Claypool Publishers 出版的 "人类语言技术综合讲座" (Synthesis Lectures on Human Language Technologies) 系列中的一部。这套英文系列丛书立足于自然语言处理、计算语言学、信息检索、自然语言人机接口等与人类语言技术相关的学科，以综合讲座的形式介绍各个学科领域的发展概貌、着重突出各学科最新出现的重要的技术和方法及其在相关研究中的实际应用。人类自然语言计算机处理作为一个学科已有几十年的发展历史。随着计算机和互联网技术的成熟和普及，人类语言活动中各种语言材料的搜集、加工、存储和提取正变得更加迅捷与便利，进而带动了自然语言计算机处理学科的飞跃性发展。但从自然语言处理的整个学科的发展来看，这一领域的主要研究成果大都是在以英语为主的西方语言的基础上取得的。相比之下，中文的自然语言处理研究起步较晚，基础薄弱，且由于汉语与英语在类型学上的显著差异，面临着许多特殊的挑战。随着汉语地位在全球范围内的提升，特别是汉语在国际互联网和商业软件开发上使用比例的飞速增加，商业信息提取、企业与客户关系管理、机器翻译、自动文摘、汉语语音识别、语言学研究、辅助汉语教学系统的开发等领域越来越需要从汉语出发的自然语言处理技术的支持与跟进。在这样的背景下，《中文自然语言处理导论》一书的出版正是适应了日益增长的对汉语语言处理技术的需求，从汉语类型学的角度深化和扩展了普通自然语言处理的研究，为丰富和完善自然语言处

理学科的理论与实践做出了一份重要贡献。

全书主体内容共分八章，另外包括一个列举与中文自然语言处理相关的语言学资源的附录、一个参考文献以及一份作者简介。全书共分八章，主体内容大致可分为三个部分：基本概念（第一、第二章）、自动识别（第四、第五章）和汉语语词的语义特征（第六、第七、第八章）。

作为全书的导引，第一章首先在人类自然语言、普通语言学、计算语言学的大背景下，把自然语言处理定位为一门将语言理论转化为实际应用的技术，并将这一技术在语言处理过程中的实施平台定位在词法、句法和语义三个层面上。作者以汉语形态分析为基础，通过一系列具体的实例，列举出汉语的形态特征给汉语语言处理造成的困难和挑战，如汉语词的切分、词类标注、句法与语义歧异等。基于汉英两种语言在词语层面上的形态区别，以及由此决定的对两种语言处理的不同的技术要求，作者确立了汉语的形态分析在本书中的核心主导地位。

第二章从普通语言学的角度，介绍汉语的字、语素和词的概念，汉语词的形成过程以及汉语词的基本特征。作者首先提供了汉语的字、语素和词三个核心形态单位的语言学定义，并详尽论述了三者之间的区别与联系。作者指出字为汉语的书写单位，呈线性等距排列，不具备代表独立语素的功能。语素为最小的语义单位，通常为单音节，以单一汉字的形式出现，可经过语素组合形成词。词是介于语素与词组之间的语言单位，受到分布调控与词汇整体性的制约。在本章接下来的篇幅中，作者详细描写了汉语合成词的构词方式。作者首先根据词的音节数量，按双音节、三音节、四音节三类分别描写，然后讨论带有词缀（包括前缀、后缀以及动词后缀）和由重叠构成的合成词的构词特点，最后讨论了离合词的特征。通过以上详尽的分析，作者指出，汉语复杂多样的构词方式是造成分词困难的重要原因，是汉语自然语言处理中无法回避的关键所在。这一章为全书提供了一个必要的语言学基础，明确了汉语语言处理所面对的关键问题。

作为第二章的深化和延续，第三章在自然语言处理框架下具体勾勒出直接造成技术处理困难的汉语语词的语言学个性与文本特征。作者将这一章所涉及到的影响汉语机器分析的汉语特征归纳为汉字、文本和语言学特征三类。与汉字有关的影响技术处理的特征包括：汉字总量的不确定性、繁简转化、异体字、方言用字、汉字编码的多样化。与文本有关的特征包括：排印格式和标点符号。与语言学特征相关的包括：缺乏语法和词性的形态标记、同音异义词与同形异义词、歧义以及以缩略语、专用人名地名、音译词、地域变体以及风格变体为代表的未登录词。第二和第三章对困扰机器处理的汉语语言与文本特征的分析为以后各章有关技术性处理对策的讨论做好了准备。

第四章集中探讨汉语的分词问题。分词被认为是汉语语言处理的第一步，分词的精确度直接关系到分析结果的优劣。作者首先通过对比英汉两种语言在分词上的差异，指出汉语句子无标记的线性字符排列决定了汉语分词必须解决确认字词顺序、加注词的分界的问题，并以此为出发点，为汉语分词归纳出一个技术性的定义。作者随后利用具体实例，说明汉语分词过程中存在的两大挑战：对歧义和未登录词的处理。针对这两大挑战，作者将现有的汉语分词方法归纳为两大类：以字为基础的方法和以词为基础的方法，详细比较、讨论了这两类方法在计算上的差别以及各自的优缺点，并着重介绍了能有效解决分词中歧义问题的两种计算方法：词典法与统计法。此外，作者还在这一章中，介绍了现有的三个大型语料库所采用的汉语分词的评估标准。这三个语料库分别为：北京大学中文系现代汉语语料库、台湾中研院现代汉语平衡语料库和宾夕法尼亚大学汉语树形结构语料库。最后，作者对一些免费的汉语分词工具进行了简要的介绍。

第五章讨论的是未登录词的识别问题。作者认为在汉语分词过程中出现的未登录词的识别问题主要是由于所需处理的未登录词尚未加入到作为分词依据的分词词典中，导致分词程序无法找到针对未登录词的分词依据，因而无法作出有效的分词判断。汉语新词的不断出现也是造成未登录词问题的一方面的原因。汉语新词的产生主要是以语素合成和词缀附加的方式实现的。未登录词主要是指那些指代人名、地名以及机构等的专用名词、特定范畴内的技术性名词以及缩略语等。作者在这一章中讨论了识别各类未登录词的计算方法，并着重介绍了对人名、组织机构名称和地名的识别方法。识别未登录词的形式依据主要包括：常用名称的内部结构、名称中的常用字以及文本信息等。

在接下来的第六至第八章，作者将讨论的重心从汉语语词的结构层面转移到语义层面。对于缺乏形态标记的汉语来说，比起形式结构，语义在语言理解过程中所起的作用似乎更为关键。正因为如此，不少语言学家将汉语归为语义型语言。不考虑语义的因素，许多汉语机器处理的任务都不可能获得满意的结果。第六章开篇介绍了与词汇语义学相关的基本概念，如：义元、多义、同义、反义、上位、下位、整体、部分、专指等，并对接下几章将涉及到的语义框架、连用语、动词配价（施事、受事、工具等）进行了说明。这一章的主要篇幅集中对三种有代表性的汉语分类辞典进行介绍和评价。这三种辞典是：《同义词词林》、知网（HowNet）和《中英文概念词典》。《同义词词林》是中国第一部纸质现代汉语语义类词典，它以三层等级树形结构模式勾画出所收常用词的语义关系，由多所大学输入汉语电脑词库后，被广泛应用在写作、翻译和自然语言处理上。知网是一个以汉语和英语的词语所代表的概念为描述对象，揭示概念与概念之间以及概念所具有的属性之间的关系为内容的常识知识库。作者通过与英文 WordNet 的对比，总结出知网的独到之处：以义元为分析单位、以图形结构描写语义关系、以英汉词汇概念的对比为分析基础。《中英文概念词典》是由北京大学计算语言所开发的英汉双语词汇概念知识库。它采用 WordNet 的结构布局，在保证与 WordNet 兼容的同时，对算法和功能进行了改进。这些改进包括更细化的名词分类、更精密的关系描写、真实语料库的支持以及具有统计学意义的量化处理等。

第七章主要论述了与汉语连用语（collocation）相关的基本概念，包括定义、特征、类别以及语料来源。针对自然语言研究领域对于连用语同现搭配这一概念的不同理解和争议，作者首先列举了一系列以英语为基础的连用语的不同定义，指出这些不同的定义源于定义者对连用语不同特点的关注。通过比对，作者进一步总结出汉语连用语与英语连用语在宏观层面上的显著不同：即汉字串的连续性、汉语字词使用的灵活性和以实词为主要对象的连用语提取特点，并据此给出了一个针对汉语的，较为严密的定义：连用语是一个由两个或两个以上词语组合而成的，具有句法和语义关联，能够重复出现并符合使用习惯的表达结构（p. 98）。以这一定义为出发点，在接下来的篇幅中，作者从定性、定量、类别（成语、结合度等）以及语料来源等方面详细论述了汉语连用语的具体特性，为下一章讨论汉语连用语的自动提取方法和运算规则奠定了基础。

第八章重点介绍汉语连用语的自动提取方法。作者首先在本章导言部分指出汉语连用语的自动提取过程实际上是连用语提取技术在汉语自动分词和词类标记上的具体应用。根据主要的区别特征和目标搜寻策略的不同，作者将当今通行的自动提取技术划分为以下三种：统计提取、句法提取和语义提取。统计提取以目标关键词为切入点，将在关键词周边限定范围内出现的字词列为候选连用语，进而依据关键词与其周边字词组合的统计显著性确定连用语。句法提取利用关键词与连用语的组合必须合乎句法规范这一要求，根据预先设定的句法规则，通过句法剖析程序（parser）对目标关键词与同现词的组合进行过滤，然后再依照统计显著性确定连用语。语义提取利用语义限定测试来确定连用语。语义限定测试主要包括同义词测试和翻译测试两种。同义词测试利用同义词替换的有限性，以排除的方式提取。如果在语料库中某一关键词的同义组合出现频率超过一定的限度，其连用语的合法性将会被质疑并可据此予以排除。翻译测试利用候选连用语的非组合性特点进行提取。如果一个词语的组合不能逐字翻译成另一种语言，与其搭配的字词则被认为不具有组合性，因而可据此确立该组合的连用词地位。针对汉语连用语的语法特性，作者又特别介绍了一种综合性的提取方法：类别提取。这一方法主要是针对不同类型的连用语而设计的。它综合了以上三种基本的提取方式，包含六种不同的运算程序。提取过程中，首先由程序确定被检测的搭配的类型，而后根据检测结果，选取匹配的运算方式进行连用语提取。作者指出，跟前面三种单一的基本提取方法相比，类别提取更适合汉语的特点，更能获得理想的提取结果。

作为一部汉语自然语言处理导论性质的专著，本书从汉语的实际出发，选取汉语的形态分析作为全书的切入点，针对汉语自然语言处理中存在的难题，按照字词切分、词类标记、未登录词识别、语义分析和连用语自动提取编排章节，展开论述，对现有的处理方案进行了详尽的归纳、总结和评估，既反映了当前汉语处理技术的概貌，又突出了学科的重点成就。

本书结构完整、条理清晰、论述缜密、循序渐进。特别是作者利用汉语描写词汇学和语义学的研究成果，通过与英语的对比，突出汉语中制约技术处理的语言特征，为讨论技术性处理方案作出铺垫的行文方式，将汉语语言学与汉语计算处理自然地联系起来，增加了本书的目的性和可读性。

作为英文系列丛书中的一部，本书的出版有着十分特殊的意义。它将汉语自然语言研究的成果以专著的形式介绍给英语世界，为整个人类语言技术领域提供了一个汉语案例，也为英语世界的同行了解汉语自然语言处理的现状和成果打开了一个窗口、为进一步的技术交流奠定了基础。

本书设定的阅读对象为已经具备初级语言处理知识的读者，因此对从事自然语言处理、计算语言学、信息检索、机器翻译、网络文字处理等工作的专业人员有着重要的参考价值。不仅如此，作为一部论述清晰、内容翔实的学科导论，本书对于自然语言处理、计算机与应用、汉语应用语言学、作为第二语言的汉语教学等专业的学生来说也可以作为理想的入门教科书来使用。此外，本书对有志于或正在从事计算机辅助汉语教学研究的汉语教育工作者也具有一定的指导意义。计算机辅助教材编写、现行课本的分析研究、汉语水平等级大纲的制定、汉语教学词频统计、汉语中介语语料库的建立等，都离不开汉语自然语言处理技术的支持。对于不具备专业的语言处理知识的大多数汉语教育工作者来说，本书不仅能为他们提供一个了解相关技术知识的途径，而且能够使他们从计算分析的角度获得对汉语特征的新认识，提高教学应用程序的开发与评估能力，因而值得在此推介。然而，对于对外汉语教育者来说，如果本书能在介绍和评价一些汉语处理工具的同时，适当增加有关具体操作的说明，将更能满足他们的需求。另外，本书个别地方在排印和文字拼写上还存在一些疏漏，有待再版时纠正。